Clinical Assessment of Dangerousness

Violence touches the lives of many in our society. When people are victimized by violent crime, the general public assumes that the victim could have been spared if the perpetrator had been identified as potentially dangerous by mental health agents. Yet the prediction of dangerousness remains an inexact science and depends upon many complex factors.

Clinical Assessment of Dangerousness provides a thorough and clear description of research findings in order to help clinicians make sound decisions concerning their patients' dangerousness. The book covers a broad spectrum of violent behavior – from parricide and filicide, to stalking and harassment – as well as crucial issues such as biological factors, domestic violence, and the influence of drugs and alcohol on violent behavior.

The book is divided into the following sections: Basic Issues in Violence Research, Mental Health Issues and Dangerousness, Family Issues and Dangerousness, and Individual Characteristics and Dangerousness. It will serve as an important reference book that covers the most recent scientific literature and provides views on future directions for research and practice in this increasingly valuable field.

Georges-Franck Pinard is Psychiatrist at the Louis-H. Lafontaine Hospital and Assistant Professor of Psychiatry at the University of Montreal.

Linda Pagani is Senior Investigator at the Research Unit on Children's Psycho-Social Maladjustment and Associate Professor at the School of Psycho-Education, University of Montreal.

Clinical Assessment of Dangerousness

Empirical Contributions

Edited by

GEORGES-FRANCK PINARD

Louis-H. Lafontaine Hospital and Department of Psychiatry
University of Montreal

LINDA PAGANI

School of Psycho-Education and
Research Unit on Children's Psycho-Social Maladjustment
University of Montreal

CAMBRIDGE
UNIVERSITY PRESS

PUBLISHED BY THE PRESS SYNDICATE OF THE UNIVERSITY OF CAMBRIDGE
The Pitt Building, Trumpington Street, Cambridge, United Kingdom

CAMBRIDGE UNIVERSITY PRESS
The Edinburgh Building, Cambridge CB2 2RU, UK   http://www.cup.cam.ac.uk
40 West 20th Street, New York, NY 10011-4211, USA http://www.cup.org
10 Stamford Road, Oakleigh, Melbourne 3166, Australia
Ruiz de Alarcón 13, 28014 Madrid, Spain

First published 2001

Printed in the United States of America

Typeface Palatino 10/13   *System* QuarkXPress™   [HT]

A catalog record for this book is available from the British Library

Library of Congress Cataloging-in-Publication Data

Clinical assessment of dangerousness: empirical contributions/edited by Georges-Franck Pinard, Linda Pagani.
    p. cm.
    Includes index.
    ISBN 0 521 64123 3
    1. Violence. 2. Violence – Psychological aspects. I. Pinard, Georges-Franck, 1961-II. Pagani, Linda, 1964-

RC569.5.V55 C564 2000
616.85'82—dc21
00-023779

ISBN 0 521 64123 3 hardback

Contents

Contributors   *page* vi
Prologue   ix
PAUL S. APPELBAUM

Introduction

1 Clinical Assessment of Dangerousness: An Overview
   of the Literature   1
   LINDA PAGANI AND GEORGES-F. PINARD

Basic Issues in Violence Research

2 Biology, Development, and Dangerousness   23
   ELIZABETH J. SUSMAN AND JORDAN W. FINKELSTEIN

3 The Development of Physical Aggression During
   Childhood and the Prediction of Later Dangerousness   47
   RICHARD E. TREMBLAY

4 Predicting Adult Official and Self-Reported Violence   66
   DAVID P. FARRINGTON

Mental Health Issues and Dangerousness

5 Major Mental Disorder and Violence: Epidemiology
   and Risk Assessment   89
   JOHN MONAHAN

6 Axis II Disorders and Dangerousness   103
   KENNETH TARDIFF

7 Recidivistic Violent Behavior and Axis I and Axis II
Disorders   121
JARI TIIHONEN

Family Issues and Dangerousness

8 Risk Assessment for Intimate Partner Homicide   136
JACQUELYN C. CAMPBELL, PHYLLIS SHARPS, AND
NANCY GLASS

9 Parents at Risk of Filicide   158
MAUREEN MARKS

10 Parricide   181
CHARLES P. EWING

Individual Characteristics and Dangerousness

11 Alcohol and Dangerousness   195
JOAN McCORD

12 Violence and Substance Abuse   216
PHILIP BEAN

13 Threats, Stalking, and Criminal Harassment   238
J. REID MELOY

Conclusion

14 Discussion and Clinical Commentary on Issues in
the Assessment and Prediction of Dangerousness   258
GEORGES-F. PINARD AND LINDA PAGANI

Index   279

Contributors

Paul S. Appelbaum, M.D., Department of Psychiatry, University of Massachusetts Medical School, Worcester, Massachusetts 01655, USA

Philip Bean, Ph.D., Department of Social Sciences, Loughborough University, Loughborough, Leicestershire LE11 3TU, UK

Jacquelyn C. Campbell, Ph.D., R.N., F.A.A.N., School of Nursing, Johns Hopkins University, Baltimore, Maryland 21205, USA

Charles P. Ewing, J.D., Ph.D., School of Law, State University of New York, Buffalo, New York 14260, USA

David P. Farrington, Ph.D., Institute of Criminology, University of Cambridge, Cambridge CB3 9DT, UK

Jordan W. Finkelstein, M.D., Department of Biobehavioral Health and Department of Pediatrics, Pennsylvania State University, University Park, Pennsylvania 16802, USA

Nancy Glass, M.S.N., M.P.H., R.N., School of Nursing, Johns Hopkins University, Baltimore, Maryland 21205, USA

Maureen Marks, DPhil., Perinatal Psychiatry, Institute of Psychiatry, London SE5 8AF, UK

Joan McCord, Ph.D., Department of Criminal Justice, Temple University, Narberth, Pennsylvania 19072, USA

J. Reid Meloy, Ph.D., Department of Psychiatry, University of California, San Diego, California, 92101, USA

John Monahan, Ph.D., School of Law, University of Virginia, Charlottesville, Virginia 22903, USA

Linda Pagani, Ph.D. GRIP-Research Unit on Children's Psycho-Social Maladjustment, Université de Montréal, Montréal, QC, H3C 3J7, CANADA

Georges-F. Pinard, M.D., F.R.C.P., Clinique Rivière-des-Prairies, Montréal, QC, H1E 4H7, CANADA

Phyllis Sharps, Ph.D., R.N., School of Nursing, Johns Hopkins University, Baltimore, Maryland 21205, USA

Elizabeth J. Susman, Ph.D., Department of Biobehavioral Health, Pennsylvania State University, University Park, Pennsylvania 16802, USA

Kenneth Tardiff, M.D., M.P.H., Cornell University Medical College, Payne Whitney Clinic, The New York Hospital, New York, New York 10021, USA

Jari Tiihonen, M.D., Ph.D., Department of Forensic Psychiatry, University of Kuopio, Niuvanniemi Hospital, FIN-70240 Kuopio, FINLAND

Richard E. Tremblay, Ph.D., F.R.S.C., GRIP-Research Unit on Children's Psycho-Social Maladjustment, Université de Montréal, Montréal, QC H3C 3J7, CANADA

Prologue

PAUL S. APPELBAUM

Interpersonal violence is an inescapable reality of contemporary society. Pick up any newspaper or listen to any news broadcast and witness the litany of violence it reveals. Murder, sexual assault, child abuse, hate crimes, terrorism – the list seems endless, the details numbingly familiar, until the day's stories blend into yesterday's, and those into the accounts of last week and the week before.

Only a fraction of this violence, of course, comes to clinical attention and that is either because the victims seek assistance or, more pertinent to the focus of this volume, because the perpetrators believe themselves or are believed by others to have a mental disorder. Indeed, although persons with mental disorders account for a small proportion of violence in most societies, the public, stoked by the media, are disproportionately concerned about the risks posed by this group. A recent estimate in the United States put percentage of violent acts accounted for by the mentally ill at about three percent, (Swanson, 1994) and data from England suggest that the proportion of murders attributable to persons with mental illness has actually been falling over time. (Taylor & Gunn, 1999) But popular estimates of the proportion of psychiatric patients who are likely to commit violent crimes vastly exceed the actual number (Pescosolido, Monahan, Link, Stueve, & Kikuzawa, 1999).

The simultaneous fascination with and terror of violence committed by persons with mental disorders was illustrated graphically quite recently in the pages of a major newspaper. There at the front of the local news section, positioned precisely in the middle of the page, was a lengthy story describing a murder committed by a man whom the headline advertised as a "mental patient." His life, the crime itself, and the events leading up to it were all laid out in stark detail, in this article

– one of a series of articles the murder had evoked. Only when one finished reading the piece might one notice the column on the edge of the page, a compilation of shorter stories judged on some basis or other less newsworthy. Two of these brief accounts dealt with murders and one with the murder of a wife and child by their husband and father. Why did neither of these equally horrific crimes warrant center-page treatment? As best one could tell, the answer appeared to be that neither perpetrator on the page's periphery was "mentally ill."

What are the roots of this popular preoccupation with crimes of violence by the mentally disordered? Some data suggest that mental disorders, especially psychotic disorders, may be associated with an increased risk of violence, (Link & Stueve, 1994; Swanson, Borum, Swartz, & Monahan, 1996) but one recent large-scale study has challenged that conclusion, suggesting that any heightened propensity for violence is better attributed to the consequence of substance abuse than to any effect of mental illness (Steadman et al., 1998). In any case, as already noted, even studies pointing to an increased risk suggest that the effect is small compared to other variables, and that its elimination – if it could be achieved – would not render our societies materially more secure. Reality, therefore, does not account for the extent of popular concern about the relationship between violence and mental disorder.

Clearly, less rational factors are at play. Persons with mental illnesses, especially psychoses and severe affective disorders, often behave oddly, inducing apprehension, frequently without warrant, in those around them. That fear is undoubtedly augmented by the more primal terrors elicited by contact with a mentally disordered person and inevitable anxiety that one might be susceptible to such a fate. Moreover, with many of the usual inhibitions governing speech and behavior apparently loosened in these conditions, there is natural concern that controls on violent actions might also be impaired. Hence the stereotype – data to the contrary notwithstanding (Steadman et al., 1998) – of the crazy person on the street, selecting targets at random for the discharge of aggressive impulses.

If the public fear persons with mental disorders – and it is quite clear that they do – they have come to expect that those charged with caring for these unfortunates will prevent them from acts of harm. Thus, mental health professionals have been called upon in numerous venues to assess the risk of violence presented by a disordered person and to manage the situation to insure that the anticipated acts do not ensue. These expectations are reflected in civil commitment statutes based, at least in part, on criteria of dangerousness to others; the recruitment of psychiatrists and psychologists to assist in determinations related to bail, sentencing, probation, and parole; the imposition of liability on clinicians when they fail to prevent violence (Anfang & Appelbaum, 1996); and the public outcry and calls for inquiry that so often follow violent acts perpetrated by persons under psychiatric care (Geddes, 1999).

This volume addresses the resulting need that clinicians have for guidance in performing the tasks of assessment and prediction. Rather than providing a "how to" guide, which in the current circumstances would be of limited utility, the editors have assembled contributions from some of the leading experts on violent behavior. In place of opinions based on "clinical experience", all too often misleading, authors have been asked to focus on what is known about the factors that contribute to violence in general and also violence by persons with whom clinicians are likely to come into contact. The richness of these presentations defies summary here, but it may be worthwhile to underscore some of the messages that are latent in the text.

Given the rewards for successful prediction of violence and, even more important, the aversive consequences of failures in assessment, it is understandable that researchers have sought and clinicians have relied upon single variables that would explain violence and allow it to be anticipated. Were there a single cause, there might well be a single cure – a "magic bullet" as it were – that would simplify at one pass the complex tasks of managing the care of persons who may have some propensity for violence. To list the variables that have attracted such attention would take the writing of a history of research and practice in the field. Past and current explanatory and predictive enthusiasms have embraced, among others – the presence of an extra Y chromosome (XYY syndrome); elevated levels of testosterone; subictal discharges in the temporal lobes; reduced brain serotonin levels; physical or sexual abuse as a child; absence of a paternal figure in early adolescence; use of alcohol and other disinhibiting substances; psychopathic traits; the influence of a culture of violence; delusions that one is being persecuted or controlled by external forces. The list ends arbitrarily here, but it could be extended by a factor of ten.

A wise professor, during my medical training, noted that the greater the number of treatments for a given condition, the less understood the condition is likely to be. One might well say the same about variables thought to be *sine qua non* for the prediction of violence. Their very multiplicity suggests that none of them represents the holy grail of prediction, and serves as an indicator of how poorly comprehended the antecedents of violence truly are. Indeed, the chapters compiled here indicate that we ought to be thinking very differently about the assessment of a person's capacity for violence, whether or not that person is mentally ill.

To begin with, violence is not a unitary phenomenon, but a diverse one. Typologies abound, none of them entirely satisfactory, but most probably shedding some additional light on the matter. Violence, to focus on one dichotomy, may be motivated by a desire for gain or by overwhelming emotion. It may occur but once in a person's life, or constitute a habitual pattern of conduct. There is no a priori reason to believe, considering the types of violence addressed in this book, that the rejected suitor who turns into a stalker and the parricidal child who commits the ultimate horror derive from similar etiologies, nor is it likely that they share many characteristics with the barroom brawler – a model citizen when not intoxicated – or the violent psychotic. Since violence is diverse, it is likely that its wellsprings are equally varied, and thus that the predictors of violence and the measures that will prevent its occurrence are several and not one.

Moreover, the large number of variables that correlate with violence – well explicated in the chapters that follow – each seem to play a relatively small role in explaining or predicting the behavior. Only rarely does a given variable account for more than twenty percent of the variance in any explanatory model. Thus, it seems likely that violence risk is related to multiple variables, the effects of which cumulate and perhaps interact to lower the threshold at which an act of aggression will occur. No one variable need always be present, no matter how potent its influence on behavior, so long as a number of less powerful variables combine to take its place. The correspondence between this cumulative model and the findings of many studies in the field is both gratifying and reassuring.

Putting these insights together, it appears that improvements in the methodology of assessing the potential for violence will be dependent on a closer focus on the type of violence at issue and the use of multivariate models of the relevant predictors. Such models already exist, ranging from standard linear regression approaches to innovative decision tree models (Monahan et al., 2000; Steadman et al., 2000). All would be improved by the greater availability of data from large-scale studies of violence that employ a sufficient number of predictors to allow their interactions to be assessed. The more homogeneous the group being studied and the more carefully types of violence are dissected one from another, the more useful the resulting data are likely to be. In the great epistemological war between the lumpers (those who would aggregate similar phenomena for study) and the splitters (those who would break phenomena down into the smallest achievable units), when it comes to assessment of the potential for violence, the splitters are likely to triumph.

While waiting for that epiphany, what is the clinician to do today and tomorrow as the need to assess violence potential remains omnipresent in clinical work? The task is somewhat easier when the evaluees have committed previous acts of violence. People being the creatures of habit that they are, it seems probable – though the theory awaits empirical validation – that those variables that were associated with violence in the past will, if present at some point in the future, increase the likelihood of a violent outcome. Close inspection of the previous acts of violence perpetrated by any person, most experts believe, will yield the best predictions of future events. At a minimum, the clinician who follows this protocol will be conforming to what the relevant professionals generally recognize as the appropriate standard of care.

More difficult by far is the task confronting the clinician who faces a person believed at risk of committing violence by virtue of a threat or behavior, but without a history of having committed violent acts. Here, at best, one searches for the presence of the generally accepted predictors of violence, to which this book is a most enlightening guide. As their numbers mount, so does the risk of violence. The young, impulsive male, easy to anger, somewhat suspicious, and abusing alcohol represents a violence risk of much greater degree than the evaluee who lacks most or all of these characteristics, as well as their equally robust substitutes. If that seems like a thin reed on which to base predictive practices that may have such profound consequences for individual liberty – it is. But, with rare exceptions, this is where we are today.

Will we ever move forward from here? It is difficult to resist the positivist assumption that the riddle of human behavior must ultimately fall to the approaches of modern clinical, behavioral, and social sciences. Whether this arrogance is warranted remains to be seen. Without question, therefore, if progress is to be made, it will come from the careful empirical explanation of these issues exemplified by the chapters that follow.

REFERENCES

Anfang, S. A., & Appelbaum, P. S. (1996). Twenty years after *Tarasoff*: reviewing the duty to protect. *Harvard Review of Psychiatry, 4,* 67–76.

Geddes, J. (1999). Suicide and homicide by people with mental illness. *British Medical Journal, 318*, 1225–1226.

Link, B., & Stueve, A. (1994). Psychotic symptoms and violent/illegal behavior of mental patients compared to community controls. In J. Monahan & H. Steadman (Eds.), *violence and mental disorder*. Chicago: University of Chicago Press.

Monahan, J., Steadman, H. J., Appelbaum, P. S., Robbins, P. C., Mulvey, E. P., Silver, E., Roth, L. H., & Grisso, T. (2000). Developing a clinically useful tool for assessing violence risk: Results from the MacArthur Violence Risk Assessment Study. *British Journal of Psychiatry, 176*, 312–319.

Pescosolido, B., Monahan, J., Link, B., Stueve, A., & Kikuzawa, S. (1999). The public's view of the competence, dangerousness, and need for legal coercion among persons with mental illness. *American Journal of Public Health, 89*, 1339–1345.

Steadman, H. J., Monahan, J., Silver, E., Appelbaum, P. S., Grisso, T., Roth, L. H., & Banks, S. (2000). A classification tree approach to the development of actuarial violence risk assessment tools. *Law and Human Behavior, 24*, 83–100.

Steadman, H. J., Mulvey, E. P., Monahan, J., Robbins, P. C., Appelbaum, P. S., Grisso, T., Roth, L. H., & Silver, E. (1998). Violence by people discharged from acute psychiatric inpatient facilities and by others in the same neighborhoods. *Archives of General Psychiatry, 55*, 393–401.

Swanson, J. W. (1994). Mental disorder, substance abuse, and community violence: An epidemiological approach. In J. Monahan & H. Steadman (Eds.), *Violence and mental disorder*. Chicago: University of Chicago Press.

Swanson, J., Borum, R., Swartz, M., & Mohanan, J. (1996). Psychotic symptoms and disorders and the risk of violent behavior in the community. *Criminal Behavior and Mental Health, 6*, 317–338.

Taylor, P. J., & Gunn, J. (1999). Homicides by people with mental illness: Myth and reality. *British Journal of Psychiatry, 174*, 9–14.

1. Clinical Assessment of Dangerousness: An Overview of the Literature

LINDA PAGANI AND GEORGES-F. PINARD

"I think you have to define for yourself the word 'danger' and then having decided that in your mind, you go see the patient and look for it with every conceivable means that you have at your command, and if you wind up not knowing something, you ought to say so. This is a complex business"

(John A. Ordway in Rappeport, 1967) (p. 53)

In spring 1965, this was in reply to audience demands for a definition of dangerousness at the first panel discussion ever held on the topic at a meeting of the American Psychiatric Association. Almost a decade after the symposium proceedings were published, Steadman (1973) once again grappled with the concept of dangerousness. He offered that it represents a probability estimation that something "dangerous" will happen in the presence of an individual. In attempts to further clarify the concept, he added that dangerousness is not an inherent characteristic of a person or situation and that it does not represent a quality, but rather an attribution of a quality.

Because of such vague conceptualizations, misguided public perceptions, and the tendency to clinically overestimate violence potential, the prediction of dangerousness among persons with mental disorders has been viewed as an inherently dangerous proposition (Shah, 1975). While the risks are not underestimated, more than ever, the assessment of dangerousness has important consequences in numerous decision-making processes: (1) Mental health professionals remain accountable to the public and courts, for their clinical judgments regarding future violence potential of patients (Lidz & Mulvey, 1995); (2) Estimates of dangerousness represent essential components of day-to-day management of many patients (Jones, 1995); and (3) There is a duty to protect potential victims (Monahan, 1993). Hence, concerns of the new millennium will focus on improving the accuracy of clinical predictions by developing empirically driven models of dangerousness for specific populations.

Empirical approaches to improving clinical judgments suggest that the "complex business" referred to by our predecessors can be broken down into simpler parts. This chapter reviews the components of the dangerousness assessment equation.

Dangerousness: Clinical Concept and Operationalized Variable

Although clinical conceptualizations of dangerousness reflect concern about potential harm to others, their components vary (reviewed in Foucault, 1981; Jones 1995): risk of inflicting serious, irreversible injury or destruction, or to induce others to engage in this risk; propensity to cause serious and lasting physical harm; risk of inflicting serious violence on others (physical and/or psychological) or damaging property that places others at risk of physical injury. The common thread among these is the concept of probability.

Gunn (1982) underscored three key elements: destructiveness, prediction, and fear. In a later publication (Gunn, 1993), he added that dangerousness represents an attribution that is made to people (or things) that is partially influenced by actuarial risk (based on computations of probability) and gut feelings (subjective fear). Hence, predictions of this attribute refer to overall clinical impressions of the likelihood that an individual will engage in something destructive in the future.

The clinical assessment of dangerousness represents an inexact science, partially because it is subjectively driven, but also because of factors such as individual choice and triggering contextual influences (Foucault, 1981; Gunn, 1993). The accuracy of such estimates further depends on patient management issues (i.e., patient compliance, symptom control, and abstinence from illicit drug and alcohol use; Norko, 1999). There is a consensus that dangerousness represents a state and not a trait and that an individual's potential for violence should be viewed on a continuum (Melton, Petrila, Poythress, & Slobogin, 1997). That is, violence potential should not be treated as a fixed level of risk, but rather as a fluctuating level of risk that varies with time, symptoms, and situations (Mulvey, 1994).

Empirical approaches are challenged by the concept of dangerousness because it does not have the measurable characteristics of matter like weight, length, or speed (Jones, 1995). As such, research studies typically use officially recorded violence (arrests, convictions, incarcerations, etc.) to represent this variable in their prediction models. Hospitalizations serve as another official source of data as well. Both strategies can bias the results because violent individuals are more likely to be "medicalized or criminalized" (Link, Andrews, & Cullen, 1992). There is always the chance that violent individuals may be more easily hospitalized or that psychiatric patients may be more easily apprehended by the police. As a result, studies using this approach are likely to have the greatest power to detect more severe disorders (i.e., schizophrenia) or crimes (e.g., homicide). The operationalization of dangerousness through official records will be most relevant to disorders and crimes that are most likely to be detected and officially documented. This is an important consideration when examining the potential for violence in populations with mental disorders.

The Link

Using a number of approaches (i.e., prospective, retrospective, and epidemiological), researchers have established a significant relationship between mental disorders and violent behavior (Link & Stueve, 1998; Marzuk, 1996). Several caveats are in order prior to appreciating its predictive power. While significant, the magnitude of this link is comparable to that of sociodemographic factors (Swanson, Holzer, Ganju, & Jono, 1990). This relationship is also limited to specific disorders and symptom constellations (Link & Stueve, 1994). Finally, persons with mental illness represent a small percentage of the population, most of which are neither criminal nor violent (Marzuk, 1996). This is in far contrast to increasing beliefs by the general public that stereotype individuals with mental illness as dangerous (Phelan, Link, Stueve, & Pescosolido, 1997). These considerations provide a perspective for interpreting this link.

The link between mental disorders and dangerousness is robust, even after controlling for socioeconomic characteristics (Marzuk, 1996). Although this link appears strongest for severe mental disorders, active psychotic symptoms are more reliable as predictors than diagnosis per se (Mulvey, 1994). Perhaps this explains why, for persons without diagnosed mental illness, the potential for dangerous behavior is increased by the use of alcohol and psychoactive substances (Marzuk, 1996).

Recent strategies have focused on establishing the magnitude of risk associated with specific mental disorders (see Litwack & Schlesinger, 1999 for an extensive historical review of earlier generation studies). By doing so, we can learn more about the risks associated with different subgroups of individuals. Epidemiological studies have been most promising in achieving this objective. These assess violence rates among *all* individuals in their community samples, treated or not, over a specified time period. These have noted elevated rates of violence for some disorders but not all (Link & Stueve, 1998).

Swanson et al. (1990) used data from the NIMH Epidemiological Catchment Area (ECA) survey to examine the relationship between violence and psychiatric disorder among 10,000 American adults from Baltimore, Raleigh-Durham, and Los Angeles. More than half of the adults who reported violent behavior met *DSM-III* criteria for one or more psychiatric disorders. Among those who met the criteria for one disorder, subjects with a diagnosis of substance abuse were more than twice as likely to report violent behavior than those with schizophrenia (21.30% versus 8.36%). The risk of violent behavior significantly increased with the number of psychiatric disorders. One could argue that the ECA survey data are biased by a cultural context marked by urban standards of higher levels of interpersonal violence. Would this link be robust in a less violent culture? Stueve and Link (1997) addressed this question with a large, community-based, epidemiological sample from Israel (N = 2678). The 5-year prevalence of interpersonal violence (fighting and weapon use) was lower than that observed in an upper Manhattan sample (Link et al., 1992). This sample also had lower base rates of substance abuse and antisocial personality disorders. Self-reports of recent interpersonal violence were significantly elevated among adults diagnosed with psychotic or bipolar disorders compared to respondents without psychiatric disorders. However, they were not elevated among adults diagnosed with nonpsychotic depression, generalized anxiety disorder, or phobias. These results were independent of lifetime substance abuse, antisocial personality disorder, and sociodemographic factors that moderate the link between mental illness and violence.

Is this link robust for more extreme violence? Homicidal behavior in cultures with a relatively low crime rate (and a high rate of solved cases) appears to be linked with some specific mental disorders classified according to *DSM-III-R* classifications. Using a Finnish sample, Eronen, Hakola, and Tiihonen (1996) found that the risk of homicidal violence was substantially highest in both men and women with schizophrenia, antisocial personality disorder, and alcoholism compared to the general population. It is important to note that this study took place in a cultural context where violent crime is not significantly influenced by organized crime and drug abuse. In another Finnish study, Tiihonen and Hakola (1994) investigated the relationship between psychiatric disorders and homicide recidivism. Their sample included all homicide recidivists from prisons or high-security hospitals who had committed their last offense during a three-year period (1988–1991). All recidivists (13 subjects) suffered from either severe alcoholism combined with personality disorder (85%) or from schizophrenia (15%). Based on 30 years of experience conducting studies on homicide recidivism, these authors concluded that homicidal recidivists are almost always affected by a mental disorder. Severe alcoholism, schizophrenia, paranoid psychosis, and paranoid personality disorders are the most common diagnoses (by order of frequency).

Prediction

Given that this link has been suspected for quite some time (Hamilton, 1916), researchers in the past several decades have tried to assess just how correct clinicians are in their assessments of dangerousness. Until the early 1990s, many doubted the validity and legitimacy of such clinical predictions, to the point that some have suggested that mental health professionals are not competent in that capacity (e.g., American Psychological Association, 1978; Dershowitz, 1969; Megargee, 1981). However, hindsight tells us that such conclusions were drawn from a literature plagued by serious methodological problems (see Gunn, 1993; Litwack & Schlesinger, 1999; or Melton et al., 1997 for a more detailed discussion). That is, the studies cited in numerous reports and reviews of the research were flawed in ways that increased the risk of inflating false-positive predictions (i.e., overestimation of someone's potential for violence). Moreover, the true test of whether such predictions are correct would be to conduct naturalistic observations (i.e., not interfering with the environment) and see if the person would indeed be dangerous as predicted. Of course, this is unethical and, as a result, challenges the literature. Finally, the fact that we are trying to predict a variable that is based, to begin with, on a weak link that is not well understood (in terms of mediating and moderating variables) is not helpful.

A more cautious look at dangerous assessment as a variable suggests that: (1) clinical judgments are valuable (Otto, 1992); (2) clinical predictions are not wrong most of the time (Litwack & Schlesinger, 1999); and (3) although there is need for improvement, clinicians do better than chance in their evaluations of dangerousness (Lidz, Mulvey, & Gardner, 1993). When we think about accountability to either patients (in the event of a false-positive prediction) or potential victims (in the event of a false-negative prediction), better than chance is simply not good enough.

Inter-rater reliability among clinicians must also improve if this field is to move forward. One study found that, although they were no better than other professionals, levels of agreement between psychiatrists were as low as 35% (Harding & Montandon, 1982). This extreme variability may be attributable to semantics. That is, perhaps for some, clinical determinations of dangerousness could mean making a prediction (i.e., clinical prognosis) and, for others, it could mean expressing concern (i.e., clinical impression). These two approaches could theoretically generate two different assessment statements, with the former yielding a more conservative judgment (i.e., dangerous and thus confine) in borderline cases (Melton et al., 1997). Dangerous assessments might become more reliable if we distinguish between predictions and expressions of concern regarding risk of violence. Mulvey & Lidz (1994) recommend that clinicians express their degree of concern about the probability of future violence in specific circumstances. As such, clinical concerns about risk of causing serious harm that warrant further confinement would not equate to a prediction of definite violence if the patient is released into the community and unsupervised. This suggestion seems to be consistent with making a medical prognosis (Gunn, 1993).

Tardiff (1989) maintains that the clinical assessments are more reliable if they address short-term risk. In this case, short-term refers to a few days to a week at most. Beyond that time frame, other factors that might change the condition may come into play (noncompliance with medication, resuming alcohol/drug use, etc.). Others, developing a new psychometric technology, show promise for longer-term risk assessment (to be discussed later in this chapter).

Whether short-term or long-term, a proper dangerous assessment demands consideration of all known risk factors. As a general rule, the cumulative number of risk factors is proportional to the degree of risk for future violence. Some factors are modifiable, but some are not. A risk factor assessment affects not only the clinical impression of probability for future violence but also the clinical management of the individual.

Components of the Risk Assessment Equation

Sociodemographic Factors

Although factors indicating access to or control of wealth (i.e., SES) have long been considered predictors of violence (Hamilton, 1916), current research has clarified the role of specific sociodemographic characteristics as moderators of the relationship between mental disorders and violence.

SES. Those who were violent in the study by Swanson et al. (1990) were more likely to come from low SES groups. Similarly, the study reported by Stueve and Link (1997) found the association between mental disorders and violence stronger among those with less education.

Age. Youth is generally associated with violence risk (Swanson et al., 1990). In psychiatric populations, this is especially noted for males under 20 and females under 34 years of age (Tardiff & Sweillam, 1982). While geriatric status also predicts some risk for violence, this risk is associated with less severe injury (Tardiff, 1989). The means used suggest the etiology of geriatric violence (Petrie, 1982). When a weapon is used, violence on the part of senior citizens is often the result of paranoid delusions and first experiences with psychiatric treatment. When no weapon is used, the act seems more disorganized and accompanied by a clouded sensorium, indicating possible organicity.

Sex. This is an easily misunderstood variable. Men do commit the majority of violent crimes in every culture (Marzuk, 1996). However, when we refer to the relationship between mental disorders and violence, the sex ratio is approximately equal (Binder & McNeil, 1990; Eronen et al., 1996; Tardiff, 1992).

Race. When controlling for diagnosis, the significant relationship between nonwhite racial status and aggression disappears (Lawson, Yesavage, & Werner, 1984). There are no significant racial differences as inpatients, outpatients, or preceding admission (Tardiff & Koenigsberg, 1985).

Historical Factors

A history of childhood deprivation influenced by harsh and inconsistent parenting seems to be an important theme in the lives of those individuals who are at greatest risk of violence (Faulk, 1994). A childhood history of abuse and neglect also figures prominently as a risk factor (Widom, 1989).

Virkkunen, Eggert, Rawlings, and Linnoila (1996) found that paternal violence, alcoholism, and absence were associated with recidivism (of violence or fire setting) among forensic psychiatric patients. In the study by Tiihonen and Hakola (1994), we note that, when data were available, paternal alcoholism played a significant role in the lives of homicide recidivists.

Early signs of persistent antisocial behavior, difficulties in peer relationships, and deep hostility toward authority are established risk factors for later violence risk (Farrington, Loeber, Stouthamer-Loeber, Vankammen, & Schmidt, 1996; Melton et al., 1997). A childhood history triad of fire setting, enuresis, and cruelty to animals should be of particular concern (Festhouse & Kellert, 1987). Early onset represents a significant predictor of later antisocial behavior (Robins, 1978). It is not surprising that past history of violent behavior represents the best "objective" indicator of future risk (Monahan, 1981; Tardiff, 1992). The risk of violence increases with a past history of "making threats" of assault (MacDonald, 1963) and each additional previous act of aggression (Shah, 1978). Antisocial personality disorder increases the risk of homicidal behavior in both sexes (Eronen et al., 1996). Such individuals typically engage in violence proactively or reactively, especially during periods of heavy drinking (Kausch & Resnick, 1999).

Situational Factors

Although earlier research indicated otherwise (e.g., Steadman, 1982), more recent epidemiological data suggest similar contextual factors for violence in both the general and mentally disordered populations. Steadman, Mulvey, Monahan, Clark Robbins, Appelbaum, Grisso, et al. (1998) found that family members and close friends were the most likely victims for both populations. This represents a narrow class of victims who are readily available, since the violent acts either took place in the home of the victim or the perpetrator. Risk of violence may be enhanced if there is a history of previous domestic violence and when family members are involved in limit-setting (Gondolf, Mulvey, & Lidz, 1991). Among more specific contextual factors, the risk of violence is enhanced when arms are readily available (Melton et al., 1997). This is especially true for more lethal forms of violence.

Mental Status as a Risk Factor

For violence that is detected, rates of violence peak around the time of hospital admission or contact with the police. Most violence occurs in the 10 weeks prior to contact with treatment, with violence peaking around the time of hospitalization (Steadman et al., 1998). Interestingly, 10 to 17% of psychiatric emergency visits involve homicidal ideation (Norko, 1999).

Thought processes and intentions represent factors of critical importance (Gunn, 1993). Summarized by Litwack & Schlesinger (1999), the following thought processes indicate significantly greater risk of violence in comparison to individuals with similar risk profiles who do not exhibit these symptoms: Active psychotic symptoms, accompanied by substance abuse and a history of antisocial behavior; delusions of threat or control by outside forces; delusions that a significant other has been replaced by an impostor; command hallucinations to commit violence; erotomania, accompanied by multiple delusional objects and prior serious antisocial behavior unrelated to the delusions; recent and current narcisistic injury (feelings of having been humiliated); or a history of sadistic fantasies.

The dynamics and risks vary according to diagnostic profile. For the same reasons they contemplate suicide or extended suicide, depressed persons may become violent due to despair (Resnick, 1969). Many persons in a manic state threaten and/or assault others, but serious violence is rare (Kausch & Resnick, 1999). Because they maintain an ability to organize a plan and retain some contact with reality, it has been suggested that paranoid schizophrenics pose the most serious risk for violence (Wessely, Castle, & Douglas, 1994). Persecutory delusions are most likely to be acted upon, with the violent act being directed at the perceived persecutor. Violence is rationalized as an effort to protect oneself. It is not surprising that the accumulation of weapons is associated with paranoid features (Meloy, 1995). Paranoid symptoms may also be influenced by another major mental disorder, personality traits, or substance abuse.

The occurrence or hint of threat represents an important indicator of violence potential. A threat's seriousness is in direct proportion to how well the threat is articulated and organized (Tardiff, 1989). Timing and duration of the threat is important as well. Threats based on longstanding delusional beliefs are less serious than recently developed plans that are influenced by a current mental state.

Substance Abuse

As it has for the general population, the increasingly pervasive use of illicit psychoactive drugs and alcohol has increased the chances of violence among persons with mental disorders (Marzuk, 1996). This applies to both the intoxicated state and withdrawal (Tardiff, 1989). Substance abuse is also associated with the accumulation of weapons (Meloy, 1995). This especially applies to the illicit use of stimulants.

In the epidemiological study by Steadman et al. (1998), the presence of a co-occurring substance abuse disorder was a key factor in violence potential. A large proportion of cases with a primary diagnosis of mental disorder had a co-occurring diagnosis of substance abuse (49.6% for depression; 41% for schizophrenia; 37.7% for bipolar disorder; 45% for other psychotic disorder). At a one-year follow-up, the prevalence of violence was 17.9% for individuals with a major mental disorder and no substance abuse disorder; 31.1% for those with a major mental disorder and substance abuse disorder; 43.0% for those with some other form of mental disorder (personality or adjustment disorder, and several cases of suicidality) and a substance abuse disorder. The prevalence of violence among patients without symptoms of substance abuse was not significantly different from the prevalence of violence among their neighbors without symptoms of substance abuse (Steadman et al., 1998). Swanson et al. (1990) found that substance abuse and the presence of more than one diagnosis increases the risk of violence substantially.

Alcohol intoxication is implicated in the majority of violent crimes, including murders, physical and sexual assaults, and domestic violence (Brain, 1986). When looking at extreme forms of violence, Tiihonen and Hakola (1994) found that 85% of homicide recidivists were classified as type 2 alcoholics combined with antisocial personality disorder. This is not surprising given previous studies relating alcohol intake to crime (Guze et al., 1962) and homicide (Felson & Steadman, 1983). Moreover, it is not just a male problem. Alcohol and drug abuse have been underscored as the most common disorder among the increasing female inmate population (Jordan, Schlenger, Fairbank, & Caddell, 1996; Teplin, Abram, & McClelland, 1996).

Biological Factors

Organic Factors. A good differential diagnosis of violent behavior considers the possibility of brain injury (Kausch & Resnick, 1999). Cognitive impairment from brain damage has been associated with violent behavior in prison inmates (Bryant, Scott, Golden, & Tori, 1984), previously normal individuals following a brain insult (Krakowski, Convit, Jaeger, Lin, & Volavka, 1989), and geriatric patients experiencing the consequences of an organic brain disease (Kalunian, Binder, & McNiel, 1990). Tardiff (1992) identified a number of medical conditions associated with violent behavior including (but not being limited to) various systemic infections, hypoxia, electrolyte imbalances, hepatic disease, renal disease, syphilis, thyroid disease, encephalitis, tuberculosis, fungal meningitis, Wilson's disease, and intoxication from heavy metals or psychoactive substances (including alcohol). Organic factors are suspected in cases where the individual is violent without provocation, appears impulsive, and is behaving completely out of character (Kausch & Resnick, 1999).

Gunn (1991) describes how violence, a universal in the animal kingdom, may create the sanctions and hierarchies of social life in its members. The search for biological markers (anatomic, biochemical, or genetic) may tell us about how violence comes about and how we can better predict it. The understanding of biopsychosocial interactions promises more accurate clinical assessment techniques in the future.

Genetic Underpinnings. In his commentary on the state of violence research, Marzuk (1996) astutely referred to genetic research on violence as still being "in utero." A link between impulsive aggression and a point mutation in the monoamine oxidase A gene, resulting in monoamine oxidase A deficiency, was recently discovered among the male members of one Dutch kindred (Brunner, Nelen, Breakfield, Ropers, & van Oost, 1993). This link was also tested and confirmed in mice (Cases et al., 1995). This is very encouraging. However, a direct causal relationship between a single gene and a specific behavior is highly unrealistic because, by definition, genes are simple and behavior is complex in nature (Brunner, 1996). Therefore, even if the relationship is confirmed in other families, the data do not support the hypothesis that monoamine oxidase A constitutes an "aggression gene."

Neuroanatomic and Neurochemical Pathways. Animal research suggests that aggression is controlled by specific excitatory and inhibitory centers of the brain (Marzuk, 1996). These include the frontal lobe, septal area, hippocampus, amygdala, caudate, thalamus, hypothalamus, midbrain, tegmentum, pons, and the cerebellum (see Elliott, 1992; Garza-Trevino, 1994 for a more extensive discussion). A number of corresponding excitatory and inhibitory neurotransmitters have been suggested as mediators of aggressive behavior. Of these, the pathway between hyposerotonergic functioning and impulsive aggression has received the most research attention.

Among 114 alcohol violent offenders and fire setters, Virkkunen and colleagues (1989) found a link between low cerebrospinal fluid (CSF) concentrations of the principal serotonin metabolite (5-HIAA) and a family history of paternal violence and alcoholism. Recidivistic violence four and a half years after prison release was associated with low serotonin metabolite concentrations, earlier parental absence, and presence of brothers in the home, indicating an interaction between biological and environmental variables (Virkkunen et al., 1996). In their conceptual model (Linnoila & Virkkunen, 1992), this group postulates a heritable defect in serotonergic functioning that is temporarily relieved by alcohol intake. This, in turn, further exacerbates the serotonin defect, thus increasing the likelihood of violent behavior.

Because working with CSF poses many methodological and ethical challenges, many have turned to platelet binding models, which are identical in structure to the corresponding sites on serotonergic neurons (Marzuk, 1996). Coccaro, Kavoussi, Sheline, Lish, and Csernansky (1996) found that a history of provocation-induced serious violence in individuals with personality disorders was inversely correlated with the maximal number of platelet tritiated paraoxetine binding sites. This suggests that reduced numbers of platelet 5-HT transporter sites may be related to life history of aggressive behavior of patients with personality disorders and brings forth another source of serotonergic dysfunction that can result in violent behavior.

Animal models have also been informative. A prospective study using naturalistic observations of free-ranging monkeys confined to an island off the coast of South Carolina suggests that low CSF 5-HIAA may be a biological marker associated with excessive risk taking (being caught in food traps more than once) and aggression (aggressive encounters with other monkeys), which increases the chances of early mortality (Higley et al., 1996; Mehlman et al., 1994).

Tiihonen, Räsänen, and Hakko (1997) tested and found support for the seasonal variation in the occurrence of homicide. They analyzed a large database on the monthly occurrence of all murders and manslaughters between 1957 and 1995. The results indicated that this seasonal variation and the correlation between monthly occurrence of homicides and violent suicides are associated with the observed circannual rhythms of serotonin transmission (circannual peaks around January and February, and nadirs in May and August). During the winter the homicide rate was significantly below the expected rate. During the summer, there was a significant elevation beyond the expected homicide rate. They observed an association between monthly occurrences of homicide and violent suicide.

Research on the neuroanatomic and neurochemical pathways not only tells us about biological influences on violence but also gives us clues as to how they interact with psychological and social factors. The rapid development of this research area promises a more unified and coherent theory of violence.

Assessment of Risk Factors

The evaluation of an individual's potential for violence is conducted for a number of important reasons: whether to admit or not to admit for treatment; in situations where a third party may be at risk and there is a duty to protect; when discharge is imminent; and for the courts. These represent relatively short-term estimates, given that we cannot lock people up indefinitely because they pose an unspecified risk over the long term.

It is reasonable to assume that risk assessment models should differ according to the characteristics of the individual, situation, potential victim involved, and type of behavior we intend to predict. Common sense also tells us that they should vary according to the number of cumulative risk factors experienced by the potential perpetrator. It is hoped that, with a better knowledge-base on risk models, clinicians will ultimately produce more accurate estimates of potential for violence in a number of clinical contexts (Grisso & Tomkins, 1996).

There are four "musts" in any professionally adequate assessment of violence risk (Monahan, 1993): (1) We must distinguish what information is key; (2) We must gather it using all reasonably available sources; (3) All relevant information should be included in the risk assessment equation; and (4) If we are not responsible for making a clinical decision, we must report the information and the risk estimate to the person who is in that capacity. In order to fulfill these important tasks, clinicians must be comfortable with the identification of risk factors for violent behavior.

Clinical Issues in the Assessment of Dangerousness

Two *clinical* approaches are typically used in evaluating the potential for violence. The traditional approach represents data gathering and synthesis techniques that are guided by the clinician's knowledge of risk factors for violence and reasoning about the relationship between mental illness and violence. The anamnestic approach, rooted in the traditional approach, attempts to identify factors that distinguish a repetitive theme in an individual's previous history of violent acts. Both methods rely on somewhat unstandardized methods of data collection and are subjective. The advantage, however, is that case-specific information is considered (i.e., insight about past transgressions and present threats, fantasies, characteristics of delusional systems).

An important obstacle for the clinician is that the evaluation invariably occurs in an out-of-context situation that is more artificial than real (Melton et al., 1997), allowing the individual the chance to minimize the impression given of risk for violence. In light of this challenge, the accuracy of one's clinical impression is maximized when interviews are conducted with the patient's significant others (family and friends), the police, and others with relevant information including employers, family physicians, parole agents, and social workers (Tardiff, 1989). One must also study all relevant documentation that is available or that could be made available. For validation and clarification purposes, Faulk (1994) suggests a thorough review of all available documentation prior to the clinical interview.

There are parallels between assessing dangerousness and assessing suicide risk (Gunn, 1993; Tardiff, 1989). Gunn outlines seven steps of risk assessment: (1) A detailed history from birth using every possible source of validation; (2) A detailed assessment of the intake of alcohol, illicit substances, and prescribed medication; (3) Inquiry into sexual interests, attitudes, and ideas; (4) A detailed account of criminal, antisocial, and violent activities (including intentions, fears, and feelings during the incidents), corroborating as much as possible with police documents (i.e., statements by victims); (5) In-depth psychological, intelligence, and personality testing; (6) A mental status assessment that also includes thoughts, feelings, and intentions during a violent or potentially violent episode; and (7) Past attitudes and behaviors in response to treatment. These steps in assessment should focus on episodes of violence (loss of temper, feelings of revenge, irritability associated with intoxication or withdrawal), the individual's appearance, any available means, and the presence of risk factors discussed in the previous section.

When threats or homicidal ideas are expressed, they should be fully addressed in the clinical interview. Details about how the act would be carried out and the expected consequences should be elucidated and discussed (Kausch & Resnick, 1999). Not only does this indicate the degree of judgment and insight characterizing the individual's mental state, but it also influences a discussion of alternative strategies that could achieve the desired effect without the consequences, such as facing charges of aggravated assault or even homicide. A postal worker who feels victimized by his supervisor on a daily basis could opt for quitting his job instead of killing his superior when confronted with the likelihood of spending many years in prison. A wife who is convinced of her husband's constant infidelity could decide to leave him instead of facing further misery knowing that, while she is behind bars for aggravated assault, he not only has custody of the children but continues to enjoy the company of other women. Both alternative coping strategies have an important element of revenge without the serious consequences incurred by violence.

The *actuarial* approach represents an increasingly popular strategy in the assessment of risk for violence. The chances that violent behavior will be perpetrated by an individual are expressed. That is, this approach yields a probability estimate that a specific kind of violence will occur by a specific individual, in a specific time frame, in more or less specific circumstances. Such probability estimates are rooted in research findings that address the occurrence of violence in individuals from different diagnostic categories. Trained scorers are required for actuarial approaches. The techniques are much like those used by insurance companies for establishing the risk that an individual will experience illness or death at different ages, depending on his or her inherent characteristics.

Clinical assessments collect the same data as actuarial assessments, but generate their conclusions about potential for violence via reasoning rather than computation. A major debate has ensued about which method is best (for an extensive discussion see review by Litwack & Schlesinger, 1999). This debate, among clinicians, resembles the qualitative versus quantitative controversy among researchers. It is important to note that actuarial instruments are meant to predict violence, whereas clinicians communicate the individual's potential for violence. This, in addition to a multitude of methodological differences, remains a challenge for recent research that tests the reliability of one estimate versus the other. Although clinical approaches are valuable (Lidz et al., 1993), actuarial techniques do show promise as an adjunct to clinical assessments of dangerousness (Melton et al., 1997).

The dichotomy between actuarial and clinical assessments is blurring to the point where they have shared characteristics (Litwack & Schlesinger, 1999). For example, the most powerful actuarial instrument to date is the PCL-R (Hare, 1996). This instrument is largely composed of clinical data. Generating a score on this instrument does not simply derive from calculations; it represents clinical judgment about the extent to which the evaluator detects superficial charm, narcissism, a lack of remorse, a lack of empathy, and manipulativeness. Hence, perhaps the debate should not really address which data collection method is best, but rather, which proportion of each should we use in order to maximize reliability and validity.

Easier identification will alert professionals and assist in decisions for safety (Jones, 1995). Of course, an equally important second step is risk communication (Schopp, 1996). Some have recommended that risk communication be expressed in probabilistic terms (Monahan & Steadman, 1996). Yet, because they use qualitative and categorical information, clinicians remain uncomfortable with the expression of explicit probabilities. Clinicians also find communication of risk assessments using a 100-point probability scale both pretentious and open to misinterpretation (Lidz et al., 1993). Probability of violence expressed (and perceived) may vary according to the scale used (i.e., categorical versus probabilistic, Monahan & Steadman, 1996; percentages versus chances, Slovic & Monahan, 1995). Borum (1996) recommends that practice guidelines and training curricula be developed to improve the practice of risk assessment and communication.

The approach used influences the communication statement that will be made. Clinical methods remain as reliable as actuarial methods for short-term prediction (e.g., emergency room). Because actuarial strategies are helpful for long-term prediction (e.g., one year or more, Faulk, 1994; Mossman, 1994), the use of clinical assessment methods with actuarial support (where possible) would yield a better understanding of an individual's risk level. This practice would simultaneously provide both a categorical statement (influenced by the clinical method) and a probabilistic term (influenced by the actuarial method).

Upon drawing an analogy between the forecasting of violence and the weather, Monahan and Steadman (1996) suggest a categorical risk format or communication on multiple levels (e.g., low violence risk, moderate violence risk, high violence risk, very high violence risk). The risk communication message should be context dependent and express the need for additional data on the case if necessary. It should also suggest risk management strategies. The categorical messages would address the number of risk factors present that cause concern. An accompanying message about the individual's likelihood of being violent over a specified period of time under specified conditions would be most ideal. Ultimately, the goals, as with most warning systems, are to alert us to a probable event and influence the actions of decision-makers for safety and security.

Conclusion

Although early generation studies revealed that clinical estimates of violence were not very accurate (Monahan, 1981), recent research promises a better hit rate (Monahan, 1992). Moreover, a reevaluation of the early generation research indicates that those studies were not designed to assess the reliability and validity of dangerousness assessments (Litwack & Schlesinger, 1999). What is clear is that research is meant to help practitioners and, if the latter are showing difficulty in making accurate assessments, then the former has not obtained/ disseminated the necessary information to improve the practice of making assessments. By gathering field experts on specific risk factors, this book aims to underscore the empirical contributions that have been made toward a better understanding of what influences dangerousness.

A number of risk factors have been identified in this chapter. Nevertheless, the impact of a given risk factor and how it is gauged remains a challenge to the clinician who must interpret the risk profile, regardless of whether it is generated by qualitative or quantitative methods. The assessment of dangerousness is important because of its implications for management of dangerousness (Gunn, 1993). This entails measures of security, supervision, and support in both the institution and the community (Lidz & Mulvey, 1995). The goal is to assess factors that led the individual to be aggressive in the past, ascertain how many of these factors are amenable to change, and then to intervene to alter the triggering factors so that the risk of violence is reduced.

What next? Researchers must manage the methodological problems in the study of violence and mental disorders. These problems are rooted in weak measurement of both predictors and outcomes, ethical constraints, poor collaboration, and the absence of a unified theoretical perspective (Gunn, 1993). In his reflections, Marzuk (1996) suggested five strategies to improve the state of research on violence, including more prospective studies, greater focus on possible mediating variables such as impulsivity and temperament, the development of a comprehensive typology of violent behavior, further exploration of biological influences on violence, and the investigation of how exposure to violence propagates further violence. Finally, we propose that continued attempts to understand the synergistic influence of certain variables over others (as is found in cases of comorbidity, e.g., alcohol on Axis I or Axis II disorders, the influence of multiple diagnoses) and how different systems interact (psychological, social, and biological) will have an important impact on how dangerousness can be assessed and managed.

REFERENCES

American Psychological Association (1978). Report of the task force on the role of psychology in the criminal justice system. *American Psychologist, 33,* 1099–1113.
Binder, R. L., & McNeil, D. E. (1990). The relationship of gender of violent behavior in acutely disturbed psychiatric patients. *Journal of Clinical Psychiatry, 51,* 110–114.
Borum, R. (1996). Improving the clinical practice of violence risk assessment: Technology, guidelines, and training. *American Psychologist, 51*(9), 945–956.
Brain, P. F. (1986). *Alcohol and aggression.* New York: Croom Helm.
Brunner, H. G. (1996). MAOA deficiency and abnormal behaviour: Perspectives on an association. *CIBA Foundation Symposium, 194,* 155–164.
Brunner, H. G., Nelen, M., Breakfield, X. O., Ropers, H. H., & van Oost, B. A. (1993). Abnormal behavior associated with a point mutation in the structural gene for monoamine oxidase A. *Science, 262,* 578–580.
Bryant, E. T., Scott, M. L., Golden, C. J., & Tori, C. D. (1984). Neuropsychological deficits, learning disability, and violent behavior. *Journal of Consulting and Clinical Psychology, 52,* 323–324.

Cases, O., Seif, I., Grimsby, J., Gaspar, P., Chen, K., Pournin, S., Muller, U., Aguet, M., Babinet, C., Shih, J. C., et al. (1995). Aggressive behavior and altered amounts of brain serotonin and norepinephrine in mice lacking MAOA. *Science, 268*(5218), 1763–1766.

Coccaro, E. F., Kavoussi, R. J., Sheline, Y. I., Lish, J. D., & Csernansky, J. G. (1996). Impulsive aggression in personality disorder correlates with tritiated paroxetine binding in the platelet. *Archives of General Psychiatry, 53*(6), 531–536.

Dershowitz, A. (1969). The psychiatrist's power in civil commitment. *Psychology Today, 47.*

Elliott, F. A. (1992). Violence, the neurologic contribution: An overview. *Archives of Neurology, 49*, 595–603.

Eronen, M., Hakola, P., & Tiihonen, J. (1996). Mental disorders and homicidal behavior in Finland. *Archives of General Psychiatry, 53*, 497–504.

Farrington, D. P., Loeber, R., Stouthamer-Loeber, M., Vankammen, W. B., & Schmidt, L. (1996). Self-reported delinquency and a combined delinquency seriousness scale based on boys, mothers and teachers: Concurrent and predictive validity for African-Americans and Caucasians. *Criminology, 34*(4), 493–517.

Faulk (1994). *Basic forensic psychiatry* (2nd ed.). London: Blackwell Scientific.

Felson, R. B., & Steadman, H. J. (1983). Situational factors in disputes leading to criminal violence. *Criminology, 21*, 59–74.

Festhouse, A. R., & Kellert, S. R. (1987). Childhood cruelty to animals and later aggression against people. *American Journal of Psychiatry, 144*, 710–717.

Foucault, M. (1981). L'évolution de la notion de l'individu dangereux" dans la psychiatrie légale. *Déviance et Société, 5*(4), 403–422.

Garza-Trevino, E. S. (1994). Neurobiological factors in aggressive behavior. *Hospital and Community Psychiatry, 45*, 690–699.

Gondolf, E. W., Mulvey, E. P., & Lidz, C. W. (1991). Psychiatric admission of family violent versus nonfamily violent patients. *International Journal of Law & Psychiatry, 14*(3), 245–254.

Grisso, T., & Tomkins, A. J. (1996). Communicating violence risk assessments. *American Psychologist, 51*(9), 928–930.

Gunn, J. (1982). Defining the terms. In J. R. Hamilton & H. Freeman (Eds.), *Dangerousness: Psychiatric assessment and management* (pp. 7–11). London: Gaskell.

Gunn, J. (1991). Human violence: A biological perspective. *Criminal Behaviour and Mental Health, 1*, 34–54.

Gunn, J. (1993). Dangerousness. In J. Gunn & P. Taylor (Eds.), *Forensic psychiatry: Clinical, legal and ethical issues* (pp. 624–645). Oxford: Butterworth-Heinemann.

Guze, S. B., Tuason, V. B., Gatfield, P. D., et al. (1962). Psychiatric illness and crime with particular reference to alcoholism: A study of 233 criminals. *Journal of Nervous and Mental Disease, 134*, 512–521.

Hamilton, A. M. (1916). *Recollections of an alienist.* New York: George H. Doran.

Harding, T. W., & Montandon, C. (1982). Does dangerousness travel well? In J. R. Hamilton & H. Freeman (Eds.), *Dangerousness: Psychiatric assessment and management.* London: Gaskell.

Hare, R. D. (1996). Psychopathy: A clinical construct whose time has come. *Criminal Justice and Behavior, 23,* 25–54.

Higley, J. D., Mehlman, P. T., Higley, S. B., Fernald, B., Vickers, J., Lindell, S. G., Taub, D. M., Suomi, S. J., & Linnoila, M. (1996). Excessive mortality in young free-ranging male nonhuman primates with low cerebrospinal fluid 5-hydroxyindoleacetic acid concentrations. *Archives of General Psychiatry, 53*(6), 537–543.

Jones, D. (1995). Predictions of dangerousness. In B. Kidd & C. Stark (Eds.), *Management of violence and aggression in health care* (pp. 12–26). London: Gaskell.

Jordan, B. K., Schlenger, W. E., Fairbank, J. A., & Caddell, J. M. (1996). Prevalence of psychiatric disorders among incarcerated women. II. Convicted felons entering prison. *Archives of General Psychiatry, 53,* 513–519.

Kalunian, D. A., Binder, R. L., & McNiel, D. E. (1990). Violence by geriatric patients who need psychiatric hospitalization. *Journal of Clinical Psychiatry, 51*(8), 340–343.

Kausch, O., & Resnick, P. J. (1999). Psychiatric assessment of the violent offender. In V. B. Van Hasselt & H. Hersen (Eds.), *Handbook of psychological approaches with violent offenders: Contemporary strategies and issues* (pp. 439–457). New York: Kluwer Academic/Plenum.

Krakowski, M. I., Convit, A., Jaeger, J., Lin, S., & Volavka, J. (1989). Neurological impairment in violent schizophrenic inpatients. *American Journal of Psychiatry, 146*(7), 849–853.

Lawson, W. B., Yesavage, J. A., & Werner, P. D. (1984). Race, violence, and psychopathology. *Journal of Clinical Psychiatry, 45,* 294–297.

Lidz, C. W., & Mulvey, E. P. (1995). Dangerousness: From legal definition to theoretical research. *Law and Human Behavior, 19*(1), 41–48.

Lidz, C. W., Mulvey, E. P., & Gardner, W. P. (1993). The accuracy of prediction of violence to others. *Journal of the American Medical Association, 269,* 1007–1011.

Link, B., Andrews, H., & Cullen, F. (1992). The violent and illegal behavior of mental patients reconsidered. *American Sociological Review, 57,* 275–292.

Link, B. G., & Stueve, A. (1998). Commentary. New evidence on the violence risk posed by people with mental illness: On the importance of specifying the timing and the targets of violence. *Archives of General Psychiatry, 55,* 403–404.

Link, B. G., & Stueve, C. A. (1994). Psychotic symptoms and the violent/illegal behavior of mental patients compared to community controls. In J. Monahan & H. J. Steadman (Eds.), *Violence and mental disorders: Developments in risk assessment* (pp. 137–160). Chicago: University of Chicago Press.

Linnoila, M., & Virkkunen, M. (1992). Aggression, suicidality, and serotonin. *Journal of Clinical Psychiatry, 53*(supp. 1), 46–51.

Litwack, T. R., & Schlesinger, L. B. (1999). Dangerousness risk assessments: Research, legal, and clinical considerations. In A. K. Hess & I. B. Weiner (Eds.), *The handbook of forensic psychology* (2nd ed., pp. 171–217). New York: Wiley.

MacDonald, J. M. (1963). The threat to kill. *American Journal of Psychiatry, 120,* 120–130.

Marzuk, P. M. (1996). Editorial. Violence, crime, and mental illness: How strong a link? *Archives of General Psychiatry, 53,* 481–486.

Megargee, E. I. (1981). Methodological problems in the prediction of violence. In J. R. Hays, T. K. Roberts, & K. S. Solway (Eds.), *Violence and the violent individual* (pp. 179–191). New York: Spectrum.

Mehlman, P. T., Higley, J. D., Faucher, I., Lilly, A. A., Taub, D. M., Vickers, J., Suomi, S. J., & Linnoila, M. (1994). Low CSF 5-HIAA concentrations and severe aggression and impaired impulse control in nonhuman primates. *American Journal of Psychiatry, 151*(10), 1485–1491.

Meloy, J. R. (1995). *The psychopathic mind origins, dynamics, and treatment.* Northvale, NJ: Jason Aronson.

Melton, G. B., Petrila, J., Poythress, N. G., & Slobogin, C. (1997). *Psychological evaluations for the courts* (2nd ed.). New York: Guilford Press.

Monahan, J. (1981). *The clinical prediction of violent behavior.* Washington, DC: National Institute of Mental Health.

Monahan, J. (1992). Mental disorder and violent behavior: Perceptions and evidence. *American Psychologist, 47*(4), 511–521.

Monahan, J. (1993). Limiting therapist exposure to Tarasoff liability. *American Psychologist, 48*(3), 242–250.

Monahan, J., & Steadman, H. J. (1996). Violent storms and violent people: How meteorology can inform risk communication in mental health law. *American Psychologist, 51*(9), 931–938.

Mossman, D. (1994). Assessing predictions of violence: Being accurate about accuracy. *Journal of Consulting & Clinical Psychology, 62*(4), 783–792.

Mulvey, E. P. (1994). Assessing the evidence of a link between mental illness and violence. *Hospital and Community Psychiatry, 45,* 663–668.

Mulvey, E. P., & Lidz, C. W. (1994). Conditional prediction: A model for research on dangerousness to others in a new era. *International Journal of Law and Psychiatry, 18*(2), 129–143.

Norko, M. A. (1999). 1998 Presidential Address. Dr. Binder: Are the mentally ill dangerous? *American Academy of Psychiatry and the Law, 24*(1), 1–3.

Otto, R. K. (1992). Prediction of dangerous behavior: A review and analysis of second generation research. *Forensic Reports, 5,* 103–133.

Petrie, J. (1982). Violence in geriatric patients. *Journal of the American Medical Association, 248,* 443–448.

Phelan, J., Link, B., Stueve, A., & Pescosolido, B. (1997, August). *Public conceptions of mental illness in 1950 and today: Findings from the 1996 General Social Survey module on mental health.* Paper presented at the Annual meeting of the American Sociological Association. Toronto, ON.

Rappeport, J. R. (1967). *The clinical evaluation of the dangerousness of the mentally ill.* Springfield, IL: Charles C Thomas.

Resnick, P. J. (1969). Child murder by parents: A psychiatric review of filicide. *American Journal of Psychiatry, 126*(3), 325–334.

Robins, L. N. (1978). Study childhood predictors of adult antisocial behavior: Replications from longitudinal studies. *Psychological Medicine, 8*(4), 611–622.

Schopp, R. F. (1996). Communicating risk assessments: Accuracy, efficacy, and responsibility. *American Psychologist, 51*(9), 939–944.

Shah, S. (1975). Dangerousness and civil commitment of the mentally ill: Some public policy considerations. *American Journal of Psychiatry, 132,* 501–505.

Shah, S. (1978). Dangerousness: A paradigm for exploring some issues in law and psychology. *American Psychologist, 33,* 224–238.

Slovic, P., & Monahan, J. (1995). Probability, danger, and coercion: A study of risk perception and decision making in mental health law. *Law & Human Behavior, 19*(1), 49–65.

Steadman, H. J. (1973). Implications from the Baxstrom Experience. *Bulletin of the American Academy of Psychiatry and the Law, 1,* 189–197.

Steadman, H. J. (1982). A situational approach to violence. *International Journal of Law & Psychiatry, 5*(2), 171–186.

Steadman, H. J., Mulvey, E. P., Monahan, J., Clark Robbins, P., Appelbaum, P. S., Grisso, T., Roth, L. H., & Silver, E. (1998). Violence by people discharged from acute psychiatric inpatient facilities and by others in the same neighborhoods. *Archives of General Psychiatry, 55,* 393–401.

Stueve, A., & Link, B. G. (1997). Violence and psychiatric disorders: Results from an epidemiological study of young adults in Israel. *Psychiatric Quarterly, 68*(4), 327–342.

Swanson, J. W., Holzer, C. E., Ganju, V. K., & Jono, R. T. (1990). Violence and psychiatric disorder in the community: Evidence from the epidemiologic catchment area surveys. *Hospital and Community Psychiatry, 41*(7), 761–770.

Tardiff, K. (1989). A model for the short-term prediction of violence potential. In D. A. Brizer & M. L. Crowner (Eds.), *Current approaches to the prediction of violence* (pp. 3–12). Washington, DC: American Psychiatric Press.

Tardiff, K. (1992). The current state of psychiatry in the treatment of violent patients. *Archives of General Psychiatry, 49,* 493–499.

Tardiff, K., & Koenigsberg, H. W. (1985). Assaultive behavior among psychiatric outpatients. *American Journal of Psychiatry, 142,* 960–963.

Tardiff, K., & Sweillam, A. (1982). Assaultive behavior among chronic inpatients. *American Journal of Psychiatry, 139,* 212–215.

Teplin, L. A., Abram, K. M., & McClelland, G. M. (1996). Prevalence of psychiatric disorders among incarcerated women. I. Pretrial jail detainees. *Archives of General Psychiatry, 53,* 505–512.

Tiihonen, J., & Hakola, P. (1994). Psychiatric disorders and homicide recidivism. *American Journal of Psychiatry, 151*(3), 436–438.

Tiihonen, J., Räsänen, P., & Hakko, H. (1997). Seasonal variation in the occurrence of homicide in Finland. *American Journal of Psychiatry, 154*(12), 1711–1714.

Virkkunen, M., De Jong, J., Bartko, J., Goodwin, F. K., & Linnoila, M. (1989). Relationship of psychobiological variables to recidivism in violent offenders and impulsive fire setters: A follow-up study. *Archives of General Psychiatry, 46,* 600–603.

Virkkunen, M., Eggert, M., Rawlings, R., & Linnoila, M. (1996). A prospective follow-up study of alcoholic violent offenders and fire setters. *Archives of General Psychiatry, 53,* 523–529.

Wessely, S. C., Castle, D., & Douglas, A. J. (1994). The criminal careers of incident cases of schizophrenia. *Psychological Medicine, 24,* 483–502.

Widom, C. S. (1989). The cycle of violence. *Science, 244*(4901), 160–166.

2. Biology, Development, and Dangerousness

ELIZABETH J. SUSMAN AND
JORDAN W. FINKELSTEIN

Introduction

The purpose is to present a developmental perspective on biological factors and dangerousness. The developmental perspective proposed is that biological factors and violence can only be understood by considering the dialectical nature of the interactions between physiological and psychological processes and the environmental contexts in which individuals develop. The chapter aims to define domains of behavior relevant to understanding biology and dangerousness; describe biopsychosocial models of dangerousness; present literature on the endocrine and serotonergic systems, autonomic nervous system, and dangerousness; and suggest clinical implications based on what is known about biological processes and dangerousness.

Behavioral Domains of Dangerousness and Biological Processes

The concept of dangerousness is difficult to define because it entails both psychological and behavioral risks that predispose to physical aggression and violent behavior. Furthermore, violence, aggression, and other forms of antisocial behavior are defined in diverse ways in the literature and tend to refer to constructs rather than specific behaviors. These constructs include antisocial behavior, externalizing behavior, norm breaking, violence, and illegal behavior. In contrast, when biological processes are included in research, measures representing one biological system tend to be considered: Hormones, neurotransmitters, or psychophysiological measures. Thus, conclusions regarding the relationships between interactive biological systems and violence are exceedingly simplistic even though multidimensional behaviors, attitudes, and various forms of violent behavior are immeasurably complex. An added layer of complexity entails the changing phenotypic nature of antisocial behavior throughout development.

Childhood physical aggression may become transformed to overt and covert forms of deviant behavior as development progresses in social, emotional, and behavioral domains. Similarly, physiological systems are changing during successive periods of development. For instance, at puberty, gonadal and adrenal hormone levels increase rapidly whereas these same hormones begin to decline in adulthood. In spite of these complexities, specific biological substances are somewhat reliably associated with various forms of antisocial behavior.

The manifestations of antisocial behavior included in biobehavioral studies are diverse. Generally accepted definitions of antisocial behavior include the following. Physical aggression refers to acts designed to injure another person and tend to be the focus of studies with children. Violence refers to acts that induce physical harm toward another individual. Domestic violence refers to aggression within a family. Antisocial behavior is a more inclusive construct that refers to relational and physical aggression, behavior problems and early and risky sex, substance use, conduct disorder, delinquency, and violence. The discussion that follows will include physical aggression and violence as components of the larger construct of antisocial behavior. We will use the term *antisocial behavior* to refer to the constructs mentioned above unless the literature cited uses a specific term like violence.

Models for Considering Biological Processes and Antisocial Behavior

The history of the biology of violence is short even though the need to integrate biological, psychological, and contextual (i.e., peers, family, communities) processes and antisocial behavior has been articulated for decades. The neglect of biology can partially be attributed to the arcane assumption of the primacy of biology as a causal influence on violence. Factors contributing to the current increase in research on biology and violence include the rejection of the primacy of biology. The models for considering biology and antisocial behavior now consider the complex bidirectional influences between biological, social, and contextual processes (Cairns & Stoff, 1996). The previous lack of integration of biological processes in studies of antisocial behavior is inconsistent with contemporary developmental perspectives that individuals develop and function as biologically and socially integrated organisms. Developmental theorists propose that maturational (biological), experiential, and cultural contributions are fused in ontogeny (Lerner & Foch, 1987; Magnusson & Cairns, 1996). Single aspects of development, like antisocial behavior, do not develop in isolation. Alternatively, it can be argued that antisocial behavior, similar to other developmental problems – depression (Compas & Hammen, 1994), adolescent violence, and pregnancy (Sells & Blum, 1995) – reflect exclusively social processes. To the extent that biological processes can explain individual differences in development and that behavior can explain individual differences in biology, then biological processes seem worthy of consideration in relation to antisocial behavior.

Current Developmental Models and Antisocial Behavior

For earlier developmental theorists, the concept of development was synonymous with biological change (e.g., Harris, 1957; Schneirla, 1957). "The concept of development is fundamentally biological" (Harris, p. 3). Within this early and still relevant perspective the concept of development refers to progressive changes in physical structures, systems and processes, systems of ideas and the organization of living structures and life processes that include emotional, social, and cognitive development as well as the contexts of development. Contemporary theorists consider development as successive changes that entail structural (biological change), as well as functional changes in psychological and behavioral capabilities that are molded by the contexts of development (Lerner, 1986). These contexts include the history of the individual, peers, family, and extra-familial institutions.

Two very different disciplinary paradigms are reflected in past approaches to antisocial behavior. Biologically oriented research focused on the role of evolution, genetics, endocrinology, neurobiology, and morphology. In contrast, behavioral research was concerned with processes within the person and the social environment. From the latter perspective, aggression is viewed as an atypical outcome derived from early familial and childhood experiences and learning experiences with deviant peers. These research models and methods did not traverse the multiple levels of analysis involved in complex antisocial behavior. The challenge for modern scientific paradigms is to explain how integration occurs across genetic, physiological, psychological, and social levels to influence the development of antisocial behavior

(Cairns & Stoff, 1996; Brain & Susman; 1997; Magnusson & Cairns, 1996; Susman, 1997).

A biobehavioral science recognizes that behaviors are simultaneously determined by processes within the individual, in the social ecology, and in interactions between the two. A focus on either social or biological factors can yield only part of the story of aggressive and violent behaviors: integrative investigations are essential to complete the picture. (Cairns & Stoff, 1996, p. 338)

Recent studies are beginning to accomplish the aim of biobehavioral integration by incorporating indexes of physiological functioning (e.g., hormones, psychophysiological indexes, neurotransmitters) with psychological and contextual measures of antisocial behavior. Biology and antisocial behavior are consolidated at multiple levels of analysis (Cairns & Stoff, 1996). Dialectical relations exist between successive layers of development: cells, organs, organ systems, whole organisms, social environment (Hinde, 1987). There are different implications for the prevention of antisocial behavior when antisocial behavior is viewed from one level of analysis.

Specific Models for Considering Biology and Violence

Four basic models for considering biological processes and development are represented by the paths in Figure 2.1 (see also Susman, 1997). Model I represents the direct effects of biological influences on antisocial behavior. Model II shows the effect of antisocial behavior on biological processes. This model became increasingly popular during the last few decades as a result of studies showing the effects of challenging and stressful experiences on physiological systems, particularly the hypothalamic-pituitary-gonadal (HPG) and hypothalamic-pituitary-adrenal (HPA) axes (Booth, Shelley, Mazur, Tharp, & Kittok, 1989; Brooks-Gunn, Graber, & Paikoff, 1994; Mazur, Susman, & Edelbrock, 1997). As reviewed above, inherent in models of development are the reciprocal influences of biology and antisocial behavior as represented in Model III. Antisocial behavior may alter biological processes, which then accelerates or decelerates the probability of future antisocial behavior. Success in dominance encounters, for instance, may elevate testosterone (T), in turn, accelerating dominance (Mazur & Booth, 1998). The final model depicts the reciprocal effects of the contexts of development, biology, and antisocial behavior (Model IV). Contexts can include both biological (e.g., endocrine system) and social-environmental contexts. The models and corre-

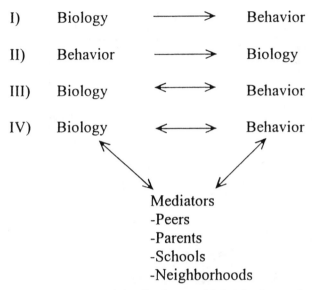

Figure 2.1. Four models of biology and behavior interactions.

sponding statistical strategies can be used to simultaneously test the validity of competing hypotheses regarding biology and behavior interactions (see Brooks-Gunn & Warren, 1989; Raine, Brennan, & Farrington, 1997; Susman & Ponirakis, 1997; Susman et al., 1987). Thus, the models of biological processes as influencing behavior and behavior as influencing biology gain validity if considered in conjunction but invalid if considered in isolation.

Raine et al. (1997) proposed a biosocial model of violence that includes genetics, environment, biological risks, social risks, biosocial interactions, biological and social protective factors, and violence. The Model appears in Figure 2.2. Genes and environmental factors are considered building blocks for influences on risk and protective factors. These factors interact to produce antisocial outcomes. Similarly, reciprocal relationships can exist between biological and social risk factors. For example, the biological risk factor of lower HPA axis arousal may stimulate an adolescent to engage in high-risk fighting in deviant peer groups. In addition, biological and social factors also can have direct effects on violence. Finally, the pathways to violence can be deterred by protective factors that interrupt the progression of certain paths. The majority of the pathways are not yet supported by empirical findings but the models described above have heuristic value for formulating hypotheses.

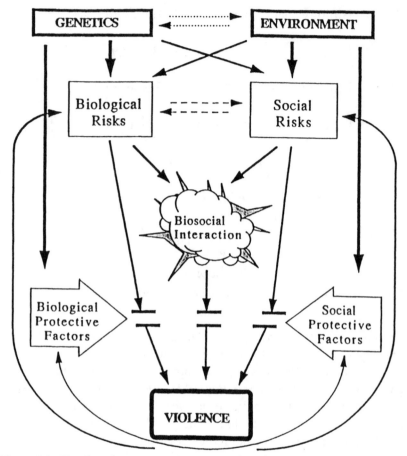

Figure 2.2. Heuristic biosocial model of violence. From Raine, A., Brennan, P., & Farrington, D. P. (1997). Biosocial bases of violence: Conceptual and theoretical issues. In A. Raine, P. A. Brennan, D. P. Farrington, & S. A. Mednick (Eds.), *Biosocial bases of violence* (pp. 1–20), New York, Plenum.

Biological Systems and Antisocial Behavior

Multiple systems are implicated in the biology of violence: endocrine, serotonergic, dopaminergic, autonomic nervous, and other systems. Herein we consider the most frequently considered systems: endocrine, serotonergic, and autonomic nervous system (see Henry & Moffitt, 1997; Raine, Farrington, Brennan, & Mednick, 1997; Stoff & Cairns, 1996 for reviews of biological systems). Noteworthy is that interacting products of biological systems are more likely to be reliable indicators of risk for antisocial behavior than specific products.

Endocrine System and Antisocial Behavior

Products of the endocrine system, principally, the steroid hormone, T, often are implicated in physical aggression in animals and antisocial behavior in humans (see Brain, 1994 for an extensive review). The effects of gonadal steroids on antisocial behavior are hypothesized to derive from the regulatory functions of hormones during pre- and post-natal periods as well as in later development. Speculation was that during brief, sensitive periods in pre- and early post-natal development, hormones are capable of affecting brain development such that behavior is influenced later in development. The early structural changes are referred to as organizational influences (Phoenix, Goy, Gerall, & Young, 1959). Activational influences stem from contemporaneous influences of hormones on behavior and refer to regulatory effects of previously established neural circuits. Commonly observed human sexual dimorphisms in brain structure, function, and behavioral expression are believed to originate from the differential organizational and activational effects of gonadal hormones. Recent thinking implicates hormones as having organizational influences throughout the life span as well as during the pre- and early post-natal periods of development. Adult neural circuits can respond to hormonal manipulation with structural changes in avian model studies (Gould, Woolley, & McEwen, 1991). Steroidal hormones collectively modulate brain neurochemistry and neurotransmitter functioning in multiple ways. Hormones can be viewed as substances that change the probability, versus cause antisocial behavior, that antisocial behavior will occur in certain situations in individuals with specific developmental experiences (Brain & Susman, 1997). In addition, behavior and experiences change the concentrations of specific hormones, thereby increasing or decreasing the probability of antisocial behavior.

Gonadal Steroids and Antisocial Behavior

Testosterone. Testosterone is the hormone most often linked to a variety of antisocial behaviors: physical aggression, dominance, and violence. In an extensive review of the literature, Mazur and Booth (1998) conclude that dominance is more closely linked to T than is physical aggression. Dominance may entail physical aggression with the intent of inflicting harm, although dominance also can be expressed nonaggressively such as in competitiveness.

Evidence for the role of T on antisocial behavior is derived from both correlational and experimental studies. In correlational studies in adult males, higher T is associated with aggressive behavior, dominance, and hostility (Persky, Smith, & Basu, 1971; Ehrenkranz, Bliss, & Sheard, 1974; Olweus, Mattson, Schalling, & Low, 1980; 1988). The links between relatively high T and specific antisocial acts are somewhat consistent. Dabbs, Frady, Carr, and Besch (1987) report that males with higher T committed more violent crimes, were judged more harshly by parole board members, and violated prison rules more often than men with lower T levels. Others studies have not found a relationship between T and aggressive behavior (see Archer, 1991). Inconsistencies across studies likely stem from differences in sample characteristics and measures. Developmental differences between children, adolescents, and adults add complexity to explaining relationships between T and antisocial behavior. Overall, the relationships between T and antisocial behavior are less consistent in pubertal age boys than would be anticipated given the theory that hormones bring to expression at puberty, activational influences, behaviors such as physical aggression that have been sensitized to androgens in the pre- and peri-natal period. Activational influences were not observed in the association between T and aggressive behavior in young adolescents (Susman et al., 1987) or in 4- to 10-year-old children with diagnoses of conduct problems (Constantino et al., 1993). In older adolescents, Olweus and colleagues (1988) found evidence for the causal role of T on provoked and unprovoked aggression. Testosterone at grade 9 exerted a direct causal influence on provoked aggressive behavior. Testosterone appeared to lower boys' frustration tolerance. A higher level of T appears to lead to an increased readiness to respond with vigor and assertion to provocation. For unprovoked aggressive behavior (starting fights and verbal aggression) at grade 9, the findings were somewhat different. Testosterone had no direct effects on unprovoked aggressive behavior. There was an indirect effect of T with low frustration tolerance as the mediating variable. Higher levels of T made the boys more impatient and irritable, in turn, increasing readiness to engage in unprovoked aggressive behavior. It is noteworthy that the associations between antisocial behavior and T are less apparent in children and younger adolescents (Brooks-Gunn & Warren, 1989; Constantino et al.,

1993; Nottelmann et al., 1987; Susman et al., 1987) than in older adolescents (Olweus, 1986; Olweus et al., 1988) and adults (Archer, 1991). These inconsistencies should be expected given the different measures of antisocial behavior. Nonetheless, some measures do capture subtle differences in adolescents with higher T levels. Adolescents with higher levels of T exhibit behaviors that are distinguishable from behavior in boys with lower T. Boy's perceptions of peer dominance were reflected in T concentrations (Schaal, Tremblay, Soussignan, & Susman, 1996). Testosterone was significantly higher in perceived leaders than in nonleaders.

The developmental differences in findings for children, adolescents, and adults indicate that elevated T and antisocial behavior may be a consequence rather than a cause of aggressive behavior during adulthood (Constantino et al., 1993; Susman, Worrall, Murowchick, Frobose, & Schwab, 1996). Model II postulates the effects of behavior on hormone concentrations. Longitudinal evidence of Model II is derived from a study of disruptive boys followed from age 6 to 13 (Schaal et al., 1996). Boys consistently displaying disruptive behavior problems across 6 years were significantly lower on T and were later in pubertal maturation compared to nondisruptive boys. The effect of antisocial behavior on suppression of gonadal steroids may result from the secretion of stress-related products of the HPA axis (corticotropin releasing hormone [CRH], adrenocorticotropin hormone [ACTH], and cortisol [Susman, Nottlemann, Dorn, Gold, & Chrousos, 1989]). Overall, the role of T in antisocial behavior is supported, but the periods of development when antisocial behavior will emerge and contextual factors that facilitate expression of T-related antisocial behavior are yet to be identified. Situations that threaten dominance may be especially notable to explore in future studies. Mazur and Booth (1998) conclude that high levels of endogenous T encourage behavior intended to dominate others.

Estrogen. The effects of estrogen on antisocial behavior only recently was considered. The lack of research on estrogen and antisocial behavior is reflective of two issues. First, males only are included in the majority of studies on hormones and antisocial behavior as physical aggression and violence are not considered a major problem in women. Second, T was considered the major hormone associated with antisocial behavior until recently when estrogen effects began to be considered as paralleling those of T. In adult males, estradiol (E_2) correlated positively with reports of physical, verbal, and impatient aggression (Gladue, 1991). Of note is that girls with higher concentrations of E_2 were likely to show greater dominance while interacting with their parents (Inoff-Germain et al., 1988). The current interest in gender phenotypic antisocial behavior (i.e., relational aggression), is likely to lead to greater specification of the role of estrogen in antisocial behavior. The role of estrogen in antisocial behavior in males also appears possible because T can be aromatized to estrogen. The extensive distribution of estrogen receptors in the brain indicates that estrogen can influence a variety of behaviors in both sexes.

Experimental studies are the preferred research design for establishing T or estrogen effects on antisocial behavior. Thus, we conducted a study in adolescents with delayed puberty who were being treated with physiological doses of T (boys) or conjugated estrogen (girls) in a placebo controlled, randomized, double-blind, cross-over design (Finkelstein et al., 1997; Finkelstein et al., 1998; Susman et al., 1998). Each 3-month treatment period was preceded and followed by a 3-month placebo period. The doses of gonadal steroids were calculated to simulate the concentrations of gonadal steroids in blood in normal early, middle, and late pubertal adolescents. Aggressive behaviors were measured by self-reports about physical and verbal aggression against peers and adults, aggressive impulses, and aggressive inhibitory behaviors. Significant increases in self-reported aggressive impulses and in physical aggression against both peers and adults were seen in girls at the low and middle dose. Significant increases in aggressive impulses and physical aggression against peers and adults were seen in boys but only at the middle dose. The findings demonstrate the influential role of gonadal steroid hormones in the initiation of aggression at puberty in adolescents with delayed puberty.

Adrenal Androgens. The adrenal androgens traditionally receive little attention in relation to antisocial behavior. Nonetheless, adrenal androgens are associated with aggressive behavior, affective expression, psychiatric disorders, and sexual behavior (Brooks-Gunn & Warren, 1989; Susman et al., 1987; Udry, Bill, Morris, Groff, & Raj, 1985; Udry & Talbert, 1988). The adrenal androgens are considered "weak" bonding androgens relative to T (Bondy, 1985). Adrenal androgen actions may parallel those of T in relation to behavior as one of the adrenal androgens, androstenedione, is a precursor of both T and estrogen. The rationale for examining antisocial behavior and adrenal androgens stems from both animal and human model studies. In the female spotted hyena, androstenedione concentrations are high and the females are highly aggressive and masculinized both anatomically and behaviorally (Glickman, Frank, Davidson, Smith, & Sitteri, 1987). High androstenedione concentrations during pregnancy may organize the sex-reversed traits of female spotted hyenas (Yalcinkaya et al., 1993). The role of androstenedione in humans is not clear beyond its role in the development of secondary sex characteristics during puberty.

In the last decade, four studies report relationships between adrenal androgens and antisocial behavior in adolescents. In pubertal age girls (Brooks-Gunn & Warren, 1989), higher dehydroepiandrosterone sulphate (DHEAS) correlated negatively with aggressive affect. The interaction between negative life events and DHEAS and aggressive affect showed that girls with lower concentrations of DHEAS and experienced negative life events had more aggressive affect than girls with fewer negative life events. The second study included 9- to 14-year-old adolescents. A consistent pattern of high adrenal androgens and low gonadal steroids was associated with problem behaviors and negative affect (Nottelmann et al., 1987; 1990; Susman et al., 1987; 1991). Adrenal androgens also correlate with dominance (Inoff-Germain et al., 1988). The third study demonstrates the contribution of adrenal androgens to sexual behavior and activities (Udry et al., 1985; Udry & Talbert, 1988). A fourth study with conduct disordered boys reported significantly higher levels of dehydroepiandrosterone (DHEA) and DHEAS and the intensity of aggression and delinquency (van Goozen, Matthys, Cohen-Kettenis, Thijssen, & van Engeland, 1998). Thus, the consistent association between adrenal androgens and antisocial behavior indicates further study.

Cortisol and Antisocial Behavior. In the 1980s, studies began to assess the relationship between products of the HPA axis, principally cortisol, and antisocial behavior. In general, antisocial behavior is associated with lower concentrations of HPA products. Virkunnen et al. (1994) showed that cerebrospinal fluid CRH was low in substance abusers and offenders and cortisol was low in habitually violent offenders. Similarly, in males with a violent history of abusing others, cortisol levels were lower than levels in comparison males (Bergman & Brismar, 1994). Lower cortisol levels are also characteristic of children who are at risk for behavior problems. Cortisol levels were lower in preadolescent sons whose fathers had conduct disorder as children and who subsequently developed antisocial personality (Vanyukov, Moss, Plail, Mezzick, & Tarter, 1993). Lower levels of cortisol also were reported in prepubertal children of parents with a psychoactive substance use disorder (PSUD) (Moss, Vanyukov, & Martin, 1995). Boys at high risk for PSUD secreted less salivary cortisol than controls in anticipation of a stressful task (Moss et al., 1995). Finally, adolescents with lower levels of plasma cortisol prior to a stressful situation (a phlebotomy procedure), but showed an increase across 40 minutes, had significantly more symptoms of conduct disorder a year later than children who decreased or those who maintained consistent levels (Susman, Dorn, Inoff-Germain & Nottelmann, Chrousos, 1997). Low HPA axis responsivity and antisocial behavior correspond to the cardiovascular system underarousal and aggressive behavior relationships observed in adolescents and adults (Raine, 1996). Individuals low on HPA axis arousal may seek out stimulating and risky situations that entail antisocial behavior.

Neurotransmitters

Serotonin. The monoamines, specifically, serotonin, represent the neurotransmitter system extensively examined in relation to antisocial behavior, although a variety of neurotransmitters may be implicated in antisocial behavior (Berman, Kavoussi, & Coccaro, 1997; Virkkunen & Linnoila, 1990). Serotonin is the most widely distributed monoamine neurotransmitter in the brain, is an inhibitory neurotransmitter (Berman et al., 1997), and plays a role in sexual behavior, analgesia, appetite, sleep, and mood. The three primary methods for measuring serotonergic function are: measurement of the primary serotonin (5-HT) metabolite in cerebrospinal fluid (CSF 5-HIAA [5-hydroxyindoleacetic acid]), endocrine responses to drug challenges, and serotonin in blood (whole blood 5-HT or platelet 5-HT uptake) (Moffitt et al., 1998). Measures of serotonin function can reflect either presynaptic availability of serotonin (e.g., reuptake) or postsynaptic neuronal sensitivity (e.g., receptor density). Studies that include assessment of serotonin tend to be carried out in clinical or forensic samples (see exception below). In these samples, the distribution of violence scores can be distorted because of a restricted range, which may reduce the sensitivity of a biological marker (Rasmusson, Riddle, Lechman, Anderson, & Cohen, 1990). The information regarding the causal role of serotonin in the development of antisocial behavior remains limited.

Dysfunctions of the serotonergic system are hypothesized to reduce the regulation of human aggression (Coccaro, 1989, Virkkunen & Linnoila, 1993). Serotonin dysregulation related disorders, such as violence and depression, are associated with low levels of serotonin. Serotonergic parameters are lower in adults with aggressive behavior (e.g., Brown et al., 1982; Brown & Linnoila, 1990; Coccaro et al., 1989; Virkkunen et al., 1994; LeMarquand, Pihl, & Benkelfat, 1994) and in suicide attempters and completers (Asberg, Schalling, Traksman-Bendz, & Wagner, 1987). The magnitude of the involvement of serotonin in antisocial behavior and psychiatric disorders varies developmentally. In children or adolescents, findings link the serotonergic system and aggression but less consistently than in adults (Zubieta & Alessi, 1993). Specifically, there was no relationship between disruptive behavior and platelet serotonin receptor density in boys at risk for delinquency but there was a negative relationship between receptor density and physically abusive family environments (Pine et al., 1996). Developmental differences may be attributed to the longevity of the antisocial behavior, psychiatric history, and interactions with family and peers may suppress serotonin synthesis, reuptake, or degradation.

Studies measuring CSF 5-HIAA generally report a negative relationship with antisocial behavior. Specifically, reduced frontal lobe serotonin turnover rate, as indexed by low CSF 5-HIAA concentrations, is reported for impulsive, violent patients with antisocial personality disorder (Berman et al., 1997; Linnoila, 1997). Children with disruptive and aggressive problems also had lower concentrations of CSF 5-HIAA (Kruesi et al., 1992). The pharmacological challenge studies also support the findings that 5-HT is inversely related to antisocial behavior. Hormone response to fenfluramine was blunted in depressed, personality-disordered subjects, and violent criminal offenders (Berman et al., 1997; O'Keane et al., 1992). The direction and magnitude of the response to fenfluramine may be affected by depression (Coccaro et al., 1989) and substance abuse (Fishbein, Lozovsky, & Jaffe, 1989). Assessing concurrently both emotional states and antisocial behavior appears essential for an accurate interpretation of challenge tests.

Pharmacological challenges also have been used to assess serotonin and familial patterns of aggression, impulsivity, and alcohol use (Coccaro, Silverman, Klar, Horvath, & Siever, 1994). Blunting of prolactin response to fenfluramine challenge was characteristic of first-degree relatives with impulsive personality traits. Questionnaire measures of aggression were not linked with problem behaviors in relatives suggesting that the challenge test may be a better predictor of problem behaviors than questionnaires. Coccaro and colleagues (Coccaro, Berman, Kavoussi, & Hauger, 1996) did find associations between self-reported aggression in personality disordered men and prolactin response to d-fenfluramine. In contrast, in children, no relationship emerged between aggression and prolactin response to fenfluramine (Stoff et al., 1992). The findings of these challenge studies and questionnaire assessments support the perspective that analysis across biological and behavioral levels offers a more valid assessment of antisocial behavior than any analysis at one level.

Studies using whole blood 5HT or [³H] imipramine binding yield inconsistent results. Imipramine binding sites appear to be involved in the transport of serotonin from the exterior to the interior of the platelet cell surface (Berman et al., 1997). Stoff and colleagues (1987) and Birmaher et al. (1990) report a negative relationship between externalizing behavior and platelet [³H] imipramine binding in children. This relationship is not consistent across studies. Unis et al. (1997) report that whole blood 5-HT was higher in adolescents with conduct disorder, childhood type, than in others with conduct disorder, adolescent type.

Personality disorders also appear to mediate the relationship between serotonin and antisocial behavior. The often reported negative relationship between CSF 5-HIAA and aggressive behavior was not found in male or female personality-disordered patients (see Berman et al. [1997] for other instances of personality characteristics and serotonin relationships). Kruesi and Jacobsen (1997), show the importance of traits (persistent response), states (response under specified conditions), and scars (response appearing after the onset of illness or insult and then persists) as mediators of CSF 5-HIAA and human violence. The scar of early and persistent aggression related to deviant parenting represents one important environmental mediator of serotonin. The evidence for environmental scar mediation of serotonin and aggression derives from the peer-reared monkey studies. Mother-reared monkeys show significant correlations between CSF 5–HIAA, social behavior, and aggression whereas peer-reared monkeys do not exhibit this correlation (Kramer, 1997). Overall, the evidence indicates that early developmental experiences may mediate serotonin-antisocial relationships. This evidence is encouraging in that early behavioral interventions may alter the serotonergic system and thereby reduce the incidence of serotonergic-related disorders.

The problems of linking serotonin and antisocial behavior in clinical or forensic samples partially is resolved by the Moffitt et al. (1998) epidemiological study. The birth-cohort sample, measurement and analytic characteristics of the community-sample report evidence of serotonin and antisocial behavior relationships. The validity of the measures was improved over previous studies as both self-report and court records were used to assess violence. Violent men were significantly higher on serotonin than nonviolent men on both self-report and court measures even after controlling for possible confounds. Peripheral serotonin is negatively related to brain serotonin, thus, these epidemiological findings are consistent with previous findings. No relationships emerged between serotonin and violence in women.

An array of evidence supports the connections between serotonin and antisocial behavior that has been derived from clinical, forensic, and community samples of adults and children using observational and experimental methodologies. Proposed is that dysfunctions in serotonergic activity (e.g., reuptake) predispose individuals to engage in behaviors that are otherwise suppressed. In impulsive or reactive aggressive individuals, reduced central 5-HT may predispose an individual to engage in aggressive behavior that would normally not be expressed (Coccaro, 1989). The evidence that serotonin and aggressive behaviors are related in children suggests that indexes of serotonin might be a useful diagnostic tool. The mediation of serotonin by trait and state characteristics of individuals, seasonal variations, and contextual considerations indicate the need for multilevel assessments when considering a serotonin marker as a diagnostic tool.

Psychophysiology of Antisocial Behavior. The relationship between psychophysiological parameters (e.g., heart rate, skin conductance) and antisocial behavior reflects functioning of the autonomic nervous system and the brain (e.g., electroencholography). Excellent reviews of the psychophysiological correlates of antisocial behavior currently exist (Fowles, 1993; Raine, 1993; 1996; 1997). The summary here derives primarily from Raine (1996; 1997). Findings from studies of resting electroencephalograms (EEG), skin conductance (SC), and heart rate (HR) generally show characteristic underarousal in antisocial individuals. Prospective studies show a relationship between low resting heart rate and later antisocial behavior (Farrington, 1987). Low resting heart rate in children as young as 4 months predicted disinhibited behavior (Kagan, 1989). Similarly, low resting heart rate at age 3 predicted antisocial behavior at age 11 (Raine, Reynolds, Venables, & Mednick, 1997). The interpretation of these findings is that antisocial individuals are relatively fearless stimulation seekers, which entails high risk and anti-social behavior. A pattern of underarousal in children suggests that an early pattern of autonomic underarousal may be a risk factor for anti-social behavior later in development (Kagan, 1989). Underarousal may predispose to both a disinhibited temperament and later antisocial behavior.

Deficits in attentional processes also are a risk for later antisocial and criminal behavior. Event-related potential (ERP) research reviews indicate that antisocial individuals are characterized by enhanced attentional processing to events of interest (Raine, 1993). ERPs are recorded from electrodes placed on the scalp and record electrical activity of the brain in response to experimental stimuli. Responses to stimulation vary depending on early, middle, or late latency ERPs corresponding to reduced arousal and excessive filtering of environmental stimuli (stimulus deprivation), increased ERP amplitude to stimulus intensity (sensation seeking), and enhanced P300 amplitudes to stimuli that have been selectively attended to (attention to stimulating events). The behavioral consequences of these ERP patterns are suspected to be causally linked to antisocial behavior. Individuals with chronically low levels of arousal seek out stimulating events to increase their arousal to more optimal levels. Stimulation-seeking focuses attention to events of interest, such as dangerous situations, in which violence is committed.

A prefrontal dysfunction theory summarizes the relationship between psychophysiology and antisocial behavior. The prefrontal dysfunction theory posits that damage to the frontal lobe results in arousal, orienting, and anticipatory fear deficits that predispose to antisocial behavior (Linnoila, 1997; Raine, 1997). Future studies will benefit from well conceptualized and hypothesis-driven approaches to the complexity of antisocial behavior and psychophysiology (Raine, 1996). It is likely that personality, family, and psychophysiological correlates interact to propel an individual toward or away from antisocial behavior.

Clinical Implications

Given it is not yet proven that biological substances cause antisocial behavior, the ultimate cause cannot then be assumed to be biological, experiential, or social (Brain & Susman, 1997). Biological factors might be considered risk factors comparable to behavioral risk factors. Since interventions are rarely designed on a one-to-one basis of one risk factor per intervention, it follows that interventions to prevent biological risk factors can be similar to interventions to prevent behavioral risks. Consistent with a developmental perspective, the implications that follow urge that prevention and treatment efforts be based on a multilevel and interdisciplinary level of analysis of antisocial behavior. Developmental models inherently result in assessments that go beyond the individual and consider family and community in the treatment of antisocial behavior.

How can health service providers and others prevent and manage dangerousness in the populations with which they are involved? The populations of interest include individuals of both sexes from all stages of development (birth to senescence) from differing social classes, from an increasing array of racial and ethnic groups and from groups with co-occurring mental and physical disabilities. A single group of providers will not be capable of identifying and managing dangerousness in this diverse population. Health care providers seldom learn in their academic training programs how to manage the problem of dangerousness. Academic training curricula rarely include the concept of dangerousness and those conducting research concerning dangerousness rarely have clinical experience in managing dangerousness. Thus, an important first step is to recognize inadequacies in requisite background and experience to address the problem of dangerousness. Next is the need to form interdisciplinary collaborations with professionals from a variety of disciplines who have expertise in dealing with dangerousness. These interdisciplinary teams might include professionals representing biology, criminology, psychiatry, psychology, and sociology. Professional teams could collectively recognize training shortcomings and be willing to share information and experience to deal with dangerousness. One such group in the United States are pediatricians, since violence toward and by children, adolescents, and young adults is a major clinical problem.

The role of researchers and clinicians as advocates of social policy for the prevention of dangerousness should not be underestimated. If these professional groups can influence significant others in the community to join health professionals to institute change, we will have accomplished what is needed to build prevention and intervention programs and to support the development of adequate programs for evaluations. It is essential that professionals, families, and communities be willing to collaborate to prevent antisocial behavior. If this collaboration is not accomplished, individuals will most likely continue to struggle with the problem of dangerousness, each doing important work, yet not identifying the causes, prevention, and treatment of dangerousness.

REFERENCES

Archer, J. (1991). The influence of testosterone on human aggression. *British Journal of Psychology, 82,* 1–28.
Asberg, M., Schalling, D., Traksman-Bendz, L., & Wagner, A. (1987). Psychobiology of suicide, impulsivity and related phenomena. In H. Y. Melzer (Ed.), *Psychopharmacology: Third generation of progress* (pp. 655–688). New York: Raven Press.
Bergman, B., & Brismar, B. (1994). Hormone levels and personality traits in abusive and suicidal male alcoholics. *Alcoholism, Clinical and Experimental Research, 18,* 311–316.
Berman, M. E., Kavoussi, R. J., & Coccaro, E. F. (1997). Neurotransmitter correlates of human aggression. In D. M. Stoff, J. Breiling, & J. Maser (Eds.), *Handbook of antisocial behavior.* (pp. 305–313). New York: Wiley.
Birmaher, B., Stanley, M., Greenhill, L., Twomey, J., Gavrilescu, A., & Rabinovich, H. (1990). Platelet imipramine binding in children and adolescents with impulsive behavior. *Journal of the American Academy of Child and Adolescent Psychiatry, 29,* 914–918.
Bondy, P. K. (1985). Disorders of the adrenal cortex. In J. D. Wilson & D. W. Foster (Eds.), *Williams textbook of endocrinology* (pp. 816–890). Philadelphia: Saunders.
Booth, A., Shelley, G., Mazur, A., Tharp, G., & Kittok, R. (1989). Testosterone and winning and losing in human competition. *Hormones and Behavior, 23,* 556–571.
Brain, P. F. (1994). Hormonal aspects of aggression and violence. In A. J. Reiss Jr, K. A., Miczek, & J. I. Roth (Eds.), *Understanding and Preventing Violence, Vol. 2 Biobehavioral Influences* (pp. 173–244). Washington, DC: National Academy Press.
Brain, P. F., & Susman, E. J. (1997). Hormonal aspects of aggression and violence. In D. M. Stoff, J. Breiling, & J. D. Maser (Eds.), *Handbook of antisocial behavior* (pp. 314–323). New York: Wiley.
Brooks-Gunn, J., Graber, J., & Paikoff, R. (1994). Studying links between hormones and negative affect: Models and measures. *Journal of Research on Adolescence, 4,* 469–486.
Brooks-Gunn, J., & Warren, M. (1989). Biological and social contributions to negative affect in young adolescent girls. *Child Development, 60,* 40–55.
Brown, G. L., Ebert, M. H., Goyer, P. F., Jimerson, D. C., Klein, W. J., Bunney, W. E., & Goodwin, F. K. (1982). Aggression, suicide, and serotonin: Relationships to CSF amine metabolites. *American Journal of Psychiatry, 139,* 741–746.
Brown, G. L., & Linnoila, M. I. (1990). CSF serotonin metabolite (5-HIAA) studies in depression, impulsivity, and violence. *Journal of Clinical Psychiatry, 51,* 42–43.

Cairns, R. B., & Stoff, D. M. (1996). Conclusion: A synthesis of studies on the biology of aggression and violence. In D. M. Stoff & R. B. Cairns (Eds.), *Aggression and violence: Genetic, neurobiological and biosocial perspectives*. Mahwah, NJ: Erlbaum.

Coccaro, E. F. (1989). Central serotonin and impulsive aggression. *British Journal of Psychiatry, 155*, 52–62.

Coccaro, E. F., Berman, M. E., Kavoussi, R. J., & Hauger, R. L. (1996). Relationship of prolactin response to d-fenfluramine to behavioral and questionnaire assessments of aggression in personality-disordered men. *Biological Psychiatry, 40*, 157–164.

Coccaro, E. F., Siever, L. J., Klar, H. M., Maurer, G., Cochran, K., Cooper, T. B., Mohs, R. D., & Davis, K. L. (1989). Serotonergic studies in patients with affective and personality disorders: Correlates with suicidal and impulsive aggressive behavior. *Archives of General Psychiatry, 51*, 318–324.

Coccaro, E. F., Silverman, J. M., Klar, H. K., Horvath, T. B., & Siever, L. J. (1994). Familial correlates of reduced central serotonergic system function in patients with personality disorders. *Archives of General Psychiatry, 51*, 318–324.

Compas, B. E., & Hammen, C. L. (1994). Child and adolescent depression: Covariation and comorbidity in development. In R. J. Haggerty, L. R. Sherrod, N. Garmezy, & M. Rutter (Eds.), *Stress, risk, and resilience in children and adolescents: Processes, mechanisms, and interventions* (pp. 225–267). New York: Cambridge University Press.

Constantino, J. N., Grosz, D., Saenger, P., Chandler, D. W., Nandi, R., & Earls, F. J. (1993). Testosterone and aggression in children. *Journal of the American Academy of Child and Adolescent Psychiatry, 32*, 1217–1222.

Dabbs, J., Jr., Frady, R., Carr, T., & Besch, N. (1987). Saliva testosterone and criminal violence in young adult prison inmates. *Psychosomatic Medicine, 49*, 174–182.

Ehrenkranz, J., Bliss, E., & Sheard, M. (1974). Plasma testosterone: Correlation with aggressive behavior and social dominance in men. *Psychosomatic Medicine, 36*, 469–475.

Farrington, D. P. (1987). Implications of biological findings for criminological research. In S. A. Mednick, T. E. Moffitt, & S. A. Stack (Eds.), *The causes of crime: New biological approaches* (pp. 42–64). New York: Cambridge University Press.

Finkelstein, J. W., Susman, E. J., Chinchilli, V. M., D'Arcangelo, M. R., Kunselman, S. J., Schwab, J., Demers, L. M., Liben, L. S., and Kulin, H. E. (1998). Effects of estrogen or testosterone on self-reported sexual responses and behaviors in hypogonadal adolescents. *Journal of Clinical Endocrinology and Metabolism, 83*, 2281–2285.

Finkelstein, J. W., Susman, E. J., Chinchilli, V. M., Kunselman, S. J., D'Arcangelo, M. R., Schwab, J., Demers, L. M., Liben, L. S., Lookingbill, G., & Kulin, H. E. (1997). Estrogen or testosterone increases self-reported aggressive behaviors in hypogonadal adolescent. *Journal of Clinical Endocrinology and Metabolism, 82*, 2423–2438.

Fishbein, D. H., Lozovsky, D., & Jaffe, J. H. (1989). Impulsivity, aggression, and neuroendocrine responses to serotonergic stimulation in substance abusers. *Biological Psychiatry, 25*, 1049–1066.

Fowles, D. C. (1993). Electrodermal activity and antisocial behavior. In J. C. Roy, W. Boucsein, D. C. Fowles, & J. Gruzelier (Eds.), *Electrodermal activity: From physiology to psychology* (pp. 223–238). New York: Plenum.

Gladue, B. A. (1991). Aggressive, behavioral characteristics, hormones, and sexual orientation in men and women. *Aggressive Behavior, 17,* 313–326.

Glickman, S., Frank, L. G., Davidson, J. M., Smith, E. R., & Sitteri, P. K. (1987). Androstenedione may organize or activate sex-reversed traits in female spotted hyenas. *Proceedings of the National Academy of Sciences, 84,* 3444–3447.

Gould, E., Woolley, C. S., & McEwen, B. S. (1991). The hippocampal formation: Morphological changes induced by thyroid, gonadal, and adrenal hormones. *Psychoneuroendocrinology, 16,* 67–84.

Harris, D. B. (1957). *The concept of development.* Minneapolis: University of Minnesota Press.

Henry, B., & Moffitt, T. E. (1997). Neuropsychological and neuroimaging studies of juvenile delinquency and adult criminal behavior. In D. M. Stoff, J. Breiling, & J. D. Maser (Eds.), *Handbook of antisocial behavior* (pp. 280–288). New York: Wiley.

Hinde, R. A. (1987). *Individuals, relationships and culture: Links between ethology and the social sciences.* New York: Cambridge University Press.

Inoff-Germain, G. E., Arnold, G. S., Nottelmann, E. D., Susman, E. J., Cutler, G. B., Jr., & Chrousos, G. P. (1988). Relations between hormone levels and observational measures of aggressive behavior of early adolescents in family interactions. *Developmental Psychology, 24,* 129–139.

Kagan, J. (1989). Temperamental contributions to social behavior. *American Psychologist, 44,* 668–674.

Kramer, G. W. (1997). Social attachment, brain function, aggression and violence. In A. Raine, D. Farrington, P. Brennan, & S. A. Mednick (Eds.), *Unlocking crime: The biosocial key* (pp. 207–229). New York: Plenum.

Kruesi, M. J., Hibbs, E. D., Zahn, T. P., Keysor C. S., Hamburger, S. D., Bartko, J. J., & Rapoport, J. L. (1992). A 2-year prospective follow-up study of children and adolescents with disruptive behavior disorders: Prediction by cerebrospinal fluid 5-hydroxy indoleacetic acid, homovanillic acid, and autonomic measures. *Archives of General Psychiatry, 49,* 429–435.

Kruesi, M. J., & Jacobsen, T. (1997). Serotonin and human violence: Do environmental mediators exist? In A. Raine, D. Farrington, P. Brennan, & S. A. Mednick (Eds.), *Unlocking crime: The biosocial key.* New York: Plenum.

LeMarquand, D., Pihl, R. O., & Benkelfat, C. (1994). Serotonin and alcohol intake, abuse, and dependence: Findings of animal studies. *Biological Psychiatry, 36,* 395–421.

Lerner, R. M. (1986). *Concepts and theories of human development* (2nd ed.). New York: Random House.

Lerner, R. M., & Foch, T. T. (1987). *Biological-psychosocial interactions in early adolescence.* Hillsdale, NJ: Erlbaum.

Linnoila, M. (1997). On the psychobiology of antisocial behavior. In D. M. Stoff, J. Breiling, & J. D. Maser (Eds.), *Handbook of antisocial behavior* (pp. 336–340). New York: Wiley.

Magnusson, D., & Cairns, R. B. (1996). Developmental science: Toward a unified framework. In R. B. Cairns, G. Elder, & J. Costello (Eds.), *Developmental Science* (pp. 7–30), New York: Cambridge University Press.

Mazur, A., & Booth, A. (1998). Testosterone and dominance in men. *Behavioral and Brain Sciences, 21,* 353–397.

Mazur, A., Susman, E. J., & Edelbrock, S. (1997). Sex difference in testosterone response to a video game contest. *Evolution and Human Behavior, 18,* 317–326.

Moffitt, T. E., Brammer, G. L., Caspi, A., Fawcett, J. P., Raleigh, M., Yuwiler, A., & Silva, P. (1998). Whole blood serotonin relates to violence in an epidemiological study. *Biological Psychiatry, 43,* 446–457.

Moss, H. B., Vanyukov, M. M., & Martin, C. S. (1995). Salivary cortisol responses and the risk for substance abuse in prepubertal boys. *Biological Psychiatry, 38,* 546–555.

Nottelmann, E. D., Inoff-Germain, G., Susman, E. J., & Chrousos, G. P. (1990). Hormones and behavior at puberty. In J. Bancroft & J. M. Reinisch (Eds.), *Adolescence and puberty* (pp. 88–123), New York: Oxford University Press.

Nottelmann, E. D., Susman, E. J., Inoff-Germain, G. E., Cutler, G. B., Jr., Loriaux, D. L., & Chrousos, G. P. (1987). Developmental processes in American early adolescents: Relationships between adolescent adjustment problems and chronological pubertal stage and puberty-related serum hormone levels. *Journal of Pediatrics, 110,* 473–480.

O'Keane, V., Moloney, E., O'Neill, H., O'Connor, A. et al. (1992). Blunted prolactin responses to d-fenfluramine in sociopathy: Evidence for subsensitivity of central serotonergic function. *British Journal of Psychiatry, 160,* 643–646.

Olweus, D. (1986). Aggressions and hormones: Behavioral relationships with testosterone and adrenaline. In D. Olweus, J. Block, & M. Radke-Yarrow (Eds.), *Development of antisocial and prosocial behavior: Research, theories, and issues* (pp. 51–72). Orlando, FL: Academic Press.

Olweus, D., Mattson, A., Schalling, D., & Low, H. (1980). Testosterone, aggression, physical, and personality dimensions in normal adolescent males. *Psychosomatic Medicine, 42,* 253–269.

Olweus, D., Mattson, A., Schalling, D., & Low, H. (1988). Circulating testosterone levels and aggression in adolescent males: A causal analysis. *Psychosomatic Medicine, 50,* 261–272.

Persky, H. K., Smith, K., & Basu, G. (1971). Relation of psychologic measures of aggression and hostility to testosterone production in man. *Psychosomatic Medicine, 33,* 265–277.

Phoenix, C. H., Goy, R. W., Gerall, A. A., & Young, W. C. (1959). Organizing action of prenatally administered testosterone propionate on the tissues mediating mating behavior in the female guinea pig. *Endocrinology, 65,* 369–382.

Pine, D. S., Wasserman, G. A., Coplan, J., Fried, J. A., Huang Y., Kassir, S., Greenhill, L., Shaffer, D., & Parsons, B. (1996). Platelet serotonin 2A (5-HT2a) receptor characteristics and parenting factors for boys at risk for delinquency: A preliminary report. *American Journal of Psychiatry, 153,* 538–544.

Raine, A. (1993). *The psychopathology of crime: Criminal behavior as a clinical disorder.* San Diego: Academic Press.

Raine, A. (1996). Autonomic nervous system and violence. In D. M. Stoff & R. F. Cairns (Eds.), *The neurobiology of clinical aggression* (pp. 145–168). Hillsdale, NJ: Erlbaum.

Raine, A. (1997). Antisocial behavior and psychophysiology: A biosocial perspective and a prefrontal dysfunction hypothesis. In D. M. Stoff, J. Breiling, & J. Maser (Eds.), *Handbook of antisocial behavior* (pp. 289–304). New York: Wiley.

Raine, A., Brennan, P., & Farrington, D. P. (1997). Biosocial bases of violence: Conceptual and theoretical issues. In A. Raine, D. Farrington, P. Brennan, & S. A. Mednick (Eds.), *Unlocking crime: The biosocial key* (pp. 1–20), New York: Plenum.

Raine, A., Farrington, D., Brennan, P., & Mednick, S. A. (Eds) (1997). *Unlocking crime: The biosocial key.* New York: Plenum.

Raine, A., Reynolds, C., Venables, P. H., & Mednick, S A. (1997). Biosocial bases of aggressive behavior in childhood, In A. Raine, D. Farrington, P. Brennan, & S. A. Mednick (Eds.), *Unlocking crime: The biosocial key,* (pp. 107–126), New York: Plenum.

Raine, A., Venables, P. H., & Mednick, S. A. (1997). Low resting heart rate at age 3 years predisposes to aggression at age 11 years: Evidence from the Mauritius Child Health Project. *Journal of the American Academy of Child and Adolescent Psychiatry, 36,* 1457–1464.

Rasmusson, A. M., Riddle, M., Lechman, J. F., Anderson, G. M., & Cohen, D. J. (1990). Neurotransmitter assessment in neuropsychiatric disorders of childhood. In S. I. Weizman, A. Weizman, & R. Weizman (Eds.), *Applications of basic neuroscience to child psychiatry* (pp. 33–60). New York: Plenum.

Schaal, B., Tremblay, R. E., Soussignan, R., & Susman, E. J. (1996). Male testosterone linked to high social dominance but low physical aggression in early adolescence. *Journal of the American Academy of Child and Adolescent Psychiatry, 35,* 1322–1330.

Schneirla, T. C. (1957). The concept of development in comparative psychology. In D. B. Harris (Ed.), *The concept of development* (pp. 78–108). Minneapolis: University of Minnesota Press.

Sells, C. W., & Blum, R. W. (1995). Current trends in adolescent health. In R. J. DiClemente, W. B. Hansen, & L. E. Ponton (Eds.), *Handbook of adolescent health risk behavior* (pp. 5–34). New York: Plenum.

Stoff, D. M., & Cairns, R. B. (Eds.)(1996). *Aggression and violence: Genetic, neurobiological, and biosocial perspectives.* Mahwah, NJ: Erlbaum.

Stoff, D. M., Pasatiempo, A. P., Yeung, J., Cooper, T. C., Bridger, W. H., & Rabinovich, H. (1992). Neuroendocrine responses to challenges with dl-fenfluramine and aggression in disruptive behavior disorders of children and adolescents. *Psychiatry Research, 43,* 263–276.

Stoff, D. M., Pollock, L., Vitiello, B. D., & Bridger, W. H. (1987). Reduction of 3H-imipramine binding sites on platelets of conduct-disordered children. *Neuropsychopharmacology, 1,* 55–62.

Susman, E. J. (1997). Modeling developmental complexity in adolescence: Hormones and behavior in context. *Journal of Research on Adolescence, 7,* 283–306.

Susman, E. J., Dorn, L. D., & Chrousos, G. P. (1991). Negative affect and hormone levels in young adolescents: Concurrent and longitudinal perspectives. *Journal of Youth and Adolescence, 20,* 167–190.

Susman, E. J., Dorn, L. D., Inoff-Germain, G. E., Nottelmann, E. D., & Chrousos, G. P. (1997). Cortisol reactivity, distress behavior, and behavioral and psychological problems in young adolescents: A longitudinal perspective. *Journal of Research on Adolescence, 7,* 81–105.

Susman, E. J., Finkelstein, J. W., Chinchilli, V. M., Schwab, J. E., Liben, L. S., D'Arcangelo, M. R., Meinke, J., Demers, L. M., Lookingbill, G., & Kulin, H. E. (1998). The effect of sex hormone replacement therapy on behavior problems and moods in adolescents with delayed puberty. *Journal of Pediatrics, 133,* 521–525.

Susman, E. J., Nottelmann, E. D., Inoff-Germain, G. E., Dorn, L. D., & Chrousos, G. P. (1987). Hormonal influences on aspects of psychological development during adolescence. *Journal of Adolescent Health Care, 8,* 492–504.

Susman, E. J., Inoff-Germain, G. E., Nottelmann, E. D., Cutler, G. B., Loriaux, D. L., & Chrousos, G. P. (1987). Hormones, emotional dispositions and aggressive attributes in young adolescents. *Child Development, 58,* 1114–1134. (Reprinted in C. N. Jacklin, *The Psychology of Gender,* [1990]).

Susman, E. J., Nottelmann, E. D., Dorn, L. D., Gold, P. W., & Chrousos, G. P. (1989). The physiology of stress and behavioral development. In D. S. Palermo (Ed.), *Coping with uncertainty: Behavioral and developmental perspectives* (pp. 17–37). Hillsdale, NJ: Erlbaum.

Susman, E. J., & Ponirakis, A. (1997). Hormones-context interactions and antisocial behavior in youth. In A. Raine, D. Farrington, P. Brennan, & S. A. Mednick (Eds.), *Unlocking crime: The biosocial key* (pp. 251–269). New York: Plenum.

Susman, E. J., Worrall, B. K., Murowchick, E., Frobose, C., & Schwab, J. (1996). Experience and neuroendocrine parameters of development: Aggressive behavior and competencies. In D. Stoff & R. Cairns (Eds.), *Neurobiological approaches to clinical aggression research* (pp. 267–289). Hillsdale, NJ: Erlbaum.

Udry, J. R., Billy, J. O., Morris, N. M., Groff, T. R., & Raj, M. H. (1985). Serum androgenic hormones motivate sexual behavior in adolescent boys. *Fertility and Sterility, 43,* 90–94.

Udry, J. R., & Talbert, L. M. (1988). Sex hormone effects on personality at puberty. *Journal of Personality and Social Psychology, 54,* 291–295.

Unis, A. S., Cook, E. H., Vincent, J. G., Gjerde, D. K., Perry, B. D., Mason, C., & Mitchell, J. (1997). Platelet serotonin measures in adolescents with conduct disorder. *Biological Psychiatry, 42,* 553–559.

van Goozen, S. H., Matthys, W., Cohen-Kettenis, P. T., Thijssen, J. H., & van Engeland, H. (1998). Adrenal androgens and aggression in conduct disorder prepubertal boys and normal controls. *Biological Psychiatry, 43,* 156–158.

Vanyukov, M. M., Moss, H. B., Plail, J. A., Mezzick, A. C., & Tarter, R. E. (1993). Antisocial symptoms in preadolescent boys and in their parents: Associations with cortisol. *Psychiatric Research, 46,* 9–17.

Virkkunen, M., & Linnoila, M. (1990). Serotonin in early onset, male alcoholics with violent behavior. *Annals of Internal Medicine, 22,* 327–331.

Virkkunen, M., & Linnoila, M. (1993). Serotonin in personality disorders with habitual violence and impulsivity. In S. Hodgins (Ed.), *Mental disorder and crime* (pp. 227–243). Newbury Park, CA: Sage.

Virkkunen, M., Rawlings, R., Tokola, R., Poland, R. E., Guidotti, A., Nemeroff, C., Bissette, G., Kalogeras, K., Karonen, S. L., & Linnoila, M. (1994). CSF biochemistries, glucose metabolism, and diurnal activity rhythms in alcoholic, violent offenders, impulsive fire setters and healthy volunteers. *Archives of General Psychiatry, 51*, 20–27.

Yalcinkaya, T. M., Siiteri, P. K., Vigne, J. L., Licht, P., Pavgi, S., Frank, L. G., & Glickman, S. E. (1993). A mechanism for virilization of female spotted hyenas in utero. *Science, 260*, 1929–1931.

Zubieta, J. K., & Alessi, N. E. (1993). Is there a role of serotonin in the disruptive behavior disorders? *Journal of Child and Adolescent Psychopharmacology, 3*, 11–35.

3. The Development of Physical Aggression During Childhood and the Prediction of Later Dangerousness

RICHARD E. TREMBLAY

When Does Violent Behavior Start?

The Adolescent Years

Using data on the prevalence of serious violent crimes from the American National Youth Survey, Elliott (1994) reported that black and white adolescent males and females in the United States became more and more at risk of committing serious violent crimes as they grew older, from 12 to 17 years of age. This sharp increase of violence was then followed, from ages 18 to 27, by an equally dramatic fall in the prevalence of serious violence. Violence appeared to peak at 17 years of age for both black and white adolescents in this national probability sample born between 1959 and 1965. This phenomenon has been labeled the age-crime curve (Farrington, 1987) and appears to have first been published by the Belgian astronomer-statistician-criminologist Adolfe Quetelet in his 1833 book entitled *Research on the Propensity for Crime at Different Ages.*

The author wishes to acknowledge the generous support of the National Science Foundation through the National Consortium on Violence Research, the Molson Foundation, the Donner Foundation, the Canadian Institute of Advanced Research, the Québec funding agencies CQRS, FCAR, FRSQ, the Québec Ministry of Health and Social Services, Santé Québec, the Canadian funding agencies NHRDP, SSHRC, the Canadian Ministry of Human Resources Development, and Statistics Canada. A large number of colleagues have contributed to the work presented in this chapter. Special thanks go to Daniel Nagin, Frank Vitaro, Michel Boivin, Mark Zoccolillo, Raymond Baillargeon, Lisa Broidy, Christa Japel, Daniel Pérusse, Jean Séguin, Robert Pihl, Linda Pagani, Jacques Montplaisir, and Ronald G. Barr. A still larger number of support personnel have been instrumental in making this longitudinal work possible. The author is especially grateful to Lyse Desmarais-Gervais, Hélène Beauchesne, Pierre McDuff, Chantal Bruneau, and Katia Maliantovitch.

The observation that the frequency of criminal activity increases steadily during adolescence, together with the observation of the male-female difference in the frequency of criminal behavior, has been used as proof that criminal behavior is strongly influenced by testosterone levels (Ellis & Coontz, 1990; Eysenck & Gudjonsson, 1989; Tremblay & Schaal, 1996). However, the age-crime curve starting during early adolescence also fits the social learning hypothesis that individuals learn to be violent and to commit crimes from their environment (Akers, 1977; Bandura, 1973; Elliott, Huizinga, & Ageton, 1985; Eron, 1990). As children become adolescents they also become physically stronger and sexually mature. There is clearly competition for finding mates and jobs. More generally, there is competition for resources and status. These developmental changes fit well with the hypothesis that the increase in steroid hormones which underlie the physical maturation during adolescence could explain the increase in criminal behavior, and more specifically the increase in physical violence. However, adolescents also ask and obtain greater freedom to spend their time without adult supervision. Having access to more resources, such as money and transportation, increases their capacity to satisfy their needs. Their cognitive competence also enables them to attempt to satisfy their needs without being dependent on the mediation of their parents. This greater freedom enables them to choose with whom, how, and where they will spend their time. Thus it is not surprising that as they become adolescents, humans have more opportunities to learn from the social environment they choose to live in.

The Middle Childhood Years

If adolescence is the period when humans are most at risk of being violent, physical aggression clearly does not start with the advent of adolescence. Using retrospective data from a Pittsburgh, Pennsylvania USA sample assessed when they were in seventh grade, Loeber and Hay (1997) reported that from 3 to 13 years of age there was a steady increase in the number of boys who started to display minor aggression, fighting, and serious violence: at age 3, fewer than 5% of the boys had started to engage in minor physical aggression; the 10% level was reached around age 8 and the 20% level around age 10. Fewer than 5% recalled fighting before age 9 and close to 20% by age 13. Thus, 13-year-old boys and their mothers recall the development of physical aggression as if children become more inclined to initiate physical aggression as they grow older. This memory of childhood events fits the image of children born good and becoming bad under the influence of their environment, which dates back to at least Jean-Jacques Rousseau's (1762) model of child development and the more recent social learning hypothesis of aggression (Bandura, 1973). It also fits the idea that steroid hormones play an important role in the development of physical violence. However, can we rely on retrospective reports of age of onset of physical aggression? This is clearly an important question for clinicians since the *DSM-IV* diagnosis for Conduct Disorder (CD) and other disorders require retrospective information on age of onset of symptoms.

Interestingly, the few studies that have focused specifically on the development of physical aggression during the elementary school years indicate that the mean frequency of physical aggression decreases with age. For example, a prospective longitudinal study of North Carolina children, using both teacher- and self-reports (Cairns & Cairns, 1994; Cairns, Cairns, Neckerman, Ferguson, & Gariépy, 1989) showed that the mean frequency of physical aggression decreased with relative steadiness from 10 to 18 years of age. Similar results were obtained from a cross-sectional study of a random sample of more than 10,000 Canadian children from 4 to 11 years of age (Tremblay et al., 1996). Figure 3.1 shows that mothers report, as expected, higher levels of physical aggression for males compared to females for each age group. It also shows that, with age, both females and males are reported to be less and less physically aggressive. Using a random sample of more than 12,000 students from secondary schools in France, Choquet and Ledoux (1994) also showed that 11- to 18-year-old males and females reported less physical aggression with age. Similar results were observed in a prospective longitudinal study of more than 1,000 males who attended kindergarten classes in schools of low socioeconomic status (SES) areas in Montreal. Their level of physical aggression was assessed by their teachers at age 6, and then from ages 10 to 15. The mean level of physical aggression for the group shows a slight decline from ages 6 to 10 and a dramatic decline from 10 to 15 years of age (Tremblay et al., 1999).

It could be argued that although most children are less and less physically aggressive with time, a minority of children start or increase the frequency of their physical aggression as they grow older. Nagin and Tremblay (1999) addressed this issue by identifying the main developmental trajectories of the teacher-rated physical aggression in the

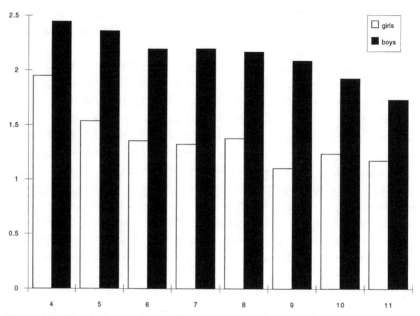

Figure 3.1. Physical aggression of boys and girls from 4 to 11 years of age.

Montreal sample of low SES area boys followed from 6 to 15 years of age. They found four categories of trajectories: the first included 4% of the boys, which could be labeled chronically physically aggressive, since their teachers regularly reported them showing a high frequency of physical aggression; a second group (28%) started with a high level of physical aggression at age 6 and, with time, became less and less physically aggressive; the majority of boys (53%) had a low level of physical aggression at age 6 and also became less and less physically aggressive with time; the last group, 14% of the boys, was never reported by the teachers to have been physically aggressive. In contrast to hypotheses of late onset antisocial behavior (Moffitt, 1993; Patterson, DeBaryshe, & Ramsey, 1989), Nagin and Tremblay did not find any group that could be labeled "late onset" for physical aggression (i.e., boys with an "onset" and maintenance of a moderate or high level of physical aggression for a significant number of years after age 6). Similar results were obtained by Broidy, Nagin, and Tremblay (1999) when the trajectory analyses were done with elementary school boys and girls from a Dunedin (New Zealand) sample (Moffitt, Caspi, Dickson, Silva, & Stanton, 1996), a Christchurch (New Zealand) sample (Fergusson & Horwood, 1999), a Quebec (Canada) provincial sample (Pagani,

Boulerice, & Tremblay, 1997; Zoccolillo, Vitaro, & Tremblay, 1999), a Nashville, Tennessee (USA) sample (Dodge, Bates, & Pettit, 1990), and a Pittsburgh (USA) male cohort (Loeber, Keenan, & Zhang, 1997).

These robust findings are clearly in complete contradiction with the idea that the frequency of physical aggression increases with age. The frequency of schoolchildren's physical aggression appears to be at its highest level during their kindergarten year. This is clearly the case for the majority of children who show a decrease of physical aggression from their kindergarten year onward, but it is also true for the chronic cases (i.e., for those who tend to regularly show the highest levels of physical aggression from ages 6 to 15). Except for the two American male samples in the Broidy et al. (1999) study, the frequency of their physical aggression does not increase with age, it simply remains at a high level.

The results from these descriptive studies also challenge the notion that there is a significant group of children who show chronic physical aggression during late childhood or adolescence after having shown no physical aggression throughout childhood. The idea of an adolescent-onset type and a childhood-onset type of CD was apparently introduced into the *DSM-IV* (American Psychiatric Association, 1994) to underscore a developmental view of the origins of CD (Lahey et al., 1998). The results described above suggest that adolescent-onset cases of CD with physical aggression do not exist.

The Preschool Years

If the violent type of CD does not start in adolescence, can we conclude that it starts during the elementary school years? Based on longitudinal studies which started collecting data in kindergarten, it would be tempting to conclude that physical aggression does start with the kindergarten year. But, as one needed to look before the adolescent years to see that there was much going on, one also needs to look before the kindergarten year to identify the age of onset of physical aggression.

It will be argued by some that it is difficult to talk of serious violence or dangerousness when we talk of kindergarten children, and still more outrageous to think that preschoolers can be violent. There are probably not many kindergarten murderers or rapists, but there are some. In 1994 two 6-year-old Norwegian boys beat a 5-year-old girl and left her to die in the snow (Bellemare & Nahmias, 1998).

Having shown that the chronic cases are at their highest level of physical aggression during their kindergarten year (Nagin & Tremblay, 1999), the search for the "onset" of physical violence must focus on the preschool years. Unfortunately there are very few studies of physical aggression before school entry. Although more than a quarter of a century ago, de Wit and Hartup (1974) made a convincing plea for studying the early development of aggression, there are still very few longitudinal studies that have tried to chart the development of physical aggression during the preschool years.

Two longitudinal studies using small samples of children found physical aggression to be relatively stable from around the end of the second year after birth onward. Keenan and Shaw (1994) observed a sample of 89 boys and girls with low SES mothers. Direct observations of behavior during laboratory assessments when the children were 18 and 24 months of age yielded significant Pearson correlations of .23, .30, and .45, respectively, for physical aggression toward mothers, objects, and examiners. Cummings, Iannotti, and Zahn-Waxler (1989) assessed the physical aggression of 22 boys and 21 girls by direct observations in a play situation with a friend at 2 and 5 years of age. They found high correlations for boys ($r = .59$) and somewhat lower correlations for girls ($r = .36$). These two studies indicate levels of stability of physical aggression similar to those observed in older children. Other studies of preschool children's aggression have generally used definitions of aggression that include a variety of disruptive and competitive behaviors. For example, Kingston and Prior (1995, p. 349) describe their focus on aggression in the following way: "we focus on the development and correlates of what we call, for brevity, `aggressive behavior' but which incorporates both verbally and physically aggressive behavior... More specifically, our definition of aggression includes behaviors such as temper outbursts; damage or destruction to property; verbal and physical threats; bullying; fighting; hurting others by hitting, biting, or scratching; and frequent disobedience." Competitive behavior was also included in their aggression scale for 2- to 4-year-olds. Because such studies do not distinguish physical aggression from verbal aggression, disobedience, competition, and temper tantrums, they cannot inform us on the age of onset and stability of physical aggression.

Also, even though longitudinal studies show relatively high correlations of physical aggression scores between 2 and 5 years of age, this does not mean that the frequency of physical aggression does not change during the preschool years. It simply means that the rank order among a group of individuals does not change. The first descriptions of these developmental trends can be found in a number of cross-sectional studies undertaken by the child development pioneers of the 1920s and 1930s (e.g., Bridges, 1931; Dawe, 1934; Murphy, 1937) who targeted conflicts and tantrums in small samples of children. These studies suggested that with age, physical aggression decreased, while verbal aggression and conflicts increased. A recent study of a large cross-sectional sample of Canadian children also indicated that, according to maternal reports, the frequency of physical aggression declined from 2 to 11 years of age, while the frequency of indirect aggression increased (Tremblay et al., 1996).

Again, if the frequency of physical aggression is at its highest at the end of the second year after birth, when is the age of "onset" of physical aggression? Published studies of physical aggression during the first two years after birth are extremely rare. In a British longitudinal study of 49 second-born children, Dunn and Munn (1985) observed physical aggression of the subjects toward their eldest sibling at ages 14, 18, and 24 months. The observed trend indicated an increase in physical aggression. In a cross-sectional study of social interactions in French day-care centers, Restoin and colleagues (Restoin, 1985; Restoin et al., 1985) reported an increase in the proportion of physical aggression compared with other forms of social interactions, from the end of the first to the end of the second year after birth. That study also showed a decrease in physical aggression from the end of the second year after birth to the end of the third year.

The frequency of different forms of physical aggression reported by mothers for their 17-month-old child, as well as the age of onset of these behaviors was studied by Tremblay et al. (1999). They interviewed a population sample of 511 mothers (260 girls and 251 boys) living in the main urban areas of the province of Quebec. The mothers were asked how often their child showed the following behaviors: took away things from others, pushed others to get what he wanted, threatened to hit others, hit others, kicked others, bit others, physically attacked others, fought, started a fight, bullied others, and was cruel to others. Most of the children were reported to have exhibited one of these behaviors at least sometimes. Half of the children were reported by their mothers to sometimes take away things from others, and 17.7% were reported to often show this behavior. As such, the inclusion of this behavior in a scale of physical aggression could be questioned because it involves a minimum level of physical aggression. However, direct observations of these behaviors (see e.g., Restoin, 1985) show that children often resist, and sometimes strongly resist, by holding on to the object while the other is trying to pull it away. The same event involving adults could lead to a robbery charge.

The second most frequently reported physical aggression at 17-months was pushing others to get what the child wants (40.1% sometimes, 5.9% often). This behavior probably occurs most often in the same context as the previous behavior, taking away things from others, but appears to indicate a higher level of physical aggression. Instead of only pulling on an object the other is holding, the child actually physically pushes the other. Taking away things and pushing to get these things were clearly the most frequent of the aggression items presented to the mothers. These results replicate direct observation studies of children which conclude that object struggles are the most frequent agonistic behaviors among young children (e.g., Hay & Ross, 1982; Restoin et al., 1985).

Biting, kicking, fighting, threatening to hit, and physically attacking others were reported for 1 in 4 to 1 in 5 of the children. Starting fights was reported for 12% of the children. Although few mothers endorsed the two most serious descriptors, there were still 8.2% who reported their 17-month-old child to bully and 3.9% who described their child as cruel.

Differences were observed between males and females, but these differences depended on whether or not the child had a sibling. Observational studies of sibling interactions have shown that children between 14 and 24 months tend to initiate physically aggressive interactions with their older siblings (Dunn & Munn, 1985). For both males and females, having a sibling clearly increased the likelihood of mothers reporting physically aggressive behavior. No significant differences in the use of physical aggression were observed between boys and girls who had siblings, except for more frequent kicking of others. However, a number of significant differences were observed between males and females who did not have siblings. Behaviors such as taking away things from others, hitting, and biting were more prevalent among boys without siblings than girls without siblings. The interaction effect between sex and presence of a sibling was seen most clearly when the percentage of boys and girls who had received a positive rating on at least one of the 10 physical aggression scales was compared (i.e., excluding taking away things from others). For those with a sibling,

80% of the boys and girls were reported to have sometimes resorted to physical aggression. For those without a sibling, 70% of the boys and only 50% of the girls were reported to have used physical aggression. This suggests that sex differences in physical aggression at that age are highly dependent on context.

Tremblay et al. (1999) also tried to understand at what age the 17-month-old had started to physically assault others. Using the approach that Loeber and Hay (1994) had with 13-year-old boys, they asked mothers who reported that their 17-month-old child had sometimes or often manifested one of the physically aggressive behaviors, and at what age they had manifested the behavior for the first time. This gave an estimate of the age of onset for each of the behaviors. The difference between the two studies is that the period of recall for the infant study was 10 to 12 months compared to 10 to 12 years for the study of young adolescents.

Some of the children were reported to have started these physically aggressive behaviors before their first birthday, but the action actually started in the first few months after that first birthday. The cumulative onset rate of some behaviors was clearly faster than others. For example, the onset rate of pushing was faster than that of kicking and hitting. Pushing appeared to precede kicking, and the latter appeared to precede hitting. The developmental trend was very similar to the one described by Loeber and Stouthamer-Loeber (1998) for the cumulative onset of minor aggression, fighting, and serious violence from 3 to 16 years of age, except that it occurred between 6 and 17 months.

Does Childhood Physical Aggression Predict Adolescent or Adult Physical Violence?

To our knowledge, no study has been published on the links between physical aggression in the preschool years and adolescent or adult physical violence. As mentioned above, this is because longitudinal studies that started in early childhood did not assess levels of physical aggression. There are many reasons why the years when humans are most frequently physically aggressive have not been of interest to "aggression" specialists.

First, it is much easier to study school children than to study infants and toddlers. A random sample of a population of school-age children can be more readily gathered since all children must go to school. Teachers and peers know the students well and will generally agree to assess subjects' behavior. Second, it has been argued that the label "aggressive" should be used only if there is an intention to hurt, and that infants and toddlers generally do not have that intention (Kagan, 1974). However, most studies of aggression in humans and animals do not assess the intention to hurt.

A third reason is that learning theory dominated research on children's aggression over the past 40 years. It proposed that because children learn to aggress from their environment, they needed time to learn before they were clearly aggressive. In his presidential address to the International Society for Research on Aggression, Eron (1990) concluded that aggressive antisocial behavior crystallizes around 8 years of age. It is of interest to note that this was the age at which 30 years earlier Eron and his colleagues (Lefkowitz, Eron, Walder, & Huesmann, 1977) started collecting data for the Columbia County longitudinal study of children's aggression. Paradoxically, they had started a longitudinal study of the development of aggression once it had already "crystallized." They obviously did not know this, and almost 30 years of prospective research was needed to reach that conclusion. Interestingly, since 1990 many new studies of the onset of aggression start with school-age children.

Two other methodological details concerning the Columbia County study shed light on the developmental models of aggression, which guided research on aggression over the past 40 years. First, the 10-item peer-rated scale for aggression at 8 years of age clearly did not respect the criteria of "intentionality" which Kagan (1974) was advocating for infants and toddlers, and it included only two physical aggression items (who pushes and shoves others; who starts fights over nothing). The other items included a range of oppositional and disruptive behaviors: who does not obey the teacher; who often says "give me that"; who gives dirty looks or sticks out their tongue at other children; who makes up stories and lies to get other children into trouble; who does things that bother others; who is always getting in trouble; who says mean things; who takes other children's things without asking.

In case some readers may believe that the aim of this study was not focused on violent behavior, the following is an excerpt from the preface of the 1977 book entitled *Growing Up to Be Violent* (Leftkowitz et al., 1977): "During the decade that elapsed between the two periods of data collection, 1960 and 1970, violence appears to have reached epidemic proportions in the United States ... Although we cannot demonstrate that this violent milieu systematically affected the behavior of our subjects, we do have evidence indicating that exposure to violence or violent models increased their aggressive behavior" (pp. vii–viii).

The failure to focus on physical aggression in this study of the development of children's "violent behavior" was not an exception. The original plan of the Montreal longitudinal study of kindergarten children initiated 24 years after the Columbia County study was based on a 13-item aggression scale that included only three physical aggression items (Tremblay et al., 1991). One of the few studies that clearly targeted physical aggression was the Carolina Longitudinal Study which started in 1981 with a sample of 4th-grade children, and which also included only three physical aggression items (Cairns & Cairns, 1994). To this day, aggression scales for children have very few physical aggression items (see Achenbach & Edelbrock, 1986; Kingston & Prior, 1995; Pekarik, Prinz, Liebert, Weintraub, & Neale, 1976) and do not assess intentionality.

The distance between the time 1 and time 2 measurement points in the Columbia County longitudinal study is also indicative of the developmental model of violent behaviors. The first measurement point at 8 years of age was followed by a second measurement point 10 years later. The authors showed that there was a small but significant correlation between the age 8 peer-rated aggression score and the age 18 self-reported aggression score (r = .18). The Cambridge Study in Delinquent Development (see Chapter 4) initiated in 1961, one year after the start of the Columbia County study, had a similar design. The first assessment point was between 8 and 10 years of age, the second between 12 and 14, and the third at age 18. Cost may have been a key issue in the decision to collect data only at one point during childhood, but certainly such studies would not have been initiated if the researchers did not believe that one assessment during middle childhood, and one assessment at the end of adolescence would reveal to what extent there is continuity in the propensity toward "aggression" or delinquency over long periods of time.

Thus, the longitudinal studies that started long enough ago to have assessed adult violent behavior did not collect data during early childhood, and the data they did collect during childhood were limited to one data point and did not specifically target physical aggression. From this, we can conclude that developmentalists of the 1960s did not believe that children's physical aggression played any role in our understanding of the development of delinquent and violent behavior.

A number of prospective longitudinal studies have shown that disruptive behavior during childhood is correlated with physical aggression during adolescence and adulthood (Farrington, Chapter 4 in this book; Huesmann, Eron, Lefkowitz, & Walder, 1984; Magdol, Moffitt, Caspi, & Silva, 1998). Disruptive behavior in childhood usually refers to oppositional, hyperactive, and physically aggressive behavior (APA, 1994).

It has been argued that hyperactivity is a major ingredient of disruptiveness, which leads to later antisocial behavior (Farrington, et al., 1990; Farrington, Loeber, & Van Kammen, 1990; Moffitt, 1990; Satterfield, 1987). Nagin and Tremblay (1999) tested this hypothesis with the trajectory approach. Using the Montreal sample of kindergarten boys in low SES area schools they identified developmental trajectories for opposition, hyperactivity, and physical aggression. For each of these behavioral dimensions they identified a chronic group, a group that started with a high level in kindergarten and over time desisted, a group that started lower in kindergarten and desisted, and a group that appeared to never show any meaningful level of the problem behavior. Although some children were chronic cases on each of the three dimensions, the overlap was far from perfect: 47% of the chronic aggressive were also chronic oppositional, and only 13% of the chronic aggressive were also chronic hyperactive, while 23% of the chronic oppositional were also chronic hyperactive.

The probability of group membership for the three dimensions was then used to predict violent and nonviolent offending during adolescence. Results clearly showed that the chronic cases for each of the dimensions were at highest risk for any of the delinquent assessments in adolescence. For example, at age 17 the boys on the chronic physical aggression trajectory reported an average of 3.58 violent episodes in the past year, while those on the high-level desistor trajectory reported 1.95; those on the low-level desistor trajectory reported 1.03; and the never aggressive trajectory reported an average of 0.72.

Multiple regression analyses were then used to assess to what extent the three disruptive dimensions made independent contributions to the predictions. Results showed that hyperactivity did not significantly predict any of the delinquent outcomes in adolescence, once opposition and physical aggression had been taken into account. Chronic oppositional behavior was the best predictor of the frequency of self-reported theft at 16 and 17 years of age, while chronic physical aggression was the best predictor of physical violence at ages 16 and 17. Interestingly, both chronic opposition and chronic physical aggression predicted the total number of juvenile infractions recorded by the juvenile courts.

These results suggest that children who show high levels of physical aggression from school entry to high school are at highest risk of physical violence at the end of adolescence. Some of these children will also show high levels of hyperactivity and high levels of opposition, but if one had to rely on only one predictor it should be physical aggression. This, of course, makes sense considering that there appears to be much behavioral continuity over time for different types of disruptive behaviors. Broidy et al. (1999) have indeed shown this to be true in six large longitudinal studies of children's behavior development in Canada, New Zealand, and the United States.

Conclusions

The aim of this chapter was to discuss the available knowledge on the development of physical aggression during childhood and its predictive value for adolescent and adult physical violence. It was argued that very few studies have specifically studied physical aggression during childhood and that the development of physical aggression during the preschool years has been especially neglected. The few studies that do exist show that, contrary to the general belief, the frequency of physical aggression does not increase with age. It does appear that the age at which humans are most frequently physically aggressive is not during adolescence, but at the end of the second year after birth. Most 1½-year-olds engage in physical aggression and most have learned to use alternative ways of achieving their aims by the time they enter kindergarten. However those who have not learned by that time are at an increased risk of maintaining that behavior and becoming the physically aggressive adolescent or adult. By that time physical aggression is much more lethal because of increased physical strength, increased cognitive power, and easier access to weapons.

These conclusions have important implications for future research on the development and prevention of violent behavior. First, instead of continuing to study why children learn to be violent after entry in the school system, we should focus on how children learn not to physically assault from early childhood to the elementary school years. Second, if the preschool years are the period when most humans learn to inhibit physical aggression, it may be an indication that there is a sensitive period for this learning. Programs should be implemented to help those who appear to have difficulty learning. Most programs for preschoolers with behavior problems have not targeted inhibition of physical aggression. Third, because the children who still show relatively high levels of physical aggression during the elementary school years are at high risk of later violence and are beyond the apparently sensitive period for learning to inhibit these behaviors, it would seem extremely important that intensive programs be offered to these elementary schoolchildren on alternatives to physical aggression, and inhibition of physical aggression. The most effective programs may be those offered to all children (e.g., Hawkins et al., 1998; Kellam, 1992). These programs reduce the negative effects of labeling and the iatrogenic effects of putting deviant individuals together (Dishion, McCord, & Poulin, in press). They also provide an opportunity to use the prosocial children as models (Tremblay, Pagani-Kurtz, Mâsse, Vitaro, & Pihl, 1995; Tremblay, LeMarquand, & Vitaro, 1999; Vitaro & Tremblay, 1994). Finally, preadolescents and adolescents who frequently use physical aggression are at very high risk of continued physical aggression and should be offered intensive programs to learn alternatives to these behaviors. It is obvious yet that the majority of these individuals need support throughout the adolescent years to help them get through this high-risk period.

Clinicians need to remember that retrospective assessments of age of onset of physical violence clearly lead to major underestimation. Adults and adolescents who are physically aggressive were most certainly physically aggressive preschoolers. Since most humans were physically aggressive during early childhood, one would expect that, under the right circumstances, most adolescents or adults will use physical aggression. However, these cases are probably rare and would not be considered chronic unless the triggering situation is recurrent. Cases of chronic physical aggression during adolescence and adulthood among individuals who had learned to inhibit physical aggression during childhood must be extremely rare.

In closing this chapter, it may be useful to consider what is meant by chronic physical aggression. Nagin and Tremblay (1999) showed that the chronically physically aggressive boys were those most likely to report violent offenses by late adolescence. They were also those most at risk of having been arrested and found guilty before turning 18 years of age. Recent analyses have helped to shed light on the behavior of the subjects in the chronic group. Using latent class analyses, Baillargeon (1999) showed that it is extremely difficult to predict the level of physical aggression of an individual beyond a one-year interval. His analyses and those of Nagin and Tremblay (1999) show that there is both intraindividual stability and change, depending on the perspective that is taken. When the data are analyzed from the perspective of stability over a 9-year period, as in Nagin and Tremblay, there is clearly a group of individuals who are regularly assessed highly physically aggressive, and which we call chronic. However, when analyzed from the perspective of year-to-year behavior (as in Baillargeon), there is evidence of much variability. Although one tends to think of a chronic case as a case who should be reported highly physically aggressive at each measurement point, there is good evidence that the chronic cases are the most variable. This is because the most highly physically aggressive child is not hitting everyone with whom he interacts on a daily basis. Physical aggression is a rare event, even for the most chronic cases, especially from early adolescence onward. Thus for each of the measurement points the probability that a chronic case will score high is relatively weak. This explains why attempts to predict dangerousness from one measurement point to another is a risky operation. Trajectories of behavior over long periods of time should be easier to predict.

> Man is not "bad" from birth onwards, but he is not good enough for the demands of cultivated society which he has imposed upon himself.
>
> In contrast to the wild animal, the cultivated human being ... can no longer rely blindly on his instincts: many of these are so obviously ... antisocial.
>
> Lorenz (1958, p. 183)

REFERENCES

Achenbach, T. M., & Edelbrock, C. (1986). *Manual for the teacher's report form and teacher version of the child behavior profile.* Burlington, VT: University of Vermont, Department of Psychiatry.

Akers, R. L. (1977). *Deviant behavior: A social learning perspective.* Belmont, CA: Wadsworth.

American Psychiatric Association (1994). *Diagnostic and statistical manual of mental disorders* (4th ed.). Washington, DC: Author.

Baillargeon, R. (1999). *Modeling intraindividual change in physical aggression between 6 and 12 years of age using a Markov model.* Paper presented at the Society for Research in Child Development, Albuquerque, NM.

Bandura, A. (1973). *Aggression: A social learning analysis.* New York: Holt.

Bellemare, P., & Nahmias, J.-F. (1998). L'enfant criminel. Paris: Albin Michel.

Bridges, K. M. B. (1931). The social and emotional development of the preschool child. London: Kegan Paul.

Broidy, L., Nagin, D., & Tremblay, R. E. (1999). The linkage of trajectories of child-hood externalizing behaviors to later violent and nonviolent delinquency. Paper presented at the Biennial Meeting of the Society for Research in Child Development, Albuquerque, NM.

Cairns, R. B., & Cairns, B. D. (1994). Life lines and risks: Pathways of youth in our time. New York: Cambridge University Press.

Cairns, R. B., Cairns, B. D., Neckerman, H. J., Ferguson, L. L., & Gariépy, J. L. (1989). Growth and aggression: 1. Childhood to early adolescence. Developmental Psychology, 25(2), 320–330.

Choquet, M., & Ledoux, S. (1994). Adolescents: Enquête nationale. Paris: Les éditions INSERM.

Cummings, E. M., Iannotti, R. J., & Zahn-Waxler, C. (1989). Aggression between peers in early childhood: Individual continuity and developmental change. Child Development, 60(4), 887–895.

Dawe, H. C. (1934). An analysis of 200 quarrels of preschool children. Child Development, 5, 139–157.

de Wit, J., & Hartup, W. W. (Ed.). (1974). Determinants and origins of aggressive behavior. The Hague, Netherlands: Mouton.

Dishion, T. J., McCord, J., & Poulin, F. (in press). Iatrogenic effects in early adolescent interventions that aggregate peers. American Psychologist.

Dodge, K. A., Bates, J. F., & Pettit, G. S. (1990). Mechanisms in the cycle of violence. Science, 250, 1678–1683.

Dunn, J., & Munn, P. (1985). Becoming a family member: Family conflict and the development of social understanding in the second year. Child Development, 56, 480–492.

Elliott, D. S. (1994). Serious violent offenders: Onset, developmental course and termination: The American Society of Criminology 1993 Presidential Address. Criminology, 32(1), 1–21.

Elliott, D. S., Huizinga, D., & Ageton, S. S. (1985). Explaining delinquency and drug use. Beverly Hills, CA: Sage.

Ellis, L., & Coontz, P. D. (1990). Androgens, brain functioning, and criminality: The neurohormonal foundations of antisociality. In L. Ellis & H. Hoffman (Eds.), Crime in biological, social and moral contexts (pp. 162–193). New York: Praeger.

Eron, L. D. (1990). Understanding aggression. Bulletin of the International Society for Research on Aggression, 12, 5–9.

Eysenck, H. J., & Gudjonsson, G. H. (1989). The causes and cures of criminality. New York: Plenum.

Farrington, D. P. (1987). Epidemiology. In H. C. Quay (Ed.), Handbook of juvenile delinquency (pp. 33–61). New York: Wiley.

Farrington, D. P., Loeber, R., Elliott, D. S., Hawkins, D., Kandel, D. B., Klein, M. W., McCord, J., Rowe, D. C., & Tremblay, R. E. (1990). Advancing knowledge about the onset of delinquency and crime. In B. B. Lahey & A. E. Kazdin (Eds.), Advances in clinical child psychology. Vol. 13, chap. 8 (pp. 283–342). New York: Plenum.

Farrington, D. P., Loeber, R., & Van Kammen, W. B. (1990). The long term criminal outcomes of conduct problem boys with or without impulsive-inattentive behavior. In L. N. Robins & M. Rutter (Eds.), *Straight and devious pathways from childhood to adulthood*, (pp. 62–81). New York: Cambridge University Press.

Fergusson, D., & Horwood, J. (1999). *Dimensions and trajectories of disruptive behavior*. Paper presented at the Society for Research in Child Development, Albuquerque, NM.

Hawkins, J. D., Farrington, D. P., & Catalano, R. P. (1998). Reducing violence through the schools. In D. S. Elliott, B. A. Hamburg, et al. (Eds.), *Violence in American schools: A new perspective* (pp. 188–216). New York: Cambridge University Press.

Hay, D. F., & Ross, H. S. (1982). The social nature of early conflict. *Child Development, 53*, 105–113.

Huesmann, L. R., Eron, L. D., Lefkowitz, M. M., & Walder, L. O. (1984). Stability of aggression over time and generations. *Developmental Psychology, 20*(6), 1120–1134.

Kagan, J. (1974). Development and methodological considerations in the study of aggression. In J. de Wit & W. W. Hartup (Eds.), *Determinants and origins of aggressive behavior* (pp. 107–114). The Hague, Netherlands: Mouton.

Keenan, K., & Shaw, D. S. (1994). The development of aggression in toddlers: A study of low-income families. *Journal of Abnormal Child Psychology, 22*(1), 53–77.

Kellam, S. G., & Rebok, G. W. (1992). Building developmental and etiological theory through epidemiologically based preventive intervention trials. In J. McCord & R. E. Tremblay (Eds.), *Preventing antisocial behavior: Interventions from birth through adolescence* (pp. 162–195). New York: Guilford Press.

Kingston, L., & Prior, M. (1995). The development of patterns of stable, transient, and school-age onset aggressive behavior in young children. *Journal of the American Academy of Child and Adolescent Psychiatry, 34*, 348–358.

Lahey, B. B., Loeber, R., Quay, H. C., Applegate, B., Shaffer, D., Waldman, I., Hart, E. L., McBurnett, K., Frick, P. J., Jensen, P. S., Dulcan, M. K., Canino, G., & Bird, H. R. (1998). Validity of *DSM-IV* subtypes of conduct disorder based on age of onset. *Journal of the American Academy of Child and Adolescent Psychiatry, 37*(4), 435–442.

Lefkowitz, M. M., Eron, L. D., Walder, L. O., & Huesmann, L. R. (1977). *Growing up to be violent. A longitudinal study of the development of aggression.* New York: Pergamon.

Loeber, R., & Hay, D. F. (1994). Developmental approaches to aggression and conduct problems. In M. Rutter & D. F. Hay (Eds.), *Development through life: A handbook for clinicians* (pp. 488–516). Oxford: Blackwell Scientific Publications.

Loeber, R., & Hay, D. F. (1997). Key issues in the development of aggression and violence from childhood to early adulthood. *Annual Review of Psychology, 48*, 371–410.

Loeber, R., Keenan, K., & Zhang, Q. (1997). Boys' experimentation and persistence in developmental pathways toward serious delinquency. *Journal of Child and Family Studies, 6*, 321–357.

Loeber, R., & Stouthamer-Loeber, M. (1998). Development of juvenile aggression and violence. Some common misconceptions and controversies. *American Psychologist, 53*(2), 242–259.

Lorenz, K. (1958). *Man meets dog.* Hardmondsworth, UK: Penguin Books.

Magdol, L., Moffitt, T. E., Caspi, A., & Silva, P. A. (1998). Developmental antecedents of partner abuse: A prospective-longitudinal study. *Journal of Abnormal Psychology, 107*(3), 375–389.

Moffitt, T. E. (1990). Juvenile delinquency and attention deficit disorder: Developmental trajectories from age 3 to age 15. *Child Development, 61,* 893–910.

Moffitt, T. E. (1993). Adolescence-limited and life-course persistent antisocial behavior: A developmental taxonomy. *Psychological Review, 100*(4), 674–701.

Moffitt, T. E., Caspi, A., Dickson, N., Silva, P. S., & Stanton, W. (1996). Childhood-onset versus adolescent-onset antisocial conduct problems in males: Natural history from ages 3 to 18 years. *Development and Psychopathology, 8*(2), 399–424.

Murphy, L. B. (1937). *Social behavior and child personality.* New York: Columbia University Press.

Nagin, D., & Tremblay, R. E. (1999). Trajectories of boys' physical aggression, opposition, and hyperactivity on the path to physically violent and non-violent juvenile delinquency. *Child Development, 70*(5), 1181–1196.

Pagani, L., Boulerice, B., & Tremblay, R. E. (1997). The influence of poverty upon children's classroom placement and behavior problems during elementary school: A change model approach. In G. Duncan & J. Brooks-Gunn (Eds.), *Consequences of growing up poor* (pp. 311–339). New York: Sage.

Patterson, G. R., DeBaryshe, B. D., & Ramsey, E. (1989). A developmental perspective on antisocial behavior. *American Psychologist, 44,* 329–335.

Pekarik, E. G., Prinz, R. J., Liebert, D. E., Weintraub, S., & Neale, J. N. (1976). The Pupil Evaluation Inventory: A sociometric technique for assessing children's social behavior. *Journal of Abnormal Child Psychology, 4,* 83–97.

Quetelet, A. (1833). *Research on the propensity for crime at different ages.* Brussels: M. Hayez, Printer to the Royal Academy.

Restoin, A. (1985). *Aspects fonctionnels et ontogénétiques des comportements de communication chez le jeune enfant. Concomitants chronobiologiques.* Grade de docteurs es sciences naturelles, Université de Franche-Comté.

Restoin, A., Montagner, H., Rodriguez, D., Girardot, J. J., Laurent, D., Kontar, F., Ullmann, V., Casagrande, C., & Talpain, B. (1985). Chronologie des comportements de communication et profils de comportement chez le jeune enfant. In R. E. Tremblay, M. A. Provost, & F. F. Strayer (Eds.), *Ethologie et développement de l'enfant* (pp. 93–130). Paris: Editions Stock/Laurence Pernoud.

Rousseau, J. J. (1762). *Émile, de l'éducation.* Paris: Firmin Didot Frères et Fils.

Satterfield, J. H. (1987). Childhood diagnostic and neurophysiological predictors of teenage arrest rates: An eight-year prospective study. In S. A. Mednick, T. E. Moffitt, & S. A. Stack (Eds.), *The causes of crime: New biological approaches. Vol. 9* (pp. 146–167). New York: Cambridge University Press.

Tremblay, R. E., Boulerice, B., Harden, P. W., McDuff, P., Pérusse, D., Pihl, R. O., & Zoccolillo, M. (1996). Do children in Canada become more aggressive as they approach adolescence? In Human Resources Development Canada & Statistics Canada (Eds.), *Growing up in Canada: National Longitudinal Survey of Children and Youth* (pp. 127–137). Ottawa: Statistics Canada.

Tremblay, R. E., Japel, C., Pérusse, D., Boivin, M., Zoccolillo, M., Montplaisir, J., & McDuff, P. (1999). The search for the age of "onset" of physical aggression: Rousseau and Bandura revisited. *Criminal Behavior and Mental Health, 9,* 8–23.

Tremblay, R. E., Pagani-Kurtz, L., Mâsse, L. C., Vitaro, F., & Pihl, R. O. (1995). A bimodal preventive intervention for disruptive kindergarten boys: Its impact through mid-adolescence. *Journal of Consulting and Clinical Psychology, 63*(4), 560–568.

Tremblay, R. E., LeMarquand, D., & Vitaro, F. (1999). The prevention of ODD and CD. In H. C. Quay & A. E. Hogan (Eds.), *Handbook of disruptive behavior disorders* (pp. 525–555). New York: Kluwer Academic/Plenum Publishers.

Tremblay, R. E., Loeber, R., Gagnon, C., Charlebois, P., Larivée, S., & LeBlanc, M. (1991). Disruptive boys with stable and unstable high fighting behavior patterns during junior elementary school. *Journal of Abnormal Child Psychology, 19,* 285–300.

Tremblay, R. E., & Schaal, B. (1996). Physically aggressive boys from age 6 to 12 years: Their biopsychosocial status at puberty. In G. Ferris & T. Grisso (Eds.), *Understanding aggressive behavior in children. Vol. 794* (pp. 192–208). New York: Annals of the New York Academy of Sciences.

Vitaro, F., & Tremblay, R. E. (1994). Impact of a prevention program on aggressive-disruptive children's friendships and social adjustment. *Journal of Abnormal Child Psychology, 22*(4), 457–475.

Zoccolillo, M., Vitaro, F., & Tremblay, R. E. (1999). Problem drug and alcohol use in a community sample of adolescents. *Journal of the American Academy of Child and Adolescent Psychiatry, 38*(7), 900–907.

4. Predicting Adult Official and Self-Reported Violence

DAVID P. FARRINGTON

The main aim of this chapter is to investigate how far *adult* violence (after age 21) could be predicted in the Cambridge Study in Delinquent Development. The Cambridge Study is a prospective longitudinal survey of 411 South London males from age 8 to age 40. As explained later, previous analyses have focused on predicting youth violence (under age 21), violence at any age, or specific types of violence (e.g., spouse assault or soccer hooliganism). This chapter compares the prediction of convictions for violence in official records for offenses committed between ages 21 and 40 with the prediction of self-reported violence between ages 27 and 32.

This chapter investigates the efficiency of predictors of adult violence at different ages (10, 14, and 18). It distinguishes behavioral and explanatory predictors of adult violence. Childhood aggression is an example of a behavioral predictor, whereas harsh parental discipline is an example of an explanatory predictor. Childhood aggression probably leads to adult violence because of the persistence over time of an underlying construct such as aggressive personality. Harsh parental discipline may lead to adult violence because it has causal effects on an underlying construct such as an aggressive personality; perhaps children learn by observation that aggression is a legitimate way of solving interpersonal problems. Behavioral and explanatory predictors have different implications for intervention. Behavioral predictors identify people who should be targeted in intervention programs, whereas explanatory predictors identify not only people but also causal mechanisms to be targeted. For example, parent training techniques could be implemented to improve parental discipline.

Previous Relevant Research

Surprisingly, almost nothing is known about childhood and adolescent predictors of *adult* violence (age 21 or over) in large-scale community samples. Most relevant research on community samples is concerned with predictors of youth violence (under age 21: see Farrington, 1998; Hawkins et al., 1998), with predictors of violence up to a certain age (e.g., up to age 32: McCord & Ensminger, 1997; up to age 30: Eron, Huesmann, & Zelli, 1991), or with predictors of adult crime in general (e.g., Kolvin et al., 1990; Sampson & Laub, 1993). There are, of course, prediction studies based on mentally disordered samples (now concerned with "risk assessment"; see Monahan & Steadman, 1994) or on clinic samples (e.g., Mannuzza et al., 1989), but these are outside the scope of this chapter.

Prospective longitudinal surveys are needed to investigate the early predictors of adult violence. The best of these surveys include interview as well as record data and span a follow-up period of at least 5 years. These minimal requirements eliminate most surveys. For example, Mossman (1994) reviewed 44 studies of the prediction of violence, and only two (Farrington, 1989a; Kandel et al., 1989) met these criteria. Studies of self-reported violence by adults are also quite uncommon; most self-report surveys are based on youth under age 21 (for an exception, see Weiler and Widom, 1996).

In extensive reviews of longitudinal surveys of youth violence, Farrington (1998) listed 28 major studies of large community samples (several hundreds), and Hawkins et al. (1998) listed 33 major longitudinal surveys. For obvious reasons, however, the more recently mounted projects have not yet extended far enough into the adult years to study adult violence (e.g., the Pittsburgh Youth Study: Loeber et al., 1998; the Rochester Youth Development Study: Thornberry et al., 1991; the Denver Youth Survey: Huizinga, Esbensen, & Weiher, 1991; the Oregon Youth Study: Capaldi & Patterson, 1996; the Dunedin study: Henry et al., 1996; the Chicago Youth Development Study: Gorman-Smith et al., 1996).

Most longitudinal surveys that do extend into the adult ages do not provide specific information about adult violence after age 21. Often, the number of violent offenders in European studies is very small; for example, there were only 35 violent offenders up to age 26 (out of 540 males) in the Orebro project (Klinteberg et al., 1993), and only 14 violent offenders up to age 27 (out of 196 males) in the Jyvaskyla longitudinal study (Hamalainen & Pulkkinen, 1996). Also, with a few notable exceptions (e.g., the Cambridge Study and McCord, 1979), most surveys mounted before 1980 measured a very limited range of risk factors. As pointed out by Steadman et al. (1994), in violence prediction it is important to measure a wide variety of risk factors, including demographic, behavioral, personality, cognitive, educational, family, contextual, and clinical ones.

What, then, are the major conclusions about the predictors of adult violence that can be drawn from existing research? First, demographic factors matter. Males are more violent than females and African Americans are more violent than whites (e.g., Maxfield & Widom, 1996), and lower-class people are more violent than those in the upper-class (e.g., Wikström, 1985). Second, childhood aggression (e.g., Stattin & Magnusson, 1989) and juvenile violence (e.g., Hamparian et al., 1985) predict adult violence. Third, violent fathers tend to have violent sons (McCord, 1977) and children who are physically punished, abused, or neglected tend to become adult violent offenders (Eron et al., 1991; Maxfield & Widom, 1996). Fourth, a variety of family factors (e.g., criminal or alcoholic fathers, parental conflict, poor parental supervision, broken families) predict adult violence (McCord, 1979; Moffitt, Mednick, & Gabrielli, 1989). Fifth, individual factors such as low intelligence (McCord & Ensminger, 1997) and hyperactivity (Klinteberg et al., 1993) predict adult violence.

It is difficult to draw firm conclusions about the predictors of adult violence because so few projects have presented specific results on adult violence. It is likely that predictors of violence up to age 30 (say) or of youth violence are also predictors of adult violence, but it is not certain. More research is needed specifically on the predictors of adult violence.

The Cambridge Study in Delinquent Development

The Cambridge Study in Delinquent Development is a prospective longitudinal survey of the development of offending and antisocial behavior in 411 males. At the time they were first contacted in 1961–1962, these males were all living in a working-class inner-city area of South London. The sample was chosen by taking all the boys who were then aged 8–9 and on the registers of six state primary schools within a 1-mile radius of a research office that had been established. Hence, the most common year of birth of these males was

1953. In nearly all cases (94%), their family breadwinner at that time (usually the father) had a working-class occupation (skilled, semi-skilled, or unskilled manual worker). Most of the males were white (97%) and of British origin. The study was originally directed by Donald J. West, and since 1982 it has been directed by David P. Farrington, who has worked on it since 1969. It has been funded mainly by the Home Office. The major results can be found in four books (West, 1969, 1982; West & Farrington, 1973, 1977) and in summary papers by Farrington and West (1990) and Farrington (1995). These publications should be consulted for more details about the predictor variables discussed here.

A major aim in this survey was to measure as many factors as possible that were alleged to be causes or correlates of offending. The males were interviewed and tested in their schools when they were aged about 8, 10, and 14, by male or female psychologists. They were interviewed in a research office at about 16, 18, and 21, and in their homes at about 25 and 32, by young male social science graduates. At all ages except 21 and 25, the aim was to interview the whole sample, and it was always possible to trace and interview a high proportion: 389 out of 410 still alive at age 18 (95%) and 378 out of 403 still alive at age 32 (94%), for example. The tests in schools measured individual characteristics such as intelligence, attainment, personality, and psychomotor impulsivity, while information was collected in the interviews about such topics as living circumstances, employment histories, relationships with females, leisure activities such as drinking and fighting, and offending behavior.

In addition to interviews and tests with the males, interviews with their parents were carried out by female social workers who visited their homes. These took place about once a year from when the male was about 8 until when he was aged 14–15 and was in his last year of compulsory education. The primary informant was the mother, although many fathers were also seen. The parents provided details about such matters as family income, family size, their employment histories, their child-rearing practices (including attitudes, discipline, and parental disharmony), their degree of supervision of the boy, and his temporary or permanent separations from them. The teachers completed questionnaires when the boys were aged about 8, 10, 12, and 14. These furnished data about their troublesome and aggressive school behavior, their attention deficits, their school attainments, and their truancy. Ratings were also obtained from the boys' peers when they were in the primary schools, about such topics as their daring, dishonesty, troublesomeness, and popularity.

Information on Offending

Searches were carried out in the central Criminal Record Office (National Identification Service) in London to try to locate findings of guilt of the males, of their parents, of their brothers and sisters, and (in recent years) of their wives and female partners. The latest search of conviction records took place in the summer of 1994, when most of the males were aged 40.

Between ages 10 and 16 inclusive (the years of juvenile delinquency in England at that time), 85 males (21%) were convicted. Altogether, up to age 40, 164 males (40%) were convicted (Farrington, Barnes, & Lambert, 1996; Farrington, Lambert, & West, 1998). In this chapter, the recorded age of offending is the age at which an offense was committed, not the age on conviction. Delays of several months or even more than a year can occur between offenses and convictions, making conviction ages different from offending ages.

Convictions were counted only if they were for offenses normally recorded in the Criminal Record Office, thereby excluding minor crimes such as common assault, traffic infractions, and drunkenness. The most common offenses included were thefts, burglaries, and unauthorized takings of vehicles, although there were also numerous offenses of violence, vandalism, fraud, and drug abuse.

Violent Offenses

Of the 760 recorded offenses, 119 were classified as violent: 52 assaults causing bodily harm, 28 offenses of threatening behavior, 18 robberies, 18 offensive weapon offenses, and 3 sex offenses. Assaults had to be relatively serious (involving visible damage worse than bruises, swelling, or a black eye) to be counted as indictable bodily harm offenses rather than common assault. Convictions for domestic violence were almost invariably for common assault, as in the following example:

Case 870 (age 37). After an argument with his wife, who was applying for a divorce, hit her in the face and pushed her around the house, causing red marks to her face and arm. [Common assault—not counted]

Sometimes, more serious assaults led to a conviction for common assault, probably as a result of plea bargaining:

Case 141 (age 17) and Case 301 (age 18). After an argument and a fight in a pub, attacked the male victim outside with his girlfriend; knocked him to the ground, kicked him, hit him about the head and back with broken beer glasses, cut him. [Pleaded not guilty to unlawful wounding but guilty to common assault—not counted]

Assaults causing bodily harm were often connected with alcohol use, as the following four examples show:

Case 781 (age 22). After an argument in a pub, pushed the male victim to the floor and kicked him in the face and ribs, causing cuts and bruises to the face.

Case 781 (age 27). Head-butted the male victim in a pub, causing a cut nose.

Case 781 (age 27, 6 months later). Hit the male victim over the eye in a pub with a pint glass that broke.

Case 781 (age 36). Was a guest at a party, became jealous of a man dancing with a girl he liked, head-butted the man in the face, breaking his nose.

Robberies were almost invariably serious offenses, as in the following example:

Case 562 (age 26). With two others robbed two restaurants and attempted to rob a gas station while armed with a sawn-off shotgun and handgun. On each occasion fired the shotgun to frighten the victim. No person was injured. [Convicted of three robbery offenses and two offenses of possessing a firearm; counted as one robbery, since all were committed on the same day]

Threatening behavior offenses usually involved a serious threat of violence; for example, Case 660 threatened prostitutes with a replica gun at age 26.

Offensive weapon offenses usually involved sheath knives, flick knives, crowbars, shotguns, and the like. Half of those convicted for possessing an offensive weapon also had a conviction for some other violent crime.

Only 10 of the males were convicted of sex offenses, and 7 of these did not involve violence (three indecent exposure, one obscene telephone call, two consensual homosexual offenses, one sexual intercourse with his younger sister). The other three were counted because they involved violence: one alleged rape that led to a conviction for unlawful sexual intercourse, one violent indecent assault on a female, and one man (Case 403, age 33) who used a 13-year-old boy for homosexual buggery and then passed the boy on to other homosexuals for the purpose of buggery. [Convicted of indecent assault on a male]

Up to age 40, 65 of the males were convicted for violence: 16% of 404 at risk, excluding 7 not convicted for violence who died up to age 32. The vast majority of these males (54 out of 65) also had convictions for nonviolent offenses. *The 41 males (10%) convicted for violence between ages 21 and 40 (committing 66 violent crimes) are the main focus of this chapter.* About one third of those convicted for violence between ages 10 and 20 (34%, or 12 out of 35) were also convicted between ages 21 and 40, compared with 8% of those not convicted of youth violence (Odds Ratio (OR) = 6.1; 95% Confidence Interval 2.8–13.5, so $p < .05$). Odds Ratios are used here as the main measure of strength of relationships. Essentially, the OR indicates the increase in risk associated with a risk factor; ORs of 2 or greater, indicating a doubling of the risk, suggest strong predictive relationships.

In order not to rely on official records for information about offending, self-reports of offending were obtained from the males at every age from 14 to 32. In this chapter, the adult self-reported violent males are the 61 (16% of 377 known) who, between ages 27 and 32, had either (a) been involved in four or more physical fights in which blows were struck, or (b) had hit their wife or female partner without her hitting them (Farrington, 1989b, pp. 230 and 235). About a quarter of self-reported adult violent males (26%, or 16 out of 61) were also convicted for violence as adults, compared with 7% of the remainder (OR = 4.5, $p < .05$).

Previous Analyses of Violence

West and Farrington (1973) reported the prevalence of official and self-reported violence at ages 14 and 16 in the Cambridge Study, while West and Farrington (1977) reported the comparable prevalence at age 18–19. Both books also showed relationships between aggression and delinquency; for example, West and Farrington (1977, p. 11) reported that 80% of young adults convicted for violence also had convictions for dishonesty. West and Farrington (1977, p. 149) also found that violent offenders at age 18 were deviant in many respects, including heavy drinking, drunk driving, drug use, sexual promiscuity, heavy smoking, heavy gambling, and having an unstable job record.

The first analysis of predictors of self-reported violence (at age 14) was published by Farrington and West (1971). Significant predictors at age 8–10 included childhood misconduct, daring, low nonverbal IQ, large family size, and low family income. Farrington and West (1971) concluded that self-reported violent boys were similar in many respects to early delinquents (those convicted up to age 14), but that the delinquents were more deprived in regard to low income and poor housing.

Farrington (1978) carried out a more extensive study of predictors of aggression at age 8–10 (difficult to discipline, rated by teachers), 12–14 (aggression rated by teachers), 16–18 (self-reported violence), and convictions for violence between ages 10 and 20. The most important independent predictors of convictions for violence were harsh parental discipline, a convicted parent, poor parental supervision, a broken family, high daring, and low nonverbal IQ. There was considerable continuity from aggression at age 8–10 to violence at age 16–18 (see also Farrington, 1982).

Farrington, Berkowitz, and West (1982) analyzed physical fights reported by the males at age 18 (most occurring in pubs or streets). Group fights were more serious than individual fights, in involving weapons, injuries, and police intervention. A category of aggressive frequent group fighters was identified. The best predictors of these boys at age 8–10 were low family income, large family size, low verbal IQ, daring, troublesomeness, and low school track.

Farrington (1989a) investigated the predictors of aggression at age 12–14 (rated by teachers), self-reported violence at age 16–18, self-reported fights at age 32, and convictions for violence between ages 10 and 32. Regression analyses showed that the best predictors of convictions included high daring, authoritarian parents, a convicted parent, low verbal IQ, and harsh parental discipline. The best predictors of self-reported fights at age 32 included the father rarely joining in the boy's leisure activities at age 12, high self-reported delinquency at age 18, and high daring at age 8–10. Farrington (1991b) showed that the predictors of convictions for violence up to age 32 and of frequent nonviolent offenders were very similar, a result later replicated by Capaldi and Patterson (1996).

Farrington (1993) studied the predictors of bullying at ages 14, 18, and 32, while Farrington (1994) compared the predictors of soccer violence at age 18, aggressive frequent group fighters at age 18, spouse assault at age 32, and convictions for violence up to age 32. In regression analyses, Farrington (1997b) showed that a low heart rate at age 18 (possibly indicating fearlessness or low arousal) was an independent predictor of convictions for violence up to age 40 and of self-reported violence at age 18. Farrington (1997a) investigated the ability of various combined scales to predict convictions for violence between ages 10 and 20 and self-reported violence at age 18, and Farrington (1998) reviewed a variety of risk factors for these two outcomes.

No previous report on the Cambridge Study has investigated predictors of the two outcomes studied here: convictions for violence between ages 21 and 40, and self-reported violence (frequent fights and spouse assault) between ages 27 and 32.

Behavioral Predictors

Table 4.1 shows behavioral predictors, at ages 8–10, 12–14, and 16–18, of adult violence. For example, 17% of boys rated as dishonest by peers at age 10 were convicted of violence as adults, compared with 8% of the remainder (OR = 2.5). Troublesomeness, which was the best predictor of juvenile delinquency, and being difficult to discipline, which was used as a measure of childhood aggression in previous analyses, did not significantly predict adult violence.

At age 12–14, the best predictors of convictions for violence were a hostile attitude to the police, high self-reported violence, high self-reported delinquency, stealing outside home (according to mothers), and aggressiveness (rated by teachers). Frequent lying, frequent truancy, and delinquent friends also predicted adult violence. (Delinquent friends was regarded as a behavioral variable because most offending was committed in small groups.) At age 12–14, the best predictors of adult self-reported violence were self-reported delinquency, self-reported violence, frequent lying, delinquent friends, and aggressiveness. Surprisingly, self-reported bullying and fighting outside the home (according to mothers) were not significant predictors.

Also surprisingly, previous convictions for nonviolent offenses (at age 10–20) were better predictors of adult convictions for violence than previous convictions for violent offenses, according to the OR. Of 117 males convicted for nonviolence in their youth, 26% had adult convictions for violence, compared with 4% of the remaining 286 (OR = 8.6). This result is concordant with the previous finding that violent offenders are versatile rather than specialized. Youthful convictions were less strong predictors of adult self-reported violence.

At age 16–18, other important predictors of adult convictions for violence were self-reported delinquency, self-reported violence (weaker

Table 4.1. Behavioral Predictors of Adult Violence

	Odds Ratio	
Variable (% identified)	Convictions	Self-Reports
Age 8–10		
Difficult to discipline (23)	1.4	1.3
Troublesome (22)	1.6	1.7
Dishonest (25)	2.5*	1.7
Age 12–14		
Frequent liar (30)	2.6*	2.5*
Frequent truant (18)	2.8*	1.3
Early smoker (17)	1.4	1.6
Early sex (29)	1.8	1.3
Aggressive (33)	3.0*	2.4*
Bully (17)	1.9	1.1
Hostile to police (27)	4.3*	2.0*
Delinquent friends (25)	2.4*	2.5*
Fights outside home (29)	1.3	1.1
Steals outside home (17)	3.8*	2.1*
Self-reported delinquent (23)	3.8*	2.8*
Self-reported violence (15)	4.1*	2.7*
Age 16–18		
Hangs about (16)	1.2	0.7
Heavy gambler (22)	2.6*	1.2
Heavy smoker (27)	1.7	1.6
Heavy drinker (25)	2.8*	2.4*
Binge drinker (21)	1.8	2.2*
Drunk driver (22)	2.2*	1.9*
Drug user (31)	2.7*	2.9*
Motoring offense (16)	2.5*	1.1
Promiscuous sex (29)	2.3*	1.8
Irresponsible sex (20)	2.6*	1.5
Aggressive attitude (26)	1.2	1.3
Bully (22)	0.9	0.8
Antiestablishment (25)	2.4*	1.3
Conflict with parents (22)	2.3*	1.5
Antisocial group (17)	1.5	2.0*
Fights after drinking (32)	1.0	2.1*
Self-reported delinquent (25)	4.4*	3.0*
Self-reported violence (20)	3.0*	2.3*
Convicted violence (9)	6.1*	3.6*
Convicted nonviolence (30)	8.6*	3.4*

*$p < .05$.

than self-reported delinquency), heavy drinking (40 units of alcohol or more per week), drug use (mostly marijuana), heavy gambling, irresponsible sex (never using contraceptives), motoring convictions, and antiestablishment attitudes. Other important predictors of adult self-reported violence were self-reported delinquency, drug use, heavy drinking, self-reported violence, binge drinking (more than 12 units of alcohol drunk in one evening in an average week), getting involved in fights after drinking, and being a member of an antisocial group. Surprisingly, spending time hanging about on the street, bullying, and proaggressive attitudes did not predict adult violence.

These results are generally concordant with the previous conclusion that violence is one element of an antisocial personality syndrome that emerges in childhood and continues into adolescence and adulthood. Convictions for violence are associated with a generally criminal lifestyle, whereas self-reported violence is more specifically associated with heavy drinking and fighting.

Explanatory Predictors

Table 4.2 shows explanatory predictors, at ages 8–10, 12–14, and 16–18, of adult violence. Generally, most risk factors measured at age 8–10 were explanatory, whereas most risk factors measured at age 16–18 were behavioral. Explanatory variables were usually poorer predictors than were behavioral variables. At age 8–10, the strongest predictor of adult convictions for violence was having a convicted parent; 20% of boys with a convicted biological parent before age 10 were convicted for adult violence, compared with 7% of the remainder (OR = 3.4).

Other important predictors at age 8–10 of adult convictions for violence were low verbal IQ, low family income, coming from a broken family (separated from a biological parent, usually the father), harsh parental discipline, low junior school attainment, high daring (rated by parents and peers), low social class of the family breadwinner (an unskilled manual job), and a large family (four or more biological siblings by age 10). The most important predictors of adult self-reported violence were a broken family, low social class, a young mother (having her first child as a teenager), and a large family.

Surprisingly, lack of concentration or restlessness, high psychomotor impulsivity, parental conflict, poor housing, and attending a school with a high delinquency rate were not strong predictors of adult violence. Whereas small height was one of the best predictors of soccer violence at age 18 (Farrington, 1994), it did not predict adult violence.

Table 4.2. Explanatory Predictors of Adult Violence

Variable (% identified)	Odds Ratio	
	Convictions	Self-Reports
Age 8–10		
High daring (30)	2.1*	1.7
Lacks concentration (20)	1.8	0.7
High impulsivity (25)	1.1	1.0
Low nonverbal IQ (25)	1.6	0.7
Low verbal IQ (25)	2.9*	1.4
Low attainment (23)	2.2*	1.7
Low school track (29)	1.7	0.7
Unpopular (32)	1.0	1.3
Nervous–withdrawn (24)	1.2	1.8
Small (18)	1.0	0.8
Convicted parent (27)	3.4*	1.8*
Harsh discipline (30)	2.3*	1.1
Poor supervision (19)	2.1	1.2
Broken family (22)	2.5*	2.3*
Parental conflict (24)	1.7	1.6
Large family (24)	2.0*	2.0*
Young mother (22)	1.3	2.1*
Low income (23)	2.8*	1.6
Low social class (19)	2.1*	2.3*
Poor housing (37)	1.7	1.3
Delinquent school (21)	1.1	1.2
Age 12–14		
Lacks concentration (26)	4.0*	2.3*
Low nonverbal IQ (29)	1.6	0.8
Low verbal IQ (23)	1.6	1.4
Unpopular (17)	1.8	1.2
Nervous (30)	1.3	1.0
Small (24)	1.4	1.1
Father uninvolved (28)	3.1*	2.1*
Authoritarian parents (24)	2.2	1.9
Parental conflict (18)	3.2*	2.2*
Large family (21)	1.3	1.3
Low social class (32)	1.1	1.3
Poor housing (20)	1.9	1.0
Age 16–18		
Impulsive (27)	2.0*	1.6
Extraverted (22)	2.4*	1.0
Neurotic (27)	1.7	1.1
Small (15)	0.8	1.6
Low job status (16)	5.0*	2.2*
Unstable job record (24)	3.4*	1.8*
Low pay (24)	0.7	0.6
Convicted parent (30)	4.3*	1.9*
Low pulse rate (43)	1.7	1.4

* $p < .05$.

The predictive ability of low social class at age 8–10 was also surprising, because it was conspicuously poor as a predictor of juvenile delinquency (unlike low family income).

At age 12–14 the strongest predictors of adult convictions for violence and of adult self-reported violence were lack of concentration or restlessness (rated by teachers), parental conflict, and the father not joining in the boy's leisure activities. It was unclear why the first two of these factors predicted adult violence at age 12–14 but not at age 8–10. Conversely, it was unclear why low verbal IQ predicted at age 8–10 but not at age 14. Low social class was a more inclusive variable at age 14 (including partly skilled as well as unskilled manual workers). Large family size at age 14 referred to the number of people in the house rather than to the number of biological siblings (as at age 10).

At age 16–18, the strongest predictors of adult convictions for violence and of adult self-reported violence were the boy's own job status (an unskilled manual job), having a convicted parent by age 18, and the boy's unstable job record (reflecting many changes of job, periods of unemployment, and being fired). A high extraversion score (on the Eysenck Personality Inventory at age 16) and impulsiveness on an attitude questionnaire at age 18 (measured by items such as "I generally do and say things quickly without stopping to think") also predicted adult convictions for violence.

Low take-home pay at age 18 was negatively related to adult violence. This was because the more antisocial males at age 18 tended to have relatively well-paid dead-end jobs when they were working (e.g., as unskilled manual workers), whereas the more prosocial males at age 18 were students or in low-paid jobs with future prospects (e.g., apprentices or bank clerks). Disappointingly, a low pulse rate (heart rate) at age 18 did not significantly predict adult violence, although it was related to convictions for violence at any age and to self-reported violence at age 18 (Farrington, 1997b).

Multivariate Analyses

In order to investigate which variables predicted adult violence independently of other variables, forward stepwise multiple regression analyses were carried out. Strictly speaking, logistic regression analysis should be carried out with dichotomous data. However, a problem with logistic regression is that a case which is missing on any one variable has to be deleted from the whole analysis, causing a considerable loss of data. Fortunately, with dichotomous data, ordinary least squares (OLS) regression produces results very similar to logistic regression (Cleary & Angel, 1984), and the results obtained by the two methods are mathematically related (Schlesselman, 1982). Missing data were handled in the OLS regression by pairwise deletion, using all the available data for estimation of the relationships between all possible pairs of variables. Behavioral and explanatory predictors were included in each regression analysis.

Table 4.3 shows the results of these regression analyses. Variables significant at $p < .10$ in one-tailed tests are shown in this table; one-tailed tests were used because all predictions were directional. At age 8–10, the four independent predictors of adult convictions for violence were having a convicted parent, low family income, peer-rated dishonesty, and harsh parental discipline. The five independent predictors of adult self-reported violence were coming from a broken family, low social class, a nervous-withdrawn temperament (rated by parents), a young mother, and high daring. The most surprising predictor is a nervous-withdrawn temperament, because it has often been suggested that such a temperament might inhibit the expression of aggression.

At age 12–14, the five independent predictors of adult convictions for violence were a hostile attitude toward the police, lack of concentration or restlessness, stealing outside the home, the father not joining in the boy's leisure activities, and high self-reported violence. The five independent predictors of adult self-reported violence were high self-reported delinquency, frequent lying (according to teachers and parents), the father not joining in the boy's leisure activities, aggressiveness, and parental conflict.

Youthful convictions for violent and nonviolent offenses were independent predictors of both adult convictions for violence and adult self-reported violence. At age 16–18, the other independent predictors of adult convictions for violence were the boy's low job status, high extroversion, having a criminal parent, and high self-reported delinquency. The other independent predictors of adult self-reported violence were drug use, heavy drinking, and high self-reported delinquency.

When all the variables were put together, there were eight independent predictors of adult convictions for violence: a youthful conviction for nonviolence, a hostile attitude to the police at age 14, the boy's low job status at age 18, the father not joining in the boy's leisure activities at age 12, having a criminal parent at age 18, a youth-

Table 4.3. Results of Multiple Regression Analyses

Convictions	F Change	Self-Reports	F Change
Age 8–10		**Age 8–10**	
Convicted parent	12.16***	Broken family	7.38***
Low income	4.03*	Low social class	5.76**
Dishonest	2.78*	Nervous-withdrawn	2.78*
Harsh discipline	1.94	Young mother	2.80*
		High daring	2.14
Age 12–14		**Age 12–14**	
Hostile to police	15.48***	Self-reported delinquency	9.80**
Lacks concentration	10.91***	Frequent liar	4.90*
Steals outside home	5.23*	Father uninvolved	3.32*
Father uninvolved	5.75**	Aggressive	2.56
Self-reported violence	2.62*	Parental conflict	2.02
Age 16–18		**Age 16–18**	
Convicted nonviolence	45.46***	Convicted nonviolence	19.41***
Low job status	10.20***	Drug user	9.05***
Convicted violence	5.32*	Heavy drinker	3.70*
Extroverted	4.74*	Self-reported delinquent	3.40*
Criminal parent	4.43*	Convicted violence	1.75
Self-reported delinquent	2.10		
Age 8–18		**Age 8–18**	
Convicted nonviolence	34.18***	Convicted nonviolence	14.99***
Hostile to police 14	8.12**	Drug user 18	6.98**
Low job status 18	6.80**	Nervous-withdrawn 8	4.92*
Father uninvolved 12	4.33*	Low social class 10	4.01*
Criminal parent 18	4.35*	Aggressive 14	3.50*
Convicted violence	3.46*	Young mother	2.02
Extroverted 16	3.15*	Self-reported delinquent 18	2.01
Lacks concentration 14	2.50	Heavy drinker 18	1.82
		Father uninvolved 12	1.69

*** $p < .001$; ** $p < .01$; * $p < .05$; otherwise $p < .10$.

ful conviction for violence, high extroversion at age 16, and lack of concentration or restlessness at age 14. There were nine independent predictors of adult self-reported violence: a youthful conviction for nonviolence, drug use at age 18, a nervous-withdrawn temperament at age 8, coming from a low social class family at age 8–10, aggressiveness at age 14, a young mother, high self-reported delinquency at age 18, heavy drinking at age 18, and the father not joining in the boy's leisure activities at age 12.

Risk Scores

In order to assess the accuracy of predictions of adult violence, risk scores were calculated for each boy, based on the independently important predictors shown in Table 4.3. Each risk score was a simple count of the number of risk factors possessed by each boy. For example, the age 8–18 risk score for adult convictions for violence was a simple count of the number of risk factors out of the eight shown at the bottom left of Table 4.3. Where a boy was not known on a risk factor, his score was scaled up accordingly. For example, if a boy was not known on one of these eight risk factors, his score out of 7 was multiplied by 8/7. Therefore, all boys had a score in all cases.

More complicated risk scores could have been calculated, for example by weighting each risk factor according to its weight in the multiple regression equation. However, the simple points score suffers less shrinkage between construction and validation samples and is often a better predictor in validation samples (Farrington, 1985). Each risk score was collapsed into four categories, as far as possible: the highest 50 boys (category 4), the next 50 (category 3), the next 150 (category 2), and the lowest 150 (category 1).

Table 4.4 shows the percentage violent in each category of each risk score. For example, on the age 8–10 risk score for convictions for violence, 15 of the 50 highest scoring boys (30% of category 4) were convicted, compared with 12% of the 51 in category 3, 8% of the 142 in category 2, and 5% of the 160 lowest scoring boys (category 1). The OR comparing the worst 50 or so boys with the remainder was 5.4, and the OR comparing the worst 100 or so boys with the remainder was 3.7.

As expected, the age 12–14 risk score was a better predictor of adult convictions for violence, with 37% of boys violent in category 4 and an OR of 8.9 from comparing category 4 with the remainder. The age 16–18 risk score was also better, with 38% of boys violent in category 4 and an OR of 9.0 from comparing category 4 with the remainder. The combined (age 8–18) risk score was the best, with 44% of boys violent in category 4 and an OR of 17.3 from comparing category 4 with the remainder; 44% of 59 identified boys were convicted, compared with 4% of the remaining 344.

The prediction of adult self-reported violence was generally poorer according to the OR. However, false positive rates were lower, because of the higher prevalence of self-reported violence (16%, as opposed to 10% for convictions). Nearly half (46%) of boys in category 4 of the age 8–10 risk score for self-reported violence became violent, with a corre-

Table 4.4. Percent Violent versus Risk Scores

	Percent Violent				Odds Ratio	
	1	2	3	4	12/34	123/4
Convictions						
Age 8–10	5	8	12	30	3.7*	5.4*
Age 12–14	3	8	11	37	5.3*	8.9*
Age 16–18	2	7	26	38	10.3*	9.0*
Age 8–18	1	5	9	44	10.4*	17.3*
Vulnerable 8–10	7	5	14	24	3.7*	3.9*
Antisocial 10	5	12	14	18	2.1*	2.2
Antisocial 14	5	8	15	37	5.6*	7.9*
Antisocial 18	4	7	31	28	8.4*	4.3*
Self-Reports						
Age 8–10	9	15	16	46	2.3*	5.6*
Age 12–14	5	17	26	40	3.8*	4.3*
Age 16–18	7	15	31	52	5.2*	6.9*
Age 8–18	5	13	30	45	5.4*	5.8*
Vulnerable 8–10	14	13	19	25	1.8*	1.9
Antisocial 10	12	20	15	21	1.1	1.4
Antisocial 14	10	15	29	32	3.2*	2.8*
Antisocial 18	12	13	23	36	3.0*	3.5*
NV Convictions						
Vulnerable 8–10	14	19	24	45	2.7*	3.9*
Antisocial 10	11	24	33	45	3.1*	3.6*
Antisocial 14	11	20	39	58	5.5*	6.5*
Antisocial 18	10	21	42	60	6.5*	7.1*

*$p < .05$.

sponding OR of 5.6. The equivalent figures were 40% and 4.3 for the age 12–14 risk score; 52% and 6.9 for the age 16–18 risk score; and 45% and 5.8 for the combined (age 8–18) risk score. On the combined score, 45% of 42 identified boys showed self-reported violence, compared with 13% of the remaining 335.

Arguably, these risk scores tell us how far adult violence could have been predicted retrospectively rather than prospectively, since they were constructed in light of observed relationships with adult violence. Arguably, prospective predictions would be less accurate. This was tested by investigating prospective prediction scales. The *vulnerability* scale at age 8–10 was based on five explanatory variables: low family income, large family size, a convicted parent, low nonverbal IQ, and poor parental child-rearing behavior (a combination of harsh discipline and parental conflict). It was developed at an early stage as a predictor of juvenile delinquency (West & Farrington, 1973, p. 131). Each boy was scored according to the number of risk factors (out of five) that he possessed.

The *antisocial personality* scales at ages 10, 14, and 18 were devised to measure the components of an antisocial personality (Farrington, 1991a). They were not constructed in light of any prediction exercise. For example, the age 18 scale comprised convictions, self-reported delinquency, self-reported violence, antisocial group membership, drug use, heavy smoking, heavy drinking, drunk driving, irresponsible sex, heavy gambling, an unstable job record, antiestablishment attitudes, being tattooed, and impulsiveness. Each boy was scored according to the number of risk factors (out of 14) that he possessed.

Table 4.4 shows that the vulnerability scale predicted adult convictions better than adult self-reported violence; 24% of boys in category 4 were convicted (OR = 3.9), while 25% showed adult self-reported violence (OR = 1.9). The antisocial personality scale at age 10 was a relatively poor predictor of both. The antisocial personality scale at age 14 predicted adult convictions for violence better than adult self-reported violence: 37% of boys in category 4 were convicted (OR = 7.9), while 32% showed self-reported violence (OR = 2.8). The predictability of the two outcomes was more similar for the antisocial personality scale at age 18; 28% of boys in category 4 were convicted, compared with 8% of the remainder (OR = 4.3), while 36% showed self-reported violence, compared with 14% of the remainder (OR = 3.5).

Table 4.4 also shows the predictability of adult convictions for non-violent offenses, according to the vulnerability and antisocial personality scales. False positive rates were lower because of the higher prevalence of adult nonviolent convictions (22%, compared with 10% for adult violent convictions). However, the predictability for nonviolent offenses was not consistently higher or lower than for violent offenses. Comparing category 4 with the remainder, the OR was higher for nonviolent offenses for antisocial personality at age 10 (3.6 compared with 2.2) and at age 18 (7.1 compared with 4.3), lower for antisocial personality at age 14 (6.5 compared with 7.9) and equal for vulnerability at age 8–10 (3.9).

Conclusions

There is a widespread belief that the best predictor of future violence is past violence. The present results show that this belief is too simplistic, and that there are many different important predictors of future violence. Generally, past convictions for nonviolent crimes predicted adult violence better than past convictions for violent crimes. This is because offenders are versatile rather than specialized. A potential for future violence can be indicated by past nonviolent offending, and especially by frequent nonviolent offending.

Similarly, past antisocial behavior can indicate a potential for future violence. Boys who were heavy drinkers, drug users, aggressive as adolescents, and hostile to the police tended to be violent as adults. Generally, these results tell us about the development of an individual potential for violence and other types of antisocial behavior. To explain how the potential becomes the actuality of violent behavior in any given situation, it is necessary also to investigate situational triggers for violence (see e.g., Farrington, 1998), but these are outside the scope of the present chapter.

Adult violent offenders tended to lack concentration or to be restless as adolescents, tended to be daring or risk-takers, and tended to be extroverted or impulsive. They often had criminal parents and young mothers and were exposed to harsh parental discipline. They tended to experience parental conflict and broken families, and their fathers tended not to join in their leisure activities. They tended to come from low-status, low-income families, and in turn they tended to have unskilled manual jobs themselves when they grew up. All of these factors can help to identify children with a high potential for violence. They can also help in explaining the development of violence, but this is outside the scope of the present chapter (see e.g., Farrington, 1998).

Can adult violence be predicted? It all depends on the criterion for predictive efficiency. Based on the odds ratio as a measure of strength of relationship, adult violence can be predicted. Based on the criterion of a low false positive rate, adult violence (with a low prevalence) cannot be predicted. For example, consider the age 8–18 prediction score for adult convictions for violence: only 1% of boys with the lowest scores were convicted, compared with 44% of boys with the highest scores. On the basis of the odds ratio (17.3 for the comparison of the highest boys with the remainder), adult convictions for violence could be predicted. However, the majority of predicted boys (56%) did not have convictions for violence.

Could the results presented here be useful in developing risk assessment instruments for adult violence? In most cases, the answer to this question must be yes. A wide variety of different factors were measured, and many behavioral and explanatory predictors have been identified. However, it may not be possible to use some of them in practical risk assessment. For example, people might be unlikely to provide accurate self-reports of violence if these would affect their future disposals. In developing risk assessment instruments, careful consideration needs to be given to data sources, validity, and corroboration of evidence.

Could the results presented here be useful in informing violence prevention programs? To the extent that explanatory predictors have causal effects, this will be true. Factors such as daring, impulsiveness, poor concentration, and restlessness might be reduced by cognitive-behavioral skills training; harsh discipline, parental conflict, and low parental involvement might be reduced by parent management training; and low family income might be combatted by income maintenance or antipoverty programs. Violence prevention experiments are needed to test these hypotheses and to establish which risk factors have causal effects.

What further prediction research is needed in the future? Better measures of a wide range of predictor and criterion variables are needed derived from different sources. Risk assessment instruments developed in one sample need to be validated in another. New methods of assessing predictive efficiency need to be developed, preferably incorporating measurements of the costs and benefits of different outcomes (e.g., failing to identify a violent person as opposed to a false positive). Prediction has always been an important topic both theoretically and practically, and the current interest in risk assessment ensures that it will remain so for the foreseeable future.

REFERENCES

Capaldi, D. M., & Patterson, G. R. (1996). Can violent offenders be distinguished from frequent offenders? Prediction from childhood to adolescence. *Journal of Research in Crime and Delinquency, 33,* 206–231.

Cleary, P. D., & Angel, R. (1984). The analysis of relationships involving dichotomous dependent variables. *Journal of Health and Social Behavior, 25,* 334–348.

Eron, L. D., Huesmann, L. R., & Zelli, A. (1991). The role of parental variables in the learning of aggression. In D. J. Pepler & K. H. Rubin (Eds.), *The development and treatment of childhood aggression* (pp. 169–188). Hillsdale, NJ: Erlbaum.

Farrington, D. P. (1978). The family backgrounds of aggressive youths. In L. Hersov, M. Berger, & D. Shaffer (Eds.), *Aggression and antisocial behavior in childhood and adolescence* (pp. 73–93). Oxford, England: Pergamon.

Farrington, D. P. (1982). Longitudinal analyses of criminal violence. In M. E. Wolfgang & N. A. Weiner (Eds.), *Criminal violence* (pp. 171–200). Beverly Hills, CA: Sage.

Farrington, D. P. (1985). Predicting self-reported and official delinquency. In D. P. Farrington & R. Tarling (Eds.), *Prediction in criminology* (pp. 150–173). Albany, NY: State University of New York Press.

Farrington, D. P. (1989a). Early predictors of adolescent aggression and adult violence. *Violence and Victims, 4*, 79–100.

Farrington, D. P. (1989b). Later adult life outcomes of offenders and non-offenders. In M. Brambring, F. Losel, & H. Skowronek (Eds.), *Children at risk: Assessment, longitudinal research, and intervention* (pp. 220–244). Berlin, Germany: De Gruyter.

Farrington, D. P. (1991a). Antisocial personality from childhood to adulthood. *The Psychologist, 4*, 389–394.

Farrington, D. P. (1991b). Childhood aggression and adult violence: Early precursors and later life outcomes. In D. J. Pepler & K. H. Rubin (Eds.), *The development and treatment of childhood aggression* (pp. 5–29). Hillsdale, NJ: Erlbaum.

Farrington, D. P. (1993). Understanding and preventing bullying. In M. Tonry (Ed.), *Crime and justice*, vol. 17 (pp. 381–458). Chicago: University of Chicago Press.

Farrington, D. P. (1994). Childhood, adolescent and adult features of violent males. In L. R. Huesmann (Ed.), *Aggressive behavior: Current perspectives* (pp. 215–240). New York: Plenum.

Farrington, D. P. (1995). The development of offending and antisocial behavior from childhood: Key findings from the Cambridge Study in Delinquent Development. *Journal of Child Psychology and Psychiatry, 36*, 929–964.

Farrington, D. P. (1997a). Early prediction of violent and non-violent youthful offending. *European Journal on Criminal Policy and Research, 5*(2), 51–66.

Farrington, D. P. (1997b). The relationship between low resting heart rate and violence. In A. Raine, P. A. Brennan, D. P. Farrington, & S. A. Mednick (Eds.), *Biosocial bases of violence* (pp. 89–105). New York: Plenum.

Farrington, D. P. (1998). Predictors, causes and correlates of male youth violence. In M. Tonry & M. H. Moore (Eds.), *Youth violence* (pp. 421–475). Chicago: University of Chicago Press.

Farrington, D. P., Barnes, G., & Lambert, S. (1996). The concentration of offending in families. *Legal and Criminological Psychology, 1*, 47–63.

Farrington, D. P., Berkowitz, L., & West, D. J. (1982). Differences between individual and group fights. *British Journal of Social Psychology, 21*, 323–333.

Farrington, D. P., Lambert, S., & West, D. J. (1998). Criminal careers of two generations of family members in the Cambridge Study in Delinquent Development. *Studies on Crime and Crime Prevention, 7*, 85–106.

Farrington, D. P., & West, D. J. (1971). A comparison between early delinquents and young aggressives. *British Journal of Criminology, 11*, 341–358.

Farrington, D. P., & West, D. J. (1990). The Cambridge Study in Delinquent Development: A long-term follow-up of 411 London males. In H-J. Kerner & G. Kaiser (Eds.), *Kriminalitat: personlichkeit, lebensgeschichte und verhalten Criminality: Personality, behavior and life history* (pp. 115–138). Berlin, Germany: Springer–Verlag.

Gorman-Smith, D., Tolan, P. H., Zelli, A., & Huesmann, L. R. (1996). The relation of family functioning to violence among inner-city minority youths. *Journal of Family Psychology, 10,* 115–129.

Hamalainen, M., & Pulkkinen, L. (1996). Problem behavior as a precursor of male criminality. *Development and Psychopathology, 8,* 443–455.

Hamparian, D. M., Davis, J. M., Jacobson, J. M., & McGraw, R. E. (1985). *The young criminal years of the violent few.* Washington, DC: Office of Juvenile Justice and Delinquency Prevention.

Hawkins, J. D., Herrenkohl, T., Farrington, D. P., Brewer, D., Catalano, R. F. & Harachi, T. W. (1998). A review of predictors of youth violence. In R. Loeber & D. P. Farrington (Eds.), *Serious and violent juvenile offenders: Risk factors and successful interventions* (pp. 106–146). Thousand Oaks, CA: Sage.

Henry, B., Caspi, A., Moffitt, T. E., & Silva, P. A. (1996). Temperamental and familial predictors of violent and nonviolent criminal convictions: Age 3 to age 18. *Developmental Psychology, 32,* 614–623.

Huizinga, D., Esbensen, F-A., and Weiher, A. W. (1991). Are there multiple paths to delinquency? *Journal of Criminal Law and Criminology, 82,* 83–118.

Kandel, E., Brennan, P. A., Mednick, S. A., & Michelson, N. M. (1989). Minor physical anomalies and recidivistic adult violent criminal behavior. *Acta Psychiatrica Scandinavica, 79,* 103–107.

Klinteberg, B. A., Andersson, T., Magnusson, D., & Stattin, H. (1993). Hyperactive behavior in childhood as related to subsequent alcohol problems and violent offending: A longitudinal study of male subjects. *Personality and Individual Differences, 15,* 381–388.

Kolvin, I., Miller, F. J. W., Scott, D. M., Gatzanis, S. R. M., & Fleeting, M. (1990). *Continuities of deprivation?* Aldershot, England: Avebury.

Loeber, R., Farrington, D. P., Stouthamer-Loeber, M., & van Kammen, W. B. (1998). *Antisocial behavior and mental health problems: Explanatory factors in childhood and adolescence.* Mahwah, NJ: Erlbaum.

McCord, J. (1977). A comparative study of two generations of native Americans. In R. F. Meier (Ed.), *Theory in criminology: Contemporary views* (pp. 83–92). Beverly Hills, CA: Sage.

McCord, J. (1979). Some child-rearing antecedents of criminal behavior in adult men. *Journal of Personality and Social Psychology, 37,* 1477–1486.

McCord, J., & Ensminger, M. E. (1997). Multiple risks and comorbidity in an African-American population. *Criminal Behavior and Mental Health, 7,* 339–352.

Mannuzza, S., Klein, R. G., Konig, P. H., & Giampino, T. L. (1989). Hyperactive boys almost grown up: IV. Criminality and its relationship to psychiatric status. *Archives of General Psychiatry, 46,* 1073–1079.

Maxfield, M. G., & Widom, C. S. (1996). The cycle of violence revisited 6 years later. *Archives of Pediatrics and Adolescent Medicine, 150,* 390–395.

Moffitt, T. E., Mednick, S. A., & Gabrielli, W. F. (1989). Predicting careers of criminal violence: Descriptive data and dispositional factors. In D. A. Brizer & M. Crowner (Eds.), *Current approaches to the prediction of violence* (pp. 13–34). Washington, DC: American Psychiatric Press.

Monahan, J., & Steadman, H. J., (Eds.) (1994). *Violence and mental disorder: Developments in risk assessment.* Chicago: University of Chicago Press.

Mossman, D. (1994). Assessing predictions of violence: Being accurate about accuracy. *Journal of Consulting and Clinical Psychology, 62,* 783–792.

Sampson, R. J., & Laub, J. H. (1993). *Crime in the making: Pathways and turning points through life.* Cambridge, MA: Harvard University Press.

Schlesselman, J. J. (1982). *Case-control studies.* New York: Oxford University Press.

Stattin, H., & Magnusson, D. (1989). The role of early aggressive behavior in the frequency, seriousness, and types of later crimes. *Journal of Consulting and Clinical Psychology, 57,* 710–718.

Steadman, H. J., Monahan, J., Appelbaum, P. S., Grisso, T., Mulvey, E. P., Roth, L. H., Robbins, P. C., & Klassen, D. (1994). Designing a new generation of risk assessment research. In J. Monahan & H. J. Steadman (Eds.), *Violence and mental disorder: Developments in risk assessment* (pp. 297–318). Chicago: University of Chicago Press.

Thornberry, T. P., Lizotte, A. J., Krohn, M. D., Farnworth, M., & Jang, S. J. (1991). Testing interactional theory: An examination of reciprocal causal relationships among family, school, and delinquency. *Journal of Criminal Law and Criminology, 82,* 3–35.

Weiler, B. L., & Widom, C. S. (1996). Psychopathy and violent behavior in abused and neglected young adults. *Criminal Behavior and Mental Health, 6,* 253–271.

West, D. J. (1969). *Present conduct and future delinquency.* London: Heinemann.

West, D. J. (1982). *Delinquency: Its roots, careers and prospects.* London: Heinemann.

West, D. J., & Farrington, D. P. (1973). *Who becomes delinquent?* London: Heinemann.

West, D. J., & Farrington, D. P. (1977). *The delinquent way of life.* London: Heinemann.

Wikström, P-O. H. (1985). *Everyday violence in contemporary Sweden.* Stockholm: National Council for Crime Prevention.

5. Major Mental Disorder and Violence: Epidemiology and Risk Assessment

JOHN MONAHAN

This chapter will consider two related but independent questions. The first question concerns epidemiology: Is the prevalence of violence to others any higher among people who have a major mental disorder than among people who do not? The second question concerns risk assessment: Among people who have a major mental disorder, how can those who will be violent in the future be distinguished from those who will not? These questions are related because the assumed answer to the first, that the prevalence of violence to others is indeed higher among people who have a major mental disorder than among people who do not, is what often motivates the asking of the second. They are independent because it is possible to be interested in the epidemiological question without being concerned with risk assessment (e.g., in studying the stigma of mental disorder) and possible to be interested in risk assessment without being concerned with epidemiology (e.g., if people with mental disorder are less competent to make decisions than people without it [Grisso & Appelbaum, 1998], interventions based on risk assessments may be justified even if violence was *less* prevalent among people with mental disorder than among other people). In attempting to answer both of these questions, I will not be exhaustive in my citation of evidence. That has been done elsewhere (Monahan, 1997). Rather, I will focus on what I consider the most important recent (i.e., 1990–2000) research and commentary that bear on these issues.

The Epidemiology of Violence Among People with Mental Disorder

A seminal study by Swanson, Holzer, Ganju, and Jono (1990) began the 1990s by providing essential epidemiological information on the prevalence of violence among populations in the community (rather than among patients in mental health facilities). Swanson and his colleagues drew their data from the U.S. National Institute of Mental Health's Epidemiological Catchment Area (ECA) study. Representative weighted samples of adult household residents of Baltimore, Durham, and Los Angeles were pooled to form a database of approximately 10,000 people. The Diagnostic Interview Schedule (DIS), a structured interview designed for use by trained laypersons, was used to detect mental disorder according to the criteria established in the American Psychiatric Association's *Diagnostic and Statistical Manual (DSM-III)*. Five items on the DIS[1]–four embedded among the criteria for antisocial personality disorder and one that formed part of the diagnosis of alcohol abuse/dependence–were used to indicate violent behavior. A respondent was counted as positive for violence if he or she endorsed at least one of these items and reported that the act occurred during the year preceding the interview. This index of violent behavior, as Swanson et al. note, is a "blunt measure": It is based on self-report without corroboration, the questions overlap considerably, and it does not differentiate in terms of the frequency or the severity of violence. Yet there is little doubt that each of the target behaviors is indeed "violent," and I believe that the measure is a reasonable estimate of the prevalence of violent behavior.

Three findings are noteworthy: (1) The prevalence of violence is more than five times higher among people who meet criteria for a *DSM-III* Axis I diagnosis (11–13%) than among people who are not diagnosable (2%); (2) The prevalence of violence among persons who meet criteria for a diagnosis of schizophrenia, major depression, or mania/bipolar disorder are remarkably similar (between 11 and 13%); and (3) The prevalence of violence among persons who meet criteria for a diagnosis of alcoholism (25%) is 12 times that of persons who receive no diagnosis, and the prevalence of violence among persons who meet criteria for being diagnosed as abusing drugs (35%) is 16 times that of persons who receive no diagnosis.

---

[1] The items were: "(1) Did you ever hit or throw things at your wife/husband/partner? [If so] Were you ever the one who threw things first, regardless of who started the argument? Did you hit or throw things first on more than one occasion? (2) Have you ever spanked or hit a child (yours or anyone else's) hard enough so that he or she had bruises or had to stay in bed or see a doctor? (3) Since age 18, have you been in more than one fight that came to swapping blows, other than fights with your husband/wife/partner? (4) Have you ever used a weapon like a stick, knife, or gun in a fight since you were 18? (5) Have you ever gotten into physical fights while drinking?"

When both demographic and clinical factors were combined in a regression equation to predict the occurrence of violence, several significant predictors emerged. Violence was most likely to occur among young, lower-class males, among those with a substance abuse diagnosis, and among those with a diagnosis of major mental disorder.

Another equally notable study not only confirms the ECA data but takes them a large step further. Link, Andrews, and Cullen (1992) analyzed data from a larger study conducted using the Psychiatric Epidemiology Research Interview (PERI) to measure symptoms and life events. Link et al. compared rates of arrest and of self-reported violence (including hitting, fighting, weapon use, and "hurting someone badly") in a sample of approximately 400 adults from the Washington Heights area of New York City who had never been in a mental hospital or sought help from a mental health professional, with rates of arrest and self-reported violence in several samples of former mental patients from the same area. To eliminate alternative explanations of their data, the researchers controlled, in various analyses, for an extraordinary number of factors: Age, gender, educational level, ethnicity (African American, White, and Hispanic), socioeconomic status, family composition (e.g., married with children), homicide rate of the census tract in which a subject lived, and the subject's "need for approval." This last variable was included to control for the possibility that patients might be more willing to report socially undesirable behavior (such as violence) than nonpatients.

The study found that the patient groups were almost always more violent than the never-treated community sample, often two to three times as violent. As in the ECA study, demographic factors clearly related to violence (e.g., males, the less educated, and those from high-crime neighborhoods were more likely to be violent). But even when all the demographic and personal factors, such as social desirability, were taken into account, significant differences between the patients and the never-treated community residents remained. The association between mental patient status and violent behavior, as the authors noted, was "remarkably robust" to attempts to explain it away as artifact.

Most important, Link et al. then controlled for "current symptomatology." They did this by using the psychotic symptoms scale of the PERI (e.g., "During the past year, how often have you heard things that other people say they can't hear?"). Remarkably, not a single difference in rates of recent violent behavior between patients and never-treated community residents remained significant when current psychotic symptoms were controlled. The psychotic symptomatology scale, on the other hand, was significantly and strongly related to most indexes of recent violent behavior, even when additional factors, such as alcohol and drug use, were taken into account. Thus, almost all of the difference in rates of violence between patients and nonpatients could be accounted for by the level of active psychotic symptoms that the patients were experiencing. In other words, when mental patients were actively experiencing psychotic symptoms like delusions and hallucinations, their risk of violence was significantly elevated compared to that of nonpatients, and when patients were not actively experiencing psychotic symptoms, their risk of violence was not appreciably higher than demographically similar members of their home community who had never been treated. Finally, Link et al. also found that the psychotic symptomatology scale significantly predicted violent behavior among the never-treated community residents. Even among people who had never been formally treated for mental disorder, actively experiencing psychotic symptoms was associated with the commission of violent acts.

Link and Stueve (1994) reanalyzed the data used in Link et al. (1992) to allow for a much more precise specification of *what kind* of "psychotic symptoms" are most related to violence. They found that three symptoms on the psychotic symptoms scale largely explained the relationship between mental disorder and violence.[2] The authors refer to these as "threat/control-override symptoms," because they either involve the overriding of internal self-controls by external factors (items 1 and 2) or imply a specific threat of harm from others (item 3).

Swanson, Borum, Swartz, and Monahan (1996) have replicated Link and Stueve's (1994) central finding with data from the Epidemiological Catchment Area (ECA) study. Link, Monahan, Stueve, and Cullen (1999) have found generally consistent results using a large Israeli database. Swanson, Estroff, Swartz, Borum, Lachicotte, Zimmer, and Wagner (1997) also found threat/control-override symptoms to relate to violent behavior, but only when the independent effect of the absence of treatment was controlled. However, Appelbaum, Robbins, and Monahan (2000), in a large prospective clinical study, failed to find any relationship between delusions in general – and threat/control-override delusions in particular – and violence in the community.

---

[2] The items were: During the past year ... (1) "How often have you felt that your mind was dominated by forces beyond your control?"; (2) "How often have you felt that thoughts were put into your head that were not your own?"; and (3) "How often have you felt that there were people who wished to do you harm?"

Steadman et al. (1998) studied the epidemiology of violence among patients discharged from mental health facilities. They monitored violence toward others every 10 weeks during the first year after discharge for 1,136 male and female civil patients between 18 and 40 years old, at three sites in the United States (Pittsburgh, PA, Worcester, MA, and Kansas City, MO). Patient self-reports of violence were augmented by reports from collaterals (usually family members) and by police and hospital records.

Findings suggest that it is crucial for future studies to use multiple measures of violence rather than the single measures that have characterized most prior research. Relying solely on agency records, Steadman et al. (1998) reported a 1-year violence rate for all discharged patients of 4.5%. By using three independent information sources, they reported a rate six times higher: 27.5%. Steadman et al. found the presence of a co-occurring substance abuse disorder to be a key factor in violence: The 1-year prevalence of violence was 17.9% for patients with an Axis I major mental disorder (i.e., schizophrenia, major depression, or bipolar disorder) and without a substance abuse diagnosis; 31.1% for patients with an Axis I major mental disorder and a substance abuse diagnosis; and 43.0% for patients with some other form of mental disorder (primarily diagnoses of personality disorder or adjustment disorder) and a substance abuse diagnosis (see also Swartz, Swanson, Hiday, Borum, Wagner, and Burns (1998) on the effects of substance abuse on violence).

At one site (Pittsburgh), Steadman et al. (1998) obtained a general-population comparison group, consisting of 519 people living in the neighborhoods in which the patients resided after hospital discharge. They found the prevalence of violence among patients without symptoms of substance abuse to be statistically indistinguishable from the prevalence of violence among others in their neighborhoods without symptoms of substance abuse. Substance abuse significantly raised the prevalence of violence in both patient and community samples. Among those who reported symptoms of substance abuse, the prevalence of violence among patients was significantly higher than the prevalence of violence among others in their neighborhoods during the first follow-up (i.e., the first 10 weeks after discharge from the hospital). The patient sample also was significantly more likely to report such symptoms of substance abuse than was the community sample.

For both the patient and the community samples, the acts that were coded as violence were primarily "kick/bite/choke/hit-beat up" and "weapon threat/weapon use." The targets of violence by the patient sample and by the community sample were most often family members, followed by friends and acquaintances. For both the patient and community samples, violence was most likely to occur in the subject's home, in the home of another, on the street, or in a bar.

Risk Assessment of Violence Among People with Mental Disorder

Research on violence risk assessment has burgeoned in the 1990s. Lidz, Mulvey, and Gardner (1993), in what is now a classic study, took as their subjects male and female patients being examined in the acute psychiatric emergency room of a large civil hospital. Psychiatrists and nurses were asked to assess potential patient violence to others over the next 6-month period. Violence was measured by official records, by patient self-report, and by the report of a collateral informant in the community (e.g., a family member). Patients who elicited professional concern regarding future violence were found to be significantly more likely to be violent after release (53%) than were patients who had not elicited such concern (36%). The accuracy of clinical prediction did not vary as a function of the patient's age or race. The accuracy of clinicians' predictions of male violence substantially exceeded chance levels, both for patients with and without a prior history of violent behavior. In contrast, the accuracy of clinicians' predictions of female violence did not differ from chance. While the actual rate of violent incidents among released female patients (49%) was higher than the rate among released male patients (42%), the clinicians had predicted that only 22% of the women would be violent, compared with predicting that 45% of the men would commit a violent act. The inaccuracy of clinicians at predicting violence among women appeared to be a function of the clinicians' serious underestimation of the base rate of violence among mentally disordered women (perhaps due to an inappropriate extrapolation from the great gender differences in rates of violence among persons without mental disorder). Lidz et al. concluded:

What this study [shows] is that clinical judgment has been undervalued in previous research. Not only did the clinicians pick out a statistically more violent group, but the violence that the predicted group committed was more serious than the acts of the comparison group. (p. 1010)

In a recent major meta-analysis of risk factors for crime and violence among mentally disordered offenders, Bonta, Law, and Hanson (1998) found those risk factors to be remarkably similar to well-known risk factors among the general offender population:

Criminal history, antisocial personality, substance abuse, and family dysfunction are important for mentally disordered offenders as they are for general offenders. In fact, the results support the theoretical perspective that the major correlates of crime are the same, regardless of race, gender, class, and the presence or absence of mental illness. (p. 139)

There is a long tradition in criminology of using statistical (often called actuarial) techniques to combine risk factors such as those mentioned above in predicting recidivism by released prisoners. Actuarial predictions are still used to determine parole eligibility in a number of American states. Actuarial techniques have recently been applied to predicting violence among people with mental disorder (Gardner, Lidz, Mulvey, & Shaw, 1996; Webster, Douglas, Eaves, & Hart, 1997). It is useful to be reminded by Borum (1996) that a wide range of instruments can be subsumed under the rubric of "actuarial" prediction:

At a minimum, these devices can serve as a checklist for clinicians to ensure that essential areas of inquiry are recalled and evaluated. At best, they may be able to provide hard actuarial data on the probability of violence among people (and environments) with a given set of characteristics, circumstances, or both. (p. 948)

The best example of the use of actuarial data to predict violence on an inpatient ward is McNiel and Binder (1994). They constructed an actuarial scale consisting of five variables, each scored Yes or No, and given one point for each Yes answer.[3]

Patients who scored three or above on this five-point actuarial scale were called "high risk," and patients who scored two or less were called "low risk." If "fear-inducing behavior" (i.e., "attacks on objects, threats to attack persons, or verbal attacks on persons," p. 581) is included along with actual physical assault as "violence," then 57% of the "high-risk" group were violent early in their hospitalization, compared with 29% of the "low-risk" group. If one restricts the criterion to actual physical assault, then the figures become 32% and 18%, respectively.

---

[3] The variables were: "(1) History of physical attack and/or fear-inducing behavior within two weeks before admission? (2) *Absence* of suicidal behavior (attempts, gestures, or threats within two weeks before admission)? (This item is checked if patient has *not* shown recent suicidal behavior.) (3) Schizophrenic or manic diagnosis? (4) Male gender? (5) Currently married or living together?"

A noteworthy advance in the development of actuarial risk assessment to predict violence in the community was reported by Harris, Rice, and Quinsey (1993; see also Harris & Rice, 1997; Rice, 1997). A sample of 618 men who were either treated or administered a pretrial assessment at a maximum security forensic hospital in Canada served as subjects. All had been charged with a serious criminal offense. A wide variety of predictive variables were coded from institutional files. The criterion variable was any new criminal charge for a violent offense, or return to the institution for an act that would otherwise have resulted in such a charge. The average time at risk after release was almost seven years. Twelve variables were identified for inclusion in the final statistical prediction instrument.[4] If the scores on this instrument were dichotomized into "high" and "low," the results indicated that 55% of the "high-scoring" subjects committed violent recidivism, compared with 19% of the "low-scoring" group.[5]

The authors conclude:

Clinical judgment can be improved ... through the use of actuarial information; this has been referred to as "structuring discretion." In this approach to decision-making about an individual, an actuarial estimate of risk is used to anchor clinical judgment. More specifically, clinicians can use dynamic (changeable) information such as progress in treatment, change in procriminal attitudes, and the amount and quality of supervision in the postrelease environment to adjust the risk level computed by the actuarial prediction instrument. If adjustments are made conservatively and *only* when a clinician believes, on good evidence, that a factor is related to the likelihood of violent recidivism in an individual case, predictive accuracy may be improved.

Several years later, however, Quinsey, Harris, Rice, and Cormier (1998) had a change of heart:

What we are advising is not the addition of actuarial methods to existing practice, but rather the complete replacement of existing practice with actuarial

---

[4] The variables were: (1) Score on the Psychopathy Checklist, (2) Separation from parents under age 16, (3) Victim injury in index offense, (4) *DSM-III* schizophrenia, (5) Never married, (6) Elementary school maladjustment, (7) Female victim in index offense, (8) Failure on prior conditional release, (9) Property offense history, (10) Age at index offense, (11) Alcohol abuse history, and (12) *DSM-III* personality disorder. For all variables except numbers 3, 4, 7, and 10 the nature of the relationship to subsequent violence was positive (i.e., subjects who injured a victim in the index offense who were diagnosed as schizophrenic, who choose a female victim for the index offense, or who were older, were significantly *less* likely to be violent recidivists than other subjects).

[5] Computed from C. Webster, G. Harris, M. Rice, C. Cormier, and V. Quinsey, *The Violence Prediction Scheme: Assessing Dangerousness in High Risk Men* (1994) at 33.

methods. This is a different view than we expressed in Webster et al (1994), where we advised the practice of adjusting actuarial estimates of risk by up to 10% when there were compelling circumstances to do so... We no longer think this practice is justifiable. Actuarial methods are too good and clinical judgment too poor to risk contaminating the former with the latter (p. 171).

Douglas and Webster (1999) reviewed research on another actuarial instrument to assess risk of violence, the "HCR-20," which consists of 20 items addressing *Historical, Clinical,* or *Risk* management variables (Webster, Douglas, Eaves, & Hart, 1997). Douglas and Webster also reported data from a retrospective study with prisoners, finding that "scores above the median on the HCR-20 increased the odds of the presence of various measures of past violence and antisocial behavior by an average of four times."

The most recent development in this area is the publication of the work of the MacArthur Violence Risk Assessment Study (Monahan et al., 2000; Steadman et al., 2000). Here, the researchers developed what they called an "iterative Classification Tree," or ICT. They sought to increase the utility of this actuarial method for real-world clinical decision making by applying the method to a set of violence risk factors commonly available in clinical records or capable of being routinely assessed in clinical practice. Results showed that the ICT partitioned three-quarters of a sample of psychiatric patients into one of two categories with regard to their risk of violence to others during the first 20 weeks after discharge. One category consisted of groups whose rates of violence were *no more than half* the base rate of the total patient sample (i.e., equal to or less than 9% violent). The other category consisted of groups whose rates of violence were *at least twice* the base rate of the total patient sample (i.e., equal to or greater than 37% violent). The prevalence of violence within individual risk groups varied from 3% to 53%.

Future Directions

With respect to changes in research methodology, Monahan and Steadman (1994), reflecting recent developments in decision theory and in public health, suggested that research on violence prediction in the coming decades, if it is to advance the state of the science, must bear seven characteristics:

1. "Dangerousness" must be disaggregated into its component parts–the variables used to predict violence ("risk factors"), the

amount and type of violence being predicted ("harm"), and the likelihood that harm will occur ("risk").

2. A rich array of theoretically chosen risk factors in multiple domains must be chosen.

3. Harm must be scaled in terms of seriousness and assessed with multiple measures.

4. Risk must be treated as a probability estimate that changes over time and context.

5. Priority must be given to actuarial research that establishes a relationship between risk factors and harm.

6. Large and broadly representative samples of patients at multiple, coordinated sites must participate in the research.

7. Managing risk as well as assessing risk must be a goal of the research (Heilbrun, 1997; Novaco, 1997; Rice & Harris, 1997).

There is one additional item that I would now add to this list. *Risk communication* as an essential adjunct to risk assessment is an issue that will become increasingly salient in the future (Monahan & Steadman, 1996). After a clinician (perhaps with the assistance of an actuarial risk device) has made an estimate of the likelihood of harm that a person represents, how is the clinician to communicate this information to decision makers? "Risk communication" has been defined by the National Research Council (1989) as

an interactive process of exchange of information and opinion among individuals, groups, and institutions; often involves multiple messages about the nature of risk or expressing concerns, opinions, or reactions to risk messages or to legal and institutional arrangements for risk management. (p. 322)

For example, most American states have adopted the language of the California "dangerousness standard": That to be admitted to a mental hospital against his or her will, a person must be mentally disordered and "dangerous to self or others." But some states refer to the "likelihood" that the individual will cause "serious harm." The National Center for State Courts (1986) spoke of "predictions of violence," and the American Bar Association (1989) made reference to "a substantial risk of serious bodily harm to others." Finally, one influential court decision phrased the issue in terms of a "probability" of future harm.

"Dangerousness," "likelihood," "risk," and "probability," therefore, often have been used fungibly to refer to the level of uncertainty of undesirable outcomes that may occur if some persons with mental disorder are left at liberty. However, the extensive literature in the area of risk perception and behavioral decision theory has uncovered many subtle and anomalous effects, which suggest that these various terms may not be fungible. They may, in fact, have differential effects on the judgments that are rendered by clinicians and courts.

For example, in Slovic and Monahan (1995) adults were shown hypothetical stimulus vignettes describing mental patients and were asked to judge (a) the probability that the patient would harm someone else, (b) whether the patient should be categorized as "dangerous," and (c) whether coercion should be used to ensure treatment. Probability and dangerousness judgments were systematically related and were predictive of the judged necessity for coercion. However, judged probability was strongly dependent upon the form of the response scale, suggesting that probability was not represented consistently and quantitatively in the subjects' minds. For example, one response scale for expressing the probability of harm went from 0 to 100% in 10% increments. Another response scale went from "less than 1 chance in 1,000" to "greater than 40%." Judgments about the probability of violence were much higher using the first response scale than using the second. In a second study, Slovic and Monahan (1995) replicated these findings with experienced forensic clinicians as subjects. Slovic, Monahan, and MacGregor (2000) again replicated these findings, this time using actual case files rather than hypothetical vignettes. Communicating a patient's dangerousness as a relative frequency (e.g., 2 out of 10 patients will be violent) led to much higher perceived risk than did communicating a comparable probability (e.g., a 20% chance of being violent). The different reactions to probability and frequency formats appear to be attributable to the more frightening images evoked by frequencies than by probabilities.

Conclusion

Substance abuse, particularly when combined with personality disorder, appears to put discharged psychiatric patients at increased risk of violence to others. Recently developed actuarial techniques show promise in distinguishing those patients who will be violent from those who will not. How to communicate the results of clinical risk forecasts to relevant audiences so as to facilitate effective risk management and risk reduction is an issue that the field will likely begin to confront in the coming decades.

REFERENCES

American Bar Association. (1989). *ABA Criminal Justice Mental Health Standards.* Chicago: American Bar Association.

Appelbaum, P., Robbins, P., & Monahan, J. (2000). Violence and delusions: Data from the MacArthur Violence Risk Assessment Study. *American Journal of Psychiatry, 157,* 566–572.

Bonta, J., Law, M., & Hanson, K. (1998). The prediction of criminal and violent recidivism among mentally disordered offenders: A meta-analysis. *Psychological Bulletin, 123,* 123–142.

Borum, R. (1996). Improving the clinical practice of violence risk assessment: Technology, guidelines, and training. *American Psychologist, 51,* 945–956.

Douglas, K., & Webster, C. (1999). The HCR-20 violence risk assessment scheme: Concurrent validity in a sample of incarcerated offenders. *Criminal Justice and Behavior, 26,* 3–19.

Gardner, W., Lidz, C., Mulvey, E., & Shaw, E. (1996). A comparison of actuarial methods for identifying repetitively violent patients with mental illness. *Law and Human Behavior, 20,* 35–48.

Grisso, T., & Appelbaum, P. S. (1998). *Assessing competence to consent to treatment: A guide for physicians and other health professionals.* New York: Oxford University Press.

Harris, G., & Rice, M. (1997). Risk appraisal and management of violent behavior. *Psychiatric Services, 48,* 1168–1176.

Harris, G., Rice, M., & Quinsey, V. (1993). Violent recidivism of mentally disordered offenders: The development of a statistical prediction instrument. *Criminal Justice and Behavior, 20,* 315–335.

Heilbrun, K. (1997). Prediction versus management models relevant to risk assessment: The importance of legal decision-making context. *Law and Human Behavior, 21,* 347–359.

Lidz, C., Mulvey, E., & Gardner, W. (1993). The accuracy of predictions of violence to others. *Journal of the American Medical Association, 269,* 1007–1011.

Link, B., Andrews, A., & Cullen, F. (1992). The violent and illegal behavior of mental patients reconsidered. *American Sociological Review, 57,* 275–292.

Link, B., Monahan, J., Stueve, A., & Cullen, F. (1999). Real in their consequences: A sociological approach to understanding the association between psychotic symptoms and violence. *American Sociological Review, 64,* 316–332.

Link, B., & Stueve, A. (1994). Psychotic symptoms and the violent/illegal behavior of mental patients compared to community controls, in J. Monahan and H. Steadman (Eds.), *Violence and mental disorder: Developments in risk assessment* (pp. 137–159). Chicago: University of Chicago Press.

McNiel, D., & Binder, R. (1994). Screening for risk of inpatient violence: Validation of an actuarial tool. *Law and Human Behavior, 18,* 579–586.

Monahan, J. (1997). Clinical and actuarial predictions of violence. In D. Faigman, D. Kaye, M. Saks, and J. Sanders (Eds.), *Modern scientific evidence: The law and science of expert testimony* (pp. 300–318). St. Paul, MN: West.

Monahan, J., & Steadman, H. (1994). Toward the rejuvenation of risk research. In J. Monahan and H. Steadman (Eds.), *Violence and mental disorder: Developments in risk assessment* (pp. 1–17). Chicago: University of Chicago Press.

Monahan, J., & Steadman, H. (1996). Violent storms and violent people: How meteorology can inform risk communication in mental health law. *American Psychologist, 51,* 931–938.

Monahan, J., Steadman, H., Appelbaum, P., Robbins, P., Mulvey, E., Silver, E., Roth, L., & Grisso, T. (2000). Developing a clinically useful actuarial tool for assessing violence risk. *British Journal of Psychiatry, 176,* 312–319.

National Center for State Courts. (1986). Guidelines for involuntary civil commitment. *Mental and Physical Disability Law Reporter, 10,* 409–514.

National Research Council. (1989). *Improving risk communication.* Washington, DC: National Academy Press.

Novaco, R. (1997). Remediating anger and aggression with violent offenders. *Legal and Criminological Psychology, 2,* 77–88.

Quinsey, V., Harris, G., Rice, M., & Cormier, C. (1998). *Violent offenders: Appraising and managing risk.* Washington, DC: American Psychological Association.

Rice, M. (1997). Violent offender research and implications for the criminal justice system. *American Psychologist, 52,* 414–423.

Rice, M., & Harris, G. (1997). The treatment of mentally disordered offenders. *Psychology, Public Policy, and Law, 3,* 126–183.

Slovic, P., & Monahan, J. (1995). Danger and coercion: A study of risk perception and decision making in mental health law. *Law and Human Behavior, 19,* 49–65.

Slovic, P., Monahan, J., & MacGregor, D. (2000). Violence risk assessment and risk communication: The effects of using actual cases, providing instruction, and employing probability versus frequency formats. *Law and Human Behavior, 24,* 271–296.

Steadman, H., Monahan, J., Appelbaum, P., Grisso, T., Mulvey, E., Roth, L., Robbins, P., & Klassen, D. (1994). Designing a new generation of risk assessment research. In J. Monahan and H. Steadman (Eds.), *Violence and mental disorder: Developments in risk assessment* (pp. 297–318). Chicago: University of Chicago Press.

Steadman, H., Mulvey, E., Monahan, J., Robbins, P., Appelbaum, P., Grisso, T., Roth, L., & Silver, E. (1998). Violence by people discharged from acute psychiatric inpatient facilities and by others in the same neighborhoods. *Archives of General Psychiatry, 55,* 1–9.

Steadman, H., Silver, E., Monahan, J., Appelbaum, P., Robbins, P., Mulvey, E., Grisso, T., Roth, L., & Banks, S. (2000). A classification tree approach to the development of actuarial violence risk assessment tools. *Law and Human Behavior, 24,* 83–100.

Swanson, J., Borum, R., Swartz, M., & Monahan, J. (1996). Psychotic symptoms and disorders and the risk of violent behaviour in the community. *Criminal Behaviour and Mental Health, 6,* 317–338.

Swanson, J., Estroff, S., Swartz, M., Borum, R., Lachicotte, W., Zimmer, C., & Wagner, R. (1997). Violence and severe mental disorder in clinical and community populations: The effects of psychotic symptoms, comorbidity, and lack of treatment. *Psychiatry, 60,* 1–22.

Swanson, J., Holzer, C., Ganju, V., & Jono, R. (1990) Violence and psychiatric disorder in the community: Evidence from the Epidemiologic Catchment Area Surveys. *Hospital and Community Psychiatry, 41,* 761–770.

Swartz, M., Swanson, J., Hiday, V., Borum, R., Wagner, H., & Burns, B. (1998). Violence and severe mental illness: The effects of substance abuse and non-adherence to medication. *American Journal of Psychiatry, 155,* 226–231.

Webster, C., Douglas, K., Eaves, D., & Hart, S. (1997). *The HCR-20: Assessing risk for violence, version 2.* Mental Health, Law, and Policy Institute, Simon Fraser University.

Webster, C., Harris, G., Rice, M., Cormier, C., & Quinsey, V. (1994). *The violence prediction scheme: Assessing dangerousness in high risk men.* Centre of Criminology, University of Toronto.

6. Axis II Disorders and Dangerousness

KENNETH TARDIFF

Introduction

Axis II disorders include a variety of personality disorders and mental retardation. A personality disorder is "an enduring pattern of inner experience and behavior that deviates markedly from expectations of the individual's culture, is pervasive and inflexible, has an onset in adolescence or early adulthood, is stable over time and leads to distress of impairment" (American Psychiatric Association [APA], 1994). Dangerous behaviors (i.e., violence or suicide attempts) are mostly found among individuals with personality disorders included in Cluster B Category: Antisocial, Borderline, Histrionic, and Narcissistic Personality Disorders. Individuals with Cluster B Personality Disorders often appear dramatic, emotional, and/or erratic. Individuals with Paranoid Personality Disorder, which is in Cluster A, talk about violence but are usually not violent (Tardiff, 1998). The other personality disorders in Cluster A, Schizoid and Schizotypal Personality Disorders, and those in Cluster C (Avoidant, Dependent, and Obsessive Compulsive Personality Disorders) are not dangerous although occasionally violent or suicidal behaviors may occur if they feel angry or depressed or have an accompanying Axis I disorder, which is linked to violent or suicidal behavior. Some individuals with mental retardation are violent as a consequence of frustration and an inability to express themselves verbally. This chapter will focus on personality disorders in Cluster B and Paranoid Personality Disorder, since these are the most frequent and challenging cases where the clinician must decide whether the patient is a short-term risk for violence or suicidal behavior. The role of alcohol and drug use in the prediction of violence and suicidal behavior will be discussed because there is an overlap of alcohol and drug use, personality disorders, and risk of violence or suicide.

Personality Disorders with Increased Dangerousness

Antisocial Personality Disorder

Individuals with Antisocial Personality Disorder have a disregard for and violation of the rights of others, including violence (APA, 1994). They tend to be irritable and repeatedly get into physical fights or otherwise attack others including spouses and children. They destroy property, steal, harass others, and are involved in other criminal activities. They are impulsive and tend not to plan ahead. Violence and other behaviors that violate the rights of others are not accompanied by remorse. Instead the violence is rationalized; for example, the victim is seen by these individuals as deserving the violence, or the behavior is seen as necessary to gain what these individuals feel they deserve (e.g., money, sex, or power). They may blame the victim for being foolish or weak. They are reckless and are a danger to themselves and others as in reckless driving, driving while intoxicated, or engaging in risky, promiscuous sexual behavior. Decisions are made quickly without thinking of the consequences to self or others. This may lead to dangerous behavior or sudden changes in jobs and relationships. They are manipulative and may mislead the clinician with glib, superficial charm.

Violence by individuals with Antisocial Personality Disorder is motivated by selfishness and facilitated by a lack of remorse. It is also associated with criminal behavior and substance abuse (Hare, 1991). Studies of autonomic responses such as skin conductance and heart rate show underarousal, thus suggesting that individuals with Antisocial Personality Disorder may be violent and manifest other antisocial behaviors because they do not fear the consequences of these behaviors (Raine, 1996). Many studies have found that inheritance plays a part in Antisocial Personality Disorder (Carey & Goldman, 1997). The molecular basis for this genetic association is still unclear. The individual with Antisocial Personality Disorder is at higher risk for alcohol abuse, perhaps reflecting another genetic association (Miczek et al., 1994). Another interesting finding is that impulsive individuals (e.g., those with Antisocial Personality Disorder) have low concentrations of the serotonin metabolite 5-HIAA in brain and spinal fluid (Roy

& Linnoila, 1990). The association between impulsivity and alcohol use raises the risk for violence as well as suicidal behavior in this group of individuals. An individual with Antisocial Personality Disorder poses a dilemma to the clinician who decides that the individual is a danger to self or others in the near future, because there are no effective treatments for Antisocial Personality Disorder (Davis-Barron, 1995). Although they may be dangerous, hospitalization may not be an option unless there is clear Axis I pathology that would justify hospitalization. The prognosis for hospital treatment is poor unless there are comorbid treatable disorders such as anxiety, depression, or substance abuse (Ogloff et al., 1990; Gabbard & Coyne, 1987). The only option in a case where an individual is at risk for violence due to Antisocial Personality Disorder without another treatable disorder may be arrest and incarceration. However, this is usually impossible to accomplish unless an actual violent act has already occurred (Table 6.1).

Borderline Personality Disorder

Individuals with Borderline Personality Disorders have a pervasive pattern of instability in interpersonal relationships, self-image, emotional states, and marked impulsivity (APA, 1994). They make frantic efforts to avoid real or imagined abandonment or rejection. Abandonment or rejection as perceived by these individuals may appear slight by external observers (e.g., if someone is a few minutes late for an appointment). They form intense relationships with caregivers or lovers and expect these persons to protect and rescue them (Benjamin, 1993). When the caregiver or lover fails to live up to these unrealistic expectations, the individual with Borderline Personality Disorder reacts with rage, verbal and/or physical violence, and suicidal behavior or other self-destructive behaviors. Anger has been traditionally recognized as the main emotion and a core component of Borderline Personality Disorder (Grinker et al., 1968). Intense relationships with caregivers, lovers, and other persons stem from a deep disturbance of identity and impaired sense of self. They have chronic feelings of emptiness and experience marked shifts in emotions from anxiety to depression to irritability and rage.

Violent and suicidal behaviors are exacerbated by a number of other factors in Borderline Personality Disorder. Impulsivity is severe and causes violence, suicide attempts, as well as other self-destructive behaviors such as risky sex, reckless driving, excessive spending, and

Table 6.1. Diagnostic Criteria for Antisocial Personality (*DSM-IV*)

A. There is a pervasive pattern of disregard for and violation of the rights of others occurring since age 15 years, as indicated by three (or more) of the following:
   1. failure to conform to social norms with respect to lawful behaviors as indicated by repeatedly performing acts that are grounds for arrest
   2. deceitfulness, as indicated by repeated lying, use of aliases, or conning others for personal profit or pleasure
   3. impulsivity or failure to plan ahead
   4. irritability and aggressiveness, as indicated by repeated physical fights or assaults
   5. reckless disregard for safety of self or others
   6. consistent irresponsibility, as indicated by repeated failure to sustain consistent work behavior or honor financial obligations
   7. lack of remorse, as indicated by being indifferent to or rationalizing having hurt, mistreated, or stolen from another
B. The individual is at least age 18 years.
C. There is evidence of Conduct Disorder with onset before age 15 years.
D. The occurrence of antisocial behavior is not exclusively during the course of Schizophrenia or a Manic Episode.

binge eating as well as substance abuse. Lifetime risk of completed suicide among individuals with Borderline Personality Disorder is roughly 10%, and the risk of suicide is even higher with alcohol or substance abuse (Stone, 1990). Impulsivity may be related to low levels of serotonin; for example, there is diminished responsiveness in individuals with Borderline Personality Disorder to fenfluramine challenge (Coccaro et al., 1989). This has implications for the treatment of violence and suicide with serotonin re-uptake inhibitors. Individuals with Borderline Personality Disorder have increased likelihood of having been physically or sexually abused as children (Perry & Herman, 1993). Being physically abused as a child increases the risk of violence as an adult (Widom, 1989). This, together with impulsivity and substance abuse, contributes to the violent nature of those with Borderline Personality Disorder.

The dilemma for the clinician in the evaluation and treatment of individuals with Borderline Personality Disorder lies in how to respond to threats or episodes of violence and/or suicide attempts. On the one hand, the clinician wants to prevent imminent violence or suicide and, on the other, the clinician does not want to become the "rescuer" and thereby exacerbate borderline psychopathology. Some advocate a low threshold for hospitalization of individuals who make threats of harm, whereas others have a higher threshold for hospitalization and attempt to have individuals with Borderline Personality Disorder develop insight into the meaning of violent and/or suicidal threats and behaviors (McGlashan, 1993; Gabbard & Wilkinson, 1994).

Both Antisocial Personality Disorder and Borderline Personality Disorder are characterized by manipulation and dangerous behaviors. Individuals with Antisocial Personality Disorders manipulate impulsivity to gain profit, power, or some other materialistic goal, while individuals with Borderline Personality Disorder manipulate to gain the concern of caregivers or lovers and to express rage at perceived rejection. Individuals with both personality disorders display little remorse or concern for the damage their violence and other dangerous behaviors produce to others around them (Table 6.2).

Histrionic Personality Disorder

Individuals with Histrionic Personality Disorder demonstrate pervasive and excessive emotionality and attention-seeking (APA, 1994). They crave attention and are very uncomfortable when they are not the center of attention. They seek attention through dramatic, enthusiastic, and flirtatious behavior. They appear inappropriately sexually provocative or seductive and pay a great deal of attention to their physical appearance, clothing, and grooming. Speech is dramatic, opinionated, but shallow in terms of details. They frequently complain of a variety of physical symptoms to attract the attention of caregivers, family, or friends. They appear overly emotional but artificial.

These efforts to attract attention eventually alienate and/or embarrass those around them. When their efforts to be the center of attention fail, they may have temper tantrums or make suicidal gestures. Violence or suicidal attempts serve to refocus attention on them as well as punish the person(s) who frustrated their need to be the center of attention (Beck & Freeman, 1990; Cloninger, 1987). True feelings of depression occasionally may result in more serious suicide attempts.

Antisocial Personality Disorder and Histrionic Personality Disorder both involve impulsivity, superficiality, recklessness, and manipulation, but Histrionic Personality Disorder involves infrequent antisocial behaviors and more exaggerated emotional displays. Borderline Personality Disorder and Histrionic Personality Disorder both involve attention-seeking and shifting emotions, but Borderline Personality

Table 6.2. Diagnostic Criteria for Borderline Personality Disorder (DSM-IV)

A pervasive pattern of instability of interpersonal relationships, self-image, and affects, and marked impulsivity beginning by early adulthood and present in a variety of contexts, as indicated by five (or more) of the following:

1. frantic efforts to avoid real or imagined abandonment. *Note:* Do not include suicidal or self-mutilating behavior covered in Criterion 5.
2. a pattern of unstable and intense interpersonal relationships characterized by alternating between extremes of idealization and devaluation
3. identity disturbance: markedly and persistently unstable self-image or sense of self
4. impulsivity in at least two areas that are potentially self-damaging (e.g., spending, sex, substance abuse, reckless driving, binge eating). *Note:* Do not include suicidal or self-mutilating behavior covered in Criterion 5.
5. recurrent suicidal behavior, gestures, or threats, or self-mutilating behavior
6. affective instability due to a marked reactivity of mood (e.g., intense episodic dysphoria, irritability, or anxiety usually lasting a few hours and only rarely more than a few days)
7. chronic feelings of emptiness
8. inappropriate, intense anger or difficulty controlling anger (e.g., frequent displays of temper, constant anger, recurrent physical fights)
9. transient, stress-related paranoid ideation, or severe dissociative symptoms

Disorder involves more frequent and more severe self-destructive behavior and violence toward others (Table 6.3).

Narcissistic Personality Disorder

Individuals with Narcissistic Personality Disorder have a pervasive pattern of grandiosity and a need for attention (APA, 1994). They overestimate their abilities and their accomplishments. They expect others to recognize their superiority and are surprised and angry when they do not. They feel that they should associate only with other people who are also special and superior. They insist on having the "top" doctor, lawyer, and others in the "best" institutions.

Individuals with Narcissistic Personality Disorder need the admiration of others because their self-esteem is fragile. They need constant attention in the form of compliments and special treatment. There is a sense of entitlement. They exploit people for their own pur-

Table 6.3. Diagnostic Criteria for Histrionic Personality Disorder (*DSM-IV*)

A pervasive pattern of excessive emotionality and attention seeking, beginning by early adulthood and present in a variety of contexts, as indicated by five (or more) of the following:

1. is uncomfortable in situations in which he or she is not the center of attention
2. interaction with others is often characterized by inappropriate sexually seductive or provocative behavior
3. displays rapidly shifting and shallow expression of emotions
4. consistently uses physical appearance to draw attention to self
5. has a style of speech that is excessively impressionistic and lacking in detail
6. shows self-dramatization, theatricality, and exaggerated expression and emotion
7. is suggestible (i.e., easily influenced by others or circumstances)
8. considers relationships to be more intimate than they actually are

poses without any insight or empathy in regard to overworking them or making excessive demands. They are not interested in or are impatient when other people are discussing their own needs or feelings. They are insensitive to derogatory comments they make about other people.

Violence by individuals with Narcissistic Personality Disorder takes two forms. They become angry and may become verbally or, occasionally, even physically violent when other people do not accord them the admiration, attention, or respect these individuals believe they deserve (Beck & Freeman, 1990). The second form of violence is more severe and pervasive in "malignant narcissism" (Kernberg, 1989; Stone, 1989). These are individuals with Narcissistic Personality Disorder who have an aggressive and paranoid orientation. Violence is goal-directed for political, sexual, or other purposes. They may have a capacity for loyalty to others in the form of political institutions, organized crime, or other groups. These individuals are the ruthless political leaders who are responsible for genocide or paid assassins who murder for organized crime. Other individuals with malignant narcissism are loners who kill for sexual gratification (e.g., Ted Bundy), who are leaders of cults (e.g., Charles Manson), or who kill parents or other family members for money or revenge (e.g., Menendez brothers) (Table 6.4).

Table 6.4. Diagnostic Criteria for Narcissistic Personality Disorder (*DSM-IV*)

A pervasive pattern of grandiosity (in fantasy or behavior), need for admiration, and lack of empathy, beginning by early adulthood and present in a variety of contexts, as indicated by five (or more) of the following:

1. has a grandiose sense of self-importance (e.g., exaggerates achievements and talents, expects to be recognized as superior without commensurate achievements)
2. is preoccupied with fantasies of unlimited success, power, brilliance, beauty, or ideal love
3. believes that he or she is "special" and unique and can only be understood by, or should associate with, other special or high-status people or institutions
4. requires excessive admiration
5. has a sense of entitlement (i.e., unreasonable expectations of especially favorable treatment or automatic compliance with his or her expectations)
6. is interpersonally exploitative (i.e., takes advantage of others to achieve his or her own ends)
7. lacks empathy: is unwilling to recognize or identify with feelings and needs of others
8. is often envious of others or believes that others are envious of him or her
9. shows arrogant, haughty behaviors or attitudes

Paranoid Personality Disorder

Individuals with Paranoid Personality Disorder have a pervasive distrust and suspicion of others so that their motives are interpreted as malevolent (APA, 1994). They believe that others want to exploit, harm, or deceive them when there is little or no evidence to support that. They doubt the loyalty of friends or associates and are reluctant to confide in others, for fear that information will be used against them. They interpret benign remarks by others as demeaning or threatening.

They believe that they have been harmed by the actions of others. This may take the form of harm to their reputation or in a more concrete way such as not being promoted at work. They bear grudges and have persistent hostile feelings toward those they believe have harmed them. They react with insults, threats, and lawsuits against employers, governmental agencies, and others whom they feel have harmed them. The individual with Paranoid Personality Disorder is the "disgruntled employee" or "paranoid worker" (Boxer, 1993). These individuals do not usually become violent, but if they do, it can be catastrophic in terms of mass murder. Another arena where paranoid thoughts may produce violence is that of intimate relationships. These individuals want to maintain complete control of intimate relationships to avoid being betrayed. They may constantly question and monitor the activities, intentions, and fidelity of their spouse or partner. They may gather circumstantial evidence to support their suspicions of infidelity. This may eventually result in arguments and physical violence against the lover or suspected third person (Table 6.5).

Short-Term Prediction of Dangerousness

The clinician in the emergency room or in an outpatient setting is often faced with evaluating dangerousness; that is, estimating the risk of a subsequent violent episode or suicide attempt by a patient who is

Table 6.5. Diagnostic Criteria for Paranoid Personality Disorder (*DSM-IV*)

A. A pervasive distrust and suspiciousness of others such that their motives are interpreted as malevolent, beginning by early adulthood and present in a variety of contexts, as indicated by four (or more) of the following:
  1. suspects, without sufficient basis, that others are exploiting, harming, or deceiving him or her
  2. is preoccupied with unjustified doubts about the loyalty or trustworthiness of friends or associates
  3. is reluctant to confide in others because of unwarranted fear that the information will be used maliciously against him or her
  4. reads hidden demeaning or threatening meanings into benign remarks or events
  5. persistently bears grudges (i.e., is unforgiving of insults, injuries, or slights)
  6. perceives attacks on his or her character or reputation that are not apparent to others and is quick to react angrily or to counterattack
  7. has recurrent suspicions, without justification, regarding fidelity of spouse or sexual partner
B. Does not occur exclusively during the course of Schizophrenia, a Mood Disorder With Psychotic Features, or another Psychotic Disorder and is not due to the direct physiological effects of a general medical condition.

Note: If criteria are met prior to the onset of Schizophrenia, add "Premorbid" (e.g., "Paranoid Personality Disorder (Premorbid)").

threatening this or who has actually been violent or suicidal before arriving in the emergency room or clinic. A number of authors have developed clinical guidelines in deciding whether a patient poses a significant risk of violence in the near future (Mulvey & Lidz, 1995; Sensky et al., 1996; Tardiff, 1996; Tardiff, 1998). These guidelines are rather consistent in describing what information should be collected in the evaluation of a patient to determine the potential for violence. Note that the types of information weighted in a decision are parallel for violence and suicide; for example, degree of formulation, intent, severity of past attempts, and so forth.

The model proposed in this chapter represents that consensus, but it has not been empirically tested for accuracy. On the other hand, this model has been used successfully by the author and others as a standard in a number of malpractice suits involving violence and suicide by patients. The model includes information that the clinician should consider so as to make a decision about a patient's potential for violence or suicide in the near future (i.e., the next few days or week at most). Beyond a week, there is the opportunity for intervening factors to change the state of the patient and the environment that existed at the time the evaluation of violence potential was done. These intervening factors can include noncompliance with medication, resumption of drinking or substance use, threats of divorce by a spouse, and other stressors. Prediction of dangerousness over the long-term is possible, but of less clinical usefulness. For example, knowing that a patient with Borderline Personality Disorder has a 10% lifetime risk of completing a suicide does not help with individual patients. Even if you knew that a specific patient is likely to kill him- or herself in a lifetime, one cannot keep the patient in a hospital indefinitely to prevent that. On the other hand, we do know that repetitive violence, particularly for patients with personality disorders, tends to follow the same pattern over time in terms of type of target and circumstances around the violent act. A study of patients admitted to my psychiatric hospital found that patients with personality disorders were more likely than other types of patients to be violent a few weeks after discharge, and that the targets of violence after discharge tended to be the same as before admission (Tardiff, 1997). Knowing that a patient has been violent in the past and that the patient will be violent in the future is relevant in this case since the past targets of violence (usually lovers and family) could be brought into treatment during a hospitalization to develop strategies of prevention of future violence.

Sources of Information

The essential components of these models for the short-term prediction of violence rely on information collected from the patient interview, but other sources of information must be sought. These include past records from treatment, police records, and other records. It is essential that the clinician speak or attempt to speak to the family, therapist, police, and others who may have knowledge of the patient.

In the routine evaluation of patients for violence, a screening question such as "Have you ever lost your temper?" should be asked just as you ask "Have you thought that life isn't worth living?" for suicide assessment. If the answer is yes, the clinician proceeds to inquire about the specifics of past violent behavior and ideation. Some patients, such as those with paranoid delusions, may be reluctant to divulge thoughts of violence, so the clinician must listen carefully and follow up on any hints of violence that may surface during the interview. If there are thoughts of violence or even threats, the degree of formulation of the ideas or threats of violence must be assessed.

Degree of Formulation

A well-formulated or detailed plan should make the clinician concerned about the risk of violence that a patient poses. This includes details about where, when, and how the patient will attack the victim as well as knowledge about the potential victim's personal life such as daily schedules and address. For example, vague thoughts of an employee "getting even" are not as serious, all other things being equal, as specific thoughts of how and when the patient has planned to attack a specific supervisor.

Intent

If a patient has thoughts of harming someone, it is important to assess his or her intent to harm the person. Just because a patient has thoughts of violence, it may not be sufficient to warrant action by the clinician. For example, a young obsessive-compulsive woman in the hospital told her therapist that she had fleeting thoughts and images of her killing her sister's newborn baby. She was very upset about these thoughts and it was clear that these thoughts were obsessive, unwanted, and distressful. She was judged not to be at risk for violence and has not harmed the baby since discharge from the hospital.

Availability of Victims

The availability of a potential victim is important. This refers to daily vulnerability of the victim as well as geographic distance between the patient and potential victim. For example, a potential victim living in an apartment with a doorman is generally safer than one living in a house in the suburbs. Geography plays a part in assessment of risk of violence to a potential victim. For example, a patient threatening his father who lives on the opposite coast is less of a danger than a patient who is threatening his father with whom he lives.

Weapons

Availability of a weapon is a major factor in whether violence will occur and in the lethality of violence. The patient should be asked, if there is a concern about violence or suicide, if there is a gun in the household, whether he/she has access to other guns, or how he/she would go about buying a gun. If there is a gun in the house, family members should be instructed to remove it, not just hide it.

History of Violence, Suicide, and Other Impulsive Behaviors

A history of violence, suicide, or other impulsive behaviors by the patient is a major factor in the assessment of potential for violence. Past violence predicts future violence. Episodes of past violence, for example the most recent episode, must be dissected in a detailed, concrete manner by the clinician. This includes details of the time and place of the violence, who was present, who said what to whom, what did the patient see, what does the patient remember, what do family members or staff remember, why was the patient violent, and what could have been done to avoid the violent confrontation. Often there is a pattern of escalation of violence, such as the dynamics of a couple interacting in domestic violence or the borderline patient responding to perceived rejection by a physician.

The "past history" of violence or suicide attempts should be treated as any other medical symptom. This includes the date of onset, frequency, place (targets), and severity. Severity is measured by degree of injury to the victim(s) from pushing, punching, to causing injuries such as bruises, broken bones, lacerations, internal injuries, or even death. Similarly for suicide attempts, severity is graded from no injury to near lethal. Severity and frequency may be measured by the Overt

Aggression Scale (Yudofsky et al., 1986). The past history of violence should include the presence of other clinical phenomena, such as disorientation, amnesia, and guilt after the violent episode. Last, past history of violence should include prior evaluations (e.g., psychological testing or imaging), and treatment (e.g., hospitalization, medications, and response to treatment).

Psychosis

Although not common with Personality Disorders, psychosis can occur. Psychosis increases potential for violent behavior if the patient has thoughts of violence or suicide. Paranoid thinking can progress to delusional proportions in individuals with Borderline, Paranoid, and occasionally Schizotypal Personality Disorders. Delusions can also be present with comorbid disorder (e.g., psychotic depression).

Alcohol Use and Substance Abuse

Alcohol has been found to increase the risk of violence in a number of ways. Alcohol is thought to disinhibit so that urges and behaviors that would be unacceptable in a sober state (in this case, violence) erupt despite one's personal and societal restraints against violence (Bushman, 1997). Alcohol produces impairment in tasks associated with the frontal lobes such as assessment, planning, organization of behavior, ability to engage in abstract thinking, and impaired memory. Communication skills may not be sufficient to allow the intoxicated individual to deal with the situation in a verbal rather than a physical manner. Cognitive impairment of the brain caused by alcohol may exaggerate provocation through misinterpretation of real events such as perceiving an insult in a bar or in a marital discussion. The intoxicated individual may not appreciate the consequences of violence because of cognitive impairment.

Cocaine produces violent behavior usually during severe intoxication and/or delirium (McCormick & Smith, 1995). Symptoms of intoxication include auditory, visual, and tactile hallucinations, paranoid and other delusions, irritability, confusion, and psychomotor agitation. Symptoms of intoxication or delirium typically disappear within two days after the last dose of cocaine. However, a delusional syndrome may linger for a week or more after the last dose. This syndrome is characterized by persecutory delusions which may elicit violence.

Violence may be elicited by cocaine alone. In addition to cocaine, however, alcohol and heroin are frequently used to counter the irritability and other unpleasant effects of cocaine. These substances may contribute to the violent behaviors observed (Denison et al., 1997). Amphetamine may cause intoxication, delirium, or a delusional disorder; these conditions are clinically indistinguishable from those produced by cocaine which have been discussed earlier. Paranoid delusions may result in assault or homicide (Miczek & Tidey, 1989).

Phencyclidine may be smoked, or taken orally, intranasally, or intravenously. Intoxication is manifested by belligerence, assaultiveness, a sense of invincibility, ataxia, dysarthria, muscle rigidity, seizures, and hyperacusis. Phencyclidine delirium may last longer than that caused by cocaine; otherwise it is clinically similar (Khajawall et al., 1982).

Anabolic steroids have been used by athletes and bodybuilders to enhance muscle growth, strength, and performance. Increased irritability and aggressiveness may occur as side effects to these drugs (Pope & Katz, 1994). Male athletes have demonstrated aggressive behavior and other psychopathology after taking steroids, sometimes at high doses.

Organicity

Brain damage increases the risk of violence. Individuals with Personality Disorders, particularly Antisocial and Borderline types are candidates for organic brain damage through several routes. Fights and reckless behavior can result in head trauma as do serious past suicide attempts. Substance abuse, particularly heavy polysubstance abuse, produces damage to neurons. These individuals are at high risk for HIV infection as a result of substance abuse and risky sexual practices with subsequent development of AIDS, which can progress to dementia.

Background of the Patient

The sociocultural background of the patient must be taken into consideration as one tries to determine whether a patient poses a risk of violence. Violence is an accepted way of expressing oneself in some segments of society usually characterized by poverty and lack of education. Although this environment may be more prevalent for African Americans and Latinos in inner-city areas, lack of legitimate means of attaining one's needs and the need to appear tough, rather than ethnicity is important in these cases. A patient from this background who talks of violence will probably be violent.

Compliance with Treatment

Compliance with treatment is a factor in determining a patient's risk of violence. This involves regular attendance for treatment sessions and compliance with medication and other treatments. Blood levels of medications assist the clinician in monitoring compliance with medication. Contact with the patient's family also helps in monitoring compliance with medication.

Threats of Violence Toward Clinicians

Patients can threaten the clinician in a number of different ways: from the impulsive, emotional outburst; the calm, serious statement; the joking, flippant manner; or through vague innuendos. Threats can be made face-to-face, on an answering machine, or by letter. All threats of violence must be taken seriously, and the clinician should not deny the existence or seriousness of a threat. Often the clinician can confront the patient and clarify the meaning of the threat. If it is resolved, then therapy can proceed. If there is uncertainty or the clinician feels the threat may be serious, it should be discussed with one's supervisor, colleagues, and family so as to assess the risk of harm and to develop a plan to deal with the threat.

A meeting should be arranged consisting of representatives of various areas of the organization, including security, legal affairs, administration, employee health, human affairs, director of clinical services, and a psychiatric consultant familiar with violence. This group will benefit from the various perspectives in terms of evaluating different options, from the legal to the therapeutic, in responding to the threat. In evaluating the risk of violence, information along the lines discussed earlier in this chapter must be obtained. This may involve meeting with the patient in a safe setting or obtaining information from other staff, patients, records, or other means. This is particularly problematic when threats by telephone or mail are anonymous.

If the risk of violence is significant, a plan of action must be in place. This includes security measures, restraining orders, and other means of preventing access to the intended victim. The mental state of the threatener must be assessed so as to determine whether grounds for involuntary hospitalization exist. It is helpful to use the institution as a buffer between the threatening patient and the victim; for example "it is the policy of the hospital to not tolerate threats of violence to other staff and patients, therefore the hospital intends to ... etc." It is hoped that this will deflect or at least not intensify the wrath of the threatener as the plan is implemented.

Summary of Prediction of Dangerousness

The assessment of violence potential for the short-term is analogous to the assessment for suicide potential. The clinician must consider the following:

Patients with Antisocial, Borderline, and Paranoid Personality Disorders are the most frequent concern in regard to dangerousness. If there is violent ideation the clinician should determine: How well planned the threat of violence is; available means of inflicting injury; past history of violence and impulsive behavior with attention to frequency, degree of past injuries to others and self, toward whom, and under what circumstances; alcohol and drug use; presence of other organic mental disorders; presence of schizophrenia, mania, or other psychosis; and noncompliance with treatment in the past.

All of these factors are weighed in the final assessment of whether the patient poses a significant risk to others so that some action is necessary on the part of the evaluator. Action may include hospitalizing the patient or warning the intended victim and/or the police. All of the data on which the decision that the patient is or is not at risk for violence must be documented in writing. The thinking process through which the decision was made should be evident in the written documentation. Reassessment of violence potential should be made at short intervals (e.g., from visit to visit or every few days) if the patient is to continue to be treated outside of the hospital or other institution.

REFERENCES

American Psychiatric Association (1994). *Diagnostic and statistical manual of mental disorders* (4th ed.). Washington, DC: American Psychiatric Association.
Beck, A. T., & Freeman, A. (1990). *Cognitive therapy of personality disorders.* New York: Guilford.
Benjamin, L. (1993). *Interpersonal treatment of personality disorders.* New York: Guilford.

Boxer, P. A. (1993). Assessment of potential violence in the paranoid worker. *Journal of Occupational Medicine, 35,* 122–131.

Bushman, B. J. (1997). Effects of alcohol on human aggression: Validity of proposed explanation. *Recent Developments in Alcoholism, 13,* 227–243.

Carey, G., & Goldman, D. (1997). The genetics of antisocial behavior. In D. M. Stoff, J. Breiling, & J. D. Moser (Eds.), *Handbook of antisocial behavior* (pp. 243–254). New York: Wiley.

Cloninger, C. R. (1987). A systematic method for clinical description and classification of personality disorders. *Archives of General Psychiatry, 44,* 573–588.

Coccaro, E. F., Siever, L. J., & Klar, H. M. (1989). Serotonergic studies in patients with affective and personality disorders with correlates of suicidal and impulsive aggressive behavior. *Archives of General Psychiatry, 46,* 587–599.

Davis-Barron, S. (1995). Psychopathic patients pose a dilemma for physicians and society. *Canadian Medical Association Journal, 152,* 1314–1317.

Denison, M. E., Paredes, A., & Booth, J. B. (1997). Alcohol and cocaine interactions and aggressive behaviors. *Recent Developments in Alcoholism, 13,* 283–303.

Gabbard, G., & Coyne, L. (1987). Predictors of response of antisocial patients to hospital treatment. *Hospital and Community Psychiatry, 38,* 1181–1185.

Gabbard, G. O., & Wilkinson, S. M. (1994). *Management of countertransference with borderline patients.* Washington, DC: American Psychiatric Press.

Grinker, R. R., Werble, B., & Drye, R. C. (1968). *The borderline syndrome.* New York: Basic Books.

Hare, R. O. (1991). *The Hare Psychopathology Checklist.* Toronto, Canada: Revised, Multihealth Systems.

Kernberg, O. (1989). The narcissistic personality disorder and the differential diagnosis of antisocial behavior. *Psychiatric Clinics of North America, 12,* 553–570.

Khajawall, A. M., Erickson, T. B., & Simpson, G. M. (1982). Chronic phencyclidine abuse and physical assault. *American Journal of Psychiatry, 139,* 1604–1606.

McCormick, R. A., & Smith. M. (1995). Aggression and hostility in substance abusers: The relationship to abuse patterns, coping style, and relapse triggers. *Addictive Behaviors, 20,* 555–562.

McGlashan, T. (1993). Implications of outcome research for the treatment of borderline personality disorder. In J. Paris (Ed.), *Borderline personality disorder: Etiology and treatment,* Washington, DC: American Psychiatric Press.

Miczek K. A., & Tidey J. W. (1989). Amphetamines: Aggressive and social behavior. *NIDA Research Monograph, 94,* 68–100.

Miczek, K. A., Haney, M., & Tidey, J. W. (1994). Neurochemistry and pharmacotherapeutic management of aggression and violence. In A. J. Reiss, K. A. Miczek, & J. A. Roth (Eds.), *Understanding and preventing violence* (Vol. 2) (pp. 245–514). Washington, DC: National Academy Press.

Mulvey, E. P., & Lidz, C. W. (1995). Conditional prediction: A model for research on dangerousness to others in a new era. *International Journal of Law and Psychiatry, 18,* 129–143.

Ogloff, J., Wong, S., & Greenwood, A. (1990). Treating criminal psychopaths in a therapeutic community program. *Behavioral Science and the Law, 8,* 181–190.

Perry, J. C., & Herman, J. (1993). Trauma and defense in the ideology of border-line personality disorder. In J. Paris (Ed.), *Borderline personality disorder: Etiology and treatment* (pp. 135–139). Washington, DC: American Psychiatric Press.

Pope, H. G. Jr, & Katz, D. L. (1994). Psychiatric and medical effects of anabolic-androgenic steroid use. A controlled study of 160 athletes. *Archives of General Psychiatry, 51*, 375–382.

Raine, A. (1996). Autonomic nervous system factors underlying disinhibited antisocial and violent behavior: Biosocial perspectives and treatment impli-cations. *Annals of the New York Academy of Sciences, 794*, 46–59.

Roy, A., & Linnoila, M. (1990). *Monoamines and suicidal behavior.* New York: Brunner/Mazel.

Sensky, T., Berney, T., & Coid, J. (1996). *Assessment and clinical management of risk of harm to other people.* Council Report CRS3, London, UK: Royal College of Psychiatrists.

Stone, M. H. (1990). *The fate of the borderline patient: Successful outcome in psychi-atric practice.* New York: Guilford.

Stone, M. H. (1989). Murder in the narcissistic personality disorder. *Psychiatric Clinics of North America, 12*, 643–651.

Tardiff, K. (1996). *Assessment and management of violent patients* (2nd ed.). Washington, DC: American Psychiatric Press.

Tardiff, K. (1997). A prospective study of violence by psychiatric patients after hospital discharge. *Psychiatric Services, 48*, 678–681.

Tardiff, K. (1998). Prediction of violence by patients. *Journal of Practical Psychiatry and Behavioral Health, 4*, 12–19.

Widom, C. S. (1989). Does violence beget violence? A critical examination of the literature. *Psychological Bulletin, 114*, 68–79.

Yudofsky, S. C., Silver, J. M., & Jackson, W. (1986). The Overt Aggression Scale: An operationalized rating scale for verbal and physical aggression. *American Journal of Psychiatry, 143*, 35–39.

7. Recidivistic Violent Behavior and Axis I and Axis II Disorders

JARI TIIHONEN

Violent crime is one of the most detrimental factors affecting the quality of life in many industrialized countries, and most persons incarcerated due to violent offenses have committed previous offenses (Hamparin, Schuster, Dinstz, & Conrad, 1978; Lindqvist, 1986; Tracy, Wolfgang, & Figlio, 1990; Vankeinhoitolaitos, 1997). The majority of all violent crime is attributable to a relatively small population exhibiting recidivistic violent behavior (Hamparin et al., 1978; Tracy et al., 1990). It is remarkable how little systematic and controlled scientific research has focused on the mental disorders underlying habitual violent behavior: The first studies on the quantitative risk assessment of recidivistic violent behavior were only published in the 1990s.

Several practical difficulties have hindered research on violent behavior. Many violent offenses are mild and are even not registered in police records. This obstacle can be avoided by focusing only on the most serious crimes, such as homicide. Even this does not help to improve the coverage of the offenders completely, since in many industrialized countries a large proportion of homicides remains unsolved (e.g., about 30% in the United States, International Criminal Police Organisation, 1991).

It is difficult to obtain comprehensive groups of recidivistic offenders for research purposes in countries with high crime rates caused by extensive use of illicit drugs, a high incidence of organized crime, and gun violence. This is probably because higher crime rates mean lower crime clearance rates. On the other hand, the findings obtained from countries with low or moderate crime rates and high crime detection and clearance rates cannot be applied directly to other countries.

The association between mental disorders and recidivistic violent behavior can be studied with the use of two different procedures. One approach is to study the prevalence of mental disorders among individuals who have committed violent offenses, and the alternative is to study the incidence of criminal acts in a population of mentally disordered subjects. Both of these procedures are prone to methodological errors. It is likely that in different countries and in different situations, mentally disordered subjects may be more–or alternatively less–likely to be arrested or imprisoned than nondisordered offenders. This may be explained by the fact that mentally disordered individuals are more likely to be arrested because of their deviant behavior while committing a minor offense. However, it is also evident that in many countries, the police do not arrest and register mentally ill offenders, but transfer them to hospitals for treatment. When studying the incidence of violent acts in mentally disordered offenders after they have been discharged from mental hospitals, it is only possible to observe the behavior of those patients who are not considered to be violent anymore (because it is not reasonable to discharge those patients who are still considered dangerous).

The most reliable way to study the occurrence of recidivistic violent behavior is to follow large unbiased cohorts in prospective studies. This kind of study with validated psychiatric diagnoses is very laborious and expensive and, therefore, only a few such studies have been done.

Studies on the Association of Mental Disorders and Recidivistic Violent Behavior

Table 7.1 shows a summary of the published studies on the relationship between recidivistic violent behavior and mental disorders.

Recidivistic Violent Behavior among Persons with Major Mental Disorders

Most of the studies with comprehensive material on recidivistic violent behavior in mentally ill subjects have been done in the Nordic countries, probably because the existing conditions for this kind of research are particularly good in Finland, Sweden, and Denmark. These countries have high clearance rates of violent crimes (e.g., 95–97% homicide clearance rate in Finland [Central Statistical Office of Finland, 1985–1992]) and comprehensive nationwide central hospital and crime registers. In Finland, more than 70% of all homicide offend-

Table 7.1. Summary of the Studies on the Association between Recidivistic Violent Behavior and Mental Disorders

Study	Study Design	Key Results
1. Studies on the prevalence of mental disorders among recidivistic violent offenders		
Lindqvist, 1986	Description of homicide offenders in Northern Sweden between 1970–1981.	3 of 64 homicide offenders were recidivists. Two thirds of offenders had previous criminal record.
Brown, 1991	Description of the psychopathology of serial sexual homicide killers in the United States.	Most offenders had antisocial personality disorder or sexual sadism.
Tiihonen & Hakola, 1994	Description of all ($N = 13$) homicide recidivistic offenders during a 3-year period in Finland.	85% had severe alcoholism combined with personality disorder, and 15% had schizophrenia (*DSM-III-R*).
Adler & Lidberg, 1995	Description of 21 recidivist killers during a 18-year period in Sweden.	86% had personality disorder and substance abuse, and 10% had schizophrenia (*ICD-9*).
Eronen, Hakola, & Tiihonen, 1996a	Description of all homicide recidivistic offenders ($N = 36$) during a 13-year period in Finland.	67% had alcoholism, 64% had personality disorder, 11% had schizophrenia, and 6% had major depression.
Geberth & Turco, 1997	Description of 68 serial killers in the United States.	All offenders had antisocial personality disorder or sexual sadism.

(continued)

Table 7.1 (*continued*)

Study	Study Design	Key Results
2. Studies on the incidence of recidivistic violent offenses among mentally ill persons		
Vartiainen & Hakola, 1992	Follow-up study of 305 patients with psychosis diagnosis (279 males and 26 females) discharged from a high-security hospital (mean follow-up period 8.2 years).	16 subjects (5%) committed a homicide or aggravated assaults. 11 (69%) of recidivists had stopped taking their medication, and 14 (88%) committed their offenses under the influence of alcohol.
MacCulloch, Bailey, Jones, & Hunter, 1993	Description of 19 reoffenders discharged direct to the community from a Special Hospital in the United Kingdom.	19 (13 with personality disorders and 6 with mental illness) of 112 discharged subjects committed new offenses.
Tiihonen, Hakola, Eronen, Vartiainen, & Ryynänen, 1996	Follow-up study during a 14-year period (mean follow-up period 7.8 years) among 281 male offenders with psychosis diagnosis discharged from a high-security hospital.	14 subjects committed aggravated violent offenses during the follow-up (7 homicides). *OR* 294 during the first-year discharge, and 53.1 during the 7.8-year period.
3. Prospective cohort studies		
Räsänen et al., 1998	A 26-year prospective follow-up study among a birth cohort (*N* = 11,017).	The risk of recidivistic crimes among alcoholic schizophrenic males was 9.5-fold when compared with healthy men.

ers have been subjected to a full-scale forensic psychiatric examination (4- to 8-week examination in a closed ward in a hospital), and most of the remaining offenders are evaluated to determine whether a forensic psychiatric examination should be done. Because all of these examination reports are scrutinized and filed by the Finnish National Board of Medico-Legal Affairs, it has been possible to calculate the odds ratios (OR) of homicidal behavior by comparing the prevalence of psychiatric disorders among offenders and in the general population.

Studies by MacCulloch, Bailey, Jones, and Hunter (1993), Vartiainen and Hakola (1992), Tiihonen, Hakola, Eronen, Vartiainen, and Ryynänen (1996), and Räsänen et al. (1998) shown in Table 7.1 suggest that mentally ill reoffenders are usually schizophrenic subjects with co-morbid alcohol or substance abuse problems and insufficient insight into their mental illness. The quantitative risk of committing a new violent offense and the risk of reoffending as a function of time after discharge among the mentally ill subjects has been the focus in only one study thus far (Tiihonen et al., 1996). It revealed that the risk is highest during the first year after the end of the obligatory 6-month follow-up after the discharge from a hospital ($OR = 294$ during 1-year follow-up vs. $OR = 53$ during the 7.8-year follow-up). The rate of reoffending probably depends on existing legislation and the setting of the outpatient treatment and follow-up, which differs from country to country. For example, in England, Germany, and Canada, there is legislation that enables obligatory, effective, and long-lasting outpatient care, whereas in Finland it is possible to arrange only a 6-month period of compulsory outpatient treatment after the discharge (which probably accounts for the relatively high observed relapse rate, Tiihonen et al., 1996).

Recidivistic Violent Behavior among Persons without Major Mental Disorders

Because a large proportion of milder violent offenses remain undetected, unregistered, and unsolved, concentrating on the most severe offenses, such as homicide, can help one to obtain a more comprehensive sample with which to reliably study the reoffenders.

The only studies on homicide offenders with comprehensive material have been done in Finland and Sweden (Tiihonen & Hakola, 1994; Adler & Lidberg, 1995; Eronen, Hakola, & Tiihonen, 1996a). They imply that about 80% of recidivistic homicide offenders are early-onset alcoholics with comorbid antisocial or borderline personality disorder.

Data shown in Table 7.2 suggest that the number of previous violent offenses (Tiihonen, Hakola, Nevalainen, & Eronen, 1995) is associated with habitual violence.

Table 7.2 demonstrates the risk of violent offending among different populations. The studies in those populations with previous violent offenses show the greatest risk.

Clinical Predictors and Prevention of Recidivistic Violent Behavior

Subjects with Major Mental Disorders

Recidivistic violent behavior in patients with a psychotic disorder after discharge from a hospital is associated with cessation of voluntary treatment in outpatient care (seeing the doctor or nurse and the use of neuroleptic medication), which is a result of an insufficient insight into their illness. In recent Finnish studies (which showed about a 300-fold risk of committing a homicide during the first year outside a hospital), about 70% of reoffenders had stopped taking their medication and seeing their doctor (Vartiainen & Hakola, 1992; Tiihonen et al., 1996). These studies, as well as the studies on homicidal recidivism by Eronen et al. (1996a) and a cohort study by Räsänen et al. (1998), suggest that coexisting alcohol or drug abuse among schizophrenic patients is an important factor in recidivistic violent behavior in this population: Most of the recidivistic violent crimes (88%) were committed under the influence of alcohol (Vartiainen & Hakola, 1992). Therefore, any substance abuse or dependence merits attention and should be treated as effectively and vigorously as the psychotic illness. Dopamine-releasing agents such as ethanol, cocaine, and amphetamine can induce impulsive violent behavior (Baggio & Ferrari, 1980; Thor & Ghiselli, 1975; Barros & Miczek, 1996; Rossetti, D'Aquila, Hmaidan, Gessa, & Serra, 1991; Sorensen, Jumphreys, Taylor, & Schmidt, 1992; Spanagel, Herz, Bals-Kubik, & Shippenberg, 1991) and substance abuse may make a substantial contribution to violent behavior, even among those mentally ill patients who offend deliberately as a result of their psychotic symptoms (delusions or hallucinations).

Intramuscular depot-neuroleptic treatment is efficient in preventing a relapse of psychotic illness (Kane, 1989; Kissling, 1994), but the typically used low-dose neuroleptics are associated with a significant risk of extrapyramidal side-effects and tardive dyskinesia. Clozapine and new atypical neuroleptics may have some specific antiaggressive effect

Table 7.2. Risk of Violent Behavior among Male Index Populations Compared with the General Male Population. Summary of the Studies on the Quantitative Risk of Violent Behavior

Diagnostic Group/Index Population	Number of Subjects Obtained from the Studies/Study Design	Odds Ratio	95% CI
Manic disorders (Eronen, Hakola, & Tiihonen, 1996b)	No males with manic disorders in 910 homicide offenders	—	
Anxiety disorders (Eronen et al., 1996b)	14 (= 1.5%) males with anxiety disorders in 910 homicide offenders	0.3	0.2–0.5
Dysthymia (Eronen et al., 1996b)	13 (= 1.4%) males with dysthymia in 910 homicide offenders	0.6	0.3–1.0
The general population		**1**	
Mental retardation (Eronen et al., 1996b)	11 (= 1.2%) males with mental retardation in 910 homicide offenders	1.2	0.7–2.2
Major depressive episode (Eronen et al., 1996b)	27 (= 3.0%) males with major depressive episode in 910 homicide offenders	1.6	1.1–2.4
Schizophrenia without alcoholism (Räsänen et al., 1998)	Three nonalcoholic schizophrenics convicted of violent crimes in a birth cohort (N = 11,017)	3.6	0.9–12.3
Men with major mental disorders (Hodgins, 1992)	In a birth cohort of 7,362 men there were 82 subjects suffering from a major mental disorder (their relative risk for violence was assessed)	4.2	2.23–7.78
Major mental disorder (Hodgins, Mednick, Brennan, Schulsinger, & Engberg, 1996)	The risk of committing violent crimes among males in a Danish birth cohort (N = 324,401)	4.5	3.91–5.14

(continued)

Table 7.2 (*continued*)

Diagnostic Group/Index Population	Number of Subjects Obtained from the Studies/Study Design	Odds Ratio	95% CI
Organic psychosis (Tiihonen, Isohanni, Räsänen, Koiranen, & Moring, 1997b)	An unselected birth cohort ($N = 11,017$) was prospectively followed up (data on crimes and psychiatric disorders were collected from the national registers in Finland)	5.0	1.00–23.6
Affective psychosis (Wallace et al., 1998)	Two male homicide offenders with affective psychosis among the total of 152 homicide offenders	5.0	1.3–20.9
Intellectual handicaps (Hodgins, 1992)	In a birth cohort of 7,362 men there were 82 subjects suffering from a major mental disorder (their relative risk for violence was assessed)	5.45	3.38–8.80
Schizophrenia without alcoholism (estimate) (Eronen, Tiihonen, & Hakola, 1996c)	48 nonalcoholic schizophrenics in 1,302 homicide offenders	7.3	5.4–9.7
Mental retardation (Hodgins et al., 1996)	The risk of committing violent crimes among males in a Danish birth cohort ($N = 324, 401$).	7.7	5.56–10.52
Schizophrenia and schizophreniformic psychoses (Eronen et al., 1996b)	58 (= 6.4%) schizophrenics in 910 homicide offenders	8.0	6.1–10.4
Schizophrenia (Wallace et al., 1998)	11 male schizophrenic homicide offenders among the total of 152 homicide offenders	10.1	5.5–18.6

*Homicide offenders who had committed one previous homicide (Eronen, Hakola, & Tiihonen, 1996a)	A 13-year sample of homicide recidivists (N = 35) among 1,584 homicide offenders	10.4	7.4–14.5
Alcoholism (Eronen et al., 1996b)	357 (39.2%) alcoholic males in 910 homicide offenders	10.7	9.4–12.2
Antisocial personality disorder (Eronen et al., 1996b)	103 (= 11.3%) males with antisocial personality disorder in 910 homicide offenders	11.7	9.5–14.4
Schizophrenia with alcoholism (estimate) (Eronen et al., 1996c)	38 (= 2.9%) alcoholic schizophrenics in 1,302 homicide offenders	17.2	12.4–23.7
Schizophrenia with alcoholism (Räsänen et al., 1998)	Four alcoholic schizophrenics convicted of violent crimes in a birth cohort (N = 11,017)	25.2	6.1–97.2
*Schizophrenia and an earlier homicide (Eronen et al., 1996a)	A 13-year sample of homicide recidivists (N = 35) among 1,584 homicide offenders	25.8	9.6–69.6
*Released forensic psychiatric patients during a 7.8 year follow-up (Tiihonen et al., 1996)	A follow-up study of released patients with a mean follow-up period of 7.8 years	53.1	25.0–112.8
*Homicide offenders after release from prison (Tiihonen, Hakola, Nevalainen, & Eronen, 1995)	Data from 163 homicide offenders; the risk of offenders with at least 4 previous aggravated violent offenses was compared with all homicide offenders compared with general population (OR = 145)	14.5	3.3–65
*Homicide offenders during first year after release from prison (Eronen et al., 1996a)	A 13-year sample of homicide recidivists (N = 35) among 1,584 homicide offenders	253.8	145.8–441.9
*Released forensic psychiatric patients during their first year outside the hospital (Tiihonen et al., 1996)	A follow-up study of released patients with a mean follow-up period of 7.8 years	293.9	119.2–724.7

* Studies on recidivistic populations.

(Citrome & Volavka, 1997), but at present, none of them are available as depot injections. However, new antipsychotics – risperidone, sertindole, and olanzapine—have very mild adverse effects, which results in better compliance.

The results indicate that effective, regular, and long-lasting compulsory outpatient care after discharge represents an absolute necessity in patients with a psychotic disorder, previous offenses, and insufficient insight into their mental illness. This was demonstrated recently in a Finnish follow-up study which revealed that 14 of 16 (88%) relapsing violent offenders had no insight about their psychotic disorder. If the mental state of the patient with previous offenses and psychotic disorder deteriorates significantly, he/she should be hospitalized immediately. Unfortunately, not all countries have legislation that allows compulsory long-term outpatient treatment and follow-up after discharge from the hospital (e.g., in Finland the duration of the compulsory outpatient follow-up and treatment period is a mere 6 months).

Subjects without Major Mental Disorders

Offenders without the diagnosis of psychosis are sentenced to incarceration in prisons or penitentiaries in most countries. However, in the United States and the United Kingdom it is possible to set the conditions that must be met before the prisoner can be paroled. Serial killers receive very long sentences in most cases, and their personal pathology is usually persistent and resistant to treatment. Early-onset antisocial behavior and sexual sadism are characteristic of the most dangerous reoffenders (Brown, 1991; Geberth & Turco, 1997). However, serial killers comprise only a small proportion of all recidivistic violent offenders. Among other habitually violent offenders, the number of previous violent offenses represents the best predictor of recidivistic behavior: If a prisoner has committed at least three aggravated violent offenses in addition to one homicide, his/her risk of committing a new homicide is about 15-fold when compared with those prisoners who have committed a single homicide but have no other criminal record (Tiihonen et al., 1995). Low CSF 5-HIAA and blood glucose levels (Virkkunen, DeJong, Bartko, Goodwin, & Linnoila, 1989; Virkkunen et al., 1994; Virkkunen, Eggert, Rawlings, & Linnoila 1996), and a high score on a psychopathy checklist, elementary school maladjustment, young age at index offense, and *DSM-III* diagnosis of personality disorder in the Risk Assessment Guide (RAG) (Webster, Harris, Rice,

Cormier, & Quinsey, 1994) have a strong association with recidivistic violent behavior.

In Finland and Sweden, about 80% of recidivistic homicide offenders are type-2 alcoholics, and about 70–80% of all homicides are committed under alcohol intoxication (Eronen, 1997). Preventing relapse of alcohol abuse (and, especially, outside the Nordic countries, illicit drug abuse) represents a crucial issue when one seeks to prevent recidivistic violent behavior in nonpsychotic offenders. Several studies indicate that impulsive and violent behavior in individuals with personality disorders can be treated with lithium (Sheard, Marini, Bridges, & Wagner, 1976) and serotonin selective re-uptake inhibitors such as fluoxetine (Salzman et al., 1995; Coccaro & Kavoussi, 1997). Naltrexone and acamprosate are now recognized as providing effective pharmacological treatment for alcoholism (O'Malley et al., 1992; Volpicelli, Alterman, Hayashida, & O'Brien, 1992; Sass, Soyka, Mann, & Zieglgänsberger, 1996) and the results from molecular biological studies are very promising concerning the immunological treatment (i.e., vaccination) for cocaine abuse (Fox et al., 1996). However, the most challenging issue is how to arrange effective treatment in an outpatient setting among persons with severe antisocial behavior and poor cooperation and compliance. The most important issues are that patients receive their treatment and take their medication regularly as instructed, and that they see their doctor or nurse on a regular basis, which makes it possible to intervene (e.g., to institutionalize the patient, if his or her mental state has deteriorated) in time and thereby prevent violent behavior.

Conclusion

The data published thus far (mainly from Nordic countries) suggest that the most important mental disorders contributing to recidivistic violent behavior are type-2 alcoholism and schizophrenia. Type-2 alcoholism (often associated with illicit drug use) is characterized by early onset of alcohol abuse, antisocial personality traits, and a reduced central serotonin turnover rate. In many countries, such as the United States, the use of illicit drugs such as cocaine is an important factor in recidivistic violence. One common etiological factor in recidivistic violent behavior among type-2 alcoholics and schizophrenics is probably dysfunction of prefrontal cortical areas, which has been revealed in brain-imaging studies performed in violent offenders (Goyer et al., 1994; Raine et al., 1994;

Tiihonen et al., 1997a). Long-lasting outpatient treatment (including neuroleptic medication) is a crucial issue in preventing recidivistic violent behavior among mentally ill patients after their discharge from the hospital. In addition to frequent observation and follow-up with psychotherapeutic and sociobehavioral therapy, recidivistic violent behavior could possibly be suppressed (even among those persons without major mental disorders) with pharmacological treatments such as fluoxetine (Coccaro & Kavoussi, 1997), naltrexone (O'Malley et al., 1992, Volpicelli et al., 1992), acamprosate (Sass et al., 1996), 5-HT_{1B}-agonists such as eltoprazine (de Koning et al., 1994; Tiihonen, Hakola, Paanila, & Turtiainen, 1993), or, in the future, possibly some kind of cocaine vaccine (Fox et al., 1996). The main problem in treating and preventing recidivistic behavior is the patient's poor compliance and attitude, which requires new approaches such as effective compulsory outpatient treatment, supervised drug administration, or use of depot-injection drugs as an alternative to long-lasting incarceration.

REFERENCES

Adler, H., & Lidberg, H. (1995). Characteristics of repeat killers in Sweden. *Criminal Behavior and Mental Health, 5,* 5–13.
Baggio, G., & Ferrari, F. (1980). Role of brain dopaminergic mechanisms in rodent aggressive behavior: Influence of (+, –) N-n-propyl-norapomorphine on three experimental models. *Psychopharmacology, 70,* 63–68.
Barros, H.M.T., & Miczek, K. A. (1996). Neurobiological and behavioral characteristics of alcohol-heightened aggression. In D. M. Stoff & R. B. Cairns (Eds.), *Aggression and violence. Genetic, neurobiological, and biosocial perspectives* (pp. 237–264). Hillsdale, NJ: Erlbaum.
Brown, J. S. (1991). The psychopathology of serial sexual homicide: A review of the possibilities. *American Journal of Forensic Psychiatry, 12,* 13–21.
Central Statistical Office of Finland. (1985–1992). *Criminality known to the police 1984–1991.* Helsinki, Finland: Author.
Citrome, L., & Volavka, J. (1997). Psychopharmacology of violence. Part II: Beyond the acute episode. *Psychiatric Annals, 27,* 696–703.
Coccaro, E. F., & Kavoussi, R. J. (1997). Fluoxetine and impulsive aggressive behavior in personality-disordered subjects. *Archives of General Psychiatry, 54,* 1081–1088.
Eronen, M., Hakola, P., & Tiihonen, J. (1996a). Factors associated with homicide recidivism in a 13-year sample of homicide offenders in Finland. *Psychiatric Services, 47,* 403–406.
Eronen, M., Hakola, P., & Tiihonen, J. (1996b). Mental disorders and homicidal behavior in Finland. *Archives of General Psychiatry, 53,* 497–501.
Eronen, M., Tiihonen, J., & Hakola, P. (1996c). Schizophrenia and homicidal behavior. *Schizophrenia Bulletin, 22,* 83–89.

Eronen, M. (1997). *Psychiatric disorders and homicidal behavior in Finland*. Kuopio University Publications D, Medical Sciences 130. Kuopio: Kuopio University Printing Office.

Fox, B. S., Kantak, K. M., Edwards, M. A., Black, K. M., Bollinger, B. K., Botka, A. J., French, T. L., Thompson, T. L., Schad, V. C., Greenstein, J. L., Gefter, M. L., Exley, M. A., Swain, P. A., & Briner, T. L. (1996). Efficacy of a therapeutic cocaine vaccine in rodent models. *Nature Medicine, 2*, 1122–1132.

Geberth, V. J., & Turco, R. N. (1997). Antisocial personality disorder, sexual sadism, malignant narcissism and serial murder. *Journal of Forensic Sciences, 42*, 49–60.

Goyer, P. F., Andreason, P. J., Semple, W. E., Clayton, A. H., King, A. C., Compton-Toth, B. A., Schultz, S. C., & Cohen, R. M. (1994). Positron-emission tomography and personality disorders. *Neuropsychopharmacology, 10*, 21–28.

Hamparin, D. M., Schuster, R., Dinstz, S., & Conrad, J. P. (1978). *The violent few: A study of violent offenders*. Lexington, MA: Lexington Books.

Hodgins, S. (1992). Mental disorder, intellectual deficiency, and crime. *Archives of General Psychiatry, 49*, 476–483.

Hodgins, S., Mednick, S. A., Brennan, P. A., Schulsinger, F., & Engberg, M. (1996). Mental disorder and crime: Evidence from a Danish birth cohort. *Archives of General Psychiatry, 53*, 489–496.

International Criminal Police Organisation (1991). *International Crimes Statistics 1989–1990*. Lyon, France: Author.

Kane, J. M. (1989). Schizophrenia: Somatic treatment. In H. I. Kaplan & B. J. Sadock (Eds.), *Comprehensive textbook of psychiatry V. Vol. 1 5th ed.* (pp. 777–792). Baltimore, MD: Williams & Wilkins.

Kissling, W. (1994). Compliance, quality assurance and standards for relapse prevention in schizophrenia. *Acta Psychiatrica Scandinavica, 89* (suppl. 382), 16–24.

de Koning, P., Mak, M., de Vries, M. H., Allsopp, L. F., Stevens, R. B., Verbruggen, R., Van den Borre, R., van Peteghem, P., Kohen, D., & Arumainayagam, M. et al. (1994). Eltoprazine in aggressive mentally handicapped patients: A double-blind, placebo-controlled and baseline-controlled multi-centre study. The Eltoprazine Aggression Research Group. *International Clinical Psychopharmacology, 9*, 187–194.

Lindqvist, P. (1986). Criminal homicide in Northern Sweden 1970–81: Alcohol intoxication, alcohol abuse and mental disease. *International Journal of Law and Psychiatry, 8*, 19–37.

MacCulloch, M., Bailey, J., Jones, C., & Hunter, C. (1993). Nineteen male serious reoffenders who were discharged direct to the community from a Special Hospital: I. General characteristics. *Journal of Forensic Psychiatry, 4*, 237–248.

O'Malley, S. S., Jaffe, A. J., Chang, G., Schottenfeld, R. S., Meyer, R. E., & Rounsaville, B. (1992). Naltrexone and coping skills therapy for alcohol dependence. *Archives of General Psychiatry, 49*, 881–887.

Raine, A., Buchsbaum, M. S., Stanley, J., Lottenberg, S., Abel, L., & Stoddard, J. (1994). Selective reductions in pre-frontal glucose metabolism assessed with positron emission tomography in accused murderers pleading not guilty by reason of insanity. *Biological Psychiatry, 36*, 365–373.

Räsänen, P., Tiihonen, J., Isohanni, M., Rantakallio, P., Lehtonen, J., & Moring, J. (1998). Schizophrenia, alcohol abuse, and violent behavior: A 26-year follow-up study of an unselected birth cohort. *Schizophrenia Bulletin, 24,* 437–441.

Rossetti, Z. L., D'Aquila, P. S., Hmaidan, Y., Gessa, G. L., & Serra, G. (1991). Repeated treatment with imipramine potentiates cocaine-induced dopamine release and motor stimulation. *European Journal of Pharmacology, 201,* 243–245.

Saltzman, C., Wolfson, A.N., Schatzberg, A., Looper, J., Henke, R., Albanese, M., Schwartz, J., & Miyawaki, E. (1995). Effect of fluoxetine on anger in symptomatic volunteers with borderline personality disorder. *Journal of Clinical Psychopharmacology, 15,* 23–29.

Sass, H., Soyka, M., Mann, K., & Zieglgänsberger, W. (1996). Relapse prevention by acamprosate. Results from a placebo-controlled study on alcohol dependence. *Archives of General Psychiatry, 53,* 673–680.

Sheard, M. H., Marini, J. L., Bridges, C. I., & Wagner, E. (1976). The effect of lithium on impulsive aggressive behavior in man. *American Journal of Psychiatry, 133,* 1409–1413.

Sorensen, S. M., Jumphreys, T. M., Taylor, V. L., & Schmidt, C. J. (1992). 5-HT$_2$ receptor antagonists reverse amphetamine-induced slowing of dopaminergic neurons by interfering with stimulated dopamine synthesis. *Journal of Pharmacology and Experimental Therapeutics, 260,* 872–878.

Spanagel, R., Herz, A., Bals-Kubik, R., & Shippenberg, T. S. (1991). β-endorphin-induced locomotor stimulation and reinforcement are associated with an increase in dopamine release in the nucleus accumbens. *Psychopharmacology (Berlin), 104,* 51–56.

Thor, D. H., & Ghiselli, W. P. (1975). Suppression of mouse killing and apomorphine-induced social aggression in rats by local anesthesia of the mystacial vibrissae. *Journal of Comparative Physiology and Psychology, 88,* 40–46.

Tiihonen, J., Hakola, P., Paanila, J., & Turtiainen, M. (1993). Eltoprazine for aggression in schizophrenia and mental retardation. *Lancet, 341,* 307.

Tiihonen, J., & Hakola, P. (1994). Psychiatric disorders and homicide recidivism. *American Journal of Psychiatry, 151,* 436–438.

Tiihonen, J., Hakola, P., Nevalainen, A., & Eronen, M. (1995). Risk of homicidal behaviour among persons convicted of homicide. *Forensic Science International, 72,* 43–48.

Tiihonen, J., Hakola, P., Eronen, M., Vartiainen, H., & Ryynänen, O-P. (1996). Risk of homicidal behavior among discharged forensic psychiatric patients. *Forensic Science International, 79,* 123–129.

Tiihonen, J., Kuikka, J. T., Bergström, K. A., Karhu, J., Viinamäki, H., Lehtonen, J., Hallikainen, T., Yang, J., & Hakola, P. (1997a). Single-photon emission tomography imaging of monoamine transporters in impulsive violent behaviour. *European Journal of Nuclear Medicine, 24,* 1253–1260.

Tiihonen, J., Isohanni, M., Räsänen, P., Koiranen, M., & Moring, J. (1997b). Specific major mental disorders and criminality. A 26-year prospective study of the 1966 Northern Finland birth cohort. *American Journal of Psychiatry, 154,* 840–845.

Tracy, P. E., Wolfgang, M. E., & Figlio, R. M. (1990). *Delinquency in two birth cohorts.* New York: Plenum Press.

Vankeinhoitolaitos.   (1997).   *Vankeinhoidon   vuosikertomus   1996.*
Oikeusministeriön vankeinhoito-osaston julkaisuja, sarja A, No 39. Helsinki:
Vammalan Kirjapaino (in Finnish).
Vartiainen, H. T., & Hakola, H.P.A. (1992). How changes in mental health law
adversely affect offenders discharged from security hospital. *Journal of
Forensic Psychiatry, 3*, 563–570.
Virkkunen, M., DeJong, J., Bartko, J., Goodwin, F. K., & Linnoila, M. (1989).
Relationship of psychobiological variables to recidivism in violent offenders
and impulsive fire setters. A follow-up study. *Archives of General Psychiatry,
46*, 600–603.
Virkkunen, M., Rawlings, R., Tokola, R., Poland, R. E., Guidotti, A., Nemeroff,
C., Bissette, G., Kalogeras, K., Karonen, S-L., & Linnoila, M. (1994). CSF bio-
chemistries, glucose metabolism, and diurnal activity rhythms in alcoholic,
violent offenders, fire setters, and healthy volunteers. *Archives of General
Psychiatry, 51*, 20–27.
Virkkunen, M., Eggert, M., Rawlings, R., & Linnoila, M. I. (1996). A prospective
follow-up study of alcoholic violent offenders and fire setters. *Archives of
General Psychiatry, 53*, 523–529.
Volpicelli, J. R., Alterman, A. I., Hayashida, M., & O'Brien, C. P. (1992).
Naltrexone in the treatment of alcohol dependence. *Archives of General
Psychiatry, 49*, 876–880.
Wallace, C., Mullen, P., Burges, P., Palmer, S., Ruschena, D., & Browne, C.
(1998). Serious criminal offending and mental disorder. *British Journal of
Psychiatry, 172*, 477–484.
Webster, C. D., Harris G. T., Rice, M. E., Cormier, C., & Quinsey, V. L. (1994). *The
violence prediction scheme. Assessing dangerousness in high risk men.* Toronto,
Canada: Centre of Criminology, University of Toronto.

8. Risk Assessment for Intimate Partner Homicide

JACQUELYN C. CAMPBELL, PHYLLIS SHARPS,
AND NANCY GLASS

Intimate partner homicide represents a serious health and social problem throughout the world. The majority of research on the topic has been conducted in the United States, Canada, and Australia, with only limited cross-national investigations disaggregating intimate partner homicide from other forms of homicide (Gartner, 1990; LaFree, 1998). Even with the limitations in worldwide databases, it is clear that men are universally most often the perpetrators in intimate partner homicide as with homicide in general. When women kill a husband, boyfriend, or estranged partner, they are far more likely to be acting in self-defense than are men (Wolfgang, 1958; Easteal, 1993; Browne, Williams, & Dutton, 1998). In intimate partner homicide overall, estrangement, jealousy, and prior beating of the *female* partner represent major risk factors (Browne et al., 1998; Smith, Moracco, & Butts, 1998). Daly and Wilson (1998) conclude that the underlying dynamics of intimate partner homicide are basically "male sexual proprietariness and female attempts to escape male control" with the actual homicide only representing the extreme of the coercive control that characterizes battering. Most data from individual countries' sources such as Africa, Australia, England, United States, and Canada support that general contention (Crawford & Gartner, 1992; Edwards, 1985; Mushanga, 1978; Easteal, 1993; Campbell, 1992).

Determination of risk of intimate partner homicide needs to be based on this underlying theoretical premise of male coercive control of females. Thus, although informed by risk of dangerousness literature from other fields (such as sexual assault and mentally disordered individuals), this chapter will concentrate on the literature specific to domestic homicide and the emerging field of risk assessment specific to domestic violence. Most experts on violence risk assessment are recommending such specialization as actuarial methods and research on particular dynamics become available (Litwack & Schlesinger, 1999; Monahan & Steadman, 1994; Quinsey & Maguire, 1986). The chapter will first present an overview of risk factors associated with intimate partner homicide. The second section is a review of the existing instruments that attempt to predict risk of intimate partner homicide and dangerousness with in-depth information on three of the instruments with available psychometric data. The state of development of these instruments will be placed within the context of the state of the science of violence risk assessment with other populations.

Review of Literature

Intimate partner homicide represents the single largest category of femicides, with women being most often killed by a husband or lover, or ex-husband or ex-lover (National Institute of Justice, 1997; Mercy & Saltzman, 1989; Bailey et al., 1997; Bachman & Saltzman, 1995). The percentage of female murder victims killed by intimates has remained at about 30% since 1976 (Bureau of Justice, 1998). This is in contrast to only 12.9% of male homicides with an intimate partner perpetrator. Since 1977, the proportion of male homicides by a female intimate partner has decreased, while the percentage of female victims of intimate partner homicide increased from 54% to 70% in 1992 (Zawitz, 1994).

The characteristics of intimate partner femicide differ markedly from those of homicide of male intimate partners. The majority of intimate partner femicides involve battering of the female by the male intimate before her death (Mercy & Saltzman, 1989; Moracco et al., 1998; Campbell, 1992; Bailey et al., 1997). Two American studies in different jurisdictions documented that two thirds of the intimate partner femicide cases had a documented history of female partner battering (Moracco et al., 1998; Campbell, 1992). In contrast, intimate partner homicides of men by women are characterized by a history of battering of the female perpetrator by the male victim in as many as 75% of the cases (Hall-Smith, Moracco, & Butts, 1998; Campbell, 1992). Other retrospective studies have associated the following factors with intimate partner femicide: use of guns, forced sex, substance abuse (both drugs and alcohol), controlling and/or stalking behavior, and threats of suicide by the perpetrator (Campbell, 1995). Intimate partner homicide involving either partner as perpetrator is also characterized by a history of estrangement (Wilson & Daly, 1993; Dawson & Gartner, 1998).

Relationship between Victim and Perpetrator in Intimate Partner Homicide

In recent decades in the United States, intimate partner homicide rates overall have declined (Rosenfeld, 1997). One possible explanation for this trend is that the concurrent lower marriage rates in recent decades have decreased women's exposure to legally sanctioned spouses. However, while relatively fewer women have been killed by their husbands, an increasing number of nonmarried women have been killed by boyfriends (Rosenfeld, 1997). The largest decreases in intimate partner homicide have been for males. A possible explanation is that decreased barriers to leaving violent relationships and more protections for battered women through legal sanctions and shelter resources have resulted in more women being able to leave rather than kill their abusive partner (Browne et al., 1998; Rosenfeld, 1997). In fact, Browne and colleagues (1998) tested this premise with statewide data and found that in states where domestic violence laws and shelter services were most available for battered women, male victim intimate partner homicide rates were lowest.

Wilson and Daly's (1993, 1995) research suggest that women who leave relationships, whether marriage or cohabitation, are more vulnerable for intimate partner femicide. They analyzed 1,748 spousal homicides from Canada, 1,758 spousal homicides from the U.S., and 398 cases from England. When physical separation and initiation of legal separation proceedings occurred simultaneously, the first 2 months following separation were the highest risk period for intimate partner femicide (Wilson & Daly, 1993; Wilson et al., 1995). From these studies and clinical experience with battered women, it has been theorized that male partners are threatened by loss of control over the relationship when women announce their decision to separate, and some men will stop at nothing to regain control, including femicide. However, it was the combination of separation and legal procedure initiation that most increased risk in the Wilson and Daly study. Women who continued to live with a partner without starting legal separation procedures were at greater risk for intimate partner homicide than women who separated but did not start legal procedures. Although it is clear that the period after separation is a time of increased risk, this has not been compared with the risk of staying in an abusive relationship. In both North Carolina and Ontario two to three times as many couples were intact as were estranged when the woman was killed (Dawson & Gartner, 1998; Smith et al., 1998).

Empirical evidence also exists of an association of intimate partner femicide and abuse during pregnancy. In an ongoing clinical trial of women battered during pregnancy ($N = 199$), 11.9% of battered women reported a knife or gun used against them within the last 12 months (McFarlane, Soeken, Campbell, Parker, Reel, & Silva, in press). All the women who reported a weapon used against them reported significantly higher levels of physical abuse as well as higher scores on a measure of risk of femicide. In two other samples, abuse during pregnancy has been associated with other risk factors for femicide (Campbell, 1986; Campbell, Soeken, McFarlane, & Parker, 1998). Two theories may explain this increased risk. First, men who abuse their partners during pregnancy are particularly violent, and the abuse during pregnancy is a sign of this violence. Second, jealous and controlling men may suspect or have evidence that the unborn child is not their biological progeny and therefore may kill their partner out of male sexual competitiveness (Daly, Wiseman, & Wilson, 1997).

Perpetrators

Like other homicides, male perpetrators of intimate partner murders in the United States are most likely to be poor, young, a member of an ethnic minority group, with a history of other violence, and substance abuse (Weiner, Zahn, & Sagi, 1990). Resource theory of domestic abuse from sociology may offer a partial explanation. This theory suggests that when male personal resources, such as education, income, job prestige, and community standing are lower than his spouse, he is likely to use violence to lower the perceived status difference (Walker, 1984; Howard, 1986). Often young ethnic minority males are poorly educated, unemployed, or underemployed (National Institute of Justice, 1997; Jaynes & Williams, 1989; Bowman, 1993; Smith & Brewer, 1990) as compared to their female partners. As a result, they may resort to violence and eventually murder as a means of exerting power and control to elevate or equalize their status in their intimate relationships.

Female perpetrators of intimate partner homicide are less likely to be substance abusers than are male perpetrators or their male victims (Smith et al., 1998; Campbell, 1992). They are also far less likely to have had a history of any kind of violence. In the vast majority (75% or more) of cases when a female kills an intimate partner, there is either immediate victim precipitation (the victim being the first to show a weapon or strike a blow) or a long history of the woman being battered (Browne et al., 1999; Campbell, 1992; Smith et al., 1998).

Weapons

Access to and availability of firearms in the United States greatly increases the risk of homicide in general and also intimate partner homicide (Kellerman et al., 1993). Statistics related to the kind of weapons for intimate partner homicide show an increasing use of firearms. Analysis of the 1992 FBI Supplemental Homicide Reports revealed 66% of the female murder victims known to have been killed by intimates were shot to death (Zawitz, 1994) compared to 19% in the 1950s (Wolfgang, 1958). A slightly lower percentage of male intimate partners (55%) were shot to death in 1992 (Zawitz, 1994). In all cases of intimate partner murder, handguns are the weapons of choice; however, female victims are more likely to be killed with shotguns and rifles than are male victims (Arbuckle et al., 1996; Zawitz, 1994). In a study of 134 homicides of American Indian, Hispanic, and non-Hispanic white women in New Mexico, researchers also found that firearms were nearly twice as likely to be used in "domestic" (intimate partner) femicides compared to other femicides (Arbuckle et al., 1996). Wilt, Illman, and Brodyfield (1995) found that 50% of 244 intimate partner femicides in New York City between 1990 and 1994 were shootings and 22% were stabbings. Bailey et al. (1997) reanalyzed the results of two population-based case-control studies and found that prior intimate partner violence and gun ownership were strongly associated with femicide in the home.

To date, one exception to handgun predominance in weapons for intimate partner homicide exists – a study of 2,556 males and females who were killed in Chicago between 1965–1993 (Block & Christakos, 1995). Firearms were the second most common weapon of choice (35%), with knives being the most commonly used weapon (37%) during the commission of intimate partner homicide. The Chicago analysis also demonstrated weapon use varied by gender. Male perpetrators were more likely to beat an intimate partner to death and slightly more likely to use a handgun.

Overkill is another gender differentiation characteristic among intimate partner homicides (Campbell, 1992; Browne et al., 1998). Overkill was first described by Wolfgang in 1958 as two or more acts of shooting or stabbing or beating the victim to death. Several North American studies have found the majority (46–90%) of women in intimate partner homicides the victims of overkill compared to 12% or less of males (Browne et al., 1998).

Homicide-Suicide and Domestic Femicide

Homicide followed by suicide occurs most frequently in a family context and most often in an intimate, long-term relationship (Buteau, Lesage, & Kiely, 1993). The demographic patterns most often found with homicide-suicide are male offender and a female victim, female victim younger than male perpetrator, and whites more often than nonwhites (Buteau et al., 1993; Stack, 1997). The older age and more often white rather than minority status of almost exclusively male perpetrators differentiates homicide-suicides from other homicides in general and from other intimate partner homicides (Stack, 1997; Buteau et al., 1993). A statewide analysis in North Carolina revealed that 26% of intimate partner femicides were homicides-suicides (Moracco et al., 1998). In Chicago, between 1965 and 1993, 15% of men who killed their female partner then killed themselves (Block & Christakos, 1995).

Buteau and associates (1993) in Canada as well as U.S. researchers (e.g., Morton et al., 1998; Stack, 1997) have divided homicide-suicide into "mercy killings" or "suicide pacts" (older and afflicted by physical illness or other serious problems) and the more usual intimate partner homicide-suicide. In the much larger (90% of cases in North Carolina), younger category, risk factors for perpetrators include being male, jealousy, being depressed or having been depressed, a longstanding relationship with the victim, a history of physical abuse or separation/reunion episodes, personality disorder, and alcohol abuse (Buteau et al., 1993; Morton et al., 1998). The typical case in Buteau and associates' (1993) review of 39 homicide-suicides between 1988–1990 in Quebec involved a man killing his spouse after waiting for her to return home to retrieve her belongings. Separation was also a factor in 45% of the North Carolina homicide-suicides (Morton et al., 1998).

In both studies, a significant proportion (but less than one quarter) of the male perpetrators (15% in North Carolina; 21% in Quebec) had consulted mental health services in the year prior to the event (Buteau et al., 1993; Morton et al., 1998). Depression was reported in 46% and substance abuse in 23% of perpetrators in Quebec. In North Carolina, 38% of the homicide-suicide perpetrators had ingested alcohol before death, but this was a slightly lower percentage than for other intimate partner femicides (Moracco et al., 1998; Morton et al., 1998).

Substance Abuse and Other Mental Illness

It is generally difficult to identify substance abuse in homicide perpetrators with certainty unless they have committed suicide, so it is less clear as to how much a risk factor it presents in the intimate partner homicides without suicide. There may also be differential risk depending on the substance used (drugs versus alcohol), use of alcohol versus intoxication at the time of the homicide, whether the victim or perpetrator or both were users, and gender. For instance, Campbell (1992) found the male perpetrators and victims of intimate partner homicide to be far more likely alcohol abusers than female perpetrators and victims. In several studies, male alcohol use seems to be a stronger risk factor for males as victims of intimate partner homicide than for males as perpetrators (Block, 1995). For women, both Wilt (1995) and Moracco et al. (1998) found alcohol use in as many nonintimate partner femicide victims as domestic femicide victims. Persuasive evidence about drug abuse was found in two large data sets (Chicago and North Carolina) where significantly less drug abuse was found among cases of intimate partner homicide than other homicides or femicides (Moracco et al., 1998; Block & Christakos, 1995).

In the Zawitz (1994) review of intimate partner violence in the United States, it was reported that 13% of perpetrators (11% of males, 15% of females) of intimate partner homicide had a history of mental illness, compared to 3% (not reported by gender) of nonfamily murderers. This is the only report of a large sample that makes such a comparison and used data from 540 prosecutor files of intimate partner homicides (Langen & Dawson, 1995). There is more convergence of evidence of a history of mental illness of perpetrators in the studies of homicide-suicide.

Summary of Risk Factors and Implications for Risk Assessment

Although the specific individual and household risk factors are as yet inadequately determined even in North America where the majority of research has been conducted, some conclusions can be drawn (Kellerman et al., 1993; Campbell, 1995; Browne et al., 1998). Clearly, prior domestic violence and handguns are the most consistent and strongest risk factors, with estrangement also strongly implicated. Although violence outside the home, alcohol abuse, minority ethnicity, and unemployment are also implicated in male perpetrated intimate partner homicide, they seem to be less strong risk factors than for other types of homicide. Homicide-suicide with a male perpetrator is a form of homicide especially associated with intimate partnership. Guns, estrangement, and prior psychopathy in the form of depression are particular risk factors for this form of intimate partner homicide. Other aspects of the intimate partner relationship, such as abuse during pregnancy, have also been implicated as risk factors, but the studies from which such information has been gleaned are not large enough nor is there enough comparison data to make definitive conclusions.

Since prior domestic violence against the female partner is the most consistent and strongest risk factor for intimate partner homicide, one of the major approaches to decrease this form of violence is to assess risk with battered women and male perpetrators of domestic violence. Clinical assessment of risk has been recommended and used by domestic violence victim advocates for more than a decade (e.g., Hart, 1988). Many professionals, including those in law enforcement, victim services, and health care are now looking for actuarial methods for risk assessment. The term *actuarial methods* is generally applied to instrumentation with fixed and explicit formulas for assignment of risk categories and decision making (Grove & Meehl, 1996).

Because of the low base rate of intimate partner homicide and the ethical necessity in intervening in the most obviously dangerous cases, we will never be able to predict intimate partner homicide (or determine predictive validity of any dangerousness instrument) with certainty (Campbell, 1995; Litwack & Schlesinger, 1998; Mulvey & Lidz, 1995). In the general field of violence, risk assessment is recognized as the appropriate terminology for the enterprise, rather than prediction of violence. There is also recognition of the importance of development of this kind of inquiry, however difficult and uncertain, because of the seriousness of the potential outcomes (loss of human life versus loss of liberty) (Mulvey & Lidz, 1995).

There has been debate as to the merits of actuarial versus clinical assessment of risk of violence. Litwack and Schlesinger (1998) represent those who interpret the state of the science as not yet proving that actuarial methods are always most accurate, while Quinsey et al. (1998) argue that actuarial methods are the only defensible approach. A dichotomy is probably oversimplistic, because the best approach is to gather as much information (clinical and instrumentation) from as many sources as possible in the time and circumstances allotted for an assessment (Litwack et al., 1993; Litwack & Schlesinger, 1999; Monahan, 1996; Mulvey & Lidz, 1995). The degree of actuarial assessment possible also depends on the development of the science in the specific area of violence and type of perpetrator involved. In Quinsey's major area of assessment, sexual assault perpetrators, there is both time, instrumentation (phallometric assessment), and actuarial science development, to conduct the kind of composite evaluation that best predicts reoffending (Quinsey et al., 1998). In the areas in which the most research has been done in assessing the risk of future violence (sexual assault and risk of the diagnosed mentally ill committing community violence), there is no clear applicability to intimate partner homicide risk. Sexual assault perpetrators and batterers have not been compared and it is unclear how much of a risk psychopathology is for perpetration of domestic violence in general or intimate partner homicide specifically.

The Psychopathy Checklist Revised (PCL-R) is well correlated with assault recidivism but has not been used with battering populations (Hare, 1991). The major program of research that has investigated perpetrator psychopathology has used the MCMI-II instrument (Dutton, 1995, 1995a) and found borderline personality organization (and PTSD symptoms from childhood abuse) to be a common pattern among batterers. However, most studies have not found consistent patterns of psychopathology among batterers, leading several researchers to propose typologies of batterers with differential patterns of mental illness (e.g., Holtzworth-Munroe & Stuart, 1994).

The development of specific instruments to assess risk in the domestic violence field is relatively new. Several instruments have been developed to assess battered women's risk of homicide and perpetrators' risk of reoffending to address the need in the criminal justice, health, and advocacy systems. The majority of these instruments are designed to be used with perpetrators to evaluate the risk of recidivism for the criminal justice system, but several were designed to assess risk of intimate homicide. Most are designed to be used as actuarial methods, but do not yet have sufficient psychometric data support to be used as the sole determinant of decision making. At this point in development they should be used as supplements to clinical judgment. The next section will briefly describe these instruments and the state of their development.

Recidivism and Lethality Risk Domestic Violence Instruments

Roehl and Guertin (1998) have compiled an excellent overview of instruments designed to assess dangerousness in domestic violence situations. Ten instruments were identified and reviewed: Danger Assessment (DA); Domestic Violence Inventory (DVI); Domestic Violence Risk Assessment Form; Domestic Violence Screening Instrument (DVSI); Kingston Screening Instrument for Domestic Violence (K-SID); Mosaic-20; Lethality Checklist and Physical Abuse Scale; Pre-Sentence Investigation (PSI) Domestic Violence Supplement; Risk Assessment and Lethality Assessment; and the Spousal Assault Risk Assessment (SARA). In addition to those reviewed by Roehl and Guertin, the Navy Risk Assessment is also designed to be an actuarial assessment but is not yet evaluated.

Three additional clinical domestic violence risk factor lists are examples of those widely used in the field in various settings, which have little or no psychometric data to support them and are not involved in any ongoing studies. Hart's (1988) clinical domestic homicide risk factor list has been widely used as the basis for safety planning in shelters and other victim service settings, whereas Sonkin's (1985) instrument was the first published and developed for use in batterer treatment settings. The Delaware State Police Domestic Violence Assessment, which is an adaptation of the Danger Assessment, was developed as a clinical instrument for police.

The DA and Mosaic-20 were specifically designed to assess risk of homicide for primary use with victims as reporters, while the other instruments were designed to identify risk of reoffending in spousal assault cases. Three of the instruments (Domestic Violence Risk Assessment Form, Lethality Checklist and Physical Abuse Scale, and Risk Assessment and Lethality Assessment) have separate lethality risk factors and reassault or abuse-related factors. The distinction between lethality and reassault or reoffending is important in terms of what risk factors are identified, usage of the instrument, and its validation. For instance, substance abuse is more of a risk factor in domestic assault than in domestic homicide and perpetrator depression more a risk factor in intimate partner femicide (because of the large proportion of homicide-suicides) than in intimate partner homicide or in domestic violence reoffending. Child abuse victimization or witnessing domestic violence in childhood are well documented as risk factors for intimate partner abuse perpetration and therefore are presumed to be risk factors for reassault (Straus & Gelles, 1990). However, neither has been implicated in intimate partner lethality.

Another distinction between the two types of instruments is that the lethality assessments were designed to be used primarily with victims from service agencies rather than in law enforcement settings. Ease of administration and brevity are extremely important in these settings. In contrast, risk of reassault instruments were developed for use in the criminal justice (or military) system for sentencing, probation, bail, and treatment-type decisions. In these settings more actuarial evaluations are feasible and important to conduct, many sources of data can be obtained, and the perpetrator is the primary object of evaluation rather than the relationship characteristics.

Both types of instruments are important and may involve different factors assessed and different approaches to assessment. In evaluating the relative value of the different instruments, their purpose must be kept in mind. In terms of validity, it is far more difficult to assess predictive validity of the lethality assessment instruments because of the even lower base rate of domestic homicide than the already low incidence of domestic reassault.

Published data on any of the instruments are meager and independent evaluations practically nonexistent (Roehl & Guertin, 1998). Many of the instruments are based on risk factor lists with no empirical research, but the Mosaic-20 (Trone, 1999), the DA (Campbell, 1992; Campbell, 1995), the Domestic Violence Risk Assessment Form, and the K-SID (Straus et al., 1990) were based on independent case evaluations or research, the first two of homicide cases and the last two of domestic violence cases. According to Roehl and Guertin (1998) and personal communication with authors, the SARA (Kropp, Hart, Webster, & Eaves, 1995; Kropp & Hart, in press), K-SID (Gelles, 1998), DVSI (Williams, 1999, personal communication), PSI (Roehl, 1998), and DA (Campbell, 1992; Campbell, 1995) are currently part of ongoing validation studies with some preliminary data having been presented at conferences (Gelles, 1998; Kropp, 1998; Kropp & Hart, in press). Studies of Mosaic-20 and the Navy Risk Assessment are also planned. Psychometric data on the DA (Campbell, 1995) have been published, and some independent research using the instrument has been conducted, which will be reviewed below.

SARA, K-SID, and DA Instruments

Because the SARA, DA, and K-SID have the most easily available psychometric data and represent three different approaches to dangerousness risk in intimate partner violence, they will be reviewed in more detail. Table 8.1 presents an overview of the three instruments. The DA

	Kingston Screening Instrument for Domestic Violence (K-SID) (Gelles, 1998)	Spousal Assault Risk Assessment (SARA) (Kropp et al., 1995; Kropp & Hart, in press)	Danger Assessment (DA) (Campbell, 1986, 1995)
Instruments			
Description	12 items each with 3 categories. Shaded categories = 1 point; 2 areas considered high risk regardless of point total. Severity & Injury Index & Poverty Chart	20 items 3-point scale (0-absent, 1-subthreshold, 2-present); critical items (evaluator choice) 0-absent, 1-present. Summary risk rating toward partner of low, moderate, or high	15 item Yes/No checklist plus Calendar Assessment of frequency and severity of past-year incidents
Type of risk	Reoffending	Reassault	Lethality
Scoring	Low 0–3, moderate 4–6, high 7–10, or very high categories (previous DV arrest &/or violation of protective order)	3 continuous scores (Total scores—sum of rating on items 0–40; number of factors present 0–20; number of critical items 0–20) & summary risk rating 0–3	Summative, no cutoff, victim and advocate collaborative interpretation
Intended system use	Criminal justice	Criminal justice	Health care, victim advocacy
Sources of information	Perpetrator assessment plus collateral criminal justice information.	As many as possible–perpetrator assessment, victim interview, collateral criminal justice records, standardized instruments (Personality Assessment Inventory, Hare Psychopathy Checklist)	Victim
Psychometric data	6 samples ($N = 2,681$) internal consistency = .62–.83; inter-rater reliability = .18–.38 on critical items; .63–.85 on other 3 scores. Discriminant group support for spousal assaulters vs. other offenders; not as much for spousal reassaulters vs. non; mixed construct validity support		10 samples ($N = 2,251$); internal consistency reliability (alpha) = .60–.86; test-retest = .60–.86; construct validity—convergent w/CTS & ISA r = .55–.75 and discriminant group support

is a measure designed to assist battered women in the assessment of their own risk of femicide, while the purpose of the K-SID and SARA is to assess risk of reoffending in the criminal justice system. The SARA is described as an instrumental means of coding professional judgment (Kropp & Hart, in press), while the K-SID is explicitly designed as an actuarial assessment.

The SARA is currently being used widely in Canada and Vermont for probation, supervision and treatment decisions, and as part of a validation study of the DVSI and the SARA in Colorado (Kropp & Hart, in press; Roehl & Guertin, 1998; Williams, 1999). It was developed in the early 1990s and is described as an assessment guide based on a thorough literature review rather than an actuarial instrument or psychological test (Kropp et al., 1995). It has four different scoring approaches, including a 0–2 assessment as well as absolute presence of each of 20 risk factors (with space for the evaluator to add other "considerations" that can also be rated or counted). In addition, there is a score consisting of the evaluator's judgment of how many of the risk factors (including the additional considerations) are "critical" and an independent overall summary risk rating (to the partner and to others). The manual urges the evaluator to use as many sources of information as possible in filling out the SARA, including both victim and perpetrator interviews, additional criminal justice records, and standardized instruments, especially the Hare Psychopathy Checklist (Hare, 1991).

In six samples (N = 2,681), the SARA has shown good internal consistency (alpha = .62–.83) and item homogeneity (Kropp & Hart, in press). The present data on the SARA are from Canada, resulting in a primarily (80%) white population. In a large sample (N = 1,010) of inmates, the SARA discriminated well between those with a spousal assault history and those without. However, in a smaller study (N = 102) of recidivist versus nonrecidivist spouse assaulters, the number of critical items score discriminated best between the two groups, and the spousal assault risk factor items were more discriminatory than the general violence items. In the other evaluation of construct validity, again with a relatively small sample (N = 86), the general violence items of the SARA had moderate (.24–.53) correlations in expected directions with other violence risk instruments. The SARA scores based on the risk factors had the strongest correlations, whereas many of the violence risk instruments did not correlate with the spousal assault items or the more clinical assessments of the SARA. Part of the explanation for these findings is that many spouse assaulters are not necessarily generally violent (Holtzworth-Munroe & Stuart, 1994). The K-SID was developed from the extensive program of research of Richard Gelles (Straus & Gelles, 1990) as a screening instrument. It consists of 10 risk markers for reassault with three categories of response for each item. Certain categories count points that are added for classification into low (0–3), moderate (4–6), high (7–10), and very high risk of reoffending. The presence of either of two additional risk factors (previous domestic violence arrest and previous violation of a temporary or permanent protective order) puts the perpetrator into the very high-risk category without considering the score on the rest of the instrument. There is also a poverty chart to determine the answer to the income risk factor, a formula for determining "binge" alcohol use, and a severity and injury chart that does not factor into the score for risk classification. Gelles (1998) has reported data from several ongoing studies indicating support for internal consistency and discriminant group validity. The K-SID is being used throughout Connecticut as a basis for criminal justice decisions including probation, incarceration, and protective order conditions.

Danger Assessment

The Danger Assessment (DA) was originally developed by Jacquelyn Campbell (1986) with consultation and content validity support from battered women, shelter workers, law enforcement officials, and other clinical experts on battering. The initial items on the Danger Assessment instrument were developed from retrospective research studies of intimate partner homicide or serious injury (Campbell, 1981; Browne, 1987; Berk et al., 1983; Fagan et al., 1983).

The first portion of the measure assesses severity and frequency of battering by presenting the woman with a calendar of the past year. The woman is asked to mark the approximate days when physically abusive incidents occurred, and to rank the severity of the incident on a 1 to 5 (1 = slap, pushing, no injuries and/or lasting pain through 5 = use of weapon, wounds from weapon) scale. The calendar portion was conceptualized as a way to raise the consciousness of the woman and reduce the denial and minimization of the abuse, especially since using a calendar increases accurate recall in other situations (Campbell, 1995; Ferraro & Johnson, 1983). In the original scale development, 38% of women who initially reported no increase in severity and frequency, changed their response to "yes" after filling out the calendar (Campbell, 1986, 1995).

The second part of the DA is a 15-item yes/no response format of risk factors associated with intimate partner homicide. Both portions of the instrument take approximately 20 minutes to complete. The woman can complete the instrument by herself with professionals from the health care, criminal justice, or victim advocate systems assisting in the interpretation within the context of her situation. The DA is scored by counting the "yes" responses with no classification or cutoff score; a higher number indicates that more of the risk factors for femicide are present in the relationship. The DA has published data on construct validity but no predictive validity information (Campbell, 1995).

The initial studies using the DA instrument are described in detail elsewhere (Campbell, 1986, 1995). In the 10 research studies in which the DA was used, reliability ranged from 0.60 to 0.86 (Campbell, 1986; Campbell, 1995; McFarlane et al., 1992; Parker, 1994; McFarlane et al., 1996; McFarlane et al., 1998). In two studies in which test-retest reliability was assessed, it ranged from 0.89 to 0.94 (Stuart & Campbell, 1989; Campbell, 1994). All samples include a substantial portion of minority women (primarily African American) and women from a variety of settings. Internal consistency reliability estimates did not vary for African-American, Latino, and White women (Campbell, 1995). Construct validity was supported by significant differences in mean scores among contrasting groups of women. The lowest mean score was found in the nonabused sample, with the highest score among the sample of women in the emergency department (Campbell, 1995).

Convergent construct validity has been supported in the majority of the studies with moderate to strong correlations with instruments measuring severity and frequency of domestic violence, including the Index of Spouse Abuse, the Conflict Tactics Scale, and injury from abuse (Campbell, 1995). Since the last overall description, at least five additional independent studies have been conducted with additional reliability support (internal consistency of .69–.78) (Table 8.2). In further support of construct validity, the DA had significant correlations (.56–.62) as expected with instruments measuring symptoms of post-traumatic stress disorder (PTSD) (Woods, in press; Silva et al., 1997) and severity and frequency of domestic violence (.75) (McFarlane et al., 1998) in the newly reported studies. In addition, in both of the preced-

Table 8.2. Recent Danger Assessment Psychometric Data

Studies	Diaz (unpublished data)	Woods (in press)	Silva et al. (1997)	Parker et al. (1994)	McFarlane et al. (1998)
N	77 abused women	160 women 53 abused 55 post-abuse 52 nonabused	131 abused women	1,203 pregnant women	199 pregnant abused women
Setting	DV community center	Community and shelter	Primary care	Prenatal care	Prenatal care
Ethnicity	100% Mexican (Mexico City)	64% Anglo 34% African American 1% Hispanic 1% Native American	34% African American 64% White 1% Latino 1% Native American	34.4% African American 34.2% Latino 31.3% White	48.6% African American 24.1% Latino 24.1% White
Reliability	alpha = .69	alpha = .78	alpha = .72	alpha = .84	alpha = .72
Validity		Construct – SCL-PTSD* $r = .65$; IES** $r = .62$		Construct validity ISA*** $r = .75$	Construct validity ISA-P*** $r = .75$
Mean score on DA	6.76	8.04 abused 2.31 post-abuse .75 nonabused			5.6 abused during pregnancy 2.92 nonabused during pregnancy

* SCL-90 scored for PTSD.

** Impact of Events Scale.

*** ISA-P Index of Spouse Abuse—Physical (ISA—Index of Spouse Abuse).

ing studies, the DA successfully discriminated between groups of abused and nonabused women.

The DA instrument has been utilized in a variety of settings including battered women's shelters and health care settings. The criminal justice system also is using the DA as a means of increasing victim safety, deterring perpetrators, and using limited resources effectively. In several jurisdictions, the DA has become a requirement for presentencing investigations to develop appropriate sentences and probation conditions for intimate partner violence offenders in at least one jurisdiction (Roehl & Guertin, 1998). The New Castle, Delaware, State Police also use a revised version of the DA to evaluate perpetrator dangerousness.

Campbell and colleagues (1996) are currently conducting a multisite case control study to investigate the relative risk of factors from the DA instrument along with other factors suggested from clinical experience and other research. This study will provide further validity data for the DA and indicate appropriate weighting of the items. One of the aims of this research is to produce a "user-friendly" short list of risk factors for intimate femicide which can be self- or clinician administered and used as a basis for safety planning with women in a variety of medical and social service settings (Campbell, 1996). Prospective studies are also needed, not only to assess predictive validity (within the limitations of safety concerns for study participants) but also to determine long-term effects of the DA on victim insights and actions.

Because the purposes and origins of the three instruments reviewed in depth differ, it is reasonable that they contain several different but many overlapping risk factors. The SARA overlaps the most with the other two instruments while the K-SID and DA have few risk factors in common. All three have promising initial psychometric data to support them, but their development is in very early stages.

Conclusion

Continued efforts to develop a valid and comprehensive list of risk factors for intimate partner homicide are necessary. The field is seeking more accurate assessment of potential lethality in domestic violence relationships than the instruments available can provide. Clinicians have been held accountable for not adequately predicting and protecting patients from potential danger (Hart, 1988; Litwack & Schlesinger, 1999; Mulvey & Lidz, 1995). Legal experts generally agree that if a patient is a serious threat to someone else, the therapist or health care provider must warn the potential victim (Campbell, 1994). Most domestic violence experts also assert a responsibility to conduct a separate assessment of the potential risk for homicide for victims as a basis for safety planning (Hart, 1988). It is recommended that some instrument be used to augment overall clinical judgment to make sure that the risk factors specific to intimate partner homicide are assessed. The subsequent safety planning discussion should include strategies for having essential documents, safe destinations, appropriate use of protective (restraining) orders and calls to the police, communication with batterer treatment clinicians, money available for quick exits, helping children plan for an emergency, and disarming a gun if present in the home (Campbell, 1995). Safety planning with victims represents an essential intervention in dangerous domestic violence relationships.

Actuarial methods for risk assessment in intimate partner violence situations are in their infancy, and well-validated instrumentation is still several years away. Several instruments have been developed, but as yet published psychometric data are sparse and predictive validity studies nonexistent on any of the instruments. However, several studies are underway that will allow more accurate assessment within the next 5 years. Until that time, sophisticated clinical judgment informed by a knowledge of the particular dynamics of intimate partner violence in general and intimate partner homicide specifically is needed. The instruments that have been developed to assess risk of intimate partner homicide and reassault, although early in their development in terms of statistical evaluation, can provide some of the necessary framework for informed clinical judgment.

REFERENCES

Arbuckle, J., Olson, L., Howard, M., Brillman, J., Ancti, C., & Sklar, D. (1996). Safe at home? Domestic violence and other homicides among women in Mexico. *Annals of Emergency Medicine, 27*(2), 210–215.

Bachman, R., & Saltzman, L. E. (1995). *Violence against women: Estimates from the redesigned survey.* Washington, DC: U.S. Department of Justice.

Bailey, J. E., Kellermann, A. L., Somes, G. W., Banton, J. G., Rivara, F. P., & Rushford, N. P. (1997). Risk factors for violent death of women in the home. *Archives of Internal Medicine, 157,* 777–782.

Berk, R. A., Berk, S., Loseke, D. R., & Rauma, D. (1983). Mutual combat and other family violence myths. In D. Finkelhor, R. J. Gelles, G. T. Hotaling, & M. A. Straus (Eds.), *The dark side of families* (pp. 197–212). Beverly Hills, CA: Sage.

Block, C. R., & Christakos, A. (1995). Intimate partner homicide in Chicago over 29 years. *Crime and Delinquency, 41*(4), 406–526.

Bowman, P. J. (1993). The impact of economic marginality among African American husbands and fathers. In H. McAdoo (Ed.), *Family ethnicity: Strength in diversity* (pp. 120–140).

Browne, A. (1987). *Battered women who kill.* New York: Free Press.

Browne, A., Williams, K. R., & Dutton, D. C. (1998). Homicide between intimate partners. In M. D. Smith & M. Zahn (Eds.), *Homicide: A sourcebook of social research* (pp. 149–164). Thousand Oaks, CA: Sage.

Bureau of Justice (1998). *Violence between intimates: Analysis of data on crimes by current or former spouses, boyfriends, and girlfriends.* Washington DC: National Institute of Justice.

Buteau, J., Lesage, A. D., & Kiely, M. C. (1993). Homicide followed by suicide: A Quebec case series, 1988–1990. *Canadian Journal of Psychiatry, 38*(8), 552–556.

Campbell, J. C. (1981). Misogyny and homicide of women. *Advances in Nursing Science, 3*(2), 67–85.

Campbell, J. C. (1986). Assessment of risk of homicide for battered women. *Advances in Nursing Science, 8*(4), 36–51.

Campbell, J. C. (1992). "If I can't have you, no one can": Power and control in homicide of female partners. In J. Radford & D.E.H. Russell (Eds.), *Femicide: The politics of woman killing* (pp. 99–113). New York: Twayne.

Campbell, J. C. (1994). Domestic homicide: Risk assessment and professional duty to warn. *Maryland Medical Journal, 43*(10), 885–889.

Campbell, J. C. (1995). Prediction of homicide of and by battered women. In J. C. Campbell (Ed.), *Assessing the risk of dangerousness: Potential for further violence of sexual offenders, batterers, and child abusers* (pp. 93–113). Newbury Park, CA: Sage.

Campbell, J. C. (1996). *Risk factors for homicide in violent intimate relationships.* Washington, DC: National Institute for Health Funded Research. #5R01 DA11156–02.

Campbell, J. C., Soeken, K., McFarlane, J., & Parker, B. (1998). Risk factors for femicide among pregnant and nonpregnant battered women. In J. C. Campbell (Ed.), *Empowering survivors of abuse: Health care for battered women and their children* (pp. 90–97). Thousand Oaks, CA: Sage.

Crawford, M., & Gartner, R. (1992). *Woman killing: Intimate femicide in Ontario: 1974–1990.* Ontario, Canada: Women We Honor Action Committee.

Daly, M., & Wilson, M. (1988). *Homicide.* Hawthorne, NY: Aldine de Gruyter.

Daly, M., & Wilson, M. (1998). An evolutionary psychological perspective on homicide. In M. D. Smith & M. Zahn (Eds.), *Homicide: A sourcebook of social research* (pp. 58–71). Thousand Oaks, CA: Sage.

Daly, M., Wiseman, K. A., & Wilson, M. (1997). Women with children sired by previous partners incur excess risk of uxoricide. *Homicide Studies, 1*(1), 61–71.

Dawson, R., & Gartner, R. (1998). Differences in the characteristics of intimate femicides: The role of relationship state and relationship status. *Homicide Studies, 2,* 378–399.

Dutton, D. G. (1995). *The domestic assault of women.* Vancouver: UBC Press.

Dutton, D. G. (1995a). Trauma symptoms and PTSD-like profiles in perpetrators of intimate abuse. *Journal of Traumatic Stress, 8*(2), 299–316.

Easteal, P. W. (1993). *Killing the beloved*. Canberra: Australian Institute of Criminology.

Edwards, S. M. (1985). A sociolegal evaluation of gender ideologies in domestic assault and spousal homicide. *Victimology, 10*, 186–205.

Fagan, J., Stewart, D. E., & Hansen, K. (1983). Violent men or violent husbands? Background factors and situational correlates. In R. J. Gelles, G. Hotaling, M. A. Straus, & D. Finkelhor (Eds.), *The dark side of families* (pp. 49–68). Beverly Hills, CA: Sage.

Ferraro, K. J., & Johnson, J. M. (1983). How women experience battering: The process of victimization. *Social Problems, 30*, 325–339.

Gartner, R. (1990). The victims of homicide: A temporal and cross national comparison. *American Sociological Review, 55*, 92–106.

Gelles, R. (1998, October). *Lethality and risk assessment for family violence cases.* Paper presented at the 4th International Conference on Children Exposed to Family Violence, San Diego, CA.

Grove, W. M., & Meehl, P. E. (1996). Comparative efficiency of informal (subjective, impressionistic) and formal (mechanical, algorithmic) prediction procedures: The clinical-statistical controversy. *Psychology, Public Policy, and Law, 2*, 293–323.

Hall-Smith, P., Moracco, K. E., & Butts, J. (1998). Partner homicide in context. *Homicide Studies, 2*(4), 400–421.

Hare, R. D. (1991). *Manual for the Hare Psychopathy Checklist-Revised (PCL-R)*. Toronto: Multi-Health Systems.

Hart, B. (1988). Beyond the "duty to warn": A therapist's "duty to protect" battered women and children. In K. Yllo & M. Bogard (Eds.), *Feminist perspectives on wife abuse* (pp. 234–248). Newbury Park: Sage.

Holtzworth-Munroe, A., & Stuart, G. L. (1994). Typologies of male batterers: Three subtypes and the differences among them. *Psychological Bulletin, 116*(3), 476–497.

Howard, M. (1986). Husband-wife homicide: An essay from a family law perspective. *Law and Contemporary Problems, 49*(1), 63–88.

Jaynes, G. D., & Williams, R. M. (1989). *A common destiny: Blacks and American society*. Washington, DC: National Academy Press.

Kellerman, A. L., & Mercy, J. A. (1992). Men, women and murder: Gender-specific differences in rates of fatal violence and victimization. *Journal of Trauma, 33*(1), 1–5.

Kellerman, A. L., Rivara, F. P., & Rushforth, N. B. (1993). Gun ownership as a risk factor for homicide in the home. *New England Journal of Medicine, 329*, 1084–1091.

Kropp, P. R. (1998, October). *Risk Assessment and Monitoring in Domestic Violence Cases: Recent Research and Practice*. Paper presented at the 4th International Conference on Children Exposed to Family Violence, San Diego, CA.

Kropp, P. R., & Hart, S. D. (in press). The Spousal Assault Risk Assessment Guide (SARA): Reliability and Validity in Adult Male Offenders. *Journal of Psychological Measurement*.

Kropp, P. R., Hart, S. D., Webster, C. D., & Eaves, D. (1995). *Manual for the Spousal Assault Risk Assessment Guide (2nd ed.)*. Vancouver, B.C.: The British Columbia Institute Against Family Violence.

LaFree, G. (1998). A summary and review of cross-national comparative studies of homicide. In M. D. Smith & M. Zahn (Eds.), *Homicide: A sourcebook of social research* (pp. 125–148). Thousand Oaks, CA: Sage.

Langen, P. A., & Dawson, J. M. (1995). *Spouse murder defendants in large urban counties.* Washington, DC: Bureau of Justice Statistics.

Litwack, T. R., Kirschner, S. M., & Wack, R. C. (1993). The assessment of dangerousness and predictions of violence: Recent research and future prospects. *Psychiatric Quarterly, 64,* 245–273.

Litwack, T. R., & Schlesinger, L. B. (1999). Dangerousness risk assessments: Research, legal, and clinical considerations. In A. Hess & I. Weiner (Eds.), *The handbook of forensic psychology* (pp. 171–217). New York: Wiley.

McFarlane, J., Parker, B., Soeken, K., & Bullock, L. (1992). Assessing for abuse during pregnancy: Severity and frequency of injuries and associated entry into prenatal care. *Journal of the American Medical Association, 267,* 2370–2372.

McFarlane, J., Soeken, K., Campbell, J. C., Parker, B., Reel, S., & Silva, C. (1998). Severity of abuse to pregnant women and associated gun access of the perpetrator. *Public Health Nursing, 15,* 201–206.

Mercy, J. A., & Saltzman, L. E. (1989). Fatal violence among spouses in the United States 1976–85. *American Journal of Public Health, 79,* 595–599.

Monahan, J. (1996). Violence prediction: The past twenty years and the next twenty years. *Criminal Justice and Behavior, 23*(1), 107–120.

Monahan, J., & Steadman, H. J. (Eds.) (1994). *Violence and mental disorder: Developments in risk assessment.* Chicago: University of Chicago Press.

Moracco, K. E., Runyan, C. W., & Butts, J. (1998). Femicide in North Carolina. *Homicide Studies, 2,* 422–446.

Morton, E., Rynyan, C. W., Moracco, K. E., & Butts, J. (1998). Partner homicide victims: A population based study in North Carolina, 1988–1992. *Violence and Victims, 13*(2), 91–106.

Mulvey, E. P., & Lidz, C. W. (1995). Conditional prediction: A model for research on dangerousness to others in a new era. *International Journal of Law and Psychiatry, 18,* 129–143

Mushanga, T. M. (1978). Wife victimization in East and Central Africa. *Victimology, 2,* 46–59.

National Institute of Justice. (1997). *A study of homicide in eight US cities: An NIJ intramural research project.* Washington, DC: U.S. Department of Justice.

Parker, B., McFarlane, J., & Soeken, K. (1994). Abuse during pregnancy: Effects on maternal complications and birthweight in adult and teenage women. *Obstetrics and Gynecology, 84,* 323–328.

Quinsey, V., Harris, G. T., Rice, M. E., & Cormier, C. (1998). *Violent offenders: Appraising and managing risk.* Washington, DC: American Psychological Association.

Quinsey, V., & Maguire, A. (1986). Maximum security psychiatric patients: Actuarial and clinical predictors of dangerousness. *Journal of Interpersonal Violence, 1*(2), 143–171.

Roehl, J., & Guertin, K. (1998). *Current use of dangerousness assessments in sentencing domestic violence offenders.* Pacific Grove, CA: State Justice Institute.

Rosenfeld, R. (1997). Changing relationships between men and women. A note on the decline of intimate partner homicide. *Homicide Studies, 1*(1), 72–83.

Saltzman, L. E., Mercy, J. A., O'Carroll, P. W., Rosenberg, M. L., & Rhodes, P. H. (1992). Weapon involvement and injury outcomes in family and intimate assaults. *Journal of American Medical Association, 267*(22), 43–47.

Silva, C., McFarlane, J., Soeken, K., Parker, B., & Reel, S. (1997). Symptoms of post-traumatic stress disorder in abused women in a primary care setting. *Journal of Women's Health, 6*(5), 543–552.

Smith, M. N., & Brewer, V. E. (1990). Female status and the "Gender Gap" in U.S. homicide victimization. *Violence Against Women, 1*(4), 339–350.

Smith, P. H., Moracco, K. E., & Butts, J. (1998). Partner homicide in context: A population based perspective. *Homicide Studies, 2,* 400–421.

Sonkin, D. J., Martin, D., & Walker, L. E. (1985). *The male batterer: A treatment approach.* New York: Springer.

Stack, S. (1997). Homicide followed by suicide: An analysis of Chicago data. *Criminology, 35*(3), 435–453.

Straus, M. A. (1979). Measuring intrafamily conflict and violence: The conflict tactics scales. *Journal of Marriage and the Family, 41,* 75–88.

Straus, M. A., & Gelles, R. J. (1990). *Physical violence in American families: Risk factors and adaptations to family violence in 8,145 families.* New Brunswick, NJ: Transaction Publishers.

Stuart, E., & Campbell, J. C. (1989). Assessment of patterns of dangerousness with battered women. *Issues in Mental Health Nursing, 10,* 245–260.

Trone, J. (1999). *Calculating intimate danger: MOSAIC and emerging practice of risk assessment.* New York: Vera Institute of Justice.

Walker, L. E. (1984). *The battered woman syndrome.* New York: Springer.

Weiner, N. A., Zahn, M. A., & Sagi, R. J. (1990). *Violence: Patterns, causes, public policy.* San Diego, CA Harcourt.

Wilson, M., & Daly, M. (1993). Spousal homicide risk and estrangement. *Violence and Victims, 8* (1), 3–15.

Wilson, M., Johnson, H., & Daly, M. (1995). Lethal and nonlethal violence against wives. *Canadian Journal of Criminology, 37,* 331–362.

Wilt, S. A., Illman, S. M., & Brodyfield, M (1995). *Female homicide victims in New York City.* New York: New York City Dept of Health.

Wolfgang, M. E. (1958). *Patterns in criminal homicide.* Philadelphia, PA: University of Pennsylvania Press.

Woods, S. J. (in press). Normative beliefs regarding the maintenance of intimate relationships among abused and non-abused women. *Journal of Interpersonal Violence.*

Zawitz, M. W. (1994). *Violence between intimates.* Washington, DC: Bureau of Justice Statistics.

9. Parents at Risk of Filicide

MAUREEN MARKS

Introduction

Homicide is a major contributor to child mortality. Moreover, official records of rates of child homicide are almost certainly underestimates. Some infant homicides are never discovered, especially those killed soon after delivery, and others are never recorded as such. For example, it is generally considered that at least 2% to 10% of registered cot deaths are probably homicides (Knowledon, Keeling, & Nicholl, 1985; Emery, 1985) and a more recent study suggests the proportion may be even greater (Wolkind, Taylor, Waite, Dalton, & Emery, 1993).

When a child becomes the victim of homicide, a parent is usually the perpetrator. In this chapter I will summarize what is known about the characteristics of children who have been killed and of the parents who killed them and what this may tell us about the underlying causes of such tragedies.

One of the major problems in understanding parental filicide is that most of the research into the subject has been obtained from either official statistics or from highly selective case samples; for example, parents referred to psychiatric or forensic services, or from anecdotal literature reports. The recording of official statistics tends to be unreliable and the range of data recorded limited, and because different countries tend to record information in different ways international comparisons are difficult. There are also cultural differences in the extent to which child homicides in themselves are consistently recorded. Although the data from selected samples tend to be more reliable and informative, the conclusions that can be drawn about child homicides in general from such samples are of limited value. They may give a biased, even erroneous picture of the typical homicidal parent. This means that results from most studies need to be interpreted with caution.

Characteristics of Victims

Age of Victim

The most consistently reproduced finding, across studies, both within and between Western cultures is that there are age-related differences in the circumstances surrounding the homicide of children. This is true in the United Kingdom (d'Orban, 1979; Marks & Kumar, 1993; Marks & Kumar, 1996) and also in the United States (Jason, Gilliland, & Tyler, 1983; Christoffel, 1989; Crittenden & Craig, 1990), in Canada (Daly & Wilson, 1988), in Australia (Wilkey, Pearn, Petrie, & Nixon, 1982), and in Japan (Shiono, Maya, Tabata Fujiwara, Azumi, & Morita, 1986). Infants under a year are at greatest risk. Figure 9.1 shows rates for different ages in England and Wales during 1987–1996: For infants under 1 year the risk is four times that of the general population; for toddlers (children aged between 1 and under 5 years) the risk is no different from the rest of the population; older children (those aged between 5 and 15) are at lowest risk.

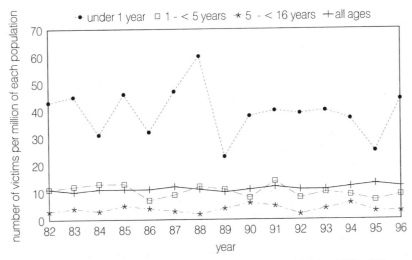

Figure 9.1. Homicide rate by age of victim, England and Wales 1982–1996. Offenses currently recorded: Criminal Statistics 1990–1996.

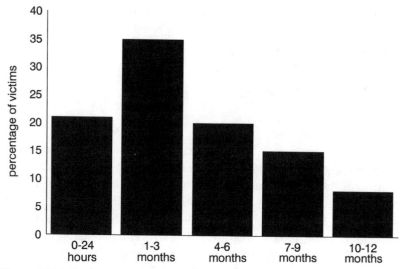

Figure 9.2. Infant homicide in England and Wales 1982–1988. Age of victims (*n*= 214) (From Marks & Kumar, 1993).

For children under a year old, the younger the infant the greater the risk. The data presented in Figure 9.2 come from UK Home Office records of all children under 1 who were the victims of homicide in England and Wales during 1982–1988 and indicate the number of children who were victims according to their age. Newly delivered infants were at greatest risk. Children under 6 months old were at greater risk than those over 6 months. The same pattern of results was also found for infants who were the victims of homicide in Scotland during 1978–1993 (see Figure 9.3).

Sex of Victim

The findings concerning sex differences in rates of child homicides are inconsistent. In our British studies, we found that infants killed within 24 hours of delivery were equally likely to be male or female but that for children aged between 1 day and 1 year, boy babies were over-represented, especially during the first 6 months of life when rates of homicide are at their highest. These effects of sex of infant were observed in two separate studies, one of infant homicides in England and Wales (RR = 1.8) and the other in Scotland (RR = 1.6). Unfortunately most studies do not differentiate between age groups

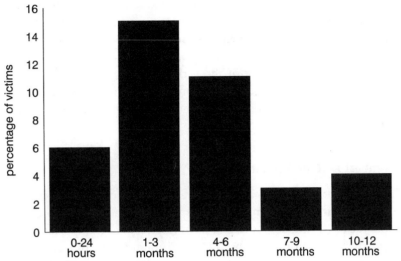

Figure 9.3. Infant homicide in Scotland 1978–1993. Age of victims ($n = 43$) (From Marks & Kumar, 1996).

when sex effects are examined, and this may account for the inconsistencies reported. However, one U.S. study (Jason et al., 1983) also found that male infant homicides predominated over female ones and a comparison of intentional and unintentional infant (< 1 year old) injury deaths in Washington State (Cummings & Mueller, 1994) found that male infants were at increased risk (RR = 1.8) of intentional injury death compared to females. This effect may be related to the increased physical vulnerability of male infants compared to female ones or it may be a consequence of parental attributions about the infant's behavior, for example that male infants are perceived as more aggressive and requiring harsher discipline than female children (Marks, 1996).

Obstetric Risk Factors

D'Orban (1979) reported that in a subgroup of women admitted to prison on remand for the killing or attempted murder of their child, nearly half of the infants had suffered from ill health at the time of the offense (e.g., had been premature, suffered from retarded development, or had respiratory infections). Cummings and Mueller (1994) found that no prenatal care, low birthweight (<2500 gm), and having a younger mother were all associated with increased risk of death from intentional injury, irrespective of who had killed the infant. In contrast, Crittenden and Craig (1990) were able to examine low birthweight, handicapping conditions, birth trauma, or twin status and reported that in their series only 14% of murdered children (and only two neonates) experienced any of these risk factors, whereas 85% of the sample experienced social risk (unmarried mother or birth order greater than two). Neither of these latter factors were found to be a function of the age of the child killed.

Parents at Risk of Neonaticide

The characteristics and causes of the homicide of infants within 24 hours of their birth (neonaticide) are very different from those of the homicide of children older than a day, which makes it important to distinguish them from the homicide of infants or older children. Unfortunately, few official records and epidemiological studies do so and those that do tend to use different definitions of what constitutes a neonate (e.g., up to 1 week or up to 1 month old). This makes the interpretation of the data obtained difficult and comparisons between studies impossible. Figure 9.4 shows the rate of homicides for children aged between 1 day and 4 weeks old, in England and Wales during 1982–1988; note the disproportionately high rate on the first day, which

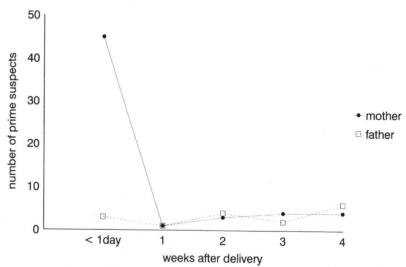

Figure 9.4. Infants killed within 1 month of delivery and prime suspect: England and Wales 1982–1988.

drops dramatically thereafter. These data suggest that Resnick's (1970) distinction of up to 24 hours is a valid one.

Anecdotal reports and case note studies suggest that demographic features of neonaticides may also be different from homicides of infants over a day. For example, compared to parents who kill older infants, neonaticidal mothers are more likely to be young (under 20), single, and often still living at home with parents. The pregnancy is often the first, unintentional, and concealed. The motivation to kill is usually because the child was unwanted (Resnick, 1970).

The infant's death is more likely to have resulted from inaction rather than the violent action that often characterizes the killing of older infants: nearly half die from neglect (Marks & Kumar, 1993). In addition, the mothers are rarely mentally ill (d'Orban, 1979). Mothers who kill their neonates are treated comparatively leniently by the legal system in the United Kingdom. A major proportion are never indicted and those who are usually receive infanticide convictions (Marks & Kumar, 1993).

The most frequent observation about women who commit neonaticide is that the pregnancy had been denied (e.g., Brozovsky & Falit, 1971; Green & Manohar, 1990). In some cases the woman may "know" she is pregnant but to all intents and purposes behaves as if she were not. This state of affairs is usually the consequence of an unconscious belief: That if you don't think about it, the pregnancy will, magically, disappear. Sometimes the woman does not seem to acknowledge (even to herself) that she is pregnant. In either case the woman does not seek medical help and makes no preparation for the delivery. After the child is born and disposed of, the mother returns immediately to her normal daily life.

The denial in these concealed pregnancies is sometimes so powerful that it seems also to influence the perceptions of the pregnant woman, and others as well. This may be related to the fact that the biological manifestations of pregnancy sometimes become attenuated; for example, there may be reduced change in body contour, continuation of menstrual bleeding during pregnancy, or no complaints of pregnancy such as nausea or increased urinary frequency. For example, Brozovsky and Falit (1971) report a neonaticidal mother who, during the pregnancy, had convinced her physician, after a positive pregnancy test and at 5 months, that she was no longer pregnant.

The labors are often fast, the woman thinks she has colic or menstrual pain, may interpret the contractions as a need to defecate, and the delivery itself as a bowel movement. The arrival of the baby is thus experienced as a traumatic shock and puts an end to the denial; the woman is then confronted with the overwhelming fear that made the denial so necessary and effective in the first place. Anxiety of such intensity sometimes leads to ego disorganization, especially when the ego is less than resilient in the first place (which is typical of these women), and in this disorganized or dissociated state the woman kills the child or allows it to die.

A typical case is a 20-year-old single woman who had successfully concealed her pregnancy. She had had a previous pregnancy, which had also been concealed. This first baby had been delivered into a toilet at the parental home, but had been rescued by a family member and subsequently adopted. During her second pregnancy this woman was able to convince not only her workmates, whom she lived with, but also her immediate family whom she saw regularly and who knew of the earlier concealed pregnancy, and even a man with whom she had a sexual relationship in the seventh month of the pregnancy, that she was not pregnant. She "knew" she was pregnant and yet when labor pains started (at term) she thought the pains were caused by something she had eaten. She was alone at the time and the infant was born into the toilet and subsequently died of neglect. The morning of the infant's delivery she returned to work complaining of a heavy period.

The overrepresentation of naive young women in studies of neonaticide may be in part a consequence of their naïveté. It is generally believed that reported rates of neonaticide underestimate true rates, because many neonaticides remain undiscovered. It is likely that more mature, sophisticated women are better able to conceal an unwanted pregnancy and dispose of the newly delivered infant in such a way that it remains undiscovered. For example, Funayama and Sagisaka (1988) report 12 recorded cases of Japanese mothers who had carried out multiple neonaticides (3 or more in each case). Eleven of the women were married, and their ages ranged from 31 to 45 years.

Sakuta and Saito (1981) distinguish between two different kinds of neonaticide, which they describe as the "mabiki" and "anomie" types. Mabiki is a Japanese term that means "thinning out," and is also used to refer to neonaticide when it is used as a form of population control, which was once culturally acceptable in Japan. The mabiki type of neonaticidal mother is typically married, has several children, and does not wish to have more. In contrast, the "anomie" type of mother is characteristically unmarried, this is her first child and the reasons for the infanticide are, for example, "avoiding ill-repute" or "loss of psychological support." It may be that a similar, if less clear-cut distinction also applies to neonaticides that occur in Western countries today.

Paternal neonaticide is rare. Kaye, Borenstein, and Donnelly (1990) review four cases, one of which involved an infant with severe congenital abnormalities; the other three men had severe psychiatric disorders (two schizophrenia, one mental impairment).

Parents at Risk of Filicide

Mothers or Fathers?

Infants aged between 1 day and under 1 year tend to be killed by either parent. In Florida, fathers and mothers are equally likely to be the perpetrator. Jason et al. (1983) analyzed national child (younger than 18 years old) homicide data from the FBI crime reporting system for 1976–1979. They found that mothers killed neonates and that slightly more fathers than mothers killed infants under 1 year. Similarly, in England and Wales (Marks & Kumar, 1993), and in Scotland (Marks & Kumar 1996), slightly more infants are killed by fathers than mothers. In the latter two studies there was no interaction between sex of perpetrator and sex of victim: Fathers and mothers were equally likely to kill boys or girls.

For children aged 1 to less than 5 years, again, the most likely perpetrator is a parent, with mothers and fathers equally likely. However, with increasing age, preschool children are more likely to be killed by someone other than the parent (Jason et al., 1983; Crittenden & Craig, 1990). For example, Crittenden and Craig report that although only 12.5% of infants were killed by someone other than a parent, 51% of those aged between 1 and under 5 years were killed by someone other than the parent.

Stepfathers?

There is some evidence to suggest that children aged between 1 and under 5 years are at increased risk of harm from stepparents compared to biological parents. Crittenden and Craig (1990) report that the most frequent perpetrator other than a parent for this age group was a parent's lover (19% of victims). In contrast, the study by Jason et al. (1982) reports only 2% of infant homicides and 3% of child homicides (aged

1–18 years) were by stepparents. Stepfathers were overrepresented in a Canadian series of child (under 5) homicides during 1974–1990 and also in England and Wales during 1977–1990 (Daly & Wilson, 1994). In the latter study Daly and Wilson were testing hypotheses about the differential effects of genetic fathers versus stepfathers. They analyzed UK Home Office records of homicides of children under 5 years, by fathers, during 1977 to 1990. They found, as predicted, that there was considerable excess risk for stepfathers – more than one third of the 378 fathers who had killed their children were stepfathers.

This is in contrast to our own analyses of a section of the same database (Marks & Kumar, 1993). We studied the records of the homicides of 214 children under a year of age during 1982–1988 and found only 6 stepfathers out of a total sample of 87 fathers (7%) who had killed an infant aged between 1 day and under 1 year. This was when we applied the broadest possible interpretation of Daly and Wilson's definition of stepfather (i.e., "those in both registered and de facto unions with the victim's mother"). It is difficult to know where this disparity comes from. It may be that stepfathers are highly overrepresented in the homicide of children aged 1 to 5 years. Or it may be that the data provided are unreliable. This example illustrates the importance of taking into account the child's age when examining child homicide data and also the difficulty in using official homicide records as a source of data rather than more direct contact with perpetrators.

Filicide Typologies

Filicide is usually attributed to either mental illness or child abuse; that is, the parent who has killed his or her child is generally considered to be either mad or bad. In England and Wales there is an Infanticide Act, particular legislation that applies to a woman who has killed her child under 1 year of age. Implicit in this legislation is the idea that childbirth may sometimes have a destabilizing impact on mothers, that the infant homicide may have occurred under these unstable psychological conditions, and that therefore there may be a case for diminished responsibility for the crime. In contrast, in Scotland and in the United States mothers who kill their children are charged as for any other homicide offense with the possibility that the filicidal mother can plead diminished responsibility within the usual terms of each country's homicide legislation. Despite these differences in legislation, in most Western countries the younger the infant, the greater the likelihood that the offense will be attributed to some form of mental illness and the perpetrator convicted of a less serious offense and given a lighter sentence. This is particularly true for mothers who kill their infants.

In England and Wales most mothers who kill their infants are convicted of infanticide and given probation sentences. In contrast, fathers who kill their infants are usually given prison sentences (Marks & Kumar, 1993). Despite there being no infanticide act in Scotland the outcome is similar. Most mothers who kill infants receive noncustodial sentences, either probation or hospital orders, and most fathers are sent to prison (Marks & Kumar, 1996).

Studies in the United States have not examined differential sentencing of mothers and fathers, but Crittenden and Craig (1990) report that in Florida, the younger the infant, the more likely the offense will be ascribed to parental mental illness, and the less serious the conviction and lighter the sentence.

Because public records provide limited information about the details surrounding these offenses, it is difficult to determine if sentencing reflects the circumstances and severity of the crime. Data we obtained from the Scottish Office included a computer record of the motive for the offense. Mothers were usually recorded as having killed their infant because of their mental state, whereas the most frequent attribution given to fathers was that of rage (Marks & Kumar, 1996). However, we were unable to determine how these motivations were ascribed and whether the difference between mothers and fathers was due to the circumstances surrounding the offense or to the effects of gender on the attributions about the causes of events.

A number of different classification systems have been devised to take into account the events leading up to the offense to ensure that filicides are more accurately classified. Resnick (1969) reviewed 131 cases of child murder reported in the literature and classified filicides according to "apparent motive" as follows: (1) altruistic filicide – either a suicidal parent could not abandon the child and so killed it, or the parent killed the child to relieve its real or imagined suffering; (2) acutely psychotic filicide—parents who kill under the influence of delusions, hallucinations, epilepsy, or delirium; (3) unwanted child filicide—the victim was not wanted by the parent; (4) accidental filicide—the killing was the result of child-battering, with no homicidal intent; (5) spouse revenge—when the offspring is killed in order to get back at the spouse.

Curiously, in Resnick's sample, accidental filicide was infrequent. Only 12% of filicides were categorized in this way. The most frequent category was that of altruism, which accounted for 50%, with psychotic filicides being the next frequent (21%). This may be due to the source of his sample – cases reported in the world scientific literature.

Scott (1973a) based his classification system on "the source of the impulse to kill" rather than motivation. His categories included: (1) victim constitutes the stimulus (exasperation, loss of temper, the battering parent); (2) mental illness; (3) stimulus arising outside the victim, including displacement of anger, with or without revenge motive; (4) elimination of unwanted child; and (5) mercy killing. In his study of 29 fathers remanded to Brixton Prison charged with killing their child under 5 years of age, Scott (1973b) found that there was always an immediate precipitating stimulus from the child (e.g., the refusal of food, vomiting, crying, staring, refusing to smile, looking scared or blank, wet, dirty, etc.). Scott reports that the father's interpretation of the child's behavior seemed to be linked to the violent act, for example, the child becoming willful, defiant, a battle of wills; or the child making him feel as though not part of the family because child preferred mother.

Similarly, a study of 12 filicidal men who were examined on a forensic psychiatric service (Campion, Cravens, & Coven, 1988) indicated that most frequently the act that killed the child was an isolated explosive outburst resulting from the father's misinterpretation of the child's behavior.

In a more systematic study of maternal filicides d'Orban (1979) studied 89 women admitted to Holloway during 1970–1975, who had been charged with the killing or attempted murder of 109 children. This constituted almost the total sample remanded in custody during the period, in London and the South East of England, because all mothers charged with the killing or attempted murder of their children during that time were remanded to Holloway for some period before trial.

D'Orban based his classification of the offenses on that of Scott's "source of the impulse to kill," with an added category, neonaticide. D'Orban found that the most frequent category of perpetrator was that of the "battering mothers." As with the fathers in Scott's study, frequently the mother had lost her temper with some aspect of the child's behavior (e.g., the child's crying, feeding, or incontinence). Only 14 of 89 women in d'Orban's study were psychotic at the time of the offense, so he concluded that puerperal psychotic illness is a relatively rare cause of maternal filicide.

However, about half the offenses in d'Orban's study had been against children aged a year or more; that is, they had occurred sometime after the postpartum period, by which time the risk of maternal mental illness has substantially declined (Kendell, Chalmers, & Platz, 1987; Cox, Murray, & Chapman, 1993). In addition a sizable number had involved neonaticide, which is unlikely to be related to either battering or mental illness. In a later reanalysis of d'Orban's data (Marks & Kumar, 1995), the relative contribution of mental illness to offenses that occurred nearer to the infant's delivery (i.e., when the mother was more likely to have a postnatally related psychological illness) was assessed. The effect of the period of time that had elapsed since delivery on the contribution of mental illness to the mother's impulse to kill was examined by comparing infants aged between 1 day and under 6 months old, with those aged between 6 months and under a year and those aged 1 year or more. Neonaticides were excluded from this analysis.

The results indicated that maternal mental illness was more likely to be implicated in the killing of *older* children. Women who killed children between 1 day and under 6 months were most frequently categorized as "battering" mothers, whereas mothers who had killed or attempted to kill older infants were most frequently categorized as mentally ill. Although maternal mental illness had contributed to some of the homicides of infants aged between 1 day and 6 months, more often infants had been killed, or nearly killed, because the mother had suddenly lost patience with the child.

In Australia, Wilkey et al. (1982) identified seven "well-defined syndromes of unlawful killing of children" (p. 32). These were: (1) neonaticide – the death of an infant within 24 hours of birth; (2) infanticide – the killing of an infant aged under 12 months by the mother classically associated with puerperal psychosis; (3) euthanasia – the killing of an abnormal child by a parent; (4) the end result of nonaccidental injury; (5) the deprived and starved child; (6) murder-suicide – where an adult kills one or more family members and then commits suicide; (7) murder. Like Scott and d'Orban, these authors also concluded that the largest group of deaths were those occurring as the end result of nonaccidental injury assaults.

Similar results have been reported in studies in the United States. A study of all victims 12 years of age or less, during 1956–1982, in Florida (Copeland, 1985) found that 45% of all deaths were due to fatal child abuse. This study notes, too, that the younger the child the more likely the death was a result of child abuse – 91% of child abuse fatalities occurred in children aged 3 or less, whereas nonchild abuse cases were more evenly distributed throughout the age range. Copeland also found that male children were more likely to be child abuse fatalities.

Similarly, Crittenden and Craig (1990) reported that children between 1 month and 5 years were more than twice as likely to be killed as a result of injuries inflicted by parents responding to noxious behavior (e.g., incessant crying or disobedience) than were neonates or older children (52% compared to 17% of neonates and 21% of school-aged children). They also found that in 60% of children aged between 1 month and under 5 years there was evidence of present or past abuse or neglect; for example, marks on the child's body, a service record of maltreatment, or an eyewitness report. Only 7% of neonates and 10% of school-aged children showed any evidence of abuse or neglect.

Similarly, another American study (Christoffel, 1989) of 437 child homicides in Cook County, Illinois, during 1977–1982, found that: "Deaths of very young children were overwhelming related to neglect or maltreatment. Often death resulted from attempts to deal with difficult but common behaviors of infants."

In a study that used a pairwise case-control design, a comparison of previously documented child maltreatment was made between 220 child homicide deaths with a group of unintentional injury deaths (matched for age, race, sex, and date of death) (Sorenson & Peterson, 1994). Only 17% of the homicide families and 15% of the unintentional death families had had prior involvement with social or child protection services. However, children who died of homicide were three times as likely as those whose deaths were unintentional to have had a documented history of both child maltreatment and social service need prior to their deaths.

It appears that the greatest number of filicides, by both mothers and fathers, and particularly those involving infants and preschool children, are the end point of an abusive parent-infant relationship, and that parents at risk of filicide may share many of the features that characterize battering parents in general

Characteristics of Abusive Parents Who Kill

Scott (1973b) identified a number of features. First, fewer than half of the men in his study were the biological father of the child. Second, disproportionate numbers of fathers were the main child-carers (the men were unemployed and their partners working). No father was considered mentally ill at the time of the offense. However, Scott considered that 22 of the 29 men studied (76%) had personality disorders. Twenty-five (86%) were considered to be "undercontrolled." Nearly 70% had one or more criminal convictions. Finally, 66% of the men came from punitive family backgrounds and 41% reported parental violence. Younger children were at increased risk. In 76% of cases there were previous indications of abuse, either to the victim or to a sibling.

In his study, d'Orban (1979) compared the women categorized as "battering" with the remaining women in his sample and found that battering mothers were characterized by chaotic and violent home backgrounds, parental separation in childhood, marital violence, financial and housing problems, came from large families (often with a history of parental discord), and had a family history of crime and a criminal record. The women were often pregnant or had more than one child or ill children at the time of the offense. In addition, 47% of the battering group had a previous history of battering, either with the index child or with a previous child.

The following is a typical case of fatal child abuse. A couple, age 21 and 18 years, both unemployed, were charged jointly with the murder of their 6-week-old daughter who had died as a result of head injury with skull fracture. There were also injuries thought to have occurred 2 to 4 weeks prior to the child's death.

The couple had an older child of 13 months. There had been previous concerns about the older child, who at 7 weeks had been admitted to the hospital with injuries, which the parents claimed were caused when they hit the child to try and make it breathe properly during a choking fit. She was placed for a time in foster care.

Both parents were the biological parents of the victim. Both were involved in the care of the children, the father more so than the mother with the victim. They both wanted the flat they lived in to be clean and orderly: "We were very house proud and neat – everything had its place and everything had to be in its place." The evidence suggested that both parents tended to use physical discipline; several witnesses reported seeing each of the parents hitting the older child about the head when she refused food or cried. The father found the child's crying difficult to bear – according to his partner, it used to get him "really wound up." Eventually it got to the stage, the mother reports, that when the older child was near the father "she realized she was likely to get a clump and therefore she started crying when he was near her."

Although only the parents had access to the victim on the day the fatal offense occurred, both denied having caused or knowing who had caused the infant's injuries. Therefore the specific circumstances at the time of the offense will never be known, but it is believed that the father had lost his temper, and swung the victim by the leg, hitting her head against a wall.

Munchausen Syndrome by Proxy

A number of fatalities resulting from a parent (usually the mother) inducing illness in her child have been reported. It is estimated that between 5% to 9% of known cases of Munchausen syndrome by proxy result in the child's death (Rosenberg, 1987; Gray & Bentovim, 1996).

Munchausen syndrome by proxy is a relatively recently acknowledged phenomenon. In 1974 DiMaio and Bernstein reported a case in which nine infants and small children had suffered a minimum of 20 episodes of cyanosis while in contact with or in the care of a particular woman. Seven of these children had died. Of the dead children, four were the woman's own (one adopted). All but one of the children were under 2 years of age. They had breathing difficulties and became cyanotic. On admission to the hospital, tests proved negative. No respiratory difficulties occurred in the hospital. Cyanosis occurred only when the perpetrator was in the vicinity.

Meadow (1977) first described the fabrication or induction of illness symptoms in children, and the subsequent medical investigations that seem intended by the perpetrator to follow, as Munchausen syndrome by proxy, and categorized it as a form of child abuse. Since then there have been increasing reports of such abuse with a proportion of these having resulted in the child's death.

Bools, Neale, and Meadow (1992) studied 56 children who had been victims of fabricated illness and 82 of their siblings. Twenty-nine percent of the index children had a history of failure to thrive and 29% a history of nonaccidental injury, inappropriate medication, or neglect. Seventy-three percent of the index children had been affected by at least one of these factors. Eleven percent of the siblings had died in early childhood, the cause of death not being identified, and 39% of the siblings had had illnesses fabricated by their mothers.

Bools, Neale, and Meadow (1994) report lifetime psychiatric histories of 47 such mothers who had either smothered or poisoned their child. Seventeen of the mothers were diagnosed as having personality disorders. Thirty-four had a history of either factitious or somatoform disorder and 26 a history of self-harm. A diagnosis of personality disorder was also made for all 14 mothers in the study of Samuels, McClaughlin, Jacobson, Poets, and Southall (1992).

Gray and Bentovim (1996) report on a series of 41 children from 37 families identified as having had illness induced by a parent. Seventeen of the children had presented in a life-threatening state. Four of the children died. Three fathers and 34 mothers were responsible. They identify four patterns of presentation: failure to thrive through the active withholding of food; allegation of allergy and withholding of food; allegation and fabrication of medical symptoms; active interference by poisoning or disrupting medical treatment. The families were characterized by histories of early abuse in the parents' own life, a high prevalence of personality disorder, a lack of understanding and tolerance of the ordinary behaviors of childhood, and problems in their current adult relationships.

In a comprehensive survey of the literature, Bools (1996) distinguishes the situation where the child is deliberately harmed by the perpetrator (e.g., by poisoning or smothering) from that in which fabrication of symptoms alone occurs. Fatalities are most likely to occur when the illness is deliberately induced. The most frequent reports were of poisoning, most commonly laxatives and tranquilizers, and smothering. Less frequently, the parent introduced infectious material directly into the child (e.g., via an intravenous line) or induced symptoms by withholding food or medicine.

The picture that is beginning to emerge is of parents with characteristics similar to those seen in other forms of child abuse. Some features, however, have been noted by many investigators as common and peculiar to factitious parents. First, a number of investigators have noted that the mothers usually had an overly close relationship, even a clinging one, with the child. They are seen to be very loving, caring mothers if a little too overinvolved. Second, mothers have high rates of somatizing and/or factitious disorder. Third, many have trained or worked in caring professions. Finally, many investigators have commented on the pervasive denial involved in these cases even when the mother is presented with compelling evidence of her complicity (see Bools [1996] for a review of these issues).

What Makes a Parent a Fatal Child Abuser?

We may add to our understanding of the precursors to child homicide by parents by regarding it as an extreme form of child abuse, and look within the child abuse arena to see what has been discovered about parents who abuse their children.

Steele (1978, 1987) suggests that the direct murder of infants is uncommon and is usually the act of a psychotic or seriously disturbed family member or stranger. He argues that more frequently, infant homicide has much in common with other forms of child maltreatment. He adds that in cases of death resulting from repeated physical abuse, parents, as a rule, do not intend to kill the child. On the contrary they have an investment in a living child who must be punished to become more obedient and satisfying. Death is an unexpected, undesired, incidental result of the abuse.

Steele outlines some common characteristics of parents who batter, and there is little to distinguish them from parents whose abuse leads to the child's death. These include: (1) A history of abuse or neglect in early life; (2) Lack of empathy for the child, involving lack of awareness of a child's physical and emotional state and needs; (3) Very high expectations of the infant, expecting the child to be like an adult; (4) A belief that abusive behavior is justified if the child didn't meet expectations – for example, if the child does not respond to its caretaker's inept or inappropriate feeding, the child is seen as defective; (5) Impaired parent-child attachment.

However, even given this set of circumstances, not all parents abuse, let alone kill their child. What might make a parent an abuser who kills? A group of Dutch psychiatrists (Lesnik-Oberstein, Koers, & Cohen, 1995) have formulated a three-factor theory of child abuse. They postulate a combination of three key factors required for abuse to take place, namely a high level of hostility in the parent, a low level of inhibition of overt aggression, and finally, a focusing of parental aggression on the child. The type of abuse that then occurs will depend on the extent to which a parent can contain covert or overt expression of his or her hostility when it is focused on the child. Figure 9.5 illustrates how this idea is formalized and how filicide may sometimes be the end point of abuse. The ratio of parental hostility to parental inhibition will determine whether no abuse occurs, or whether there is psychological or physical abuse (i.e., physical abuse that is severe enough to kill the infant).

The Role of Mental Illness

Axis I Disorders. Although many individual case examples have been published, few studies have systematically examined the circum-

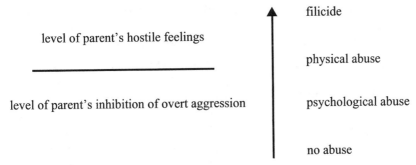

Figure 9.5. Hostility-inhibition ratio (adapted from Lesnik-Oberstein, Koers, & Cohen, 1995).

stances surrounding filicide where the parent's mental state was the main precipitating factor. McGrath (1992) studied a cohort of 115 women who were in Broadmoor Hospital, and had killed their child during 1956–1969. For 46% the diagnosis was affective psychosis, and 37% were schizophrenic. Only 5% were categorized as having personality disorder. Seventy-five percent had a history of previous psychiatric illness and 49% had attempted suicide at the time of the offense. In many cases the claimed motivation was altruistic – to relieve the child of suffering – although only one victim had severe disability. However, because Broadmoor is a high-security hospital to which only the most severely ill and dangerous patients are admitted, the psychiatric characteristics observed in this sample are likely to be typical of Broadmoor's patient population in general, as much as peculiar to women who had killed their child. Thus it would be unwise to generalize to risk factors in women in the community from this study.

The sample studied by d'Orban (1979) was more representative. In this study, 54% of the mothers who had been categorized as having killed their child as a direct consequence of mental illness had a history of previous psychiatric illness requiring inpatient or outpatient treatment; 88% suffered from psychiatric symptoms prior to the offense. Two-thirds had attempted or contemplated suicide at the time of the offense. Usually the murder and suicides were simultaneous acts. In the majority, the conscious motive was primarily self-destruction, and the killing of the child was an extension of the suicide act; less frequently was the killing the result of some delusional idea.

Axis II Disorders. D'Orban (1979) reported that many of the women he categorized as "battering" also had psychiatric diagnoses, although these diagnoses were not implicated in the offense. Forty-seven percent had personality disorder and an additional 33% were depressed at the time of the offense. The data from Scott's (1973b) study, discussed above, suggest a similar confluence of factors for fathers who kill their children; although no father was considered mentally ill at the time of the offense, 22 out of 25 had personality disorders.

The conclusion to be drawn from these studies is that a high proportion of parents who have killed a child, as a consequence of abuse, suffer from some kind of psychiatric disorder, either depression or personality disorder, particularly the latter. In turn, both personality disorder and depression are more likely to be associated with either high levels of hostility or a reduction in the capacity to inhibit the expression of hostility, or both. In fact, personality disorders are defined by these features: The *DSM-IV* criteria for personality disorder include abnormalities in cognition (ways of perceiving and interpreting), affectivity, interpersonal functioning, and impulse control (American Psychiatric Association, 1994). Individuals with personality disorder by definition experience difficulties in all areas of interpersonal functioning and these will apply in their relationships with their children as much, if not even more so, given the emotional intensity of family life, as in any social domain. It would appear that although such diagnoses may not usually be directly linked to infant homicide, they are likely to contribute indirectly because they may make the task of containing aggressive feelings (which all parents sometimes feel toward their infants) difficult, and for some, impossible.

Conclusion

The younger the infant the more likely he or she is at risk of becoming the victim of homicide, and the younger the infant the more likely the perpetrator will be a parent. Neonaticide is usually committed by mothers; fathers are rarely involved. Neonaticide is probably the least preventable of filicides.

Male infants more than a day old and under 5 years are at increased risk compared with females, especially those aged between 1 day and 6 months. A parent is the most likely perpetrator of child homicide. Both mothers and fathers are at risk, although fathers may be slightly more prone, especially if the father is the main caretaker.

The younger the child the more likely its death will be a consequence of a parent having lost patience with the child. Child abuse fatalities appear to be the most frequent type of filicide in the under 5 age group. This type of filicide usually involves a parent who is not severely mentally ill but has ways of parenting that are inherently abusive to the infant. A parent with the additional presence of low level or existing psychiatric disturbance, or personality disorder, is likely to exacerbate the risk. Children of school age and older are less likely to become the victims of homicide; when they are killed, however, someone other than a parent is increasingly likely to be the perpetrator.

As with assessing the risk of violence in psychiatric patients generally, there are difficulties in assessing the risk of filicide in a mentally ill parent. The risk of being killed by a parent as a direct consequence of the parent's mental illness is unrelated to the child's age. Most parents with mental illness do not harm their children. When they do, the most likely scenario involves a parent who is suicidal and who believes the child will also be better off dead.

Finally, Jacobsen and Miller (1998) present three examples of detailed, systematic, and extensive assessments of future parenting risk when a mentally ill mother had killed someone previously: A neonaticidal mother, a "battering" mother who had killed a 1-year-old child, and a mother who had killed an adult friend during a psychotic episode. As a result of the assessments, all three were deemed to be at *low* risk for future child maltreatment and violence. This article illustrates the highly complex and multifaceted issues involved in making assessments of parents at risk of filicide. I will summarize the examples, because they are good illustrations of the need to consider every case in its own right.

The mother who had killed her neonate had subsequently been in psychotherapy and had been able to use this to help her change. In the three years subsequent to the neonaticide, no violent incidents or suicide attempts occurred. At the time of the assessment she demonstrated positive and sensitive parenting skills with her surviving children and appeared to have a good understanding of their needs and appropriate expectations of them. She had no current psychiatric symptoms.

The filicide had occurred when the mother was a teenager with two children under 5. At the time she killed her 1-year-old she was living with a violent, possessive, substance-abusing partner who beat her regularly. She was socially isolated and severely depressed. Since the offense she had left her abusive partner, built up a social network, become engaged in and had responded well to psychotherapy. Her interactions with and expectations of her children were positive. There was no underlying hostility or intrusiveness toward them.

The third woman had killed a friend during a psychotic episode. Subsequently her psychosis responded to antipsychotic medication and she became asymptomatic as long as she remained on regular medication. Otherwise she was able to function at a high level and give adequate care to her children. It was thought she would benefit from interventions to improve her parenting. She was highly motivated and responded well to these interventions. In light of this, she was believed to be at low risk for future violence.

I present these well-documented and carefully assessed examples to illustrate that parents can and do change, and that any assessment of future risk needs to take into account not only the parent's history but also the current situation. Has the parent accepted responsibility for the past, is he or she motivated to change, is he or she able to accept the interventions necessary for change to be effected? Despite a history of highly negative risk factors, if the parent is able to demonstrate a sustained willingness for and evidence of change for the better, then there may be hope for both parent and child.

REFERENCES

American Psychiatric Association. (1994). *Diagnostic and statistical manual of mental disorders* (4th ed.). Washington, DC: American Psychiatric Association.

Bools, C. N., Neale, B. A., & Meadow, S. R. (1992). Co-morbidity associated with fabricated illness (Munchausen syndrome by proxy). *Archives of Disease in Childhood, 67,* 77–79.

Bools, C. N., Neale, B. A., & Meadow, S. R. (1994). Munchausen syndrome by proxy: A study of psychopathology. *Child Abuse and Neglect, 18,* 773–788.

Bools, C. N. (1996). Factitious illness by proxy: Maunchausen syndrome by proxy. *British Journal of Psychiatry, 169,* 268–275.

Brozovsky, M., & Falit, H. (1971). Neonaticide: Clinical and psychodynamic considerations. *Journal of American Academy of Child Psychiatry, 10,* 673–683.

Campion, J. F., Cravens, J. M., & Coven, F. (1988). A study of filicidal men. *American Journal of Psychiatry, 145,* 1141–1144.

Christoffel, K. K. (1989). Age-related patterns of violent death, Cook County, Illinois, 1977 through 1982. *American Journal of Disorders of Childhood, 143,* 1403–1409.

Copeland, A. R. (1985). Homicide in childhood. The Metro-Dade County experience from 1956–1982. *American Journal of Forensic Medicine and Pathology, 6,* 21–24.

Cox, J. L., Murray, D., & Chapman, G. (1993). A controlled study of the onset, duration and prevalence of postnatal depression. *British Journal of Psychiatry, 163,* 27–31.

Crittenden, P. M. & Craig, S. E. (1990). Developmental trends in the nature of child homicide. *Journal of Interpersonal Violence, 5*, 202–216.

Cummings P., & Mueller, B. A. (1994). Infant injury death in Washington State, 1981 through 1990. *Archives of Pediatric and Adolescent Medicine, 148*, 1021–1026.

DiMaio, V. J. M., & Bernstein, J. D. (1974). A case of infanticide. *Journal of Forensic Sciences, 19*, 744–754.

Daly, M., & Wilson, M. I. (1988). *Homicide*. New York: Aldine de Gruyter.

Daly, M., & Wilson, M. I. (1994). Some differential attributes of lethal assaults on small children by stepfathers vs genetic fathers. *Ethology and Sociobiology, 15*, 207–217.

d'Orban, P. (1979). Women who kill their children. *British Journal of Psychiatry, 134*, 560–571.

Emery, J. L. (1985). Infanticide, filicide and cot death. *Archives of Disease in Childhood, 60*, 505–507.

Funayama, M., & Sagisaka, K. (1988). Consecutive infanticides in Japan. *American Journal of Forensic Medicine and Pathology, 9*, 9–11.

Gray, J., & Bentovim, A. (1996). Illness induction syndrome: Paper I–A series of 41 children from 37 families identified at Great Ormond Street Hospital for Children NHS Trust. *Child Abuse and Neglect, 20*, 655–673.

Green, C. M., & Manohar, S. V. (1990). Neonaticide and hysterical denial of pregnancy. *British Journal of Psychiatry, 156*, 121–123.

Home Office (1997). *Criminal Statistics: England and Wales 1987–96*. London: HMSO.

Jacobsen, T., & Miller, L. J. (1998). Mentally ill mothers who have killed: Three cases addressing the issue of future parenting capability. *Psychiatric Services, 49*, 650–657.

Jason, J., Gilliland, J. C., & Tyler, C. W. (1983). Homicide as a cause of pediatric mortality in the United States. *Pediatrics, 72*, 191–197.

Kaye, N. S., Borenstein, N. M., & Donnelly, S. M. (1990). Families, murder and insanity: A psychiatric review of paternal neonaticide. *Journal of Forensic Sciences, 35*, 133–139.

Kendell, R. E., Chalmers, & J. C., Platz C. (1987). Epidemiology of puerperal psychosis. *British Journal of Psychiatry, 150*, 662–673.

Knowlden, J., Keeling, J., & Nicholl, J. P. (1985). *Post neonatal mortality*. DHSS Report, HMSO: London

Lesnick-Oberstein, M., Koers, A. J., & Cohen, L. (1995). Parental hostility and its sources in psychologically abusive mothers: A test of the three-factor theory. *Child Abuse and Neglect, 19*, 33–49.

McGrath, P. G. (1992). Maternal filicide in Broadmoor Hospital 1916–1969. *Journal of Forensic Psychiatry, 3*, 271–297.

Marks, M. N. (1996). Characteristics and causes of infanticide in Britain. *International Review of Psychiatry, 8*, 99–106.

Marks, M. N., & Kumar, R. (1993). Infanticide in England and Wales, 1982–1988. *Medicine, Science and the Law, 33*, 329–339.

Marks, M. N., & Kumar, R. (1995). Parents who kill their infants. *British Journal of Midwifery, 3*, 249–253.

Marks, M. N., & Kumar, R. (1996). Infanticide in Scotland. *Medicine, Science and the Law, 36,* 299–305.

Meadow, R. (1977). Munchausen syndrome by proxy: The hinterland of child abuse. *Lancet, 2,* 345–345.

Registrar General Scotland (1994). *Mid-1993 Population Estimates Scotland.* Edinburgh: HMSO.

Resnick, P. J. (1969). Child murder by parents: A psychiatric review of filicide. *American Journal of Psychiatry, 126,* 325–334.

Resnick, P. J. (1970). Murder of the newborn: A psychiatric review of neonaticide. *American Journal of Psychiatry, 126,* 1414–1420.

Rosenberg, D. (1987). Web of deceit: A literature review of Munchausen syndrome by proxy. *Child Abuse and Neglect, 11,* 547–563.

Sakuta T., & Saito, S. (1981). A socio-medical study of 71 cases of infanticide in Japan. *Keio Journal of Medicine, 30,* 155–168.

Samuels, M. P., McClaughlin, W., Jacobson, R. R., Poets, C., & Southall, D. (1992). Fourteen cases of imposed upper airway obstruction. *Archives of Disease in Childhood, 67,* 162–170.

Scott, P. D. (1973a). Parents who kill their children. *Medicine, Science and the Law, 13,* 120–126.

Scott, P. D. (1973b). Fatal battered baby cases. *Medicine, Science and the Law, 13,* 197–206.

The Scottish Office (1993). *Statistical Bulletin: Criminal Justice Series.* Edinburgh: Government Statistical Service.

Shiono, H., Maya, A., Tabata, N., Fujiwara, M., Azumi, J., & Morita, M. (1986). Medicolegal aspects of infanticide in Hokkaido District, Japan. *The American Journal of Forensic Medicine and Pathology, 7,* 104–106.

Sorenson, S. B., & Peterson, J. G. (1994). Traumatic child death and documented maltreatment history, Los Angeles. *American Journal of Public Health, 84,* 623–627.

Steele, B. F. (1978). Psychology of infanticide resulting from maltreatment. In M. Kohl (Ed.), *Infanticide and the value of life* (pp. 76–85). New York: Prometheus Books.

Steele, B. F. (1987). Psychodynamic factors. In R. E. Helfer & R. S. Kempe (Eds.), *The Battered Child (4th ed.)* (pp. 81–114). Chicago: University of Chicago Press.

Wilkey, I., Pearn, J., Petrie, G., & Nixon, J. (1982). Neonaticide, infanticide and child homicide. *Medicine, Science and the Law, 22,* 31–34.

Wolkind, S., Taylor, E. M., Waite, A. J., Dalton, M., & Emery, J. L. (1993). Recurrence of unexpected infant death. *Acta Paediatrica, 82,* 873–876.

10. Parricide

CHARLES P. EWING

As a boy, L. assaulted a hitchhiker and then urinated on him. As an adult, the 200-pound, alcohol and drug abuser routinely carried a pistol, stabbed and shot at his father, and terrorized his neighbors. For years, L. beat his wife. When she finally left him, he convinced a court to give him custody of their four children

For the next four years, L. kept the children in an isolated trailer with no electricity, no phone, and no running water, allowing them out only to go to school. Inside the mobile home, L. beat the children with rubber hoses and two-by-fours, and punched, slapped, and kicked them. While drunk he would line the children up against the wall and ring their heads with gunfire.

L.'s reign of terror ended when his two older children, sons 15 and 12, shot him in the head with a deer rifle while he slept. Criminal charges against both boys were ultimately dismissed.

Sixteen-year-old J. had never been in trouble. An above-average student and member of the high school swim team, he was a Boy Scout and active member of his church. At the same time, however, J. was suffering from major depression, a learning disability, and chronic feelings of inferiority. After receiving disappointing scores on college admission tests and an "F" on a Spanish quiz, J. snapped.

Initially intent upon killing himself, J. instead turned his rage outward and used the family's .22-caliber rifle to shoot and kill both his parents. Charged with murder, J. was found not guilty by reason of insanity.

G. had been in trouble on and off since he was 6, when he started riding his bicycle in front of cars and throwing objects at passing drivers. By age 11, he was banned from most nearby stores because of his shoplifting. In junior high school, he was suspended for fighting and stealing. In high school, he was suspended for carrying a knife and gun to school.

Though eventually admitted to a school for troubled youth, G. continued to act out. He ran away from home, stole cars, continued shoplifting, and fraudulently used a credit card belonging to a family friend. While arguing with a peer, G. shoved the boy to the ground and fractured his skull. As the boy lay unconscious, G. continued to assault him.

Eventually, at age 15, G. broke into his grandparents' home, stole a gun, and then shot and killed his mother, father, and 11-year-old sister.

At trial, G. claimed that the killings were the result of years of physical and psychological abuse and long-term use of Ritalin, a hyperactivity medication. G. was convicted of three counts of first-degree murder, and sentenced to life in prison without parole.

By the time they were 17 and 15 years old, brothers B. and D. had abused drugs and alcohol, shaved their heads, affiliated themselves with Neo-Nazis, and repeatedly threatened their parents. The two boys, both of whom stood more than 6 feet tall, had also tattooed their foreheads. One boy's tattoo read "Seig Heil" and the other "Berserker."

The boys' distraught mother contacted mental health professionals and even called the Anti-Defamation League in an attempt to cope with her sons' increasingly threatening behavior. Her efforts were to no avail, however, as ultimately the brothers' rage became homicidal. Together B. and D. used a knife, a baseball bat, and the handle of a pickax to brutally stab and bludgeon their mother, father, and 11-year-old brother. Charged with three counts of murder, B. and D. each pleaded guilty and was sentenced to life in prison without parole.

M. was 16 years old when he, too, bludgeoned and stabbed both his parents to death. Adopted by an older, wealthy, and childless couple when he was 4 days old, M. had for years been showered with attention and material belongings.

Though M. initially blamed his parents' deaths on his father's business partner, he later confessed to police, telling them he set an alarm clock for 5:35 A.M., got up, stripped off his clothing, crept naked into his mother's bedroom, beat her with a barbell and slashed her throat, and then went to another room, where he did the same to his sleeping father.

Police officers also said M. told them he was tired of driving his parents' old Lincoln and wanted a newer and fancier vehicle. Witnesses later testified that prior to killing his parents, M. casually told them he could have any car he chose if his parents were dead. Moreover, other witnesses said that shortly after his father died, M. bragged about his inheritance and promised to take them to a rock concert in a limousine.

M. was convicted of two counts of murder and sentenced to 50 years to life in prison.

The media-inspired stereotype of murder is that of "the innocent victim shot, stabbed, strangled or beaten to death by a total stranger – a rapist, robber, serial killer, or even mass murderer, who is drugged, deranged, sociopathic or some combination of all three" (Ewing, 1997, p. 6). While this stereotype is not entirely without foundation, at least in the United States nearly half of all homicide victims are related to or acquainted with their killers (U. S. Department of Justice, 1994).

In fact, recent U. S. Justice Department statistics indicate that approximately 16% of those slain in the United States are killed by family members and nearly 12% of these intrafamilial homicides are parricides – children killing their parents (U.S. Bureau of Justice Statistics, 1994).

Parricide, the killing of one's parent or parents, is a relatively rare but psychologically intriguing and socially troubling form of interpersonal violence. Though often regarded as the most dreadful crime, in many ways parricide is perhaps the most understandable of all forms of homicide.

The Incidence of Parricide

The true incidence of parricide is unknown, but each year in the United States, more than 300 parents are killed by their children (Heide, 1992; Ewing, 1997). Annually, since 1976, between 1.5 and 2.5% of all U.S. homicides have been parricides (see Mones, 1991; Federal Bureau of Investigation, 1995). Data compiled annually by the U.S. Federal Bureau of Investigation (FBI) suggest that among those arrested for murder or nonnegligent homicide, approximately 1% have killed their fathers, while a slightly smaller percentage have killed their mothers (Federal Bureau of Investigation, 1995).

Among intrafamilial homicides, parricides are much more common. A recent government study of urban homicides in the United States found that 11.7% of intrafamilial homicides involved one or more offspring killing a parent (U. S. Department of Justice, 1994).

Perpetrators and Their Victims

The anecdotal and limited empirical research on parricide suggests that most perpetrators are juveniles (see Ewing, 1990a; Mones, 1991; Heide, 1992; Dutton & Yamini, 1995). Generally available FBI data include arrestees of all ages, so it impossible to determine from those data how many parricide offenders are adults as opposed to juveniles. Nor do such data reveal anything about the victims or the circumstances of these killings.

However, Heide (1992) has analyzed an expanded FBI database, known as the Supplementary Homicide Report (SHR), for a 10-year period. Her analysis of SHR data for the decade between 1977 and 1986 provided a number of statistical insights about the nature of parricide in the United States. Heide found that (1) the murdered parents and stepparents were "typically white and non-Hispanic" (p. 3); (2) on average, these victims tended to be in their late 40s and 50s; (3) stepparent victims were younger than biological parent victims; (4) the majority of the perpetrators were white, non-Hispanic males; (5) more than 70% of those who killed fathers, stepfathers, or stepmothers were younger than 30; and (6) close to 70% of those who killed mothers were between 20 and 50.

Heide also found that among parricide victims, "15 percent of mothers, 25 percent of fathers, 30 percent of stepmothers, and 34 percent of stepfathers were killed by sons and daughters under 18" (p. 3).

Although this analysis suggests that the percentage of parricides committed by juveniles is relatively low (i.e., 15 to 34% depending upon the relationship between victim and perpetrator), it is still significantly higher than the percentage of all criminal homicides committed by juveniles. In recent years, roughly 10% of all criminal homicides in the United States have been committed by youngsters under the age of 18 (Ewing, 1990b, 1997).

Parricide as a Response to Child Abuse

Parricide has not been the subject of much, if any, systematic research (see Rowley et al., 1987; Ewing, 1990a, 1997). Most of the professional literature on the subject is comprised of case studies and limited analyses of small samples of convenience – generally cases in which the perpetrators were evaluated and/or treated by the author, who is usually a mental health professional (see, e.g., Maas et al., 1984; Chamberlain, 1986; Benedek & Cornell, 1989; Newhill, 1991; James, 1994). Though few in number, however, most of these reports emphasize a common theme: "Youngsters who kill a parent have generally been severely victimized by that parent" (Ewing, 1990a).

For example, Sadoff (1971), a psychiatrist who has evaluated and treated many young parricide offenders, has concluded that "a bizarre neurotic relationship exists between the victim and his assassin in which the parent-victim mistreats the child excessively and pushes him to the point of explosive violence" (p. 68). Similarly, Tanay (1976), a psychiatrist who coined the term *reactive parricide*, regards the killing of a parent as generally a reaction to overwhelming abuse: "A last resort effort to protect the psychic integrity of the perpetrator threatened with psychic disintegration" (p. 76).

Mones, an attorney, who has not only reviewed this body of literature but represented dozens of children charged with killing their parents, has concluded that most of these youngsters have been severely abused by the parent(s) they have killed. He has provided the following profile of adolescent parricide offenders:

[T]hey are raised in homes where chaos and persecution are the order of the day. These children exist on the extreme end of the child abuse spectrum, most being victims of what I call "poly-abuse." Not only have they typically been physically, mentally, and often sexually abused since they were very young (oftentimes since infancy), but they have witnessed the repeated abuse of other family members as well. (Mones, 1991, p. 12)

Heide, who has studied the phenomenon of parricide both clinically and statistically, concurs with Mones. Although she notes that some young parricide offenders are severely mentally ill and/or dangerously antisocial, she reports that:

The severely abused child is the most frequently encountered type of adolescent parricide offender ... In-depth portraits of such youths have frequently shown that they killed because they could no longer tolerate conditions at home. These children, typically adolescents, were psychologically abused by one or both parents and often witnessed or suffered physical, sexual, and verbal abuse as well. (Heide, 1992, p. 6)

Other Possible Risk Factors

In her own study of juvenile killers, Heide (1992) conducted an in-depth analysis of seven cases of parricide. Six of these perpetrators

186   CHARLES P. EWING

were boys. All were white and ranged in age from 12 to 17 years. These
seven offenders killed six fathers, three mothers, and one brother. All of
the killings were committed by firearms – guns that Heide described as
"readily available" to the young perpetrators (p. 36).

Six of the seven youthful parricide offenders studied by Heide had
been abused by their parents, five severely. The single female offender
had been both sexually abused and forcibly raped by her father. All six
abuse cases also involved evidence of "confirmed alcoholism or heavy
drinking in the home" (p. 37).

After reviewing her own study and the reports of others, Heide
(1992) identified 12 characteristics associated with adolescents who kill
their parents:

1. A pattern of violence in the family.
2. Failed efforts by the adolescents to get help.
3. Failed efforts by the adolescents to escape from the family situation.
4. Isolation and fewer social outlets among these adolescents.
5. A family situation that became increasingly intolerable.
6. Increasing feelings of helplessness on the part of these adolescents.
7. Inability to cope with increasing stress, leading to a loss of self-
   control.
8. Adolescents with little if any prior involvement with the criminal
   justice system.
9. Ready availability of a gun as a major factor in the homicide.
10. Alcohol abuse and/or alcoholism in the home.
11. Evidence that adolescent offender may have been in a dissocia-
    tive state at or near the time of the killing.
12. Evidence that the adolescent offender and other family members
    felt relieved by the victim's death.

Parricide as a Family Conspiracy

Heide is not the first to observe that in many cases, adolescent perpetrators and their family members feel relieved by the victim's death.
Many years earlier, Tanay (1973) concluded that many parricides are
"adaptive" and represent a "family integrating experience" (p. 273). As
he explained:

The statement that a parent killing may be adaptive has a blasphemous quality.
In a number of cases such a conclusion has forced itself upon me, not only by

the history that preceded the killing but also by the consequences which the slaying had upon the life of the perpetrator and the entire family (Tanay, 1973, p. 273).

In a similar vein, Sargent (1962), Ewing (1990a), and others have observed what has been called a "family conspiracy" in some cases of parricide. In an early article on this issue, Sargent speculated that "sometimes the child who kills is acting as the unwitting lethal agent of an adult (usually a parent) who unconsciously prompts the child so that he can vicariously enjoy the benefits of the act" (p. 35). Sargent cited numerous cases in support of this hypothesis, including one in which an 8-year-old shot and killed his abusive father after the boy's mother expressed a wish that the father would die.

Ewing (1990b) later cited two such cases. In the first, a 16-year-old initially refused his mother's request to kill his abusive father, but shot the man to death when the mother threatened to kill herself unless the boy killed his father. In the second case, a 17-year-old was told by his mother that she would pay $50 to have her abusive husband, the boy's stepfather, killed. The boy conveyed his mother's "offer" to a friend who communicated it on to another youth, who took the offer seriously, and killed the man. The 17-year-old, his mother, and the shooter all pleaded guilty to various homicide charges.

Ewing (1990a) also noted that: "Even where there is no 'conspiracy,' explicit or implicit, between parent and child, the killing of one parent to protect the other parent is not an uncommon scenario in juvenile parricide" (p. 37). Ewing cited two cases as examples.

In the first, a 3-year-old observed his drunken father beating his mother and threatening her with a pistol. When the man laid the pistol down, the boy grabbed it and shot him to death. Later the child told authorities: "I killed him. Now he's dead. If he would have hit my mother, I would have shot him again" (Ewing, 1990b, p. 112).

In the second case, a 15-year-old shot and killed his stepfather, who had been abusing the boy's mother for 14 years. Immediately prior to the killing, the man had slammed the boy's mother into a metal door. The teenager grabbed a gun, shot the man, and then chased him before shooting him at least three more times.

Occasionally, as in the case of L. described earlier, "family conspiracy" parricides involve siblings rather than parents. As Ewing (1997) observed, "When juveniles conspire with siblings to kill their fathers, the family dynamics generally seem to fit the typical patricidal pattern of paternal abuse" (p. 106). Ewing (1990a) describes a case in which three brothers – aged 15, 13, and 10 – conspired to kill their father who

188CHARLES P. EWING

forced them to live in squalid conditions and treated them with "extreme cruelty" (p. 38).

Mental Illness and Parricide

Given its source (i.e., mental health professionals who had evaluated and treated perpetrators), much of the early literature appeared to emphasize mental illness as a factor in many parricides, especially those committed by juveniles (see Rowley et al., 1987). While juveniles who kill their abusive parents often suffer from emotional problems secondary to the abuse they have suffered, most are not seriously mentally ill. Nor are these youngsters usually antisocial or conduct disordered, as are many juveniles who kill outside the family (see, generally, Ewing, 1990a; Heide, 1999).

Indeed, many youngsters who kill their abusive parents might best be described to be "good kids." For the most part, they tend to be conforming, perform adequately academically, stay out of trouble, and give little or no evidence of psychopathology. Their homicidal acts do not appear to result from mental illness or personality disorder, but rather in response to the brutal abuse they have endured at the hands of those they kill.

Still, a small percentage of parricide perpetrators do appear to fit into other classifications. For example, Heide (1992) has identified two other types of parricide offender: the "severely mentally ill" and "dangerously antisocial" (pp. 7–11). Maloney (1994), a psychologist who has examined many parricide perpetrators, refers to similar subtypes as "psychotic offenders" and "psychopathic parricides" (p. 22). More recently, Weisman and Sharma (1997) studied the records of 64 individuals charged with murdering or attempting to murder their parents, and found that 40% were adjudged not guilty by reason of insanity.

Nevertheless, although much of the early literature on parricide emphasized the seriously mentally ill offender, only a rather small percentage of juveniles who kill their parents are, in fact, psychotic or otherwise seriously disturbed. For example, among the seven parricidal youths discussed by Heide, only one fit her profile of the "severely mentally ill child."

In most of the cases fitting this "severely mentally ill" profile, the perpetrator has an extensive history of psychiatric impairment and treatment. As Maloney reports:

First, these individuals almost always have a previous history of treatment for a serious mental disturbance. The history is usually corroborated by formal reports from mental health professionals, psychiatric hospitals or the like. Second, they are psychotic at the time of the offense ... Third these individuals are usually overtly delusional at the time of the killing of their parents ... A fourth characteristic of these homicides is that the act of killing, itself, is bizarre. (Maloney, 1994, p. 21)

J. – a patricide offender in his late 20s – fits this pattern well. J. killed his father and was psychologically evaluated by Maloney (1994). According to Maloney, J. had been treated for a psychotic episode after his high school graduation but had experienced "serious psychological problems before that time" (p. 20). J. also has a history of substance abuse, including use of marijuana, LSD, PCP, cocaine, and alcohol. Although he eventually graduated from college, J. was never able to support himself independently, and was living with his father at the time of the killing.

In explaining the killing of his father, J. first gave Maloney a lengthy, rambling, and disorganized narrative. J. said he believed that his father was "a great evil for living with me so long and lying to me and hiding my goodness from other people" (p. 21). He added that after his father ignored J.'s request to commit suicide, "I went and got a knife and cut his head three-quarters off and cut a cross on his back..." (p. 21).

Heide (1992) described a similar case in which one of the parricide offenders she examined was also clearly psychotic at the time of the killing. Nineteen-year-old "Jonathan" stabbed his mother 40 times, slit her throat, and tried to slice off her left hand "to demonstrate his allegiance to Satan" (p. 8). Examining mental health professionals concluded that this young man was extremely delusional, suffered from paranoid schizophrenia, and acted in response to command hallucinations directing him to murder his mother.

In most cases involving psychotic or otherwise seriously disturbed perpetrators, there is often clear evidence of mental illness prior to the parricide (see, e.g., Weisman and Sharma, 1997). Moreover, in some cases, even when parricide perpetrators have been identified as psychotic or seriously mentally ill, they have no recorded history of serious mental illness prior to the parricide, and the diagnosis is made only after the killing.

This does not necessarily mean that the posthomicidal diagnoses in these cases are inaccurate. In many instances, it may be that the perpetrator's mental illness was not apparent to others around him and/or may have become acute only immediately prior to the parricide.

One classic example is the case of J. described earlier. Prior to killing both his parents and being acquitted by reason of insanity, J. had been a good student and active teenager, who had never been in any serious trouble. After the killings, J. was examined by mental health professionals, who determined that he suffered from a severe depression at the time of the killings, and that as a result of this depression and other emotional problems, he had been unable to cope with increasing stress.

The Antisocial Parricide Perpetrator

At least some who kill their parents appear to fit what Heide (1992) and Maloney (1994) call the "dangerously antisocial" or "psychopathic" parricide offender. After establishing that he was using the term "more in a colloquial than a technical psychological or psychiatric sense" (p. 22), Maloney (1994) described "psychopathic" offenders as follows:

In general, they do not have a history of child abuse, but there may be some deficit in terms of their early bonding and early relationship with their parent [which] may result in impairment in feelings of empathy and compassion for other persons ... These defendants are not grossly mentally disturbed. Conversely, upon psychological evaluation, their mental status appears to be essentially normal. Although there may be a history of drug or substance abuse, usually there is no history of treatment for serious mental disturbance. There may be some referral to counseling during the adolescent years primarily for lack of application in school or having conduct problems. (p. 22)

It should be noted, however, that in many cases in which there is a history of antisocial behavior on the part of the parricide perpetrator, labels such as "antisocial," "psychopathic," "conduct disorder," or "antisocial personality disorder" (even if clinically warranted) usually does not provide a full explanation of the killing. Even in these cases, claims of child abuse should not be rejected summarily in the search for causes of parricide. As Heide (1992) has noted:

Children who have been abused and neglected may adopt an antisocial way of responding to life as a means of psychic, if not physical, survival. Antisocial behavior can focus their attention away from the problems at home that are too difficult to handle. When faced with an [adolescent parricide offender] with any history of acting out, the question whether the adolescent is truly sociopathic (that is, lacks a conscience), or whether he or she has adopted a pattern of acting out to maintain his or her fragile mental health is one best reserved for the mental health professional. (p. 11)

Moreover, as Mones (personal communication, quoted in Ewing, 1997) says of these young offenders: "They may try to cover up what is really going on. But when you scratch the surface, you find a significant history of abuse and other family dysfunction."

Heide (1992), Maloney (1994), and Mones (1991) all make it clear that many parricide offenders do not fall neatly into any single classification. Instead, it appears that many antisocial offenders have been abused and/or neglected by their parents, as have many mentally ill offenders. In the final analysis, all three authorities agree that the most frequent common denominator among parricide perpetrators is a history of child abuse victimization.

Economically Motivated Parricides

Although most youths who kill their parents are victims of child abuse, killing to avert future abuse and/or avenge past abuse, occasionally children kill their parents for another reason: Greed. Though "infinitesimal few" in number, at least some parricide offenders are, in the words of Mones (1991), "hell bent on prematurely wrenching the family fortune from Mom and Dad" (p. 15).

For obvious reasons, those who commit parricide for money are often children of wealthy parents. Their crimes seem especially horrible, if not senseless, not simply because they are children of great wealth and privilege but because the money they kill for would, in most cases, eventually have been theirs anyway.

The highly publicized California case of the Menendez brothers, Lyle and Erik, is perhaps the best-known parricide apparently motivated at least in part by greed (see Ewing, 1997). Lyle and Erik Menendez, sole beneficiaries of their parents' $14 million estate, shot and killed their mother and father as the couple sat watching television in their $5 million Beverly Hills mansion. After a lengthy investigation and two trials, in which Lyle and Erik claimed to have been brutally abused by their father, the brothers were convicted of capital murder but spared the death penalty.

As this and other similar cases make clear, even in cases where the perpetrator appears to have had a clear economic motive to kill his or her parents, the desire for money, by itself, rarely provides a fully satisfactory explanation of parricide. Undoubtedly some of these young killers are abused children, acting out longstanding rage against their parents. Still other economically motivated parricide perpetrators appear to fall into the category Heide calls "dangerously antisocial." Their homicidal acts, though immediately motivated by the desire to speed up their inheritances, are really a manifestation of their antisocial personalities.

Finally, of course, some economically motivated parricides appear to be committed by offenders who are both antisocial personalities and victims of abuse.

Conclusion: Assessing the Risk of Parricide

Parricide is clearly an extremely low base rate phenomenon. As such, it is rarely predictable with any degree of accuracy. Still, many parricide perpetrators have been evaluated and/or treated by mental health professionals prior (sometimes immediately prior) to their crimes; and at least some parricides might have been prevented had these professionals been more attuned to factors suggesting that the would-be perpetrator was at significant risk of killing his or her parent(s).

Thus, in many cases, clinicians will rightfully be concerned about the possibility of parricide, and will want to make some effort to assess the risk that a given patient or client will kill a parent.

Although, to date, there is no universally accepted protocol for assessing the risk of parricide, the description of the phenomenon provided in this chapter suggests at least the outline of one such protocol.

As with most forms of interpersonal violence, the risk of parricide is undoubtedly greatest where the would-be perpetrator makes an explicit or implicit threat to kill. Though it has not been studied systematically, the relationship between parricide and prior threats to kill is supported anecdotally (see Ewing, 1990a, 1990b). From various clinical reports, it appears that many people who kill a parent have previously threatened (or otherwise signaled an intention) to do so. It should be obvious that, in every case, such threats must be taken seriously and investigated thoroughly. Indeed, in some cases, clinicians will have a legal duty to take steps to protect the threatened party (Ewing, 1997).

Beyond specific threats, however, and perhaps most significantly, children who are being abused or have been abused by their parents appear to be at greatest risk for parricide. Moreover, it seems that the more egregious and enduring the abuse, the more likely it is that the child-victim will act out homicidally against his or her abusive parent. Indeed, the risk of parricide seems greatest in cases of what Mones

(1991) calls "poly-abuse" (p. 12) – those in which a child is physically, psychologically, and sexually abused by a parent. Similarly, children who have repeatedly witnessed a parent abusing other family members also seem to be at heightened risk for the commission of parricide (Heide, 1992).

Additionally, race, ethnicity, and gender appear to be related to parricidal behavior, with white, non-Hispanic males apparently accounting for the majority of parricides.

Also apparently implicated in parricide are a number of family dynamics. When perpetrators are juveniles (i.e., under the age of 18), stepfathers and stepmothers appear to be at greatest risk, followed by fathers and mothers – presumably due to the greater conflict many youngsters experience with stepparents or possibly the greater conflict that seems to occur in many broken and blended families. Families that feature alcohol abuse, especially one or more alcoholic parents, also seem to be at particular risk for parricide. The same appears to be true of families living in households in which a firearm is readily available. Finally, the "family conspiracy" theory (Sargent, 1962; Ewing, 1990b) suggests that the risk for parricide is heightened where more than one family member would appear to benefit from the death of one of the parents – as, for example, where the potential parricide victim is abusing two or more members of the family.

Mental illness is another risk factor in parricide. As was indicated earlier, however, many parricide perpetrators are not grossly mentally ill. Thus, the presence or absence of a diagnosable mental illness is in no way dispositive when it comes to assessing the possibility of parricidal behavior.

Similarly, the presence of psychopathy, sociopathy, conduct disorder, or antisocial personality disorder may also be risk factors, but are certainly in no way pathognomonic.

Given the limited and sometimes disparate literature dealing with mental illness and antisocial traits among parricide perpetrators, clinicians would do well to consider these features as most significant when they are combined with an explicit or implicit threat to kill a parent, a history of abuse or family violence, or the presence of other features that have been linked to parricide: for example, alcohol abuse in the family, firearms in the home, limited social support, inability to cope with stress, feelings of helplessness, evidence of dissociation, and/or previously failed efforts to escape from the family situation or otherwise get help.

REFERENCES

Benedek, E. P., & Cornell, D. G. (1989). *Juvenile homicide.* Washington, DC: American Psychiatric Association Press.

Chamberlain, T. J. (1986). The dynamics of a parricide. *American Journal of Forensic Psychiatry, 7,* 11–23.

Dutton, D. G., & Yamini, S. (1995). Adolescent parricide: An integration of social cognitive theory and clinical views of projective-introjective cycling. *American Journal of Orthopsychiatry, 65,* 39–47.

Ewing, C. P. (1997). *Fatal families: The dynamics of intrafamilial homicide.* Thousand Oaks, CA: Sage.

Ewing, C. P. (1990a). *When children kill: The dynamics of juvenile homicide.* Lexington, MA: D. C. Heath.

Ewing, C. P. (1990b). *Kids who kill.* Lexington, MA: Lexington Books.

Federal Bureau of Investigation (1995). *Crime in America: Uniform crime reports.* Washington, DC: U.S. Government Printing Office.

Heide, K. M. (1992). *Why kids kill their parents: Child abuse and adolescent homicide.* Columbus: Ohio State University Press.

Heide, K. M. (1999). *Young killers: The challenge of juvenile homicide.* Thousand Oaks, CA: Sage.

James, J. R. (1994). Turning the tables: Redefining self-defense theory for children who kill abusive parents. *Law and Psychology Review, 18,* 393–408.

Maas, R. L., Prakash, R., Hollender, M H., & Regan, W. M. (1984). Double parricide – matricide and patricide: A comparison with other schizophrenic murders. *Psychiatric Quarterly, 56,* 286–290.

Maloney, M. (1994). Children who kill their parents: *Prosecutor's Brief.* California District Attorney's Association Journal, 16, 20.

Mones, P. (1991). *When a child kills.* New York: Pocket Books.

Newhill, C. E. (1991). Parricide. *Journal of Family Violence, 6,* 375–394.

Rowley, J. C., Ewing, C. P., & Singer, S. (1987). Juvenile homicide: The need for an interdisciplinary approach. *Behavioral Sciences and the Law, 5,* 3–10.

Sadoff, R. (1971). Clinical observations on parricide. *Psychiatric Quarterly, 45,* 65.

Sargent, D. (1962). Children who kill: A family conspiracy? *Social Work, 7,* 35.

Tanay, E. (1976). Reactive parricide. *Journal of Forensic Sciences, 21,* 76.

Tanay, E. (1973). Adolescents who kill parents: Reactive parricide. *Australian and New Zealand Journal of Psychiatry, 7,* 263–273.

U.S. Department of Justice. (1994). *Violence between intimates.* Washington, D. C.: U.S. Government Printing Office.

U. S. Bureau of Justice Statistics. (1994). *Murder in families.* Washington, D.C.: U.S. Government Printing Office.

Weisman, A. M., & Sharma, K. K. (1997). Forensic analysis and psychological implications of parricide and attempted parricide. *Journal of Forensic Sciences, 42,* 1107–1113.

11. Alcohol and Dangerousness

JOAN McCORD

The co-occurrence of misbehavior and drinking have typically colored perceptions of the role alcohol plays in criminal behavior. For example, a recent U.S. Government publication provides figures of coincidences between alcohol use and dangerous conduct as indicating "extensive and far-reaching impacts of alcohol abuse on crime and public safety" (Greenfeld, 1998, p. 1). The author notes that he and co-investigators found "that nearly 4 in 10 violent victimizations involve use of alcohol, about 4 in 10 fatal motor vehicle accidents are alcohol-involved; and about 4 in 10 offenders, regardless of whether they are on probation, in local jail, or in state prison, self-report that they were using alcohol at the time of the offense."

Although drinking, fighting, and street crimes frequently occur at the same times and places, that is insufficient grounds for concluding that drinking causes fighting or street crimes. Furthermore, although many people who do dangerous things also drink, the nature of that relationship is far from certain.

This chapter examines several types of connections between alcohol consumption and criminality. The first section considers links between criminal behavior and drinking from historical perspectives. The section shows how development of a social agenda helped shape research strategies. The second section describes alcohol-related crimes, indicating their changing patterns. The third section focuses on syndromes, rather than incidents or events. The section focuses on the overlap of symptoms attributed to antisocial behavior disorder and alcoholism, and on their etiology and development. The chapter ends with a discussion of concepts and causes regarding criminal behavior and the use of alcohol.

Criminal Behavior and Drinking

Attributed links between drinking and crime appeared in reports by the earliest criminologists. The work of those early criminologists set a pattern for many subsequent studies. Mary Carpenter (1864/1969), a leader of the Reformatory Movement in England, describing tactics to prevent crime, claimed: "The Temperance Cause stands first in importance ... The testimonies of medical men, the declarations of Judges, the evidence of Governors and Chaplains of gaols, all point to the same cause of a large proportion of the crime of our country" (vol. 2, p. 325). Enrico Ferri (1897) tracked wine consumption in France between 1829 and 1887, noting corresponding increases in drinking and crimes. Ferri concluded, "despite a certain inevitable variation from year to year, there is a manifest correspondence of increase and decrease between the number of homicides, assaults, and malicious wounding, and the more or less abundant vintage" (p. 117). Lombroso (1912/1968) made similar claims, with estimates that alcoholism was a contributing cause in about three-quarters of the crimes in England. Charles Goring (1913), who compared Cambridge students with British prisoners, found a correlation of .39 between alcoholism and criminality.

Backing a claim that alcohol was at least indirectly responsible for "degeneracy, pauperism, poverty, disease, and crime," the sociologist George Elliott Howard (1918) asserted that scientists had proven that alcohol "impairs the judgment, clouds the reason, and enfeebles the will; while at the same time it arouses the appetites, inflames the passions, releases the primitive beast from the artificial restraint of social discipline" (pp. 61–62). Howard relied partly on figures showing that in Germany, Italy, France, and the United States, crimes of violence rise sharply during holidays when liquor flows most freely. He also cited studies showing rates of crime in relation to nativity of incarcerated felons. The rates, according to Howard, showed that "the relative percentage of felonies due to intemperance for each nationality stands in direct ratio to the drinking habits of such nationality" (p. 65). The percentages ran from the Scotch, at the high end, down to the "Hebrew race which is noted for its exceptional sobriety the world over." Figures from Massachusetts suggested that the largest percentage of criminals were occasional drinkers, followed by social drinkers, with habitual or excessive drinkers having the lowest proportion. Howard argued from this evidence that only complete prohibition would be able to reduce crime.

Crime in America was widely seen to reflect inebriety. The New York Chief of Police reported in 1850 that juvenile delinquents were "the offspring of always careless, generally intemperate, and oftentimes immoral and dishonest parents" (Matsell, 1850, p. 14). Surveys of convicts were used to suggest that alcohol was a major cause of crime. According to one study, 50% of the crimes among more than 13,000 convicts from 17 prisons and reformatories in 12 states could be attributed to drinking alcohol (cited in Howard, 1918). In Philadelphia, a dramatic decline in public drinking corresponded with a drop of indictments for murder from 3.1 per 100,000 between 1869 and 1871 to 2.1, 30 years later (Lane, 1986). Obviously, a perceived connection between drinking and crime has deep historical roots.

Prohibition, Alcohol, and Crime

During the first half of the 19th century, because of problems believed to be related to public drinking, a variety of regulations had been proposed for its control. For example, a local option law regarding liquor sales was adopted by the state of Maine in 1829, a year after citizens in Gardner, Maine, had voted to grant licenses only if a proprietor agreed not to sell liquor by the glass (Dunford, 1945). In 1846, states were granted power to charge license fees for imports from other states, provided Congress had no countervening laws.

Between 1846, when the U.S. Supreme Court first endorsed them, and 1869, 13 states enacted local option laws. Yet the 14th Amendment, ratified in 1868, seemed to many to provide protection of the right to manufacture and sell liquor. In 1874, the Supreme Court clarified its position in a decision that made manufacture and sale of liquor a privilege rather than a right. The Court went a step further when it ruled, in 1887, that compensation was unnecessary for confiscated liquor or equipment to manufacture liquor.

Through decisions of 1888 and 1890, the Supreme Court ruled in such a way that dry states could not reject importation of intoxicating liquor, at least under broadly defined conditions related to shipping procedures. "Original Package" houses arose to take advantage of the rulings, but these came under attack through the Wilson Act passed by Congress in August 1890. A series of struggles between federal and state powers ensued, culminating in 1917 with the Supreme Court upholding the Webb-Kenyon Act of 1913, passed over the veto of President Taft. This act removed protection of interstate liquor commerce, providing states with the power to enforce their laws against alcohol consumption.

During World War I, social workers, joined by industrialists, backed prohibition as patriotic. Dry zones around military bases reinforced prohibitions against serving liquor to servicemen. Local elections, however, revealed resistance to the Temperance movement. In 1916, Boston voters rejected almost two to one a bill that would have prohibited the licensing of saloons. Yet by 1917, 26 states had outlawed the sale of liquor. On April 4, 1917, legislators introduced the resolution that became the 18th Amendment. That resolution prohibited "manufacture, sale, or transportation of intoxicating liquors within, the importation thereof into, or the exportation thereof from the United States and all territory subject to the jurisdiction thereof for beverage purposes."

Timberlake (1966) traced success of the Prohibition movement to a conjunction of scientific discoveries and social changes that made plausible the engineering of society represented in the Progressive movement. Although the 18th Amendment did not take effect until January 16, 1920, the War Prohibition Act, enacted on November 21, 1918, and enforced after July 1, 1919, marked the real beginning of national prohibition in the United States (Burnham, 1968).

Controversy over prohibition did not, of course, end with enactment of the 18th Amendment. Sociologists continued to see social problems emanating from failures of enforcement. For example, Edward A. Ross (1921) attributed differences in rates of drunkenness among different racial groups to "alcoholic selection." Citing industrial accidents as well as physical and mental problems putatively caused by alcohol, Ross argued that without successful enforcement of prohibition, the country would go through a period of self-destruction in which people susceptible to alcohol would annihilate one another or themselves.

In April 1926, the Committee on the Judiciary of the 69th Congress held hearings about prohibition. Stanley Shirk, a lawyer acting as research director of the Moderation League, testified that drunkenness and crime had increased during Prohibition. Fisher (1926) disputed the interpretation given by Shirk, reanalyzing the data with corrections to consider first-time offenders separately and to take into account population increases. These reanalyses showed decreased rates of convictions for drunkenness, juvenile delinquency, public use of profanity, crimes against chastity, and assaults.

Other evidence, too, suggests that criminal behavior declined during Prohibition. Ferdinand (1967), for example, reported decreasing rates of crime for Boston over the period, with the exception of a rise in rape, during war and depression, and manslaughter between 1916 and 1936. These declines in criminality extended from 1849 to 1951, however, so that it is doubtful that they should be attributed to Prohibition. Crime rates in New York City, too, decreased during the Prohibition period (Willbach, 1938). Yet in Chicago, the same author reported: "The ratios of the population arrested for crimes against the person showed an almost continuous increase up to 1927 which was followed by an almost uninterrupted decrease through 1939" (Willbach, 1941). Some evidence suggests that enforcement of Prohibition contributed to a downward shift in the age at which youths began to commit serious crimes rather than a change in the population of criminals (McCord, 1992).

In sum, the evidence does not demonstrate that legislating against the use of alcohol reduced crime. Nevertheless, the debate over Prohibition left as legacy a style of displaying rates of alcohol-related crime in isolation from contextual information valuable to its interpretation.

Post-Prohibition Studies of Crime and Alcohol

Since repeal of the 18th Amendment, many studies have reported the presence of alcohol during criminal events or among criminals. For example, Shupe (1954) analyzed reports of urine alcohol concentration of 882 suspects in Columbus, Ohio. The suspects had been apprehended during or immediately after committing a felony. The proportion whose urine exceeded 0.10% alcohol ranged from 43% for felonious assault to 88% for cutting. Wolfgang and Strohm (1956) and Wolfgang (1958), discussing homicides committed between 1948 and 1952 in Philadelphia, reported that alcohol was present in 64% of the situations. These consisted of 9% alcohol present among victims only, 11% among offenders only, and 44% among both. Alcohol was more frequently present in situations in which the victim had precipitated the violence. Also, alcohol was more likely to be present in homicides committed Friday through Sunday than in those committed Monday through Thursday (70% vs. 50%). The authors note that because they have no figures showing general drinking patterns, they cannot assess the association between drinking and homicide, though the evidence frequently has been taken to indicate that drinking contributes to violence.

In Los Angeles over the decade 1970 through 1979, 51% of male victims and 26% of female victims were found to have alcohol in their blood (Goodman et al., 1986). As in Philadelphia, alcohol was more likely to be present among weekend victims. More than half the Friday through Sunday victims had alcohol in their blood, whereas 42% of Monday victims, and between 36% and 38% of the victims from the rest of the week had alcohol in their blood. Victims killed in bars or restaurants were most likely to have been drinking. Those killed by friends or acquaintances and those killed with knives or other cutting weapons were most likely to have alcohol in their blood. Goodman and his associates, too, recognize that in the absence of information about drinking in the surrounding circumstances, the information cannot be interpreted as demonstrating cause.

In Helsinki between 1963 and 1968, among the 105 male and 9 female offenders convicted for criminal homicides, 66% definitely had been drinking as had 68% of their victims (Virkkunen, 1974). Both had been drinking in 55%, and at least one in 79% of the cases. Virkkunen also discovered that approximately two out of three homicides had been preceded by aggressiveness or altercations, a condition associated with drinking and with male perpetrator/male victim crimes. Numerous government documents focus on reporting proportions of inmates who claim to have been under the influence of drugs or alcohol at the time they committed their offenses (e.g., Flanagan & Maguire, 1992; Innes & Greenfeld, 1990; Jamieson & Flanagan, 1989).

There is little reason to doubt that a sizable number of criminals are habitual drinkers. The proportion varies by type of crime, with crimes of violence at the high end among serious crimes (Amir, 1971; Banay, 1942, 1945; Bohman, Cloninger, Sigvardsson, & von Knorring, 1982, 1983; Collins, 1981; Flanagan & McGuire, 1992; Gerson & Preston, 1979; Murdoch, Pihl, & Ross, 1990; Nicol, Gunn, Gristwood, Foggitt, & Watson, 1973; Wikström, 1985).

Pernanen (1981) suggested that alcohol tends to disorganize cognitive functions, increasing dependence on situational cues. Analysis of 749 violent crime incidents recorded by the police in Thunder Bay, Canada, indicated that 31% of the offenders and 26% of the victims had been drinking, with evidence of alcohol present in 42% of the situations (Pernanen, 1991). Male offenders with female victims were the most likely to have been drinking. Victims were more likely to have been drinking when there was more than one offender, though offenders were more likely to have been drinking when acting alone.

Because they failed to include appropriate comparisons, despite the large number of studies that report levels of alcohol use by offenders, no supportable judgments can be made about whether drinking and crime are likely to be associated. To bridge this lacuna, incarcerated youths can be compared with general populations.

Among youths in long-term, state-operated juvenile institutions during 1987, 32% reported having been under the influence of alcohol at the time they committed the offense for which they were incarcerated (Beck, Kline, & Greenfeld, 1988). In a class of 1987 high school seniors, 38% reported that they had, on at least one occasion within the prior two weeks, consumed at least five drinks in a sitting (Johnston, O'Malley, & Bachman, 1988). Among young adults, the rates were 32% at age 18, 36% for 19- and 20-year-olds, 38% for 21- and 22-year-olds, declining to 36% for 23 – 24-year-olds, and declining thereafter to 25% at ages 29 to 32 (Johnston, O'Malley, & Bachman, 1991).

Roizen (1981) showed that despite the higher rates of crime among blacks as compared with whites, their rates of drinking and of alcohol involvement in crimes were lower. Similar relative rates of drinking have been found in other studies. Use of alcohol was lower among black men and black women than among white men and women in senior classes between 1976 and 1989 (Bachman et al., 1991). In 1985, a household survey showed that among males across ages, whites were slightly more likely than Hispanics and Hispanics more likely than blacks to drink alcohol at least once a week (40%, 38%, 35%). Between the ages of 18 and 25, 48% of the white males, 43% of the Hispanic males, and 40% of the black males reported drinking at least once a week (The National Institute on Drug Abuse, 1987). Among victims of homicide, whites were more likely than blacks to have been intoxicated (Abel & Zeidenberg, 1985). Such rate comparisons tend to belie explanations of crime in terms of drinking behavior.

More direct evidence also raises doubts that alcohol is a contributing factor to violence. Bard and Zacker (1974), for example, examined police reports of their calls for family crises. These involved 1,358 occasions among 962 families. Disputes that did *not* involve assault were about twice as likely to have included alcohol as those that did.

In order to get a better idea of how alcohol is related to criminal violence, Mayfield (1976) analyzed descriptive accounts collected from male prisoners convicted for crimes ranging between assault with a deadly weapon and first-degree murder. The convicts reported that 40% of their victims had been drinking and 35% definitely had not; 57% of the convicts said they themselves had been drinking. Among those who had been intoxicated at the time of the crime, only 13% considered drinking to have been causally related to the assaultive behavior, with an additional 28% considering alcohol to have been contributory to the violence.

Pernanen (1991) asked a randomly selected sample to report on their recent experiences with violence. He learned that alcohol was involved in 54% of the incidents of physical violence, with the assailant drinking in 51% and the respondent in 30%. Women were less likely to report episodes in licensed drinking places, where alcohol was involved in all but 1%. Analyses of the information gathered from these reported incidents led Pernanen to conclude that alcohol had little influence on violence.

Fagan (1990) rightly points out that "intoxication does not consistently lead to aggressive behavior" (p. 243). He suggests a complex feedback model in which cognitive functions, setting, and expectancy both result from and produce the type and amount of substance used. In Fagan's model, only the two variables labeled "setting and social context" and "formal and informal social controls" directly affect interpersonal aggression.

Alcohol-Related Crimes

Although repeal of Prohibition ended the crimes of manufacture, sale, or transportation of intoxicating liquors, specific crimes have been identified as alcohol-related. Driving under the influence of alcohol, driving while intoxicated, public drunkenness, disorderly conduct, vagrancy, and liquor law violations are the crimes commonly considered to be alcohol-related. Disorderly conduct, a crime classified as alcohol-related in government compilations, refers to any breach of the peace. The crime of vagrancy, though considered to be alcohol-related by the U.S. government, includes vagabondage, begging, and loitering. In 1990, according to the Uniform Crime Reporting Program, there were 1,810,800 arrests in the United States for driving under the influence, 714,700 for violation of liquor laws, 910,100 for drunkenness, 733,000 for disorderly conduct, and 38,500 for vagrancy, for a total of 4,107,100 alcohol-related arrests (Flanagan & Maguire, 1992). Public drunkenness or intoxication, liquor law violations (including underage purchasing or sales, violation of open container laws, and unlicensed production or sale of liquor), and driving under the influence come closest to the core of violations related to using alcohol. The latter includes, however, operating a vehicle or common carrier while under the influence of narcotics.

With the exception of liquor laws, juveniles account for relatively low proportions of the arrests for alcohol-related crimes. In 1991, those under 18 accounted for 1% of the arrests for driving under the influence, 3% of those arrested for public drunkenness, 6% of the vagrancies, 18% of those arrested for disorderly conduct, and 23% of those who violated liquor laws (U.S. Government, August 1992).

The proportion of women arrested for alcohol-related crimes increased in every category between 1962 and 1990 (Flanagan & Maguire, 1992; Hoover, 1964). In 1990, women accounted for almost 13% of the arrests for driving under the influence, up from 6% in 1962. They accounted for 19% of the arrests for liquor law violations, as compared with 14% in 1962. In 1990, women accounted for 19% of the arrests for disorderly conduct, 10% of the arrests for public drunkenness, and 13% of the arrests for vagrancy; these figures can be compared with 13% of disorderly conduct, 8% of public drunkenness, and 9% of vagrancy arrests in 1962.

Official attitudes toward public drunkenness have changed considerably since the early 1960s. In the decisions *Easter v. District of Columbia*, 361 F.2d 50 (DC Circuit, 1966, en banc) and *Driver v. Hinnant*, 356 F.2d 761 (4th Circuit, 1966), the court argued that because alcoholism was an illness, a homeless alcoholic could not avoid public drunkenness and therefore ought not be punished. In 1967 the United States Crime Commission, the DC Crime Commission, and the Cooperative Commission on the Study of Alcoholism recommended that a public health approach be substituted for the criminal justice approach to public drunkenness. In 1969, these recommendations were followed by a "Joint Statement of Principles Concerning Alcoholism" from the American Bar Association and the American Medical Association, urging state legislatures to view alcoholism as an illness rather than as a crime. The Alcoholic Rehabilitation Act of 1968 (Public Law 90-574) included the statement that handling chronic alcoholics within the criminal justice system "perpetuates and aggravates the broad problem of alcoholism whereas treating it as a health problem permits early detection and prevention of alcoholism and effective treatment and rehabilitation, relieves police and other law enforcement agencies, and better serves the interests of the public." A Uniform Alcoholism and Intoxication Treatment Act was approved and recommended for enactment in all states during the National Conference of Commissioners on Uniform State Laws in 1971. The recommendation was never adopted by all 50 states, but at various times, more than half the states have treated public drunkenness as a health problem rather than as a crime.

Driving under the influence accounts for the highest proportion of alcohol-related crimes. Figures from 1988 through 1990 suggest that the more severe the automobile crash the greater the likelihood of alcohol involvement (Flanagan & Maguire, 1992). Estimates compiled by the National Highway Safety Administration show that for 1990, 5% of the crashes resulting only in property damage, 9% of those resulting in minor or moderate injury, and 20% of those resulting in severe or fatal injury involved alcohol.

The first recorded driving fatality occurred in 1898 (Waller, 1976). In 1989, there were 26,379 fatally injured motor vehicle drivers, 37.2% of whom had at least 0.10% blood alcohol concentration (Maguire & Flanagan, 1991).

In 1990, reporting shifted from showing fatalities of drivers to showing fatalities in motor vehicle accidents (Flanagan & Maguire, 1992). For 1982 through 1989, information about both was available. For these years, between 56% and 58% of the fatalities were drivers. The number of drivers killed rose from 24,690 in 1982 to 26,379 in 1989. But the proportion of the driver fatalities whose blood alcohol was at least 0.10% declined from 44% to 37% over the 8-year period.

According to the U.S. Department of Justice, there were 1,810,800 recorded arrests for driving under the influence in 1990 (Flanagan & Maguire, 1992). This is more than the number of arrests reported for drug abuse violations (1,089,500) and $2\frac{1}{2}$ times the rate of arrests for all Type I violent crimes (705, 500).

Popular opinion seems to favor a view that those who drive while intoxicated are an unselected mix of those who drink, suggesting that drunken drivers could be any one of us. Nevertheless, fatalities tend to occur among younger drivers, many of whom have had prior arrests both for alcohol-related behavior and for violence (Waller, 1976).

One longitudinal study shows that men convicted for driving while intoxicated could be distinguished from their classmates in elementary schools by being more self-reliant. Their families were more likely to display conflict and aggression, and they themselves were more likely to have been in trouble for drinking and to have been in fights. Furthermore, their criminal records showed that 69% had been convicted for Index crimes in comparison with 27% of the comparison group. The evidence indicated, therefore, that drunken driving typically represented part of a pattern of antisocial behavior (McCord, 1984).

Alcoholism and Antisocial Behavior

Several strains of evidence link serious criminality and alcoholism. In one study of 223 consecutive releases from prisons and reformatories, 43% were diagnosed as alcoholics (Guze, 1976). In another, criminality was found to have declined when sociopaths reduced their drinking (Goodwin & Guze, 1979). Violent criminals have been found more likely to be alcoholics, younger, and less intelligent than nonviolent ones (Nicol et al., 1973). Heavy drinking and aggressive behavior are parts of a lifestyle for many delinquents (Farrington, 1979; Pulkkinen & Hurme, 1984). Additionally, juvenile delinquents have relatively high rates of subsequent alcoholism, and alcoholics report histories of juvenile delinquency (Collins, 1981; Lindelius & Salum, 1973; McCord, 1980; McCord & McCord, 1960; Zucker & Gomberg, 1986).

Alcohol probably plays a variety of roles related to antisocial behavior. One study indicates that although most professional thieves drink heavily, they rarely drink immediately prior to committing a crime. Had they been drinking, several reported, they would have been unreliable partners. Nevertheless, these men rarely were married or legitimately employed and often hung out where drinking provided the entertainment. The researcher concluded that "the lifestyle of successful property criminals is conducive to both heavy drinking and homelessness" (Cordilia, 1985, pp. 166–167). Casual criminals, on the other hand, tend to have been drinking in conjunction with their thefts. Among these men, Cordilia suggests, participation with a drinking group provides companionship.

For both alcoholism and criminality, early onset presages particularly severe problems (Blumstein, Cohen, Roth, & Visher, 1986; Farrington, 1983, 1986; Foulds & Hassall, 1969; McCord, 1981a; Schuckit, 1973; Schuckit, Rimmer, & Winokur, 1970; Stabenau, 1984; Wolfgang, Figlio, & Sellin, 1972). Recent longitudinal evidence suggests also that early criminality is linked with the early use of alcohol (van Kammen, Loeber, & Stouthamer-Loeber, 1991).

The combination of heavy drinking with antisocial behavior seems to identify a subset of criminals particularly prone to antisocial personality disorder. In one study of 360 inmates in a maximum security institution, symptoms of alcoholism, measured by the Diagnostic Interview Schedule (Robins, Helzer, Croughan, & Ratcliff, 1981), and age at first intoxication were correlated with only one of the two factors involved in psychopathy (Hare, 1985), the factor measuring general deviant behavior. Because alcoholism was unrelated to the factor measuring such attitudes as selfishness, callousness, remorselessness, guiltlessness, and lying, the authors suggested that a general deviance factor underlies both psychopathy and alcohol abuse (Smith & Newman, 1990).

Retracing 524 lower-class white children referred to a child guidance clinic, Robins (1966) found several predictors that led to both the repetitive form of criminality, which she called sociopathic behavior, and to alcoholism. Robins suggested that the overlap between alcoholism and sociopathy may have been partially due to the fact that the children were seen in a clinic specializing in treatments for antisocial children (p. 261). Yet similar findings are reported for a community study of white, American-born, urban, predominantly middle-class subjects traced from age 10 to their mid 40s (Jones, 1968). Those who became problem drinkers had been undercontrolled, rebellious, assertive, aggressive, and sometimes sadistic in their school years. In a subsequent analysis, Robins (1978) considered the disorders to be developmentally related, with frequency of childhood behavior problems an efficient predictor of alcoholism and antisocial behavior as an adult.

In another longitudinal study, McCord (1980) found that among juvenile delinquents, those who became alcoholics were more likely to commit serious crimes as adults. As compared with nonalcoholic criminals, the alcoholic criminals also were more likely to escalate the seriousness of the crimes they committed.

To the extent that the personality correlates and etiology resemble one another for alcoholism and antisocial personality, it is reasonable to believe that these are two ways of looking at a single type of disorder. If these similarities actually mask different disorders, however, treating them as a single disorder may prevent discovering underlying causes and potential cures.

To address the question of common causes, McCord and Ensminger (1997) considered the lives of 456 males and 497 females first studied at the age of 6 and retraced when they were 32 years old. Subjects had lived in an impoverished black ghetto at the time the study began. Alcoholics were identified using *DSM-III-R* diagnostic criteria and through the CAGE test (Ewing & Rouse, 1970). Violent criminals were identified through official records. Among females, being aggressive at age 6 and skipping school predicted violence; none of the considered variables predicted alcoholism. Among males, being aggressive at age 6, skipping school, and being high in intelligence predicted violence;

being frequently spanked predicted alcoholism. At least for males, alcoholism combined with violence seemed to be a consequence of exposure to multiple risk conditions.

Although both alcoholics and criminals appear to court risks, risk taking is not characteristic of alcoholics. Combs-Orme, Taylor, Scott, and Holmes (1983), for example, retraced 1,289 alcoholics 6 to 9 years after treatment. Reported deaths were verified through vital statistics. The 22% mortality rate was 3.1 times that expected from St. Louis rates adjusted for age, but rates of death due to homicide were only slightly elevated. These results echo a study of 1,000 consecutive admissions of alcoholics to an outpatient clinic in Melbourne, Australia (Bartholomew & Kelley, 1965). Among the males, who comprised 85% of the sample, only 15% had records for any crime other than drunk and disorderly. Among the females, only 2% had records for crimes other than drunk and disorderly.

When alcoholics are grouped according to whether or not they are also criminals, the alcoholic criminals resemble nonalcoholic criminals more than noncriminal alcoholics in terms of such childhood characteristics as shyness, aggressiveness, and self-confidence (McCord, 1981b). Parents of the alcoholic criminals resemble parents of nonalcoholic criminals more than parents of noncriminal alcoholics in terms of affection, supervision, expectations, aggressiveness, and conflict.

Some research suggests that differences in family history may distinguish between antisocial alcoholics and others. Alcoholics with a high degree of familial alcoholism tend also to meet criteria for *DSM-III* antisocial personality disorder (Alterman, Gerstley, Strohmetz, & McKay, 1991; Lewis, Rice, & Helzer, 1983; Yates, Petty, & Brown, 1988). Hesselbrock, Stabenau, Hesselbrock, Roger, and Babor (1982) found that with bilineal family histories of alcoholism, probands were more likely to be arrested, have accidents, and show loss of control with drinking. Similarly, McKenna and Pickens (1981, 1983) found that among chronic alcoholic patients in a rehabilitation center, those who had two alcoholic parents were most likely to become alcoholics at earlier ages, to have been suspended from school, and to have been arrested. Schuckit (1984) analyzed family histories among 99 consecutive admissions of primary alcoholics to an alcohol treatment program. He found that those having two alcoholic parents were youngest, and were most likely to have been convicted as incorrigible. Similar results were obtained in a study of 137 men convicted for driving while intoxicated (Harwood & Leonard, 1989).

To classify alcoholism as a single disorder is tantamount to classifying fevers as though their causes were similar merely because the symptom was similar. Although there is widespread agreement among those who do research on alcoholism that a typology is necessary, no taxonomy has proven sufficiently productive to gain general acceptance.

Conceptual Issues and Discussion

A historicai picture showing the simultaneous development of the field of criminology and the prohibition movement provides a context by which to understand the claim that coincidence rates are sufficient evidence on which to argue that alcohol causes dangerous behavior. Nevertheless, the compilation of evidence showing proportions of crimes with which alcohol can be associated has led to little knowledge. People are not equally at risk for being in public drinking places. We do not know much about the people who frequent public bars nor much about their propensity for fighting. Nor do we know whether the amount of liquor consumed by assailants or their victims in or near bars is greater than that consumed by relevant others who have not been involved with crime incidents. The relatively few studies that compare drinking among offenders with similarly situated nondrinking offenders fail to show that alcohol plays a major role in criminal behavior.

Alcoholic serious criminals appear in both studies of alcoholics and of serious criminals. Because this group is not equally distributed across the socioeconomic spectrum, studies are differentially influenced by their inclusion. Future research would be enlightened by recognition that both criminal and alcoholic populations are heterogeneous.

An adequate account of relationships between the use of alcohol and crime should begin with clearer understanding of the differences between mere co-occurrence of alcohol with criminal acts and causal relations between them. Behavior caused by the influence of alcohol presumably would not occur in the absence of drinking. Behavior due to the influence of alcohol may be behavior that is judged wrong by a sober actor. Alternatively, it may be behavior permitted under ritualized circumstances that involve the imbibing of alcohol.

Laboratory studies showing that alcohol can increase the amount of pain one person gives another may be of this latter type (Gantner & Taylor, 1982; Gustafson, 1992; Murdoch & Pihl, 1985; Zeichner & Pihl,

1979, 1980). The pain-giving experiments set levels of pain that are not devastating, and liquor may reduce inhibition at such levels without necessarily having any disinhibiting effects against fundamental moral principles. The fact that effects from alcohol appear to fade in group settings suggests that the paucity of alternative cues may be a contributing factor to the importance of both expectancy effects and effects of alcohol in the laboratory.

Doubtless, there are occasions when a person drinks in order to justify doing something that would be impossible for a sober person to explain. In such cases, it would be reasonable to view alcohol as a contributing cause.

Adequate theories about the contribution of alcohol to criminal behavior require understanding intentional actions. Intentional actions must have motives as contributing causes. Causal explanations of crimes and the use of alcohol should take into account something similar to what Aristotle referred to as the material, formal, efficient, and final causes (Physics Bk. II, Ch. III). Although the terms are archaic, the distinctions they make are important to modern science.

Material causes are relatively stable conditions out of which a thing comes to be. In relation to crime and alcohol, the notion of material cause points to the existence of classes at greatest risk. If analyses of the conditions of risk mistake the role of material causes, the stable influences of these causes are likely to swamp data analyzed in relation to more transient factors. For example, in his study of violence in Thunder Bay, Pernanen (1991) allowed gender to compete with presence of alcohol in the logistic regression models. As a result, Pernanen concluded that alcohol had little influence on aggression. Men drank more often and were more prone to violence. It is a mistake, however, to assume that a statistical relationship between sex and violence provides the foundation for understanding conditions under which alcohol and violence are sometimes connected.

Formal causes provide the archetype or form under which events occur. Experimental studies demonstrate that expectations influence behavior, perhaps more strongly with alcohol than without. Some of these studies show that when males are led to believe they are drinking alcohol, whether or not the belief is true, they tend to become more aggressive (Lang, Goeckner, Adesso, & Marlatt, 1975; Steele & Southwick, 1985). Cultural expectations, a type of formal cause, might also help to explain why women are less often involved as either perpetrators or victims of crimes outside the home.

210   JOAN McCORD

Whether one ought to count alcohol as an efficient cause of crime depends in part on the degree to which alcohol contributes to risk. Ideally, one would like to consider a setting both with and without alcohol. The same, or similar individuals would be tested under both conditions. If alcohol, either through its chemical or social properties, were to enhance the likelihood of crime, then it would be reasonable to conclude that alcohol helps explain the crime through its causal role.

The perspective of participants is particularly valuable in the study of final causes, the goals or purposes served through use of alcoholic beverages. Motives have a window outward, because they explain our actions; therefore, we need not rely solely on self-reports to study them.

To help understand alcohol-related dangerousness, accounts should describe relationships among people, motives, and incidents. Within a culture, there are differences in the degree to which people turn to alcohol when they are angry. These differences seem to be related to whether or not alcohol-induced behavior is perceived to be excusable. Whether or not alcohol will be generative of crime depends partly on the nature of people's motives for their actions.

In the absence of appropriate studies, a conclusion that alcohol causes dangerous behavior is unwarranted. On the other hand, we know that dangerous behavior occurs in the presence of alcohol among men more than women, among whites more than blacks, and on weekends more often than during weekdays.

Abel, E. L., & Zeidenberg, P. (1985). Age, alcohol, and violent death: A postmortem study. *Journal of Studies on Alcohol, 46*(3), 228–231.
Alterman, A. I., Gerstley, L. J., Strohmetz, D. B., & McKay, J. R. (1991). Psychiatric heterogeneity in antisocial alcoholics: Relation to familial alcoholism. *Comprehensive Psychiatry, 32*(5), 423–431.
Amir, M. (1971). *Patterns in forcible rape.* Chicago: University of Chicago Press.
Aristotle. (1941). Physics. (R. P. Hardie and R. K. Gaye, Trans.). In R. McKeon (Ed.), *The basic works of Aristotle* (pp. 218–394). New York: Random House.
Bachman, J. G., Wallace, J. M., O'Malley, P. M., Johnston, L. D., Kurth, C. L., & Neighbors, H. W. (1991). Racial/ethnic differences in smoking, drinking, and illicit drug use among American high school seniors, 1976–89. *American Journal of Public Health, 81*(3), 372–377.
Banay, R. S. (1942). Alcoholism and crime. *Quarterly Journal of Studies on Alcohol, 2*, 686–716.
Banay, R. S. (1945). Alcohol and aggression. *Alcohol, science, and society* (pp. 143–152). New Haven: Quarterly Journal of Studies on Alcohol.

Bard, M., & Zacker, J. (1974). Assaultiveness and alcohol use in family disputes: Police perceptions. *Criminology, 12,* 281–292.

Bartholomew, A. A., & Kelley, M. F. (1965). The incidence of a criminal record in 1,000 consecutive "alcoholics." *British Journal of Criminology, 5,* 143–149.

Beck, A. J., Kline, S. A., & Greenfeld, L. A. (1988). Survey of youths in custody, 1987. *The Criminal Justice Archive and Information Network of the Inter-University Consortium for Political and Social Research,* Fall 1988, 1–3.

Blumstein, A., Cohen, J., Roth, J. A., & Visher, C. A. (Eds.). (1986). *Criminal careers and career criminals.* Washington, DC: National Academy Press.

Bohman, M., Cloninger, C. R., Sigvardsson, S., & von Knorring, A. (1982). Predisposition to petty criminality in Swedish adoptees. *Archives of General Psychiatry, 39,* 1233–1241.

Bohman, M., Cloninger, C. R., Sigvardsson, S., & von Knorring, A. (1983). Gene-environment interaction in the psychopathology of Swedish adoptees: Studies of the origins of alcoholism and criminality. In S. B. Guze, F. J. Earls, & J. E. Barrett (Eds.), *Childhood psychopathology and development* (pp. 265–278). New York: Raven Press.

Burnham, J. C. (1968). New perspectives on the prohibition "experiment" of the 1920s. *Journal of Social History, 2,* 51–68.

Carpenter, M. (1864/1969). *Our convicts.* Montclair, NJ: Patterson Smith.

Collins, J. J., Jr. (1981). Alcohol careers and criminal careers. In J. J. Collins (Ed.), *Drinking and crime* (pp. 152–206). New York: Guilford.

Combs-Orme, T., Taylor, J. R., Scott, E. B., & Holmes, S. J. (1983). Violent deaths amongst alcoholics. *Journal of Studies on Alcohol, 44,* 938–949.

Cordilia, A. (1985). Alcohol and property crime: Exploring the causal nexus. *Journal of Studies on Alcohol, 46,* 161–171.

Dunford, E. (1945). Legal aspects of prohibition. In E. M. Jellinek (Ed.), *Alcohol, science and society* (pp. 321–353). New Haven: Quarterly Journal of Studies on Alcohol.

Ewing, J., & Rouse, B. A. (1970). Identifying the hidden alcoholic. Paper presented at the 29th international congress on alcohol and drug dependence, Sydney, NSW Australia.

Fagan, J. (1990). Intoxication and aggression. In M. Tonry & J. Q. Wilson (Eds.), *Drugs and crime* (pp. 241–320). Chicago: University of Chicago Press.

Farrington, D. P. (1979). Environmental stress, delinquent behavior, and convictions. In I. G. Sarason & C. D. Spielberger (Eds.), *Stress and anxiety, Vol. 6* (pp. 93–106). New York: Wiley.

Farrington, D. P. (1983). Offending from 10 to 25 years of age. In K. T. Van Dusen & S. A. Mednick (Eds.), *Prospective studies of crime and delinquency* (pp. 73–97). Boston: Kluwer-Nijhoff.

Farrington, D. P. (1986). Stepping stones to adult criminal careers. In D. Olweus, J. Block & M. Radke-Yarrow (Eds.), *Development of antisocial and prosocial behavior* (pp. 359–384). New York: Academic Press.

Ferdinand, T. N. (1967). The criminal patterns of Boston since 1848. *American Journal of Sociology, 78,* 1, 84–99.

Ferri, E. (1897). *Criminal sociology.* New York: Appleton.

Fisher, I. (1926). *Prohibition at its worst.* New York: Macmillan.

Flanagan, T. J., & Maguire, K. (1992). *Sourcebook of criminal justice statistics 1991*. Washington, DC: U.S. Government Printing Office.

Foulds, G. A., & Hassall, C. (1969). The significance of age of onset of excessive drinking in male alcoholics. *British Journal of Psychiatry, 115*, 1027–1032.

Gantner, A. B., & Taylor, S. P. (1982). Human physical aggression as a function of alcohol and threat of harm. *Aggressive Behavior, 18*, 29–36.

Gerson, L. W., & Preston, D. Q. (1979). Alcohol consumption and the incidence of violent crime. *Journal of Studies on Alcohol, 40*, 307–312.

Goodman, R. A., Mercy, J. A., Loya, F., Rosenberg, M. L., Smith, J. C., Allen, N. H., Vargas, L., & Kolts, R. (1986). Alcohol use and interpersonal violence: Alcohol detected in homicide victims. *American Journal of Public Health, 76*, 144–149.

Goodwin, D. W., & Guze, S. B. (1979). *Psychiatric diagnosis* (2nd ed.). New York: Oxford University Press.

Goring, C. (1913). *The English convict: A statistical study*. London: Stationery Office. (Available from Montclair, NJ: Paterson Smith.)

Greenfeld, L. A. (1998). *Alcohol and crime: An analysis of national data on the prevalence of alcohol involvement in crime*. U.S. Department of Justice, Washington, DC.

Gustafson, R. (1992). Alcohol and aggression–a replication study controlling for potential confounding variables. *Aggressive Behavior, 18*, 21–28.

Guze, S. B. (1976). *Criminality and psychiatric disorders*. New York: Oxford University Press.

Hare, R. D. (1985). Comparison of procedures for the assessment of psychopathy. *Journal of Consulting and Clinical Psychology, 53*, 7–16.

Harwood, M. K., & Leonard, K. E. (1989). Family history of alcoholism, youthful antisocial behavior and problem drinking among DWI offenders. *Journal of Studies on Alcohol, 50*, 210–216.

Hesselbrock, V. M., Stabenau, J. R., Hesselbrock, M. N., Roger, E., & Babor, T. F. (1982). The nature of alcoholism in patients with different family histories for alcoholism. *Progress in Neuro-psychopharmacological and Biological Psychiatry, 6*, 607–614.

Hoover, J. E. (1964). *Crime in the United States*. Boston: Beacon Press.

Howard, G. E. (1918). Alcohol and crime: A study in social causation. *American Journal of Sociology, 24*, 61–80.

Innes, C. A., & Greenfeld, L. A. (1990). *Violent state prisoners and their victims*. BJS Special Report, Washington, DC: U.S. Department of Justice.

Jamieson, K. M., & Flanagan, T. J. (1989). *Sourcebook of criminal justice statistics – 1988*. Washington, DC: U.S. Department of Justice, Bureau of Justice Statistics.

Johnston, L. D., O'Malley, P. M., & Bachman, J. G. (1988). *Illicit drug use, smoking, and drinking by America's high school students, college students, and young adults: 1975–1987*. Rockville, MD: National Institute on Drug Abuse.

Johnston, L. D., O'Malley, P. M., & Bachman, J. G. (1991). *Drug use among American high school seniors, college students and young adults, 1975–1990* (2 volumes). Rockville, MD: National Institute on Drug Abuse.

Jones, M. C. (1968). Personality correlates and antecedents of drinking patterns in adult males. *Journal of Consulting and Clinical Psychology, 32*, 2–12.

Lane, R. (1986). *Roots of violence in black Philadelphia 1860–1900.* Cambridge, MA: Harvard University Press.

Lang, A. R., Goeckner, D. J., Adesso, V. J., & Marlatt, G. A. (1975). Effects of alcohol on aggression in male social drinkers. *Journal of Abnormal Psychology, 84,* 508–518.

Lewis, C. E., Rice, J., & Helzer, J. E. (1983). Diagnostic interactions: Alcoholism and antisocial personality. *Journal of Nervous and Mental Disease, 171,* 105–113.

Lindelius, R., & Salum, I. (1973). Alcoholism and criminality. *Acta Psychiatrica Scandinavica, 49,* 306–314.

Lombroso, C. (1912/1968). *Crime: Its causes and remedies.* Montclair, NJ: Patterson Smith.

McCord, J. (1980). Patterns of deviance. In S. B. Sells, R. Crandall, M. Roff, J. Strauss, & W. Pollin (Eds.), *Human functioning in longitudinal perspective: Studies of normal and psychopathological populations* (pp. 157–162). Baltimore: Williams & Wilkins.

McCord, J. (1981a). A longitudinal perspective on patterns of crime. *Criminology, 19,* 211–218.

McCord, J. (1981b). Alcoholism and criminality: Confounding and differentiating factors. *Journal of Studies on Alcohol, 42,* 739–748.

McCord, J. (1984). Drunken drivers in longitudinal perspective. *Journal of Studies on Alcohol, 45,* 316–320.

McCord, J. (1992). Another time, another drug. In M. Glantz & R. Pickens (Eds.), *Vulnerability to drug abuse* (pp. 473–489), Washington, DC: American Psychological Association Press.

McCord, J., & Ensminger, M. E. (1997). Multiple risks and comorbidity in an African-American population. *Criminal Behaviour and Mental Health, 7,* 229–352.

McCord, W., & McCord, J. (1960). *Origins of alcoholism.* Stanford, CA: Stanford University Press.

McKenna, T., & Pickens, R. (1981). Alcoholic children of alcoholics. *Journal of Studies on Alcohol, 42,* 1021–1029.

McKenna, T., & Pickens, R. (1983). Personality characteristics of alcoholic children of alcoholics. *Journal of Studies on Alcohol, 44,* 688–700.

Maguire, K., & Flanagan, T. J. (1991). *Sourcebook of criminal justice statistics 1990.* Washington, DC: U.S. Department of Justice, Bureau of Justice Statistics.

Matsell, G. W. (1850). Report of the chief of police concerning destitution and crime among children in the city. In T. L. Harris (Ed.), *Juvenile depravity and crime in our city. A Sermon* (pp. 14–15). New York: Norton.

Mayfield, D. (1976). Alcoholism, alcohol, intoxication and assaultive behavior. *Diseases of the Nervous System, 37,* 288–291.

Murdoch, D., & Pihl, R. O. (1985). Alcohol and aggression in a group interaction. *Addictive Behaviors, 10,* 97–101.

Murdoch, D., Pihl, R. O., & Ross, D. (1990). Alcohol and crimes of violence: Present issues. *The International Journal of the Addictions, 25,* 1065–1081.

National Institute on Drug Abuse. (1987). *National Survey on Drug Abuse: Population Estimates 1985*. Rockville, MD: National Institute on Drug Abuse.

Nicol, A. R., Gunn, J. C., Gristwood, J., Foggitt, R. H., & Watson, J. P. (1973). The relationship of alcoholism to violent behavior resulting in long-term imprisonment. *British Journal of Psychiatry, 123*, 47–51.

Pernanen, K. (1981). Theoretical aspects of the relationship between alcohol use and crime. In J. J. Collins, Jr. (Ed.), *Drinking and crime* (pp. 1–69). New York: Guilford Press.

Pernanen, K. (1991). *Alcohol in human violence*. New York: Guilford Press.

Pulkkinen, L., & Hurme, H. (1984). Aggression as a predictor of weak self-control. In L. Pulkkinen & P. Lyytinen (Eds.), *Human action and personality*. Jyvaskyla, Finland: University of Jyvaskyla Press.

Robins, L. N. (1966). *Deviant children grown up*. Baltimore: Williams & Wilkins.

Robins, L. N. (1978). Sturdy childhood predictors of adult antisocial behavior: Replications from longitudinal studies. *Psychological Medicine, 8*, 611–622.

Robins, L. N., Helzer, J. E., Croughan, J., & Ratcliff, K. S. (1981). National Institute of Mental Health Diagnostic Interview Schedule. *Archives of General Psychiatry, 38*, 381–389.

Roizen, J. (1981). Alcohol and criminal behavior among blacks: The case for research on special populations. In J. J. Collins, Jr. (Ed.), *Drinking and crime* (pp. 207–252). New York: Guilford Press.

Ross, E. A. (1921). Prohibition as the sociologist sees it. *Harper's Magazine, 142*, 186–192.

Schuckit, M. A. (1984). Relationship between the course of primary alcoholism in men and family history. *Journal of Studies on Alcohol, 45*, 334–338.

Schuckit, M. A. (1973). Alcoholism and sociopathy–Diagnostic confusion. *Quarterly Journal of Studies on Alcohol, 34*, 157–164.

Schuckit, M. A., Rimmer, J. R., & Winokur, G. (1970). Alcoholism: Antisocial traits in male alcoholics. *British Journal of Psychiatry, 117*, 575–576.

Shupe, L. M. (1954). Alcohol and crime: A study of the urine alcohol concentration found in 882 persons arrested during or immediately after the commission of a felony. *Journal of Criminal Law, Criminology, and Police Science, 44*, 661–664.

Smith, S. S., & Newman, J. P. (1990). Alcohol and drug abuse/dependence disorders in psychopathic and nonpsychopathic criminal offenders. *Journal of Abnormal Psychology, 94*, 430–439.

Stabenau, J. R. (1984). Implications of family history of alcoholism, antisocial personality, and sex differences in alcohol, dependence. *American Journal of Psychiatry, 141*, 1178–1182.

Steele, C. M., & Southwick, L. (1985). Alcohol and social behavior I: The psychology of drunken excess. *Journal of Personality and Social Psychology, 48*, 18–34.

Timberlake, J. H. (1966). *Prohibition and the Progressive Movement, 1900–1920*. Cambridge, MA: Harvard University Press.

U. S. Government. (August 1992). *Uniform Crime Reports*. Washington, DC: Government Printing Office.

van Kammen, W. B., Loeber, R., & Stouthamer-Loeber, M. (1991). Substance use and its relationship to conduct problems and delinquency in young boys. *Journal of Youth and Adolescence, 20*, 399–415.

Virkkunen, M. (1974). Alcohol as a factor precipitating aggression and conflict behavior leading to homicide. *British Journal of Addictions, 69,* 149–154.

Waller, J. A. (1976). Alcohol and unintentional injury. In B. Kissin & H. Begleiter (Eds.), *The biology of alcoholism: Social aspects of alcohol, Vol. 4* (pp. 307–349). New York: Plenum.

Wikstrom, P. H. (1985). *Everyday violence in contemporary Sweden: Situational and ecological aspects.* Stockholm: The National Council for Crime Prevention, Sweden.

Willbach, H. (1938). The trend of crime in New York City. *Journal of Criminal Law, Criminology, and Police Science, 29,* 62–75.

Willbach, H. (1941). The trend of crime in Chicago. *Journal of Criminal Law, Criminology, and Police Science, 31,* 720–727.

Wolfgang, M. E., & Strohm, M. A. (1956). The relationship between alcohol and criminal homicide. *Quarterly Journal of the Studies on Alcohol, 17,* 411–425.

Wolfgang, M. E. (1958). *Patterns in Criminal Homicide.* New York: Wiley.

Wolfgang, M. E., Figlio, R. M., & Sellin, T. (1972). *Delinquency in a birth cohort.* Chicago: University of Chicago Press.

Yates, W. R., Petty, F., & Brown, K. (1988). Alcoholism in males with antisocial personality disorder. *The International Journal of the Addictions, 23,* 999–1010.

Zeichner, A., & Pihl, R. O. (1979). Effects of alcohol and behavior contingencies on human aggression. *Journal of Abnormal Psychology, 88,* 153–160.

Zeichner, A., & Pihl, R. O. (1980). Effects of alcohol and instigator intent on human aggression. *Journal of Studies on Alcohol, 41,* 265–276.

Zucker, R. A., & Gomberg, E. S. L. (1986). Etiology of alcoholism reconsidered: The case for a biopsychosocial process. *American Psychologist, 41,* 783–793.

12. Violence and Substance Abuse

PHILIP BEAN

Introduction

For these purposes violence can be defined as behavior by persons against other persons that intentionally threatens, attempts, or actually inflicts physical harm (Reiss & Roth, 1993, p. 35). It does not include self-inflicted harm as in suicide, nor verbal abuse, harassment, or psychological humiliations in which trauma may occur. Nor does it include unintentional harm, whether to self or others, which may result from taking contaminated or unusually pure substances leading to an overdose and perhaps death. Substance abuse means using illegally controlled substances but can include alcohol.

Interest in the links between violence and substance abuse has been prompted by increasing awareness that drug markets are violent places where death is commonplace and violence a standard feature of street dealing. In Britain and elsewhere, the introduction of crack cocaine in the late 1980s led to a more fearful yet considered formulation of the existing position. Low-level crack dealers were seen to display firearms on the streets of British cities where firearms were hitherto unknown. A product of this change has been to develop strategies for intervention and control, which have included a renewed research activity aimed at explaining some of the complexities between violence and substance abuse (de la Rosa, 1990). Another has been to alert policy makers to use research to help control a burgeoning industry of drug trafficking and supply.

Too often, however, the strategies required for intervention have been threatened by defects in existing data. Some have been long-standing, others recent. For example the Criminal Statistics produced annually in England and Wales (Home Office, 1997) provide data on the numbers and legal categories of offenses reported to the police and cleared up. There is no way of knowing how many violent events, or drug events took place, some of which may involve more than one offender, nor whether violent offenders were drug users. An increase in homicides, often attributed to an increase in drug use cannot be identified from these statistics. Similarly, the official statistics give data on property offenses reported to the police, but nothing about whether they were committed by drug users.

Nor are other official statistics more helpful. Medical records from hospital casualty departments where large numbers of violent drug users are dealt with daily rarely provide data on basic sociodemographic features of their patients, nor of the assailant, let alone whether substance abuse was present. Nor do custody records in the police stations. Similarly, probation presentence reports, which would be expected to record such information, tend not to do so – about 35% of the cases we examined of known abusers (Bean, 1995). This is not true, of course, for all public agencies. Of particular value are the data provided by Drug Use Forecasting (DUF) which in 1995 surveyed 20,737 adult males and 8,065 adult females arrested in 23 and 21 sites, respectively, in major U.S. metropolitan cities. About 10% of male and 14% of females were in need of alcohol or drugs at the time of the alleged offense, and 31% of both males and females said they were similarly under the influence of drugs or alcohol (N.I.J., 1995). DUF, together with one or two other longitudinal data sets, stand alone for the quality of data they provide; a British study, using a similar methodology, produced similar results (Bennett, 1998).

Most information comes from research, but here, too, the quality varies. Some research is of the highest order, but a great deal is poorly constructed, described by Michael Tonry as "scientifically weak and scanty" (Tonry, 1990, pp. 2 and 4). On a number of central questions about drug policy Tonry reports that "very little systematic knowledge is available from methodologically rigorous research" (p. 2). Too often basic errors intrude: For example, violence is rarely confined to specific social situations, being more often part of a generalized pattern of deviancy. Therefore, distinctions are required between violence associated with substance abuse and violence not similarly associated. A great deal of research fails to differentiate this distinction. Nor is it acceptable to say that violence within communities with widespread drug use is etiologically linked to substance abuse, without presenting evidence of the extent of violence elsewhere. If levels are comparable, it is reasonable to

conclude that violence is a manifestation of the general criminal procliv-
ities of the offenders rather than attributable to substance abuse. Other
problems relate to the way samples are drawn; few studies permit gen-
eralizations to be made – the sample is either too small or biased by the
population from which it is drawn (Fagan, & Chin, 1990).

Much research does little more than establish comorbidities (i.e.,
substance abuse and violence), often confusing comorbidity and etiology. A causal link is implied when there is only statistical evidence of
comorbidity; the explanation may be due to a third unknown disorder,
a biological vulnerability perhaps, or there may be no connection
between them. The trouble is we are better in producing these than
establishing etiology. In order to assign a causal link, there must be certainty that the behavior would have occurred had no substance been
taken.[1] To muddy the waters further, drugs are bought, sold, and consumed with no resulting violence, even though the threat of and presence of violent individuals has an effect.

We should not be too pessimistic about the overall state of knowledge, because more is known today than was known a few years ago.
We have learned there is no straightforward link between substance
misuse and violence, if only because most substances are taken without
any violent act, and there is no simple progression from substance
abuse to violence. Sometimes violence precedes substance abuse. Both
may be associated with a deviant lifestyle that they have in common
(Fagan & Chin, 1990 p. 4). We have learned also that violence has
stronger associations with some drugs than others, and the impact of
the drug is unrelated to the supply system. For example, cannabis consumption may not of itself produce violence, but the suppliers can be
and often are violent. Learning some of these basic lessons gives hope
for the future, but we are still a long way from giving more sustained
help to policy makers.

Theoretical Assumptions

There is no single theory of substance misuse, just as there is no single
theory of violence. Basic terms remain ill defined: What, for example,

---

[1] Jeffrey Fagan says "the presence of alcohol or drugs in violent events do not necessarily
imply that the substances affected the behavior of any of the participants. To assign a
causal role ... requires that we be certain that the behavior could not have occurred if
the user had been sober" (Fagan, 1993, p. 68).

is a drug; what constitutes addiction; and what constitutes substance abuse?[2] What is a violent act? Physical and sexual assaults against women and children by intimates are only slowly being recognized as violent crimes (Reiss & Roth, 1993, p. 3).

Existing theories are likely to be of a general nature. For example, subcultural and gang theories have incorporated substance abuse where violence is used to control territory, claim markets, or deal with ill-disciplined members. Or violence within drug markets can be theoretically linked to other illegal markets involving prostitution, or black markets in prohibited goods (Reiss & Roth, 1993, p. 202). The influential American Panel on the Understanding and Control of Violent Behavior mentions various theories of violence that lead to "problem-solving initiatives of pragmatic focused, methodologically sound collaboration efforts by policy makers, evaluation researchers, and basic researchers" (Reiss & Roth, 1993, p. 327). Violence is heterogeneous, and violent offenders are versatile rather than specialized, having multiple etiologies. So too are substance abuse and substance abusers.

The literature on substance abuse and violence is extensive, covering numerous academic disciplines. It is however, mainly American: There is little or no research in Britain or outside the United States. Transferring what is known of one society to another is always risky, even though there may be similarities between them. Moreover, in the absence of a single theory, ordering this literature is always difficult, even with numerous typologies able to classify various components of the drugs–violence nexus. That produced by Goldstein (Goldstein, 1995), referred to as "a tripartite conceptual framework," is probably the most useful. It has three features:

---

[2] The terms *abuse* and *misuse* and *use* are used interchangeably throughout. Sir Louis Blom-Cooper notes how the term *drug* moves from a relatively value neutral term when used in pharmacology to a value laden normative term when used in criminology (Blom-Cooper, 1998). One of the best but least recognized attempts at defining drugs is Lindesmith's view, that the central feature of all addiction is the craving for drugs. This exists whether it be in 20th century young urban male heroin addicts, or elderly, middle-class opiate smokers, and is present irrespective of age, personality, country of origin, or method of administration. The tendency to relapse or continue taking drugs is a corollary or consequence of craving. This craving for drugs, Lindesmith argues, develops only when the drug-taker understands the meaning of the withdrawal symptoms and attributes them to their cause (i.e., the use of the drugs), pp. 10–11 (1974) Bean, P. T. *The Social Control of Drugs*.

1. Psychopharmacological: Some individuals, as a result of long- or short-term ingestion of specific substances, may become excitable and irrational and act out in a violent fashion.
2. Economic–compulsive: Some drug users engage in economically oriented violent crime to support their costly habit; robbery is an example.
3. Systemic: Some individuals engage in aggressive patterns of interaction within the system of drug use and distribution. Systemic violence includes disputes over territory, enforcement of normative codes within drug-dealing hierarchies, punishment for failing to pay debts, or selling adulterated drugs.

There has been much discussion about whether Goldstein's framework constitutes a model and whether there is overlap between the three features: They are not mutually exclusive so presumably an offender can move between them. There is also debate about whether the framework can act as a predictive instrument. Elaborations have been common, sometimes to the point where they confuse more than they clarify,[3] and sometimes leading to the more obvious conclusion that certain types of violent events require multiple explanations. Yet the strength of Goldstein's framework is its clarity, and its emphasis on systemic violence is important. What it does not do, because it was never intended to do, is to produce causal explanations, nor account for all forms of violence within drug use. For example, it does not take account of drug takers who are mentally disordered, the so-called dual diagnosis patients, nor does it account for gender differences; male and female violence differs according to the roles within a relationship and an organization.[4,5]

---

[3] See: The conceptual scheme for organizing understanding of the drugs – violence relationships, by James Collins (1990). Summary thoughts about drugs and violence, in de la Rosa, M. (Ed.), *Drugs and violence: Causes correlates and consequences* NIDA Research Monograph, 103, pp. 265–275. I am unable to understand the scheme and feel reassured by Collins's own comment that "the model is ambitious and clearly not fully testable by any single study," pp. 272–273.

[4] Other typologies exist. The London Probation Service for example, classifies according to drug-inspired violence, drug-induced violence, and drug-marketing violence; the first when violence occurs as a result of committing property offenses to feed a habit; the second where violence occurs as a result of taking the drugs; and the third where the drug market leads to violence. The similarity with the Goldstein typology is clear.

[5] See Collins (1990).

Who Are the Violent Substance Abusers, and Where Does Violence Occur?

Violent people involved in drug misuse are not a subset of violent offenders, nor a specific subset of offenders generally. Convergence has occurred – that is, substance abusers and other criminals have become one and the same. The increasing numbers of persons taken into police custody in Britain and America testing positive for drugs bear this out (Bennett, 1998; Inciardi, Lockwood, & Pottieger, 1993, p. 113). There is also evidence that many drug users were offenders prior to drug misuse – about 50% in most British populations – and even those who were not share many of the characteristics of those who were. Drug-selling organizations recruit those who are violent, or enjoy violence, where they fill many roles within that organization including intimidating ordinary citizens who refuse to cooperate, tacitly or otherwise, with their demands (Johnson et al., 1990).

Violent substance abusers, especially street-level dealers, tend also to be victims of crimes, and of violence in particular. The British Crime Survey (Home Office, 1996) finds that factors associated with committing crime also apply to victims, that is, being young (18–24), male, single, going out frequently in the evenings with others, and spending time drinking in pubs and discos. In our study of Nottingham drug users we found that street-level dealers who were also substance abusers had unusually high rates of offending and high rates of victimization, with violence a constant feature (Bean & Wilkinson, 1988). They were burglars and they were burgled, they were violent and victims of violence. Similar results have been found in the United States (Kingery, Pruitt, & Hurley, 1992) where the aggressors were also the victims. Goldstein incidentally drew attention to the way drug users become victims, which he linked to the effects of the drug, that is when drunk, or being so obnoxious that others were violent to them (Goldstein, 1995).

Recently, a new complicating factor has arisen – that of mental disorder. An increasing number of mental patients are involved in substance abuse as are substance abusers who are mentally disordered. Again the American literature dominates. In Britain there is a comprehensive literature on mental disorder, and an equally comprehensive literature on substance abuse, but little to link the two.[6] The growth of

---

[6] At the time of writing (1998) there were only two U.K. papers on dual diagnoses, neither of which was directly concerned with violence.

this dual diagnosis group stems from the decarceration policies of the late 1970s and early 1980s, when large numbers of mental patients were discharged from mental hospitals. About 50% of drug users have dual conditions (Swanson et al., 1990) and some having multiple conditions including alcohol addiction and HIV. High-profile cases of fatal stranger violence in Britain leading to public inquiries[7] have not always identified this group or brought out the links between them (Blom-Cooper, et al., 1990). The Epidemiological Catchment Area (ECA) study in the United States, certainly the most comprehensive with interviews of nearly 20,000 people (Eaton & Kessler, 1985), concluded that dual diagnosis patients were more violent than those with a single diagnosis. However, the data are not straightforward, for although respondents with dual diagnosis had a greater risk, they had only a slightly greater risk than those with single diagnosis of substance abuse. That is, substance abuse was associated with a high risk of violence whether or not it occurred with mental disorder; the presence of mental disorder increased the risk, but not significantly (Swanson, 1994, p. 113).

Diagnosing these patients is complex and misdiagnosis common, because one condition may mask or mimic the other. Psychosis from LSD use or from amphetamine use, for example, produces symptomatologies not greatly different from schizophrenia. Or the presence of one may exacerbate the other, or if not, then prevent successful treatment, so that florid schizophrenic patients who take cocaine may be more violent than otherwise. Managing these patients is a problem; the ward atmosphere deteriorates when dual-disordered patients are admitted, with threats and violence on staff being commonplace.[8]

The Social Conditions Under Which Violence and Substance Abuse Occur

Violence associated with substance abuse occurs under numerous social conditions and for a variety of reasons. In this sense it does not differ from other forms of violence. As shown in our Nottingham study, violence was used by substance users according to their position on the

---

[7] Perhaps the Committee was unaware of the problem, but in the case of Jason Mitchell there was clear evidence of extensive cannabis use in a highly volatile psychotic patient. The cannabis use was hardly considered.

[8] The link between illicit substance abuse and psychiatric disorder is an intriguing one, highly complex and worthy of a separate study of its own (see Swanson et al., 1990).

supply system (Bean & Wilkinson, 1988). Relatively important dealers used violence to collect debts and enforce discipline; when dealing ended ("dealing doesn't last," they often said) violence was a continuation of their deviant lifestyle used to fund their habit or for gratuitous reasons. They were violent whether they were dealing or not.

As a general rule violence was greater with street-level dealing than elsewhere. This is confirmed by Reiss and Roth (1993) who suggest that violence is greater in illegal markets where the seller has less control over the access to the purchaser (e.g., call-girl operations are less violent than open-air street walking). "Similarly in drug markets runner-beeper drug delivery systems may entail less violence than open air markets, while heavily fortified crack houses may experience still less risk" (p. 18). In later research in Nottingham we found that levels of violence in crack dealing decreased once control of the profits moved out of the local area (i.e., where the center of control was more organized) (Bean, 1995b). Violence became more focused and instrumental and was used to enforce discipline and collect debts.

The potential for violence depends on a number of factors such as face-to-face encounters, the location, and local bystanders. It can also be part of some prearranged ritual. The so-called off-the-street violence associated with substance abuse (i.e., debt collecting, enforcing discipline, etc.) is not likely to be haphazard. Exchanges taking place among higher level drug dealers are rarely documented but likely to operate according to a prearranged set of signals (Bean, 1994). Violence in high-level dealing almost always involves co-offending, that is, with two or more offenders on one victim (co-offending is probably less common at the street level), based on a predetermined scale of punishments.

The convergence between substance abusers and offenders has been a major development in Britain in the last decade, although reports in the United States suggest it goes back to the late 1970s (Inciardi, et al., 1993, p. 113). Substance abuse is most likely to be found in high crime areas where there is:

1. A concentration of poor families in geographical areas and greater income differences between rich and poor.
2. Measures associated with differential social disorganization such as population turnover, community transitions, family disruption and housing population density – all of which affect the community's capacity to supervise young males (Reiss & Roth, 1993, p. 14).

To complicate matters some areas with high substance abuse rates will have lower crime rates, and some with high crime rates have lower rates of violence. Nonetheless, in general, high crime and high substance abuse rates are correlated, and high levels of substance abuse mean high violence. Drug markets will develop where there is already a subculture of violence. For example, when violent gangs in the United States became involved in the crack trade, they used violence as they always did – to protect reputations, resources, or territory. However, the pattern is not uniform; not all gang members will be involved in crack dealing (Reiss & Ross, 1993, p. 17).

A promising area of research is to determine the nature of the convergence between drug taking, crime, and violence, and of the social conditions that promote violence, including the locations where violence occurs. Clearly the presence or absence of firearms modifies the likelihood of violence, but there are many other factors including the presence of large numbers of unsupervised young males which affect rates. Also research is needed to determine how or if passersby, bystanders, or associates can intervene to reduce or prevent violence.

A distinction should be made between sellers and users in drug markets; not all sellers are users. Ecstasy (or MDMA) in Britain is often sold by nonusers, with little violence associated with those transactions – the user buying only what he or she needs. These transactions usually take place in clubs or pubs. Those selling drugs on the street are of a different order, and this is where violence is most likely to occur (Chaiken & Chaiken, 1990). The dealer must protect the markets, determine territory, and cope with informers who are always a threat to the organization. (British police officers who deal with informers often say the drug world is the most treacherous, having more informers than elsewhere [Bean, 1996].) The dealers have to show they are in command. An important area of research would be to document the nature of violence in street markets and determine how much was related to dealing and how much was not, who did what and how.

Psychopharmacological Violence

According to Goldstein (1995), this type of violence occurs as a result of short- or long-term injection of specific substances, where the user becomes excitable and/or irrational and may exhibit violent behavior. Fagan (1993) defines it differently. He sees it as a type of violence that occurs when the use of substances produce changes or impairs cognitive features, intensifies states, or disrupts hormonal or physiological functions that motivate or restrain violence. Most of the appropriate literature concerns alcohol.

There is an extensive literature on alcohol and violence (it is also covered elsewhere in this book). Research from the 1960s onward bears out the common belief that high levels of domestic violence occur after licensed premises have closed in the evening. The casualty departments of hospitals in Britain and elsewhere experience similarly high levels with an endless procession of young people who have been drinking, victim and offender alike, seeking medical treatment. Studies of violent offenders consistently show that violent incidents take place in or near licensed premises, and almost half of all incidents of disorderly behavior dealt with by the police occur shortly after the end of permitted drinking hours (Mott, 1987). Information from two British Crime Surveys show that in England and Wales, 22% of personal violence incidents occurred in or near pubs and discos (Hough & Shacky, 1987). Recent research using a situational control model shows how street violence can be reduced by controlling entrance to licensed premises and segregating various groups.

All of this suggests alcohol is criminogenic, promoting violence. Collins (1989) concludes that alcohol and alcohol-related problems have been associated with many violent offenders, with alcohol in violent events commonplace. This is true whether for homicide (Wolfgang, 1958), or rape (Shupe, 1954, cited in Collins, 1989), where 50% of rape arrestees had been drinking and 45% were intoxicated. Johnson et al. (1990), in examining rapes occurring in Winnipeg, found alcohol in 72% of offenders, victims, or both. In Britain, a study of men charged with rape between 1972 and 1976 showed that, where more than one offender was involved, they and the victim tended to be young and more likely to have consumed alcohol than lone offenders (West & Wright, 1981).

Some of this violence is ritualistic. In domestic violence, alcohol is consumed in settings that give approval to male violence, where violent incidents are part of a considered demonstration of masculine authority. High levels of violence are associated with sporting events, such as football matches in Britain, with use and sale prohibited within a selected radius of the ground. Being ritualistic means it is no less destructive, but prevention programs need to take account of the rituals as well as the violence.

For other drugs there has been less research and less hard evidence with which to link violence. At a personal anecdotal level, it was noticed in Nottingham in 1993, while conducting research into crack cocaine supply systems, that some local pimps said they had given up using cocaine because it made them violent; they beat up the girls, which they said was bad for business. Goldstein (1989) says users describe the cocaine "crash" – going down from the high – as a period of anxiety and depression in which external stimuli may be reacted to in violent form (p. 25). And while heroin produces the typical soporific effect ("going on the nod"), withdrawal can produce irritability and violence when more heroin is required to ward off those symptoms.

Identifying the impact of a single drug among illicit users is difficult; multiple use is common. Where drug use is confined to licit use (i.e., alcohol), the impact is easier to identify. The extent of violence is affected by the amount consumed, the patterns of use, the psychological condition of the user, and the length of use. Users with a history of violence will need only small amounts for high levels of violence to occur. Long-term chronic use of alcohol tends to produce depression because it modifies the neuroreceptors that produce depression, and affects and disrupts social communication. Curiously enough schizophrenic patients rarely use heroin, which is odd because heroin would be expected to be their preferred drug, able to diminish their hallucinations. Paradoxically they often use cocaine, and as a result produce a more florid volatile state than hitherto. There seems no obvious reason why this should be so, and we await more research on this matter.[9]

There is firm evidence that morphine, heroin, and other opiate derivatives reduce aggressive and violent behavior, albeit temporary, and in the early stages of use. Again it is difficult to identify the impact of a single drug, since multiple use is common. The development of opiate blockers such as naltrexone have had an impact on the treatment of opiate addicts: Patients taking naltrexone experience no effects from opiates.

Stimulant drugs such as amphetamines produce different effects according to the doses. Low-level doses, often found in ecstasy (MDMA), tend not to produce violent or aggressive behavior, but with other amphetamines, low-level doses produce increased levels of com-

---

[9] A great deal of what follows in this section on psychopharmacological use is drawn from Reiss & Roth (1993).

petitive behavior. High-level doses taken over a long period can produce psychosis and violence, but again this depends on the user's personal history. Those with a violent history or unstable personality tend
to be more violent after chronic stimulant use where the psychotic
episodes, if accompanied by hallucinations, resemble paranoid psychoses. There is an interesting debate as to whether these hallucinations differ in nature and degree from those of the schizophrenic
patient. The general opinion is they do not, except that those for the
schizophrenic tend to last longer; those for amphetamines usually clear
up within two weeks of treatment (Turner & Tsuang, 1990).

Cocaine is also a stimulant and said to be addictive, but this is open to
debate.[10] Its links with violence are less clear, although it is thought that
chronic use can lead to a psychotic state similar to that for other long-
term amphetamine use. In Britain, cocaine is a preferred drug sold extensively on the street and often taken with heroin. This makes it difficult to
determine its effects, long-term or otherwise, and evidence of links with
violence remain equivocal. One American study reports violent and
aggressive behavior from cocaine users; another study reported no difference in the frequency of violent acts between institutionalized cocaine
users and violent patients (Reiss & Roth, 1993, p. 194).

The hallucinogenic group, which includes cannabis and LSD, are
chemically diverse (Reiss & Roth, p. 194). They have, however,
received much research attention. Five major reviews of the research
literature on cannabis concluded that violent behavior is either
decreased or unaffected by use. In animal studies, acute doses promote
submissiveness or flight responses, and in large doses, inhibit attack or
threatening behavior (Reiss & Roth, p. 195). LSD does not appear to
trigger violent behavior, but it can aggravate the effects of preexisting
psychopathology, which can promote violent outbursts in those
already prone to violence.

To repeat the point, these studies cannot be considered in isolation
from the social situation in which drugs are taken and the personal history of the user. Consider alcohol: Not all who take it become violent,
but those who do are affected by the way the social situation mediates.
For example, consuming alcohol in pubs and bars where the atmosphere is more vibrant is likely to lead to violence, while drinking in

---

[10] It all depends, of course, on what one means by addicted. Cocaine is not addictive in
the sense that heroin is addictive, but some users will continue to take it over long
periods and behave in a way that is compulsive.

more restrained conditions does not. Some drinking may be socially functional and institutional in achieving the desired behavior (i.e., violence is expected to occur in those settings). Jeffrey Fagan suggests that the focus should be on locations and contexts. "This analytic focus shifts alteration from persons to events and emphasizes location as the critical intervening construct in the occurrence of violence" (Fagan 1993, p. 76). Those include the places the alcohol was consumed, the psychology and background of the drinker, and the interactions during and after consumption.

Teasing out these situational and social factors, examining the events including ways in which some people may turn a situation away from violence while others do not, is one way forward (Mott, 1987). Psychopharmacological effects may be less important; violence is more contrived than simply a response to the drug's effects.

Economic Crime and Violence Within Drug Markets

One of the categories in Goldstein's tripartite framework (1995) was what he called economically oriented violent crime, usually robbery, where the user, not normally motivated to act violently, needs money to pay for his or her habit. Goldstein claims that heroin and cocaine are the most relevant substances: They are usually the most expensive, where violence results from "the perpetrator's own nervousness, the victim's reaction, the weaponry – or lack of it, whether of offender or victim, the intercession of bystanders and so on" (p. 256).

It is unclear why Goldstein believes heroin and cocaine should be regarded as substances most likely to lead to violence; all addictive substances that are popular and expensive would seem to qualify. Moreover, the distinction between economic violence and systemic violence is also difficult to sustain. Systemic violence, Goldstein says, is intrinsic to any involvement with illicit substances. Systemic violence refers to the traditionally aggressive patterns of interactions within the system of drug distribution and use (1995), but the overlaps with economic violence are considerable, and definitional problems add to the complications. Moreover, Goldstein used some odd examples to show what was and what was not economic crime. For example, he did not include a robbery to obtain grocery money after the offender spent the intended grocery money on drugs, nor of a robbery of drugs from a dealer in which the user and dealer were killed: These he saw as drug related, but systemic. In a study of 414 homicides in New York City, 3%

were classified as drug related, 4% had multiple causes, 8% were pharmacological, 39% systemic, and only 2% economic (1989). These figures were later confirmed in another study of cocaine use (Goldstein et al., 1991). This low level of economic crime is extraordinary, although Reiss and Roth (1993) report differences in assessments by the police and researchers – the police regarding most homicides as belonging to the "economic" crime category (p. 200).

In Britain, Joy Mott for the Home Office estimated the proportion of various types of acquisitive crimes attributed to heroin users in England and Wales in 1987 to be between 6% and 24% of all burglaries, between 6% and 23% of thefts from the person, and between 0.6% and 8% of shoplifting. The calculations were based on a set of assumptions themselves tentative (about the number of heroin addicts, frequency of offending, extent of habit, etc.). Small changes substantially affect the figures; if the extent of the habit is greater or less than calculated, the numbers and percentage of burglaries will change accordingly. The confidence intervals on Joy Mott's figures were wide, and rightly so (ACMD, 1994).

Most research suggests that crime rates, including robbery, are higher once the offender is a regular user or is addicted: the rate drops dramatically once the user enters treatment, especially for heroin users. Chaiken and Chaiken (1990) report that crime rates are strongly related to addiction; nonaddicted users commit fewer crimes. Inciardi's study of drug-abusing populations (1990) also shows that narcotic users commit more robberies per year than other drug users. Addiction, it seems, propels users to commit crime, which suggests economic crime may be higher than Goldstein believes. The British data show nearly half of the arrestees who reported taking drugs within the last year said their drug use was connected to their offending. They emphasized the need for money to buy drugs with an estimated 32% of illegal income spent on purchasing heroin and/or crack (Bennett, 1998). Nevertheless it is difficult to disentangle the crimes committed to purchase drugs from those likely to be committed anyway. This whole area cries out for more research if only to identify what is and what is not economic crime.

Economic-related drug crime clearly exists, but it is difficult to be certain it constitutes a separate category and that there is enough research data to identify the parameters necessary to place violent events in that category. We should take note of Inciardi's conclusion on a study of hard core adolescent offenders, "those more proximal to the crack distribution were more involved in violent crime," especially the dealers. What is there about this market that produces such high levels of violence? This is another area in which a major research initiative needs to be directed.

Systemic Violence

According to Reiss and Roth, systemic drug-related violence can take three distinct paths:

1. Organizational violence, which involves territorial disputes over drug distribution rights, the enforcement of organizational rules such as prohibitions against drug use while selling or trafficking, battles with police, and punishment of individual officers, informers, or anti-drug vigilantes.
2. Transaction-related violence, which involves robberies of drugs or moneys from the buyer or seller, assaults to collect debts, and the resolution of disputes over the quality or quantity of the drugs, their ownership and rights.
3. Third-party related violence, which involves bystanders to drug disputes, and participants in related markets such as protection, prostitution, and firearm rackets.[11]

They also note that data on the frequencies of those subcategories are fragmentary. "There is a need for more systematic counting of their occurrence and analysis of the frequency of their occurrence in different settings" (p. 203). Data from category (3) are especially difficult to obtain through standard research methods.

Studies in organizational violence are rare, and almost unknown outside the United States. Yet, drug markets have certain common features: Drugs are bought and sold like all other commodities, but unlike most other commodities drug markets are characterized by a high degree of immeasurable risk, by the inability to enforce contracts in a

---

[11] Goldstein gives a number of examples of systemic violence, which differ slightly from those listed by Reiss and Roth. They include disputes over territory between drug dealers, assaults and homicides within declining hierarchies as a means of enforcing normative codes, robberies of drug dealers and the usually violent retaliation by the dealer of his/her bosses, elimination of informers, punishment for selling adulterated or phony drugs, punishment for failing to pay out debts, disputes over drugs or drug paraphernalia, and robbery violence related to the social ecology of coping areas (see Goldstein, 1995).

court of law, and by inadequate information about the product (Rydell et al., 1996). Nevertheless they are markets, with buyers and sellers, and as with other markets, drugs are bought and sold according to laws of supply and demand.

The market for drugs with its high level of profits and the lack of skills required to enter as an entrepreneur, and the ease of transportation of the commodity with an enormously valuable per unit weight, is likely to be an attractive one, and the incentives for organized crime to enter these markets are positively affected by the large profits (Caulkens & Reuter, 1996). Protection of these markets may explain the frequency of corruption, whether of politicians, business persons, police, or bank employees. It may also explain the levels of organizational violence associated with the drug trade.

Policy makers and clinicians find it difficult to break into these markets, because resistance to outside intervention is built into their structure. Consider one type of intervention; that by informers. In our Nottingham study (1993), drug informers claimed they had "a license to deal"; in effect, this meant the police did not prosecute in return for information on other dealers. The informers continued trading, with other dealers fearing that they, the informers, wanted to remove all opposition, leaving them as monopoly suppliers. They devised ways of protecting themselves whether through threatening violence on the informers or acting as informers themselves.

In Britain, Dorn, Murji, and South (1992) describe how criminals familiar with intimidation and violence moved into the drug market from the 1970s onward, transforming it from one where personal safety was accepted toward a professionalism where violence became part of criminal activity. By 1996 there were about 3,000 to 4,000 major dealers in Britain able to move large consignments of drugs and 30 to 40 gangs in London controlling the market (Bean, 1995a) Many of those gang members felt comfortable with violence.

These observations fit with some American studies that cast doubt on the otherwise accepted view that the drug trade has produced a new breed of criminal, more violent than before. Rather it seems an old breed has arrived with a previous history of violence, attracted by the possibility of a share in the large expanding profits. These criminals find they can mix freely with other organized crime syndicates where competition, personal and organizational, remains intense.

At a lower level, referred to as transactional related violence which involves assaults to collect debts and such, there may well be a new breed of criminal. These are the street dealers who are attracted to the profits, who resort to violence when they might not have done so before; they may even use firearms. They operate in a Hobbesian world where no rules or guidelines exist, except those serving their own interests. These offenders cause the most concern, because once they are initiated into violence at a young age, it may be difficult to extricate them.

A Note on Gender, Substance Abuse, and Violence

It is interesting that female violence in domestic settings lacks the association with alcohol found with male violence. Nor does it appear that female violence associated with other drugs is as common as male violence. Female drug dealers are, however, as prepared as their male counterparts to use violence when necessary either to enforce discipline or collect debts. They tend not to do it themselves but get the males to undertake it for them. They change partners often when existing business partners fail to deliver as required (Bean & Wilkinson, 1988).

The number of studies concerned with women's substance abuse and violence remains small – barely any in Britain, and only a few more in the United States. Goldstein (1989) was concerned that research has overlooked social processes or situations unique to females. He devoted a special section in his drugs/violence nexus to women, but admitted that the evidence concerning links between drugs and violence was scantier for women than for men. He hypothesized that differences were determined by the social contexts; drug-related violence by women would be more of the pharmacological variety with women less likely to commit economic or systemic acts. He said they seek alternatives to violent crime such as prostitution, shoplifting, forgery, and drug selling.

Inciardi et al. would not agree (1993, p. 114). In their study of female heroin and cocaine users in Miami they found that like their male counterparts, female heroin users engage in a wide variety of offenses, including robbery, although more than half (54%) of all their offenses were for prostitution. Female crack users offended in ways similar to men; violence-related offenses significantly correlated to levels of use: The heavier the use the greater the likelihood of violent crime being committed. Nevertheless, more than half of all offenses were for prostitution.

Too few studies have been done to arrive at a meaningful conclusion, and Inciardi's population may be unusually criminal. Other research points to important differences in gender crime; Fagan for example, says female homicide victims are less likely than male homicide victims to have used alcohol prior to their death, and while alcohol use by males is a significant risk factor in husband-to-wife violence it is not a significant risk factor in wife-to-husband violence (Fagan, 1993). We cannot assume then that there is convergence between male and female levels and types of violence. Goldstein (1989) also observes that women are less likely to engage in retaliation or face-saving violence after being cheated on a drug purchase or having drugs stolen from them. But most of all "drug use is commonly perceived as a violation of the female sex role (with) implications for an analysis of drug related violence" (p. 39)

Rosenbaum's (1995) classic study of women heroin users shows how female heroin users are more likely to have a partner who also uses heroin. Initially, the drugs bring them together but later serves to weaken the relationship – the drug becomes more important than the relationship itself. Traditional roles are reversed with the women becoming the main earner, invariably through prostitution, with sex role disruption leading to violence. Resentment and bitterness intrude into the relationship, and if there are children, the woman cannot easily undertake her role as a mother. Accordingly, women are likely to seek earlier treatment than men, and "mature out" of drug use more quickly. The alternative is bleak; it is to see what Rosenbaum calls "a narrowing of the options," which is too unpleasant to face – that is, not being a woman or mother but simply a junkie.

Many studies of women in treatment point out that women are often ignored in treatment programs, or worse, required to assist men. ("Let's ask Mary to act as John's mother.") Or, if not, then they are dealt with as if they were men, so that women are given male type interpretations of their behavior; for example, being told they entered the drug world owing to a lack of external controls. The converse may be true, with excessive controls causing the trouble. Accordingly, women complain that treatment demands are too often ignored, failing to address their role differences and expectations.

Summary/Conclusion

Policy makers trying to interpret the links between substance abuse and violence may be faced with research that assists but rarely provides a conceptual framework for prevention or intervention. That research shows how substance abuse and violence are linked, but suggests that more attention be given to the context in which violence occurs (Fagan, 1993). In Fagan's terms "It (violence) occurs in situations characterized by the effects of the substances, the physical setting where they are used, the collective personalities of the people present, the social rules about violence in the setting and how they are enforced, and the cultural expectations that shape beliefs about violence" (p. 69). Violent events are more important than the pharmacology of the substance, or of the backgrounds of violent people, although background must also be considered. The policy maker and clinician must play a role in these events; that is, change the social situations in which they occur.

In practice this means *inter alia* disrupting drug markets, not just through policing but through partnership programs with other key criminal justice organizations including local authority (civic) services. Extensive literature on partnerships (Home Office, 1993) shows how effective they can be, but emphasizes the difficulties involved where agencies are required to work together and pool resources. Moreover, disrupting drug markets may appear initially counterproductive; violence may increase as the organization behind the markets disintegrates, but later decreases as the market reduces in size and quality. The partnership approach does not exclude zero-tolerance policing; it works with and alongside it.

This is not to deny individual interventions, whether through treatment programs, perhaps linked to drug courts (although most U.S. drug courts will not take offenders with a history of violence) or through incarceration, although the impact of increasing lengths of incarceration can lead to an increase in the prison population with only a meager reduction in rates of violence. Nor is it to deny the importance of programs directed at family violence, where the victim is given sanctuary, since all contribute to a reduction in drug-related violence.

The increasing levels of violence from the dual diagnosis patient need to be addressed. Patients with dual diagnosis have high levels of noncompliance in treatment, and make much greater demands on public services than the mentally disordered or single diagnosis patients. They create a decline in ward atmosphere and an increase in stress levels among members of the treatment team (Gourney, Johnson, & Thorncroft, 1997). One of the major hurdles in Britain is to make psychiatric treatment staff, whether in police stations or hospitals, aware of the nature of dual diagnosis; they are reluctant to avoid being involved with substance abuse because they do not regard it as a problem for psychiatry. But with the links firmly established and levels of violence high, this group requires urgent attention.

REFERENCES

Advisory Council on the Misuse of Drugs (1994). *Drug Misusers and the Criminal Justice System. Part 2 Police. Drug Misusers and the Community.* London: H.M.S.O.

Bean, P. T. (1974). *The social control of drugs.* Oxford: Martin Robertson.

Bean P. T. (1994). *Regional Study to collect all relevant information related to drug trafficking production, and abuse in the ACP countries in the Caribbean region.* Report to the European Commission.

Bean P. T. (1995). *The effectiveness of sentencing drug offenders.* Unpublished report to the Home Office, London.

Bean P. T. (1995a). Policing drug offenders and the Broome Report. *Journal of the Royal Society of Health,* (115), 95–101.

Bean P. T. (1995b). *Crack cocaine use in Nottingham.* Unpublished Report to the Home Office, London.

Bean P. T. (1996). Informers and the police. *Drugs Edition* No. 10. Release Publications. 1–3.–3.

Bean, P. T., & Wilkinson, C. K. (1988). Drug taking crime and the illicit supply system. *British Journal of Addiction, 83*(5), 533–539.

Bennett T. (1998). *Drugs and crime: The results of research on drug taking and interviewing arrestees.* Home Office, London (Research Study 183).

Blom-Cooper, Sir L., Grocends, A., Guinan, P., Parker, A., & Taylor, M. (1996). *The case of Jason Mitchell: Report of the Independent Panel of Enquiry.* London, Duckworth.

Blom-Cooper, Sir L. (1998). *Does treatment change the court?* Paper presented at a conference on American Drug Courts, Loughborough University (mimeo).

Caulkens, J., & Reuter, P. (1996). The meaning and utility of drug prices. *Addiction, 19* (9), 1261–1264.

Chaiken, J. M., & Chaiken, M. R. (1990). Drugs and predatory crime. In M. Tonry, & J. Wilson, *Drugs and Crime* (pp. 203–239). *Chicago: University of Chicago Press.*

Collins, J. J. (1989). Alcohol and interpersonal violence: Less than meets the eye. In N. Weiner, and M., Wolfgang, (Eds.), *Pathways to criminal violence* (pp. 49–67). London: Sage.

Dorn, N., Murji, K., & South, N. (1992). *Traffickers, drug markets and law enforcement.* London: Routledge.

Drake, R. E., McLaughlin, P., Pepper, B., & Minikoff, K. (1991). Dual diagnosis of major mental illness and substance disorder: An overview. In K. Minikoff, & R. E. Drake (Eds.), *Dual diagnosis of major mental illness and substance disorder.* New York: Jossey-Bass.

Eaton, W. W., & Kessler, L. G. (Eds.) (1985). *Epidemiological field methods in psychiatry: The NIMH Epidemiological Catchment Area Study.* New York: Academic Press.

Fagan, J., & Chin, K. (1990). Violence as regulation and social control in the distribution of crack. In M. de la Rosa (Eds.), *Drugs and violence: Causes correlates and consequences* (pp. 8–43). NIDA Research Monograph.

Fagan, J. (1993). Interaction among drugs, alcohol, and violence. *Health Affairs* (Winter), 65–77.

Goldstein, P. J. (1989). Drugs and violent crime. In N. A. Weiner, & M. E. Wolfgang (Eds.), *Pathways to criminal violence* (pp. 16–48). London: Sage.

Goldstein, P. J. (1995). The drugs/violence nexus: A tripartite conceptual framework. *Drug Issues, 15,* 493–506.

Goldstein, P., Belluccci, P. A., Spunt, B. J., & Miller, T. (1991). *Frequency of cocaine use and violence: A comparison between men and women. NIDA Research Monograph, 110,* 113–138.

Goldstein, P., Brownstein, H., Ryan, P. J., & Rellucci, P. A. (1991). Crack and homicide in New York City 1988: A conceptually based analysis. *Contemporary Drug Problems, 16,* 651–687.

Gourney, K., Johnson, S., & Thorncroft, G. (1997). Dual Diagnosis of severe mental health problems and substance abuse/dependence, a major problem for mental health nursing. *Journal of Psychiatric and Mental Health Nursing, 4,* 89–95.

Home Office (1993). *A practical guide to crime prevention through local partnerships.* London: Home Office.

Home Office (1996). *The British Crime Survey: England and Wales.* Home Office Statistical Bulletin. London: Author.

Home Office (1997). *Criminal Statistics for England and Wales.* London: Author.

Hough, M., & Shacky, K. (1987). *Incidents of violence: Findings from the British Crime Survey.* Home Office Research and Planning Unit, no. 2, 22–26.

Inciardi, J. A., Lockwood, D. A., & Pottieger, A. E. (1993). *Women and crack cocaine.* New York: Macmillan.

Inciardi, J. A. (1990). The crack cocaine connection with a population of hard core adolescent offenders. In M. de la Rosa, E. Y. Lambert, & B. Gropper, (Eds.), *Drugs and violence: causes correlates and consequences* (pp. 92–111). NIDA Research monograph.

Johnson, B. D., Williams, T., Dei, K. A., & Sanabria, H. (1990). Drug Abuse in the Inner City. In M. Tonry, & J. Q. Wilson. *Drugs and crime,* (pp. 9–67). Chicago: University of Chicago Press.

Kingery, P. M., Pruitt, B. E., & Hurley, R. S. (1992). Violence and illegal drug use among adolescents: Evidence from the U.S. National Adolescent Student Health Survey. *International Journal of the Addictions, 27,*(12) 1445–1464.

Mott, J. (1987). *The relationship between alcohol and crime: A review of the UK literature.* Paper presented to British Criminology Conference, York University.

National Institute of Justice (1996). *Drug Use Forecasting 1995* (June). U.S. Department of Justice. Washington, DC: Author.

Reiss, A. J., & Roth, J. A. (Eds.). (1993). *Understanding and preventing violence. Vols. 1 and 3.* Washington, DC: National Academy Press.

Release (undated) *Release drugs and dance survey: An insight into the culture.* London: Release Publications.

de la Rosa, M., Lambert, E. Y. & Gropper, B. (1990). Introduction: Exploring the substance abuse–violence connection. Drugs and violence: Causes, correlates, and consequences. NIDA Research Monograph, 109, 1–7.

Rosenbaum, M. (1995). *Women on heroin.* New Brunswick, NJ: Rutgers University Press.

Rydell, C. P., Caulkins, J. P., & Everingham, S. S. (1996). Enforcement or treatment? Modelling the relative efficacy of alternatives for controlling cocaine. *Operations Research, 44*(5) 687–695.

Swanson, J. W. (1994). Mental disorders, substance abuse and community violence. In J. Monahan, & H. J. Steadman (Eds.), *Violence and mental disorder* (pp. 101–136).

Swanson, J. W., Holzer, C. E., Ganju, V. K., & Tsatomo, Jono, R. (1990). Violence and psychiatric disorder in the community: Evidence from the Epidemiological Catchment Area Survey. *Hospital and Community Psychiatry, 41*(7), 761–770.

Tonry, M. (1990). Research on drugs and crime. In m. Tonry, & J. Q. Wilson (Eds.), *Drugs and Crime* (pp. 1–8). Chicago: University of Chicago Press.

Turner W. M., & Tsuang M. T. (1990). The impact of substance abuse on the course and outcome of schizophrenia. *Schizophrenia Bulletin, 16*(1), 87–95.

Wagstaff, A., & Maynard, A. (1988). *Economic aspects of the illicit drug market and drug enforcement policies in the U.K.* London: Home Office Research Study No. 95. London: Home Office.

Wolfgang M. (1958). *Patterns in criminal homicide.* New York: Wiley.

West, D., & Wright, R. (1981). Rape: A comparison of group offenders and lone assaults. *Medicine, Science, and the Law, 21,* 25–30.

13. Threats, Stalking, and Criminal Harassment

J. REID MELOY

I have had my life verbally threatened on several occasions. The most serious threat, and the most frightening, involved a paranoid schizophrenic and psychopathic patient whom I testified against and played a role in his recommitment. I received word that he was attempting to have me killed by paying a third party a sum of money – a conspiracy to murder – but fortunately, his funds were quite limited, although his potential employees were not.

I was neither approached nor attacked in any of these threat situations. They were, as expected, all false positives; but for me the affective memories remain. As Shakespeare wrote, "between the acting of a dreadful thing and the first motion, all the interim is like a phantasma, or a hideous dream" (*Julius Caesar*, II, i).

Threats against clinicians do occur (Flannery, Hanson, & Penk, 1995; Lion, 1995), and are varied in their frequency, intensity, and meaning. Unfortunately the threat literature appears minuscule when compared to the ubiquity of expressed threats in society. In this chapter I will first focus on articulated threats in the context of the chronically intrusive and sometimes violent behavior of stalking or criminal harassment. Current knowledge of the latter acts will then be summarized to suggest a clinical framework for violence risk assessment and define future research needs.

Definitions

A *threat* is a written or oral communication that implicitly or explicitly states a wish or intent to damage, injure, or kill the target. *Stalking* in the United States and *criminal harassment* in Canada are typically defined as, "the willful, malicious, and repeated following and harassing of another person that threatens his or her safety" (Meloy & Gothard, 1995, p. 258). One of the elements of the crime of stalking is often a credible threat, although it need not be overtly expressed. Threats, moreover, occur in a variety of situations for a variety of reasons, and do not necessarily suggest the crime of stalking or criminal harassment.

Threatening Communications

A computer search of four databases (National Criminal Justice Reference Service, 1972–1998; Criminal Justice Periodical Index, 1975–1997; Medline, 1966–1998; PsycInfo, 1966–1998) to locate studies on threatening communications yielded 120 records. Most of the extant studies are social-psychological experimental designs, testing various concepts such as "reactance," and there is a small body of work on threats toward clinicians. Few studies are devoted to threats in the context of stalking or criminal harassment. Table 13.1 summarizes the major findings of these studies.

Threat research in this context suggests that (a) threats are very common; (b) most individuals do not act on their threats; (c) threats may increase, decrease, or have no relationship to subsequent violence; and (d) threats are either instrumental or expressive (Meloy, 1998). *Instrumental threats* are primarily intended to control or influence the behavior of the target through an aversive consequence. *Expressive threats* are primarily used to regulate affect in the threatener. The secondary effects of these two types of threats may vary. For example, a man may instrumentally threaten to kill his spouse if she leaves the marriage. His primary intent is to control her behavior and keep her from leaving. There may be, however, a secondary gain: He feels psychologically omnipotent and emotionally relieved if the threat is delivered with intense anger.

On the other hand, a patient expressively threatens to kill his employer to vent his work frustration to his psychotherapist. Unfortunately, the doctor interprets the threat as instrumental and very serious, and feels obligated to warn his employer. He is consequently terminated from his job, an enormous secondary loss.

Threatening communications also suggest the utilization of certain unconscious psychological defenses, such as rationalization ("she deserved it"), minimization ("I didn't mean it"), and denial ("it wasn't a threat"). I have outlined and discussed these defenses in detail else-

Table 13.1. Threatening Communications Related to Stalking and
Targeted Violence

Study	Sample
Macdonald (1968)	100 homicidally threatening hospitalized patients in Colorado *After 10 years, 3% committed homicide, 4% committed suicide*
Dietz et al. (1991a)	Threatening letters to Hollywood celebrities *Threats unrelated to approach behavior*
Dietz et al. (1991b)	Threatening letters to members of U.S. Congress *Threats negatively correlated with approach behavior*
Zona et al. (1993)	74 subjects followed by Threat Management Unit, LAPD *75% false positive rate for threats*
Meloy & Gothard (1995)	20 obsessional followers evaluated in court clinic *83% false positive rate for threats, 15% false negative rate*
Harmon et al. (1995)	48 obsessional harassers evaluated in court clinic *68% false positive rate for threats, 6% false negative rate*
Meloy (1996)	Review of 10 studies, 180 obsessional followers in total sample *On average 50% threatened, 75% false positive rate*
Meloy et al. (2000)	65 obsessional followers evaluated in court clinic *75% threatened: 60% false positive rate for threats to person and property; 11% false negative rate for threats to person and property; 72% false positive rate for threats to person only; 15% false negative rate, person only*
Fein & Vossekuil (1998)	83 attackers, near attackers, and assassins of public figures *Fewer than 10% communicated a direct threat to the target or law enforcement before attack or assassination.*
Tjaden & Thoennes (1997)	Telephone survey of 16,000 adults, random probability research design *43% of male victims of stalkers were verbally threatened; 45% of female victims of stalkers were verbally threatened*
Kienlen et al. (1997)	25 stalkers in maximum security setting *76% threatened; nonpsychotic more likely to threaten than psychotic stalkers*

where (Meloy, 1998). The type of threat (instrumental or expressive) and the defensive use of a threat often illuminate the state of mind of the threatener, which will help in evaluating whether she or he actually *poses* a threat to the object (Fein, Vossekuil, & Holden, 1995).

Limitations of Threat Research

The research on threatening communications in stalking and criminal harassment cases is scant, and raises several problems. First, there is no research at present that empirically demonstrates that threatening communications account for any of the explainable variance in predicting violence risk or dangerousness. The conventional focus on threats as a predictor of risk may be misplaced in some cases, as Dietz et al. (1991a, 1991b) and Fein and Vossekuil (1998) have shown in nonrandom samples of approaches and/or attackers of public figures.

Second, nomothetic research does not necessarily help predict the relationship between a threat and subsequent behavior in a specific case. For example, if the false positive rate for threats among stalkers is typically greater than 75%, which it is, and false negative rates are often below 15%, which they are, the high *probability* is that one who doesn't threaten will not attack. But what if our case is the exception to the rule? Are we willing to risk the 15% chance that we are wrong, especially if the stakes, or consequences, are severe? For years it was assumed that those who threatened the president of the United States and those who attacked the president substantially overlapped (Clarke, 1982; Shore et al., 1985; Shore, Filson, & Johnson, 1988; Shore et al., 1989). Research now strongly suggests that this assumption was wrong: Attackers and assassins of public officials and public figures directly communicate their threat to the target or law enforcement less than 10% of the time (Fein & Vossekuil, 1998).

Evaluating Threatening Communications

I would like to suggest a brief protocol for the assessment of threatening communications:

1. Is the threatening communication primarily instrumental or expressive?
2. If other psychological data are available, does the threat illuminate the current state of mind of the threatener?

3. Does the threatener demographically and clinically fit within any of the known samples of threateners, therefore providing frequency data for true and false positives?
4. What has been the threatener's behavior following threats in the past?
5. What are the stakes (consequences) if the threat is carried out?
6. Given the totality of known information on the case, should the threatening communication change the risk management strategy, and, if so, in what way?

Stalking and Criminal Harassment

There has been a growing body of research on stalking since the first criminal stalking law was passed in California in 1990. Meloy (1996) reviewed the existing studies of "obsessional followers" who had contact with law enforcement and identified 10 peer-reviewed scientific articles, the earliest published in 1978, with an aggregate sample of 180 individuals. The vast majority of subjects were from three large urban areas in the United States (New York City, Los Angeles, and San Diego), with the remainder from Australia and Great Britain. Since the publication of this review, four clinical studies of nonrandom samples of stalkers (Kienlen, Birmingham, Solberg, O'Regan, & Meloy, 1997; Meloy, Rivers, Siegel, Gothard, Naimark, & Nicolini, 2000; Menzies, Federoff, Green, & Isaacson, 1995; Schwartz-Watts, Morgan, & Barnes, 1997), one large random probability telephone survey of stalking victims (Tjaden & Thoennes, 1997), one nonrandom clinical study of Australian stalking victims (Pathé & Mullen, 1997), and one scholarly book on stalking (Meloy, 1998) have appeared. Research has crystallized our understanding of stalking and its inherent risks of danger.

Demographics

The vast majority of individuals who stalk are males in their fourth decade of life. They have at least a high school education, are usually average or above average in intelligence, and are significantly brighter than other criminal offenders. These findings have all been replicated in a number of studies of independent samples (Zona, Sharma, & Lane, 1993; Meloy & Gothard, 1995; Harmon, Rosner, & Owens, 1995; Mullen & Pathé, 1994; Kienlen et al., 1997; Schwartz-Watts, Morgan, & Barnes, 1997).

There is suggestive research that stalkers are also unemployed or underemployed (Meloy, 1996), which raises serious questions about the wisdom of a civil (tort) action against a stalker. This finding is expected, because it takes time to stalk – something a fully employed individual does not have. Stalkers are also marked by a history of failed heterosexual relationships and are typically unattached at the time of their offending. One researcher (Kienlen et al., 1997; Kienlen, 1998) has also documented early childhood attachment disruption (a predisposing factor) and significant loss in the year prior to the stalking (a precipitating factor) in a majority of her small, nonrandom forensic sample. This empirical work has provided some validation for Meloy's (1989, 1992) early hypothesis that stalking is a disorder of "preoccupied" attachment and may be another variant, although nonerotic, of a courtship disorder (Meloy, 1996; Freund, Scher, & Hucker, 1983).

Stalkers are not disproportionately found in any racial or ethnic group (Tjaden & Thoennes, 1997), but are likely to have prior criminal histories that may or may not be related to their stalking behavior. The more extensive the criminal history, the greater the likelihood of a diagnosis of Antisocial Personality Disorder (American Psychiatric Association, 1994) or psychopathy (Hare, 1991).

Typologies

The most useful offender-victim typology for classifying stalkers was developed by Zona, Sharma, and Lane (1993):

1. *Erotomanic.* Those individuals with a diagnosis of erotomania, representing approximately 10% of stalkers, and most likely to be females pursuing male strangers or casual acquaintances.
2. *Love obsessional.* Those male individuals with a major mental disorder, fanatically "in love" with and pursuing a female stranger or casual acquaintance, representing approximately 30% of stalkers.
3. *Simple obsessional.* Those male individuals, usually diagnosed with both substance dependency/abuse and a personality disorder, pursuing a prior sexual intimate or retaliating for mistreatment in a real, nonsexual relation, perhaps in the workplace. They represent more than 50% of stalkers.
4. *False victimization syndrome.* Those individuals who claim they are being stalked, when in fact they are not. The motivation is

usually attention-seeking, alibi-creating, retaliation, or delusion, and they represent about 2% of stalking victims.

Zona et al. (1993) demonstrated some external validity for their typology in their original study. Meloy et al. (2000) further validated group differences in psychiatric diagnosis and violence risk. Mohandie, Hatcher, and Raymond (1998) developed a comprehensive model for false victimization syndrome in stalking. Other typologies have been proposed (Harmon, Rosner, & Owens, 1995; Wright et al., 1996), but they are without sufficient validation to be recommended for clinical use.

Psychiatric Diagnoses

Meloy's (1996) review suggested that the majority of individuals who stalk have both an Axis I and Axis II disorder. Further nonrandom clinical studies have validated this finding (Kienlen et al., 1997; Meloy et al., 2000), but as yet there is no epidemiological study that is random and community-based and demonstrates a correlation between stalking and mental disorder. Extant research may be biased by the clinical and forensic populations from which the samples were drawn.

The most common Axis I disorder is substance abuse or dependence, followed by a mood disorder, and then schizophrenia. Delusional disorder as a primary diagnosis is relatively rare, and is subtyped as either erotomanic or persecutory. Symptoms of erotomania, however, are more common as secondary aspects of a major mental disorder, if one exists. When stalkers are divided between those who pursue strangers or acquaintances, and those who pursue prior sexual intimates, significant differences in Axis I diagnoses emerge. Stalkers of the former group are more likely to be diagnosed with schizophrenia or another non-drug-induced psychosis, while stalkers of the latter group (all simple obsessionals) are more likely to be diagnosed with a substance abuse or dependence disorder (Meloy et al., 2000). We also found that the preferred drugs of abuse in our sample of stalkers (N = 65) were alcohol or psychostimulants, such as cocaine and amphetamine.

The most likely Axis II disorders are Cluster B (narcissistic, borderline, or antisocial), then Cluster A (paranoid) or Cluster C (compulsive). Personality Disorder Not Otherwise Specified is common, with typical traits from all three clusters (e.g., narcissistic, paranoid, and compulsive) (Meloy et al., 2000). Antisocial Personality Disorder (ASPD), however, appears to be significantly less frequent, usually at a rate of 10% among stalkers, when compared to other incarcerated criminals, where rates usually exceed 50% (Hare, 1991). This is expected given the chronic emotional detachment evident in ASPD subjects, and psychopaths in particular (Gacono & Meloy, 1994): an attachment pathology diametrically opposed to the intense, preoccupied attachment of the stalker. Psychopathy as a measurable construct is also predictably low among stalkers, with PCL-R scores <15 (S. Hart, personal communication, March 2000). Paraphilias are not frequent among stalkers (Meloy et al., 2000), contrary to some attempts to link stalking motivations, such as erotomania, and sexual desire disorders (Kaplan, 1996).

Victims

The vast majority of stalking victims are adult women, usually somewhat younger than the stalker (Meloy, 1996; Tjaden & Thoennes, 1997). Men represent a minority of stalking victims; for example, Tjaden and Thoennes (1997) estimated the annual incidence of stalking in the United States to be 1.0% for adult women and 0.4% for adult men. Women are most likely to be pursued by a prior intimate; men are most likely to be stalked by a stranger or casual acquaintance. *Erotomanic*-type stalkers of men are likely to be women.

The emotional impact of stalking on the victim is enormous. Pathé and Mullen (1997) found in a nonrandom clinical sample of Australian stalking victims ($N = 100$) that the majority reported intrusive recollections and flashbacks, while nightmares, appetite disturbances, depressed mood, and suicide ruminations were common. Thirty-seven percent met criteria for Posttraumatic Stress Disorder (American Psychiatric Association, 1994). Hall (1998), in a telephone survey of stalking victims ($N = 145$), found that they became more aggressive, paranoid, easily frightened, and cautious following the crime. Tjaden and Thoennes (1997) found that one third of the women and one fifth of the men surveyed ($N = 16,000$) sought psychological help as a result of the stalking, and were significantly more likely than nonstalking victims to be very concerned about their personal safety and to carry something to defend themselves. These three studies of stalking victims indicate that the impact is serious, in some cases psychiatrically disabling, and long term.

Pursuit Characteristics

Meloy (1992) reported that a very small sample (N = 6) of violent stalkers had an average duration of obsession of 5 years. Zona et al. (1993) confirmed the chronicity of stalking one year later in a much larger sample (N = 74) of subjects followed by the Threat Management Unit of the Los Angeles Police Department. The average duration of obsession for the erotomanic and love obsessional groups was 10 to 12 years! Subsequent research has replicated the finding that stalking behavior is predicted to last for *months or years*, the shortest duration being the simple obsessional type. The likely reasons for this inordinate length of pursuit are behavioral – the unwitting intermittent positive reinforcement of the stalker by the victim – and psychodynamic – the obsessed, preoccupied nature of the cognitions of the stalker.

The most frequent means of pursuit are physically approaching and telephoning the victim. Letter writing is the third most common method of contact, but may be diminishing in inverse proportion to the rise in electronic communication, such as e-mail.

Stalking Motivations

Why do some people stalk? The prominent conscious emotion for the *nonpsychotic* stalker appears to be anger toward the object, followed by abandonment rage or jealousy (Meloy et al., 2000; Kienlen et al., 1997). *Psychotic* stalkers, most likely to pursue casual acquaintances or strangers, are primarily motivated by delusional beliefs specific to the target, such as an erotomanic fixation, or obliquely related to the target, such as a psychotic transference – the stranger delusionally misidentified as an ex-wife or mother. The social context for stalking appears to be isolation and loneliness (Segal, 1989; Meloy, 1996).

Meloy (1989, 1992, 1996) has proposed a psychodynamic theory for stalking that may provide the characterological foundation for the more obvious and varied conscious motivations: Stalkers share a pathological narcissism that predisposes them to (a) form idealized narcissistic linking fantasies to objects (e.g., "we are special and destined to be together forever"), usually imbued with a sense of grandiosity and a feeling of pride; and (b) experience inordinately painful feelings of shame or humiliation when rejected.

These inclinations lead to a grossly abnormal behavioral reaction when rejection does, in fact, occur. Instead of the normal hurt, anger, sadness, detachment, grief, and *search for a new object* with which to bond (e.g., another sexual intimate or an interesting new job), rage

defends against the almost intolerable feelings of shame or humiliation, and the stalker begins a pursuit to hurt, injure, damage, or destroy
the abandoning object. This borderline *level* of personality functioning,
bolstered by the defense of splitting and its phenotypic offspring, such
as devaluation or projection, has a peculiar logic: to restore the idealized narcissistic linking fantasy. Tarnishing the object in real life dimin-
ishes envy for that which can no longer be possessed; reduces
real-world interference with the fantasized object or relation as perfect;
repairs the narcissistic wound through compensatory grandiose and
entitled thoughts; and satisfies primitive, retaliatory impulses to pluck
out an eye for an eye.

Violence

Personal violence is an intentional act of aggression that physically
injures, or is likely to injure, another person. In this context I will distinguish personal violence from property violence, where the intent is
to damage or destroy an inanimate object.

The research on violence and stalking began with the early work of
de Clerambault (1921/1942) who described five patients in his *Oeuvres
Psychiatriques*. One 34-year-old man,

had a morbid passion towards his ex-wife. Although she maintained she did
not love him, he claimed her attitude always belied her words. After her remar-
riage, he said she would once again become his mistress and that when he had
satisfied his pride he would again reject her. He was constantly writing,
ambushing her, and striking her in public. He carried a razor, threatening "if
you remarry, I'll get you both." (pp. 315–322)

The relationship between stalking and violence has been seriously
researched during the past decade, despite the concerted efforts of the
American commercial media to portray every stalker as a relentless,
homicidal psychopath. They are not.

The most robust finding in the research to date indicates that the
majority of all stalkers are not interpersonally violent, and if they are,
the physical injury to the victim is not severe (Meloy, 1996; Meloy et al.,
2000). Notwithstanding this expected finding for those who are familiar with violence research, the frequencies for interpersonal violence
among stalkers are strikingly high (although fewer than 50%), and
deserve both clinical concern and more research attention[1]. The sam-

---

[1] When stalkers who are prior sexual intimates are studied separately, frequencies for
violence *do* exceed 50%.

Table 13.2. Recent Data on Personal Violence in Stalking Cases

Study	Sample	Location	Personal Violence Frequency
Mullen & Pathé (1994)	14 cases	Australia	36%
Meloy & Gothard (1995)	20 cases	California	25%
Harmon et al. (1995)	48 cases	New York	21%
Garrod et al. (1995)	100 cases	British Columbia	0–42%
Kienlen et al. (1997)	25 cases	Missouri	32%
Schwartz-Watts et al. (1997)	18 cases	South Carolina	39%
Meloy et al. (2000)	65 cases	California	40%

N = 290 cases

pling of recent studies in Table 13.2 is particularly notable given the fact that violent behavior is not a legal element in any state or federal stalking law.

With frequencies averaging about 25–35% for personal violence, the likelihood of physical attack is high, even though physical injuries are relatively minor. The psychological impact of physical violence, however, is not accounted for in these numbers, and may result in what van der Kolk (1987, p. 31) described as "the loss of faith that there is order and continuity in life."

In our research (Meloy & Gothard, 1995; Meloy et al., 2000) we found that stalkers, if they are physically violent, will grab, choke, hair pull, throw, shake, hit, slap, kick, fondle, or punch the victim. A weapon is used in less than one out of three cases when violence occurs, and it is likely to be a handgun, knife, or automobile. Most interestingly, when weapons were used, the victims were not shot by the gun, cut by the knife, or hit by the car. It appears that the weapons are used to intimidate and control the victim, rather than to injure or kill her. Homicide in stalking cases appears to be rare, probably less than 2% (Meloy, 1996). The difficulty with this statistic, however, is that stalking may not be charged in homicide cases when it does precede the crime; and there are suggestive findings in the domestic violence research that stalking behavior is a serious lethality risk factor in spousal homicide by estranged male partners (A. Browne, personal communication, April, 1998). The definitive research on the relationship between stalking and homicide of estranged spouses has yet to be done.

A 25-year-old homosexual male engaged in a pattern of stalking and harassment of his 33-year-old ex-lover for a period of three years. Over the course of time, mutual restraining orders were issued, served, and violated, both individuals physically assaulted each other at various times, including sexual assault, hitting with a board and a mallet, threatening with a knife and gun, and on at least one occasion the crime of stalking was charged, but not prosecuted. On the day of the homicide, the younger male went to the older male's rented house and demanded the return of his furniture. A struggle ensued, during which the victim's .22 caliber revolver was used by the assailant to shoot him four times, the fatal wound penetrating the heart. The assailant dropped the gun in the house, went home, and waited for the police to arrest him. The victim stumbled out into the driveway and died. The assailant was prosecuted for first-degree murder and stalking.

On clinical exam, the defendant was a nonpsychotic, anxious individual with a Personality Disorder NOS with avoidant, self-defeating, and narcissistic features.

This individual's final comment after 11 hours of evaluation was reminiscent of an Othellian monologue: "I loved him deep in my heart. I still love him. He told people he'd protect me for the rest of my life. I was not stalking this man."

Stalking violence is typically affective, rather than predatory (Meloy, 1997b; Mirsky & Siegel, 1994), when the victims are prior sexual intimates. Affective violence is an emotional reaction to a perceived threat, and is accompanied by high states of autonomic arousal. Predatory violence is planned, purposeful, and emotionless, with minimal autonomic arousal. Although there are worrisome rates of false negative threats among stalkers (11–15% attack who did not previously threaten; Meloy et al., 2000), the violence that occurs without a threat appears to be unplanned, emotional, and a reaction to rejection by a prior intimate. When individuals stalk and attack in a predatory fashion without a preceding direct and threatening communication (a false negative), predatory violence is occurring, and the targets are likely to be public figures (Dietz et al., 1991a, 1991b; Fein & Vossekuil, 1998).

Third-party Violence. Violence toward third parties has been a concern in stalking cases, and early speculation asserted that individuals other than the object of desire were at greater risk for violence. The research, however, does not bear this out. Meloy (1996) found that violence toward third parties occurred in only one out of five cases when violence occurred, and was usually directed toward those perceived to be impeding access to the object. In a recent validation study the third-party assault rate was only 3%, and 90% of the threats toward third parties were false positives (Meloy et al., 2000). Although such assaults appear to be the exception to the rule in stalking cases, they do garner attention. Robert Hoskins, the man who stalked Madonna in 1995, eventually assaulted, and was shot by her bodyguard, whom he believed was keeping him from seeing "his wife" (Meloy, 1997a; Saunders, 1998). In a recent homicide case in Michigan, *People v. Gerald Atkins* (No. 97-155349-FC), the defendant staged a military assault on the Ford Motor Plant at Wixom, killing a manager and wounding several police officers, "to prove to her that I loved her and would not let anybody come between me and her. I would not let anybody ever, ever infringe on her rights. I will not let that happen" (police interrogation, Nov. 18, 1996, p. 24). The woman in this case worked at the plant, but he had met her only briefly at a bar a month earlier. They had no social or sexual relationship. His behavior was fueled by erotomanic delusions (Meloy, 1989) and his belief that she needed to be rescued.

This social dynamic, which I refer to as *triangulation,* may increase the risk of violence in stalking cases. It may be delusional, as noted in the Atkins case, or it may be actual interference by a third party, as in the Hoskins case, such as an angry husband, police investigators, security guards, a civil attorney, or the victim's psychotherapist, who are all attempting to put an end to the stalking. The psychodynamic appears to be a displacement of the rage (projectively experienced as paranoia) felt toward the rejecting object onto a third party, which protects the idealization of the object, but at the expense of stimulating persecutory fears of attack from others. This construction of a paranoid pseudocommunity increases a sense of magical connectedness to persecutory objects (Auchincloss & Weiss, 1992), but also increases fearful vulnerability that may result in a preemptive strike (often rationalized as rescuing). There are, as yet, no empirical studies that support this formulation which predicts an increase of violence risk when stalking cases are triangulated.

Dramatic Moments. There are times in every stalking case when the stalker is humiliated–rejected by the object of pursuit, third-party interference, police detention, police arrest and incarceration, service of a restraining order, prosecution, or conviction. These feelings of shame, and therefore rage, are likely to be most intense in public venues. It is very important that violence risk in stalking cases be considered a dynamic variable that may suddenly increase following these "dramatic moments" (Meloy, 1997a). They are likely to be ignored, however, since the victim may feel the most righteously indignant and euphoric at these same moments: A victory has been achieved! Wisdom counsels that such victories not be Pyrrhic, and professionals involved in risk management of stalking cases should be sensitized to these events, particularly if the stalker has retained his physical freedom to approach the victim.

Escalation. We recently attempted to construct a formula for determining whether or not a case of stalking involved escalation. Three components were chosen – posing an actual threat, intrusiveness of the stalking behavior, and decreased latency (time) between stalking events – and were operationally defined. Interjudge reliability was established (r = .88), but there was no difference in the proportion of individuals who escalated and were violent, and those who escalated and were not violent. This finding casts doubt on the validity of the widely held belief that escalating cases are more dangerous than nonescalating cases, but more research is necessary.

Property Violence. Risk toward property is substantial, but is less likely to occur, at arguably half the rate, than personal violence toward the object. Targets are most commonly property owned by the victim, such as her automobile, or symbolically representing her, such as a personal photograph. The property destruction is typically affective, but predatory violence toward property does occur, and may serve to immobilize the victim (damaging her car), impede her safety (severing of telephone lines), or intrude upon her privacy (seeking personal information, such as financial records). These acts may practically increase the stalker's access to the victim, while also psychologically enhancing his sense of omnipotent control of her.

Protection (Restraining) Orders. Another controversy in stalking cases, and domestic violence in general, is the use of protection orders to prevent future violence. A review of the research on the effectiveness of protection orders in domestic violence cases indicates that they do work in most situations.

Table 13.3 lists the studies of protection orders to date, which I have rated according to general effectiveness in suppressing threatening and violent behavior toward protectees. Unfortunately, most of these studies are nonrandom domestic violence victim surveys of short time periods following the service of the order. We found (Meloy et al., 1997) in

Table 13.3. A Review of the Effectiveness of Protection (Restraining) Orders

Study	Positive	Negative	Mixed
Berk, Berk, Loseke, & Rauma (1983)		X	
Grau, Fagan, & Wexler (1984)	X		
Sherman & Berk (1984)			X
Fiedler, Briar, & Pierce (1984)			X
Horton, Simonidis, & Simonidis (1987)	X		
Chaudhuri & Daly (1990)	X		
Finn & Colson (1990)	X		
Kaci (1992)			X
Harrell, Smith, & Newmark (1993)			X
Committee on Criminal Courts (1993)	X		
Kaci (1994)	X		
Tjaden & Thoennes (1997)		X	
National Center for State Courts (1997)	X		
Meloy et al. (1997)	X		

a large (N = 200), random, predictive study over the course of three years, that protection orders appeared to effectively suppress criminal and violently criminal behavior toward protectees >85% of the time.

Only two studies have surveyed *stalking* victims per se (Tjaden & Thoennes, 1997; National Center for State Courts, 1997) and the effectiveness of protection orders, both funded by the U.S. government. The results were grossly inconsistent. Tjaden and Thoennes (1997) conducted a random probability telephone survey of 16,000 individuals, and found that 28% of female victims and 10% of male victims who were stalked obtained a protection order. Sixty-nine percent of the women and 81% of the men said their stalker violated the order. The gender differences in both these findings were significant ($p \leq .05$). The National Center for State Courts (1997) conducted a study at three sites (Delaware, Colorado, and the District of Columbia) based upon telephone interviews (N = 285) one month after service, follow-up interviews (N = 177) six months later, civil case records of the petitioners, and criminal histories of the defendants. The majority of the participants at all three sites reported "life improvement" at both points in time, with gains over time, and 95% stated they would seek an order again. The majority of the participants also reported no incidents of physical or psychological abuse after service. The most frequently reported problem was calling the victim at home; only 7% of the victims reported being stalked at the follow-up interviews. The researchers wrote, "when orders are properly crafted and vigorously enforced, they can be an effective tool in stopping or reducing domestic violence and stalking" (p. 44).

The risk management decision to seek a protection order in individual cases should be based upon four questions:

1. What has been the effect of a protection order in the past on this individual?
2. Is there a history of physical violence (criminal record) toward the protectee?
3. How preoccupied or obsessed with the protectee is the individual?
4. How aggressive are the local police in enforcing protection orders, and how coordinated is the judicial response to such violations?

Failure to heed a protection order in the past, prior physical violence (criminal record), intense preoccupation with the victim, and poor enforcement of the protection order all may predict protection-order violations in stalking cases.

Predictive Factors. Only one published study to date has attempted to predict violence among individuals who stalk. Menzies et al. (1995) combined a small Canadian sample of hospitalized erotomanic males ($N = 13$) with reports of erotomanic men in the English language psychiatric literature ($N = 16$). Dangerous behavior was defined as serious antisocial behavior, including actual violence toward the erotomanic objects, as well as threats. Two variables discriminated between the dangerous and nondangerous groups: multiple objects of pursuit (.0005) and unrelated serious antisocial behavior (.05). The multiple objects were typically pursued concurrently, and the serious antisocial behavior was typically a history of violence convictions. A logistic stepwise regression analysis found that these two variables could accurately predict dangerousness or not 88.9% of the time. Notwithstanding the serious methodological problems of this study – combining two very disparate groups, testing for significant difference across 14 variables with a sample size of 29 (ensuring at least one "significant" finding), a sample size too small for a logistic regression, and defining "dangerousness" to also include threats – this flawed study is the first predictive attempt in the literature. Other work needs to be done, because there is no predictive model for stalking violence. In the absence of such data, clinicians should rely on established risk factors in violence assessment, such as substance abuse (Monahan, 1997; Monahan & Steadman, 1994), particularly those found in mentally ill offenders given the high rates of Axis I disorders and prior criminality in these individuals (Harris, Rice, & Quinsey, 1993).

Concluding Remarks

Although we do not know, as yet, the specific factors that predict personal and/or property violence in stalking and criminal harassment, we do have substantial knowledge of the frequency of violence, and the nature of the violent acts should they manifest. The assessment of violence risk among stalkers should be based upon known historicaldispositional and clinical-situational factors that both aggravate and mitigate violence until this prediction research is done. Such an analysis should be contextualized and refined by the data in this chapter, closely attending to the need for *periodic* assessments, since threat and risk will change over time. The passions of the stalker ebb and flow, and with them his desires to desperately idealize, or violently devalue, the object of his obsession.

REFERENCES

American Psychiatric Association (1994). *Diagnostic and statistical manual of mental disorders, fourth edition.* Washington, DC: Author.
Auchincloss, E., & Weiss, R. (1992). Paranoid character and the intolerance of indifference. *Journal of the American Psychoanalytic Association, 40,* 1013–1038.
Berk, R., Berk, S., Loseke, D., & Rauma, D. (1983). Mutual combat and other family-violence myths. In D. Finkelhor, R. Gelles, G. Hotalung, & M. Straus (Eds.), *The dark side of families: Current family-violence research* (pp. 197–212). Beverly Hills, CA: Sage.
Chaudhuri, M., & Daly, K. (1990). Do restraining orders help? Battered women's experience with male violence and legal process. In E. Buzawa & C. Buzawa (Eds.), *Domestic violence: The changing criminal justice response* (pp. 227–252). Westport, CT: Greenwood Press.
Clarke, J. (1982). *American assassins.* Princeton, NJ: Princeton University Press.
Committee on Criminal Courts (1993). The paper shield: Orders of protection in the New York City Criminal Court. *Record of the Association of the Bar of the City of New York* (pp. 891–912). New York: Author.
De Clerambault, C. G. (1921/1942). Les psychoses passionelles (The passionate psychoses). In *Oeuvres psychiatriques* (pp. 315–322). Paris: Presses Universitaires de France.

Dietz, P., Matthews, D., Van Duyne, C., Martell, D., Parry, C., Stewart, T., Warren, J., & Crowder, J. D. (1991a). Threatening and otherwise inappropriate letters to Hollywood celebrities. *Journal of Forensic Sciences, 36*, 185–209.

Dietz, P., Matthews, D., Martell, D., Stewart, T., Hrouda, D., & Warren, J. (1991b). Threatening and otherwise inappropriate letters to members of the United States Congress. *Journal of Forensic Sciences, 36*, 1445–1468.

Fein, R., & Vossekuil, B. (1998). Preventing attacks on public officials and public figures: A Secret Service perspective. In J. R. Meloy (Ed.), *The psychology of stalking: Clinical and forensic perspectives.* (pp. 175–191). San Diego: Academic Press.

Fein, R., Vossekuil, B., & Holden, G. (1995). Threat assessment: An approach to prevent targeted violence. *National Institute of Justice: Research in action.* Washington, DC: Department of Justice.

Fiedler, B., Briar, K., & Pierce, M. (1984). Services for battered women. *Journal of Sociology and Social Welfare, 11*, 540–557.

Finn, P., & Colson, S. (1990). *Civil protection orders: Legislation, current court practice, and enforcement.* Washington, DC: Department of Justice.

Flannery, R., Hanson, M., & Penk, W. (1995). Patients' threats: Expanded definition of assault. *General Hospital Psychiatry, 17*, 451–453.

Freund, K., Scher, H., & Hucker, S. (1983). The courtship disorders. *Archives of Sexual Behavior, 12*, 369–379.

Gacono, C., & Meloy, J. R. (1994). *Rorschach assessment of aggressive and psychopathic personalities.* Hillsdale, NJ: Erlbaum.

Garrod, A., Ewert, P. W., Field, G., & Warren, G. (1995). *The report of the criminal harassment unit: The nature and extent of criminal harassment in British Columbia.* Vancouver: Ministry of Attorney General.

Grau, J., Fagan, J., & Wexler, S. (1984). Restraining orders for battered women: Issues of access and efficiency. *Women and Politics, 10*, 13–28.

Hall, D. (1998). The victims of stalking. In J. R. Meloy (Ed.), *The psychology of stalking: Clinical and forensic perspectives* (pp. 113–137). San Diego: Academic Press.

Hare, R. D. (1991). *Manual for the psychopathy checklist-revised.* Toronto: Multihealth Systems, Inc.

Harmon, R., Rosner, R., & Owens, H. (1995). Obsessional harassment and erotomania in a criminal court population. *Journal of Forensic Sciences, 40*, 188–196.

Harrell, A., Smith, B., & Newmark, L. (1993). *Court processing and the effects of restraining orders for domestic violence victims.* Denver, CO: The Urban Institute.

Harris, G., Rice, M., & Quinsey, V. (1993). Violent recidivism of mentally disordered offenders: The development of a statistical prediction instrument. *Criminal Justice and Behavior, 20*, 315–335.

Horton, A., Simonidis, K., & Simonidis, L. (1987). Legal remedies for spousal abuse: Victim characteristics, expectations, and satisfaction. *Journal of Family Violence, 2*, 265–279.

Kaci, J. (1992). A study of protective orders issued under California's Domestic Violence Prevention Act. *Criminal Justice Review, 17*, 61–76.

Kaci, J. (1994). Aftermath of seeking domestic-violence protective orders: The victim's perspective. *Journal of Contemporary Criminal Justice, 10*, 204–219.

Kaplan, H. S. (1996). Erotic obsession: Relationship to hypoactive sexual desire disorder and paraphilia. *American Journal of Psychiatry Festchrift Supplement, 153*, 30–41.

Kienlen, K. (1998). Developmental and social antecedents of stalking. In J. R. Meloy (Ed.), *The psychology of stalking: Clinical and forensic perspectives* (pp. 51–68). San Diego: Academic Press.

Kienlen, K., Birmingham, D., Solberg, K., O'Regan, J., & Meloy, J. R. (1997). A comparative study of psychotic and nonpsychotic stalking. *Journal of the American Academy of Psychiatry and the Law, 25*, 317–334.

Lion, J. R. (1995). Verbal threats against clinicians. In B. Eichelman & A. Hartwig (Eds.), *Patient violence and the clinician* (pp. 43–52). Washington, DC: American Psychiatric Press.

Macdonald, J. (1968). *Homicidal threats*. Springfield, Ill.: Charles C Thomas.

Meloy, J. R. (1989). Unrequited love and the wish to kill: Diagnosis and treatment of borderline erotomania. *Bulletin of the Menninger Clinic, 53*, 477–492.

Meloy, J. R. (1992). *Violent attachments*. Northvale, NJ: Jason Aronson.

Meloy, J. R. (1996). Stalking (obsessional following): A review of some preliminary studies. *Aggression and Violent Behavior, 1*, 147–162.

Meloy, J. R. (1997a). The clinical risk management of stalking: "Someone is watching over me..." *American Journal of Psychotherapy, 51*, 174–184.

Meloy, J. R. (1997b). Predatory violence during mass murder. *Journal of Forensic Sciences, 42*, 326–329.

Meloy, J. R. (Ed.). (1998). *The psychology of stalking: Clinical and forensic perspectives* (pp. 1–23). San Diego: Academic Press.

Meloy, J. R., Cowett, P. Y., Parker, S., Hofland, B., & Friedland, A. (1997). Domestic protection orders and the prediction of subsequent criminality and violence toward protectees. *Psychotherapy, 34*, 447–458.

Meloy, J. R. & Gothard, S. (1995). Demographic and clinical comparison of obsessional followers and offenders with mental disorders. *American Journal of Psychiatry, 152*, 258–263.

Meloy, J. R., Rivers, L., Siegel, L., Gothard, S., Naimark, D., & Nicolini, R. (2000). A replication study of obsessional followers and offenders with mental disorders. *Journal of Forensic Sciences, 45*, 147–152.

Menzies, R., Federoff, J., Green, C., & Isaacson, K. (1995). Prediction of dangerous behavior in male erotomania. *British Journal of Psychiatry, 166*, 529–536.

Mirsky, A., & Siegel, A. (1994). The neurobiology of violence and aggression. In A. Reiss, K. Miczek, & J. Roth (Eds.), *Understanding and preventing violence, volume 2: Biobehavioral influences* (pp. 59–111). Washington, DC: National Academy Press.

Mohandie, K., Hatcher, C. & Raymond, D. (1998). False victimization syndromes in stalking. In J. R. Meloy (Ed.), *The psychology of stalking: Clinical and forensic perspectives* (pp. 225–256). San Diego: Academic Press.

Monahan, J. (1997). Clinical and actuarial predictions of violence. In D. Faigman, D. Kaye, M. Saks, & J. Sanders (Eds.), *Modern scientific evidence: The law and science of expert testimony, volume 1* (pp. 300–318). St. Paul, MN: West.

Monahan, J., & Steadman, H. (Eds.) (1994). *Violence and mental disorder: Developments in risk assessment*. Chicago: University of Chicago Press.

Mullen, P., & Pathé, M. (1994). Stalking and the pathologies of love. *Australian and New Zealand Journal of Psychiatry, 28,* 469–477.

National Center for State Courts (1997). Victims' perceptions of effectiveness of protective orders as an intervention in domestic violence and stalking. In *Domestic violence and stalking: The second annual report to Congress under the Violence Against Women Act* (pp. 37–44). Washington, DC: Department of Justice.

Pathé, M., & Mullen, P. (1997). The impact of stalkers on their victims. *British Journal of Psychiatry, 176,* 12–19.

Saunders, R. (1998). The legal perspective on stalking. In J. R. Meloy (Ed.), *The psychology of stalking: Clinical and forensic perspectives* (pp. 25–49). San Diego: Academic Press.

Schwartz-Watts, D., Morgan, D., & Barnes, C. (1997). Stalkers: The South Carolina experience. *Journal of the American Academy of Psychiatry and the Law, 25,* 541–545.

Segal, J. (1989). Erotomania revisited: From Kraepelin to *DSM-III-R*. *American Journal of Psychiatry, 146,* 1261–1266.

Sherman, L., & Berk, R. (1984). The specific deterrent effects of arrest for domestic assault. *American Sociological Review, 49,* 261.

Shore, D., Filson, R., Davis, T. et al. (1985). White House cases: Psychiatric patients and the Secret Service. *American Journal of Psychiatry, 142,* 308–311.

Shore, D., Filson, R., & Johnson, W. (1988). Violent crime arrests and paranoid schizophrenia: The White House case studies. *Schizophrenia Bulletin, 14,* 279–281.

Shore, D., Filson, R., & Johnson, W. et al. (1989). Murder and assault arrests of White House cases: Clinical and demographic correlates of violence subsequent to civil commitment. *American Journal of Psychiatry, 146,* 645–651.

Tjaden, P., & Thoennes, N. (1997). *Stalking in America: Findings from the National Violence Against Women survey.* Denver: Center for Policy Research.

van der Kolk, B. (1987). *Psychological trauma.* Washington, DC: American Psychiatric Press.

Wright, J., Burgess, A., Burgess, A., Laszlo, A., McCrary, G., & Douglas, J. (1996). A typology of interpersonal stalking. *Journal of Interpersonal Violence, 11,* 487–501.

Zona, M., Sharma, K., & Lane, J. (1993). A comparative study of erotomanic and obsessional subjects in a forensic sample. *Journal of Forensic Sciences, 38,* 894–903.

14. Discussion and Clinical Commentary on Issues in the Assessment and Prediction of Dangerousness

GEORGES-F. PINARD AND LINDA PAGANI

This chapter underscores the most salient and clinically pertinent elements of the book. We have chosen to organize this commentary according to components of the standard clinical evaluation process.

Sociodemographic Data

The data invariably suggest that perpetrators of violent acts are more likely to be young, male, single, limited in educational attainment, and from disadvantaged backgrounds. One has to remember that this is a general trend, and practice shows that many offenders do not necessarily correspond to these characteristics.

Medical History

With or without a history of violence, the clinical assessment of dangerousness must involve procedures that rule out organicity. Is there a head injury in the physical history of the individual that may have resulted in brain damage or dysfunction? As mentioned in Chapter 6, physical anomalies of the brain present a greater risk for violence. Of course, this does not rule out the possibility that the inherently aggressive individual placed himself in a situation for possible head injury (i.e., reckless driving, barroom brawls, missed suicide attempts, acts of revenge, etc.). Regardless of your viewpoint on the chicken or egg question, the presence and proper assessment of organicity has true implications for patient evaluation and management (Tardiff, 1992).

Different signs and symptoms with respect to orientation (person, place, time), behavior, affect, and thought and perceptual processes help localize specific cerebral areas of malfunction. Saver, Salloway,

Devinsky, and Bear (1996) have described the possible organic causes associated with violent behavior. Behavioral regulation is governed by different cerebral structures that act in conjunction, and, when injury or pathology strikes, there is a greater risk for particular syndromes of hyperaggression. According to these authors, such syndromes differ by the type (mode) and form (outburst) of behavior exhibited: Presence of eliciting stimuli like provocation; presence of complex planning; and memory and remorse for acts. An assessment should be particularly sensitive to the history or presence of orbito-frontal injury. The classic case of Phineas Gage, an individual who experienced frontal lobe injury during an explosion in the 19th century (Fuster, 1997), contributed to past literature on frontal lobe syndromes. More recently, prefrontal dysfunction has been increasingly suggested as a possible source of different acts of violence (Raine, 1997). While prefrontal dysfunction seems to be associated with recidivistic violence, type-II alcoholism, and homicidal behavior, it is also seen in depression (Kalayam & Alexopoulos, 1999) and does not automatically indicate potential for violence. Moreover, we find prefrontal dysfunction in schizophrenia (Goldman-Rakic & Selemon, 1997), and, as has been seen in different sections of this book (see Chapters 5 and 6) the percentage of violent individuals in such populations remains a stable minority. Other frontal lobe syndromes are attributable to trauma, tumors, vascular problems, degenerative diseases, infections, or other sources, and yet may not necessarily be indicative of risk for violent behavior. Different organic afflictions may also influence changes in personality. This may or may not be predictive of violence.

Intellectual limitations are another factor to consider. Individuals affected by such characteristics frequently have a lower frustration tolerance, diminished outlets to express their emotions in a socially acceptable way, and limitations in judgment than individuals of normal intellect (Hawk, Rosenfeld, & Warren, 1993; McCreary & Thompson, 1999; Murphy & Clare, 1998).

Once a good history and physical (including a neurological exam) are complete, one can conduct a series of more in-depth assessments including but not being limited to neuropsychological testing, an electroencephalogram, brain scanning (CT-Scan, MRI); or more dynamic cerebral imagery techniques (e.g., SPECT-scan) can also assist in the identification or exclusion of an organic source of behavioral abnormality.

Chapter 2 focused on different substances found in bodily fluids that have been associated with biological origins of aggressive behavior.

Studies on this topic have been conducted with different populations: Nonviolent individuals; normal individuals placed in situations of provocation or challenge; individuals with Axis I and Axis II disorders; violent delinquents; and violent and nonviolent prisoners who have committed different types of offenses.

Among the possible substances, Susman and Finkelstein noted that the research on hormones and neurotransmitters appears the most promising in better understanding the biological processes involved in aggression. Of these, testosterone and serotonin have been the most reliable substances. Both have direct behavioral effects on the central nervous system. Different regions of the brain have receptors for these two substances, most notably structures of the limbic system that are implicated in the regulation of aggression. Although they clearly have different roles, testosterone and serotonin have both been linked with violent behavior (see Chapter 2). Their impact on behavior appears mediated by specific psychological and personality characteristics. To different degrees, both substances have an impact on mood, sensation seeking, self-affirmation and dominance, frustration tolerance, risk taking, and impulsivity (Bernhardt, 1997; Daitzman & Zuckerman, 1980; De Vegvar, Siever, & Trestman, 1994; Ehrenkranz, Bliss, & Sheard, 1974; Markowitz & Coccaro, 1995; Mazur & Lamb, 1980; van Praag, 1992; Virkkunen, Goldman, Nielsen, & Linnoila, 1995; Zuckerman, 1986). Moreover, both seem to play a role during critical periods of development. Consequently, at this point it seems important to study the possible relationships between these two substances.

As interesting and clinically pertinent such endeavors might be, testosterone and serotonin remain but biological markers that are in need of established specificity as mechanisms. A dysfunction of the serotonergic system is not necessarily indicative of violent behavior. We also find such dysfunction in affective disorders (i.e., depression and suicidal behavior), anxiety disorders (obsessive-compulsive disorder, panic disorder, social phobia, post-traumatic stress disorder), different addictions (alcoholism, drug abuse, paraphilias, impulse control disorders such as pathological gambling), and certain personality disorders (Buydens-Branchey, Branchey, Noumair, & Lieber, 1989; Coccaro, Silverman, Klar, & Horvath, 1994; Davis, Clark, Kramer, Moeller, & Petty, 1999; Hewlett, Vinogradov, Martin, & Berman, 1992; Hollander et al., 1998; Insel, 1992; Kafka, 1997; Moss, Yao, & Panzac, 1990; Petty, Davis, Kabel, & Kramer, 1996; Pihl & Peterson, 1993; Siever & Trestman, 1993; Stein, Hollander, De Caria, & Trungold, 1991; van Praag, 1992; Verkes et al., 1997).

Acknowledgment of the role of testosterone and serotonin led to the use of anti-androgenic and subsequently serotonergic treatment of sex offenders. Testosterone plays a role in human sexuality, sexual motivation, and possibly sexual aggression (Rada, Laws, & Kellner, 1976; Rada, Laws, Kellner, Stivastava, & Peake, 1983). It may also be associated with personality characteristics found in many perpetrators of sex offenses (Pinard, 1997). For its part, serotonin could play a role in aggressive behavior and related personality characteristics such as impulsivity (Asberg, 1994; Brown, Botsis, & van Praag, 1994; Coccaro, Kavoussi, Sheline, Lish, & Csernansky, 1996; Constantino, Morris, & Murphy, 1997; De Vegvar et al., 1994; Evenden, 1999; Goldman, Lappalainen, & Ozaki, 1996; Markowitz & Coccaro, 1995; Staner & Mendlewicz, 1998; Stein et al., 1996; Tuinier, Verhoeven, & van Praag, 1995; Virkkunen et al., 1995; Zuckerman, 1986). Serotonergic agents have an obsession reduction effect, particularly with egodystonic paraphilias. Their antidepressive effect can improve dysphoria that often precedes deviant sexual fantasies in such populations. In fact, it seems that such agents might reduce deviant sexual urges while minimally affecting nondeviant sexual urges (Fedoroff, 1993).

A discussion about biological factors must also consider the role of both structural and genetic factors (Eley, Lichtenstein, & Stevenson, 1999; O'Connor, Neiderhiser, Reiss, Hetherington, & Plomin, 1998), because these may actually be involved with the impact of the substances discussed above. To some degree, serotonin mediates one component of genetic liability to the development of antisocial personality (Constantino et al., 1997). Perinatal factors have been associated with antisocial behavior in adults (Brennan, Mednick, & Kandel, 1991; Mednick & Kandel, 1988). Prenatal exposure to drugs and alcohol should be taken into account as factors related to mental deficiency and even disorder (Hans, 1999; van den Bree, Svikis, & Pickens, 1998). This body of research justifies the importance of assessing the gestational and birth history of the individual we evaluate for dangerousness. It is hoped that someday there will be a homogeneous theory of violent behavior which will help us piece together all the information gathered in the biology of violence.

Psychiatric History

Monahan has underscored the fact that not all mentally ill persons are dangerous and that not all dangerous persons are mentally ill. Most are not. Nevertheless, a standard dangerousness assessment must include both an extensive psychiatric history and details of compliance with treatment. Such information will facilitate both clinical and legal decisions about the individual and the clinician's responsibility thereafter.

Indeed, a number of major mental disorders have been linked to potential for violence in certain circumstances. Among these, schizophrenia (especially the paranoid form), when untreated or in an exacerbated state, seems to pose the greatest risk for violence (Wessely, Castle, & Douglas, 1994). This is why Monahan devoted much of his chapter to that disorder. However, one should be vigilant about other disorders, including major depression (with and without psychotic characteristics), postpartum depression or psychosis, bipolar disorder, and delusional disorder. In certain unfavorable conditions, these disorders can be predictive of violent behavior. This is where the clinician must be aware that statistics from huge epidemiological studies draw on groups, whereas, in daily clinical practice the clinician is faced with making a prediction about an individual's potential. Thus, a good psychiatric history should examine: tendencies toward destructive behavior in both the recent and not so recent past; threats of suicide; suicide attempts; threats toward others; use of coercion; domestic violence; violence toward animals, and so forth.

A consistent unstated theme throughout this book is the parallel risk factors for both suicide and harm toward others (see Plutchik & van Praag, 1997 for a more extensive review). Much like the assessment of suicide risk, the evaluation of dangerousness searches for violent ideation (thoughts, fantasies, etc.) and attempts. Of course, the similarities between these two end where the focus of the aggression begins.

Specific themes may surface in the interview: the search for power or dominance (that may reach extremes such as deviant sexual content in cases of pedophilia, rape, and sadism) or revenge. We should pay particular attention to the recreational use of supporting material for such themes. This includes literature, film, pictorial, and now even web sites pertaining to different kinds of aggression. If present, it is important to have a measure of the frequency and intensity of the use of such materials and the degree of satisfaction obtained from them. It is also equally important to assess whether the individual is egosyntonic about this material, whether the individual wishes to enact the sequences, the degree of control the individual has on his or her fantasy life, and any plans the individual may have with respect to this suggestive material.

History of Violent and Criminal Behavior

There is general consensus that history of past violent behavior and criminal activity represents the best predictor of future violent behavior (see Chapter 7). In a standard assessment, it is important to note the origins of such behavior in time. Evidence of early maladjustment is particularly ominous. We must also assess signs of escalation in the proclivity toward violence. This is of particular concern in cases of some offenders who characteristically escalate over time in their modus operandi, especially in the transition from fantasy to reality (e.g., many sex offenders). Another important aspect of escalation is represented by the overlap among cases of domestic violence, intimate partner homicide, and homicide-suicide (see Chapter 8).

We must explore the use of threats by the individual just as we do for previous interests/acts of violence. The target of such threats, how elaborate the threats are, the intention, and any evidence of the threats becoming concrete (i.e., evidence of planning) should be considered (see Chapters 6 and 13). There is a duty to inform the potential victim so that measures to protect can be taken, as mentioned by Ewing, Monahan, Meloy, and others in this book. The individual's judgment and insight about threats are much like those expressed for violent behavior in general (see Chapter 13): Complete denial (refusal to acknowledge the threat and the intention); denial by invoking misinterpretation (the content of the interview or incident was misreported or misinterpreted); minimizing (acknowledging the threat, denying the intention); complete acknowledgment (acknowledging both the threat and the intention).

We should also look for behaviors that could indicate stalking (obsessional following or tracking). In addition to different types of stalkers mentioned by Meloy, we may see these behaviors in pathological jealousy, abusive relationships between intimates (or aspired intimates as in erotomania), and different paraphilias. Stalking could represent a perpetrator's modus operandi for localizing and approaching a potential victim. These behaviors could be a source of gratification, revenge, or even be of a predatory nature. In the latter case, stalking behavior could accompany voyeurism, rape, pedophilia, or even sexual sadism. Reading Meloy's contribution makes us think not only of the distinguishing features of different stalkers but also the similarities in dynamics between stalkers, sex offenders, sexual and other harassers, and perpetrators of workplace violence.

Consumption of Substances

McCord described the complex relationship between alcohol use/abuse and criminal behavior. Crimes involving alcohol use can be categorized: Against public peace/order; against persons; reckless driving; and negligence. In fact, many of the individual cases of violence mentioned by Farrington involved all of these in one sitting.

Alcohol use and dependence, as comorbid conditions, are found among different personality disorders, recidivistic criminal populations, and in major mental disorders. Alcohol consumption may have an anti-anhedonic effect for many in these groups. Among the different types of alcoholism, Tiihonen and McCord appear justifiably concerned about the early origins of type-II alcoholism. As adults, such individuals are more likely to recidivate and be involved with violence on some level (domestic, pub brawls, settling of accounts, etc.). The bottom line here is that the clinical evaluation of dangerousness must examine the individual's involvement with alcohol and should also examine the role of alcohol in his or her development. In other words, did the parents consume alcohol? Is there a history of harsh punishment or domestic violence associated with consumption in the family of creation/origin as well? Management and treatment of potential violence is much more challenging with adult consumers of alcohol. On a preventive level, perhaps we can attempt to protect and treat the offspring of such individuals, given the genetic transmission and environmental problems that they provide as parents.

Much like alcohol, there are effects of illicit drugs on physical state, behavior, affect, and thought and perceptual processes. Indeed, there are cases of psychosis associated with illicit drug intoxication. Psychiatric emergency rooms must use special precautions with such individuals, given the elevated risk of a violent outburst (Pinard, 2000).

Chapter 12 focused on the link between drug use and violence. Unlike alcohol (which is no longer prohibited in most parts of the Western world) a major mechanism of the link is economic gain. Among drug consumers, we will also find cases of crime against public peace/order, against persons, and negligence. Nevertheless, it seems that some of the dynamics observed during the period of prohibition in the United States (see Chapter 11) might be acting in the link between drug use and violence. This is not to say that drugs should not be prohibited. Rather, our assessments of dangerousness should attempt to demystify the role of drugs in the individual's life and their effect on behavior. Should they be associated with a greater risk for violent behavior because they reveal, induce, or complicate a mental state or disorder, then it is our responsibility as mental health professionals to prevent, treat, and manage. Upon assessment, however, drug involvement for economic gain has no place in the management of dangerousness prescribed by mental health professionals. Instead, that problem should be referred and directed elsewhere.

There is also the issue of social dangerousness, a concern reviewed by Roques (1999) and his group. Social dangerousness refers to the behavioral states (i.e., irritability and impulsivity) caused by consumption of a substance that can engender risks for not only the consumer, but innocent others. Excellent examples of social dangerousness involve reckless driving, road rage, parking rage, air rage, and even organizational violence. Their literature review suggests that cocaine, heroin, alcohol, and benzodiazepine use engender the greatest risks for injury of innocent others and the users themselves.

Five considerations must be made when conducting an assessment of dangerousness involving drugs or alcohol: (1) Dependence (Does irritability occur during intoxication or during withdrawal?); (2) Factors related to patterns of use/abuse (Is there evidence of binge drinking or drug use?); (3) Temporal relationship between substance use and onset of irritability and violence; (4) Context in which violence occurs (Does it typically occur in place of consumption or does the individual consume and then pursue a context for violence?); (5) Individual factors (For prognostic reasons, it is important to know the age of onset of drinking or drug use. One should question motivational features of the consumption as well. Is there an intergenerational trend? Is there comorbidity with an Axis I or Axis II disorder? etc.). In some cases, substance use can reveal an underlying predisposition or vulnerability toward psychopathology. It can represent some form of inadvertent self-medication. In other cases, psychopathology could already be present, with the substance causing exacerbation or precipitating relapses of the illness.

Chapters 5 and 7 underscore the importance of acknowledging the presence of multiple diagnoses. We acknowledge that it is very difficult to tease apart two (or more) diagnoses and determine the differential impact of each. Nevertheless, noting comorbidity is key in determining dangerousness and management of such individuals. A review of the research in the first chapter indicates the increase in risk per additional diagnosis (see chapter 1). Individuals with two (or more) diagnoses present specific needs that require approaches which must be adapted to their characteristics, making them more delicate to manage (Wetzler & Sanderson, 1997).

Personal History

In order to make a proper judgment about potential for violence, it is of the utmost importance to have information on the individual's developmental history. Such a history should consider environmental factors, family issues, and socio-cultural background. It is recommended that all possible information be obtained to collect data about parental psychopathology and any indications of childhood maltreatment (sexual, physical, psychological, or negligence). A history of abuse, especially during early childhood, may contribute to perpetuating an individual style of violence during adulthood (Spatz Widom, 1997; Widom, 1989). For example, a history of sexual abuse during childhood is widespread among adult sex offenders, especially pedophiles. According to chapter 10, it appears that a history of serious abuse is not only linked to an aggressive lifestyle in general, but also increases the chances of parricide.

Educational and Professional History

Chapters 3 and 4 indicate how early maladjustment and its resulting underachievement contribute to later risk for violence. Such findings apply well to individuals who have consistently shown aggressive and oppositional behavior throughout their schooling. Some may not achieve enough in school to acquire a job in skilled labor, whereas some may. There is also that small percentage of individuals who have enough success in school to make it into white-collar jobs. Regardless of the level of prestige associated with the job, there are direct and indirect opportunities to manifest aggression, impulsivity, and defiance. Workplace violence represents an important risk for a loose cannon. Threats and harassment represent other possible risks. It is therefore an excellent idea to get a detailed educational and work history from the individual that is ideally accompanied by some corroboration from the current or previous employer(s).

Relational and Social History

In general, we should look for recurring experiences that could influence pathologies in attachment and interfere with the development of empathy. Did the individual experience inconsistent care during childhood? Does the individual live in solitude? Does the individual have a stable set of close friends? If there is a spouse and children, are there indicators of jealousy or domestic violence? Siblings may also be an excellent source of information about the individual's social adjustment history.

Psychosexual History

The age at which the individual became sexually aware and active represents an important indicator of sexual precocity (in the case of delinquency) and sexual deviance (in the case of paraphilias). When discussing a particular sexual relationship, it would be important to ask what the individual thinks the sexual partner felt about the experience (indications of forced sexual experiences, as in acquaintance rape, become more evident with responses to this question). In this part of the evaluation we also must assess the presence of deviant interests/fantasies/behaviors and any indications of escalation in such activities. Attitudes toward previous and potential sexual partners represent important avenues for exploration.

Developmental Psychopathology

Questions about the individual's developmental history crop up again here. We note that in Chapter 3, both physical aggression and oppositional defiant behaviors that are consistent in early childhood are predictive of later official records of juvenile offenses. Chapter 4 tells us that juvenile offenses are linked to later adult criminality and violence. It would be useful to have information on the individual's behavioral development, and this is where family members become helpful. Do the parents or siblings describe the individual as a "handful" during childhood?

As mentioned earlier, among the major mental disorders, schizophrenia (in an untreated or exacerbated state) shows the strongest link to violence (Wessely et al., 1994). We suggest a cumulative risk model here. That is, estimated risk should be compounded by every additional factor that appears in the individual's profile: substance use, early childhood maladjustment, childhood maltreatment, noncompliance with treatment resulting in psychotic symptoms, lack of insight, stressful life events, and such. This helps distinguish the individuals with major mental disorder who do pose a risk for violence from the majority who do not pose such a risk.

Characteristics of Violent Acts

The evaluator seeks to characterize the dynamics of the violence; that is, the interactions between the perpetrator and victim, the personal and physical context within which the violence took place, and the modus operandi (if it appeared to be a planned act). Although indications of planning behavior are particularly ominous and suggest lack of remorse, the opposite characteristic, impulsivity, represents a serious control problem as well.

In order to understand the dynamics of the violent behavior, we must understand the motivations behind it. Clear intentions and motivations, as mentioned in the previous paragraph, strongly suggest an underlying personality disorder. However, motivations can also be linked to delusions and associated psychotic states. In the literature review on filicide by Marks, we note that altruistic filicide can be distinguished as nonpsychotic or psychotic, where the child's suffering is real or perceived as real, respectively. In the latter, the parent seeks to relieve the child of imagined suffering.

It becomes obvious at this point, that the individual's mental state at the time of the offense is important. Monahan's contribution (and work by others, e.g., Binder, 1999; Hersh & Borum, 1998; Rudnick, 1999) underscores that specific signs and symptoms of mental state are better predictors of potential for violence, more than diagnosis per se. The exacerbation of an Axis I disorder can perturb orientation, behavior, affect, thoughts, and perceptions.

An exacerbated Axis II disorder can also be characterized by disturbances in affect, cognitions, perceptions, and behavior that can lead to dangerousness. The defensive strategies used by such individuals, especially in the presence of narcissistic injury, feelings of entitlement, and fears of rejection or abandonment can contribute to violent behavior as a perceived means of being self-protective. Borderline patients are particularly vulnerable in such situations (Kernberg, 1998). The degree of psychopathy seems to play an important role in predicting recidivistic violence (Grann, Langstrom, Tengstrom, & Kullgren, 1999; Hare, 1999; Hemphill, Hare, & Wong, 1998; Quinsey, Rice, & Harris, 1995; Rice & Harris, 1995, 1997; Salekin, Rogers, Ustad, & Sewell, 1998; Serin, 1996; Serin & Amos, 1995; Wong, 1995; Zamble & Palmer, 1995). This conclusion becomes quite clear in results from evaluation studies of the various actuarial risk assessment schemes available (Litwack & Schlesinger, 1999).

Characterizations of violent acts could be drastically improved by a sound typology. It is hoped that future terms used in assessments will go beyond an Axis I or Axis II diagnosis. At present, clinicians typically rely on a dichotomy of psychotic versus nonpsychotic distinction. This method is relevant given that the quality and quantity of psychotic symptoms remain two of the most reliable predictors of future violence risk. Although the state of the art needs improvement, it does help develop insight about liability issues and strategies for treatment.

Assessment of the characteristics of violent acts must consider the features of the potential victim. The first reflex is to address risk for family members and close friends. Where acquaintances and strangers may be at risk, information about victim characteristics (e.g., age, sex) and the context of potential victimization are important to ascertain, whenever possible. For example, if the individual typically looks for violence or victims in a bar (i.e., pursuing an unknown patron of the opposite sex or looking for a brawl), then perhaps the treatment plan could involve a restraining order from the courts to avoid such areas.

Risk Management Strategies

Once a dangerousness assessment is made and is judged affirmative, it is the inherent responsibility of the clinician to design a treatment program that seeks to minimize the risk of violence. Although it is beyond the scope of this chapter to fully address the topic of risk management, we would like to highlight some important considerations. This list is not exhaustive, nor are the items mentioned in order of priority. They are to be selected when indicated as appropriate and applicable. Finally, they are context dependent, since it would be necessary to consider the policies, regulations, and laws in one's place of practice.

Factors Related to Hospitalization. If it is called for, hospitalization can not only help to manage risk but also help with differential diagnosis (Axis I and/or Axis II). A secure physical environment remains fundamental. This environment must allow easy access and use of a restraints and isolation policy. The individual's behavior must be carefully scrutinized, particularly if the individual attempts violent behavior while an inpatient in a structured and controlled setting. Of equal importance is to beware of: (1) silent psychotics (i.e., "wallflowers") who do not attract much attention, but when questioned, are clearly delusional; and (2) the presence of an Axis II disorder (e.g., psychopathy). The latter may show exemplary behavioral control and appropriateness, leading to much debate among the staff members about relevance of their hospitalization and their role in incidents involving other more vulnerable patients on the unit.

Once the individual's characteristics are reliably established in terms of dangerousness, then a proper judgment about treatment facility and risk management can be made. In the case of an individual with major mental disorder who remains in the hospital for treatment, plans for eventually increasing responsibility on the unit, supervised or accompanied outings, and eventual unescorted outings can be made. Dangerousness must be reevaluated on a frequent and regular basis in order to stimulate and track patient progress.

Factors Requiring Periodic Reevaluation. These apply to both outpatient and inpatient settings. A rigorous approach to follow-up is required when the individual's characteristics include any of the following: Unresolved psychotic symptoms; medication compliance issues (spot checks on serum levels if applicable); alcohol or drug consumption (serum or urine spot checks may be recommended here too); interest in or presence of suicidal or violent ideation; self-control of sexually deviant or aggressive fantasies; stressful life events; and inclination toward risk taking or sensation seeking. Just as with suicidal behavior, the clinician must weigh the presence of risk and protective factors at each follow-up assessment. Finally, all factors related to past criminal or unethical activities must be factored into each dangerousness reevaluation equation.

Factors to Consider in Outpatient Follow-Up. Even if the patient is new or referred to outpatient facilities, it is important to have a clear understanding of the dynamics of the risk factors for violence, past and present. The outpatient facility must be prepared to rapidly care for individuals who have been discharged from the hospital. Both quality and quantity of supervision is a key factor in care. There are times when legal/judicial agencies decide on the frequency/intensity of care. The individual may be living alone or in a supervised setting. Supervision intensity must be gauged accordingly, with the lone individual receiving more vigilant monitoring from the outpatient staff.

Sudden vulnerability represents another important outpatient issue. A scheduled appointment may have to be pushed up or the frequency of clinical contacts may have to be increased (as long as it does not increase dependence or regression). The individual may have to be contacted by telephone or outreach personnel dispatched when appointments have been missed. Finally, when outpatient facilities become insufficient to manage risk, it may be important to consider rehospitalization, day hospital, or day-center care arrangements before the situation further deteriorates. This may also include parole/probation measures restricting outings from the halfway house or even reincarceration.

Legal Considerations. Some of these can apply to either inpatient or outpatient settings. Extensive and detailed documentation represents the most important strategy here. There are a multitude of scenarios with legal implications that require extensive consultation and documentation by the clinician: Court order for examination or treatment; closed treatment; and various restraining orders and injunctions. We must maintain our obligation to inform and/or protect third parties. We must consider possible prosecution of threats or violent behavior as well, especially when the individual involved has an Axis II disorder.

Administrative and Institutional Considerations. Management of potentially violent persons depends upon institutional policies, prevention policies, and security policies and measures available. It is advisable to discuss safety concerns with colleagues (staff or department meetings and other institutional meetings) in cases where one has a doubt or requires support in decision making. One can never be too careful where safety of others is concerned. The development of institutional policies represents a dynamic and iterative process where feedback from the results of a case influences future strategies. Therefore, it is wise to confer with colleagues in order to both keep abreast and influence future policies.

Collaboration and Communication. In addition to asking experienced colleagues to consult on a case, it is important to focus on the need for good communication between different professionals, especially where incident reports and doubts are concerned. When appropriate, we may need to contact or even meet with judicial or legal representatives who are connected to the individual case. Such contacts may help determine different restrictive measures for both in- and outpatient management. If possible, we must try to include community resources and family members in treatment planning and supervision.

Counseling Considerations. Apart from developing a therapeutic alliance (allowing us to keep closer tabs), counseling helps the individual develop better insight, even if such insight has its limitations. As mentioned in Chapter 7, we should address and treat the problem of substance abuse, if present in psychotic and nonpsychotic patients, in order to substantially reduce the risk of future violence. The individual can also benefit from preventive intervention programs and support groups to avoid recidivism (for psychosis, substance use, sex offending, etc.).

Pharmacological Considerations. The most important management strategy is the use of injectable neuroleptics for psychotic patients who are noncompliant with their medication (or where the risk of noncompliance engenders great risk for others). The use of mood stabilizers with individuals experiencing mood disorders, impulsivity, and/or cerebral organicity may be effective. Because of their low toxicity, serotonin reuptake inhibitors can be useful for individuals who are vulnerable to self-intoxication. These and anti-androgenic treatments can be useful with some sex offenders. More extensive information is available in a variety of literature reviews on the chemical treatment of potential violence (e.g., Karper & Krystaal, 1997; Mann, 1995; Ray-Byrne & Fann, 1997).

Other, More Universal Measures. We can address the individual as described above and in the various contributions to this book. Nevertheless, we can also invest in youth management strategies, dysfunctional families, children of Axis I and Axis II disordered parents, staff training for assessment and prevention programs (as done with suicide). Much of this can be done as early as possible, when universal measures can benefit all children. We should focus on early childhood preventive intervention where there are children with special needs (e.g., early signs of deviant behavior such as aggression or inappropriate sexual behavior, or early signs of family dysfunction). As mentioned in Chapter 3, by intervening early we could diminish violence potential and avoid costly problems that the individual might eventually develop.

We can also lobby decision makers about better coordination of outpatient services, gun control laws, drivers' licensing procedures, more effective consequences for driving under the influence of substances, and more active censuring or prohibition of suggestive and gratuitous violence in the film and television industry. One cannot argue against a more peaceful society where both vulnerable and less vulnerable individuals can live in tranquility.

REFERENCES

Asberg, M. (1994). Monoamine neurotransmitters in human aggressiveness and violence: A selected review. *Criminal Behavior and Mental Health, 4*(4), 303–327.

Bernhardt, P. C. (1997). Influences of serotonin and testosterone in aggression and dominance: Convergence with social psychology. *Current Directions in Psychological Science, 6*(2), 44–48.

Binder, R. L. (1999). Are the mentally ill dangerous? *Journal of the American Academy of Psychiatry and the Law, 27*(2), 189–201.

Brennan, P., Mednick, S. A., & Kandel, E. (1991). Congenital determinants of violent and property offending. In D. J. Pepler & K. H. Rubin (Eds.), *The development and treatment of childhood aggression* (pp. 81–92). Hillsdale, NJ: Erlbaum.

Brown, S. L., Botsis, A., & van Praag, H. M. (1994). Serotonin and aggression. In M. Hillbrand & N. J. Pallone (Eds.), *The psychology of aggression: Engines, measurement, control* (pp. 27–39). New York: Haworth Press.

Buydens-Branchey, L., Branchey, M. H., Noumair, D., & Lieber, C. S. (1989). Age of alcoholism onset: Relationship to susceptibility to serotonin precursor availability. *Archives of General Psychiatry, 46*(3), 231–236.

Coccaro, E. F., Kavoussi, R. J., Sheline, Y. I., Lish, J. D., & Csernansky, J. G. (1996). Impulsive aggression in personality disorder correlates with tritiated paroxetine binding in the platelets. *Archives of General Psychiatry, 53*(6), 531–536.

Coccaro, E. F., Silverman, J. M., Klar, H. M., & Horvath, T. B. (1994). Familial correlates of reduced central serotonergic system function in patients with personality disorders. *Archives of General Psychiatry, 51*(4), 318–324.

Constantino, J. N., Morris, J. A., & Murphy, D. L. (1997). CSF 5-HIAA and family history of antisocial personality disorder in newborns. *American Journal of Psychiatry, 154*(12), 1771–1773.

Daitzman, R., & Zuckerman, M. (1980). Disinhibitory sensation seeking, personality, and gonadal hormones. *Personality and Individual Differences, 1*, 103–110.

Davis, L. L., Clark, D. M., Kramer, G. L., Moeller, F. G., & Petty, F. (1999). D-fenfluramine challenge in posttraumatic stress disorder. *Biological Psychiatry, 45*(7), 928–930.

De Vegvar, M. L., Siever, L. J., & Trestman, R. L. (1994). Impulsivity and serotonin in borderline personality disorder. In K. R. Silk (Ed.), *Biological and neurobehavioral studies of borderline personality disorder* (pp. 23–40). Washington, DC: American Psychiatric Press.

Ehrenkranz, J., Bliss, E., & Sheard, M. H. (1974). Plasma testosterone: Correlation with aggressive behavior and social dominance in man. *Psychosomatic Medicine, 36*, 469–475.

Eley, T. C., Lichtenstein, P., & Stevenson, J. (1999). Sex differences in the etiology of aggressive and nonaggressive antisocial behavior: Results from two
twin studies. *Child Development, 70*(1), 155–168.

Evenden, J. (1999). Impulsivity: A discussion of clinical and experimental findings. *Journal of Psychopharmacology, 13*(2), 180–192.

Fedoroff, J. P. (1993). Serotonergic drug treatment of deviant sexual interests.
Annals of Sex Research, 6, 105–121.

Fuster, J. (1997). Human Neuropsychology. In J. M. Fuster (Ed.), *The prefrontal
cortex: Anatomy, physiology, and neuropsychology of the frontal lobe* (pp.
150–184). Philadelphia: Lippincott-Raven.

Goldman, D., Lappalainen, J., & Ozaki, N. (1996). Direct analysis of candidate
genes in impulsive behaviours. *Ciba Foundation Symposium, 194*, 139–152.

Goldman-Rakic, P. S., & Selemon, L. D. (1997). Functional and anatomical
aspects of prefrontal pathology in schizophrenia. *Schizophrenia Bulletin, 23*(3),
437–458.

Grann, M., Langstrom, N., Tengstrom, A., & Kullgren, G. (1999). Psychopathy
(PCL-R) predicts violent recidivism among criminal offenders with personality disorders in Sweden. *Law and Human Behavior, 23*(2), 205–217.

Hans, S. L. (1999). Demographic and psychosocial characteristics of substance-
abusing pregnant women. *Clinics in Perinatology, 26*(1), 55–74.

Hare, R. D. (1999). Psychopathy as a risk factor for violence. *Psychiatric
Quarterly, 70*(3), 181–197.

Hawk, G. L., Rosenfeld, B. D., & Warren, J. I. (1993). Prevalence of sexual
offenses among mentally retarded criminal defendants. *Hospital and
Community Psychiatry, 44*(8), 784–786.

Hemphill, J. F., Hare, R. D., & Wong, S. (1998). Psychopathy and recidivism: A
review. *Legal and Criminological Psychology, 3*(Part 1), 139–170.

Hersh, K., & Borum, R. (1998). Command hallucinations, compliance, and risk
assessment. *Journal of the American Academy of Psychiatry and the Law, 26*(3),
353–359.

Hewlett, W. A., Vinogradov, S., Martin, K., & Berman, S. (1992). Fenfluramine
stimulation of prolactin in obsessive-compulsive disorder. *Psychiatry
Research, 42*(1), 81–92.

Hollander, E., Kwon, J., Weiller, F., Cohen, L., Stein, D. J., De Caria, C.,
Liebowitz, M., & Simeon, D. (1998). Serotonergic function in social phobia:
Comparison to normal control and obsessive-compulsive disorder subjects.
Psychiatry Research, 79(3), 213–217.

Insel, T. R. (1992). Neurobiology of obsessive-compulsive disorder: A review.
International Clinical Psychopharmacology, 7(1), 31–33.

Kafka, M. P. (1997). A monoamine hypothesis for the pathophysiology of para-
philic disorders. *Archives of Sexual Behavior, 26*(4), 343–358.

Kalayam, B., & Alexopoulos, G. S. (1999). Prefrontal dysfunction and treatment
response in geriatric depression. *Archives of General Psychiatry, 56*(8), 713–718.

Karper, L. P., & Krystaal, J. M. (1997). Pharmacotherapy of violent behavior. In
D. M. Stoff, J. Breiling, & J. D. Maser (Eds.), *Handbook of antisocial behavior* (pp.
436–444). New York: Wiley.

Kernberg, O. F. (1998). The psychotherapeutic management of psychopathic, narcissistic, and paranoid transferences. In T. Millon, E. Simonsen, M. Birket-Smith, & R. D. Danis (Eds.), *Psychopathy: Antisocial, criminal, and violent behavior* (pp. 372–393). New York: Guilford Press.

Litwack, T. R., & Schlesinger, L. B. (1999). Dangerousness risk assessments: Research, legal, and clinical considerations. In A. K. Hess & I. B. Weiner (Eds.), *The handbook of forensic psychology* (pp. 171–217). New York: Wiley.

McCreary, B. D., & Thompson, J. (1999). Psychiatric aspects of sexual abuse involving persons with developmental disabilities. *Canadian Journal of Psychiatry, 44*(4), 350–355.

Mann, J. J. (1995). Violence and aggression. In F. E. Bloom & D. J. Kupfer (Eds.), *Psychopharmacology: The fourth generation of progress* (pp. 1919–1928). New York: Raven Press.

Markowitz, P. I., & Coccaro, E. F. (1995). Biological studies of impulsivity, aggression, and suicidal behavior. In E. Hollander & D. J. Stein (Eds.), *Impulsivity and aggression* (pp. 71–90). Chichester: Wiley.

Mazur, A., & Lamb, T. A. (1980). Testosterone, status and mood in human males. *Hormones and Behavior, 14,* 236–246.

Mednick, S. A., & Kandel, E. (1998). Genetic and perinatal factors in violence. In S. A. Mednick & T. E. Moffitt (Eds.), *Biological contributors to crime causation* (pp. 121–134). Boston: Martinus Nijhoff.

Moss, H. B., Yao, J. K., & Panzac, G. L. (1990). Serotonergic responsivity and behavioral dimensions in antisocial personality disorder with substance abuse. *Biological Psychiatry, 28*(4), 325–338.

Murphy, G., & Clare, I. C. (1998). People with learning disabilities as offenders or alleged offenders in the UK criminal justice system. *Journal of the Royal Society of Medicine, 91*(4), 178–182.

O'Connor, T. G., Neiderhiser, J. M., Reiss, D., Hetherington, E. M., & Plomin, R. (1998). Genetic contributions to continuity, change, and co-occurrence of antisocial and depressive symptoms in adolescence. *Journal of Child Psychology and Psychiatry and Allied Disciplines, 39*(3), 323–336.

Petty, F., Davis, L. L., Kabel, D., & Kramer, G. L. (1996). Serotonin dysfunction disorders: A behavioral neurochemistry perspective. *Journal of Clinical Psychiatry, 57*(Suppl 8), 11–16.

Pihl, R. O., & Peterson, J. B. (1993). Alcohol, serotonin, and aggression. *Alcohol Health and Research World, 17*(2), 113–116.

Pinard, G.-F. (1997). Les bases biologiques de l'agression sexuelle. In T. Albernhe (Ed.), *Criminologie et psychiatrie* (pp. 401–406). Paris: Ellipses.

Pinard, G.-F. (2000). Considérations méthodologiques pour la recherche sur les comportements violents aux urgences psychiatriques. *Revue Francaise de Psychiatrie et de Psychologie Médicale, 35,* 9–15.

Plutchik, R., & van Praag, H. M. (1997). Suicide, impulsivity, and antisocial behavior. In D. M. Stoff, J. Breiling, & J. D. Maser (Eds.), *Handbook of antisocial behavior* (pp. 101–108). New York: Wiley.

Quinsey, V. L., Rice, M. E., & Harris, G. T. (1995). Actuarial prediction of sexual recidivism. *Journal of Interpersonal Violence, 10*(1), 85–105.

Rada, R. T., Laws, D. R., & Kellner, R. (1976). Plasma testosterone levels in the rapist. *Psychosomatic Medicine, 38*(4), 257–268.

Rada, R. T., Laws, D. R., Kellner, R., Stivastava, L., & Peake, G. (1983). Plasma androgens in violent and nonviolent sex offenders. *Bulletin of the American Academy of Psychiatry and the Law, 11*(2), 149–158.

Raine, A. (1997). Antisocial behavior and psychophysiology: A biosocial perspective and a prefrontal dysfunction hypothesis. In D. M. Stoff, J. Breiling, & J. D. Maser (Eds.), *Handbook of antisocial behavior* (pp. 289–304). New York: Wiley.

Ray-Byrne, P. P., & Fann, J. R. (1997). Psychopharmacologic treatments for patients with neuropsychiatric disorders. In S. C. Yudofsky & R. E. Hales (Eds.), *The American Psychiatric Press textbook of neuropsychiatry* (pp. 943–981). Washington, DC: American Psychiatric Press.

Rice, M. E., & Harris, G. T. (1995). Psychopathy, schizophrenia, alcohol abuse, and violent recidivism. *International Journal of Law and Psychiatry, 18*(3), 333–342.

Rice, M. E., & Harris, G. T. (1997). Cross-validation and extension of the violence risk appraisal guide for child molesters and rapists. *Law and Human Behavior, 21*(2), 231–241.

Roques, B. (1999). *La dangerosité des drogues.* Paris: Éditions Odile Jacob.

Rudnick, A. (1999). Relation between command hallucinations and dangerous behavior. *Journal of the American Academy of Psychiatry and the Law, 27*(2), 253–257.

Salekin, R. T., Rogers, R., Ustad, K. L., & Sewell, K. W. (1998). Psychopathy and recidivism among female inmates. *Law and Human Behavior, 22*(1), 109–128.

Saver, J. L., Salloway, S. P., Devinsky, O., & Bear, D. M. (1996). Neuropsychiatry of aggression. In B. S. Fogel, R. B. Schiffer, & S. M. Rao (Eds.), *Neuropsychiatry* (pp. 523–548). Baltimore: Williams & Wilkins.

Serin, R. C. (1996). Violent recidivism in criminal psychopaths. *Law and Human Behavior, 20*(2), 207–217.

Serin, R. C., & Amos, N. L. (1995). The role of psychopathy in the assessment of dangerousness. *International Journal of Law and Psychiatry, 18*(2), 231–238.

Siever, L., & Trestman, R. L. (1993). The serotonin system and aggressive personality disorder. *International Clinical Psychopharmacology, 8*(2), 33–39.

Spatz Widom, C. (1997). Child abuse, neglect and witnessing violence. In D. M. Stoff, J. Breiling, & J. D. Maser (Eds.), *Handbook of antisocial behavior* (pp. 159–170). New York: Wiley.

Staner, L., & Mendlewicz, J. (1998). Heredity and role of serotonin in aggressive impulsive behavior. *Encephale, 24*(4), 355–364.

Stein, D. J., Hollander, E., De Caria, C. M., & Trungold, S. (1991). OCD: A disorder with anxiety, aggression, impulsivity, and depressed mood. *Psychiatry Research, 36*(2), 237–239.

Stein, D. J., Trestman, R. L., Mitropoulou, V., Coccaro, E. F., Hollander, E., & Siever, L. J. (1996). Impulsivity and serotonergic function in compulsive personality disorder. *Journal of Neuropsychiatry and Clinical Neurosciences, 8*(4), 393–398.

Tardiff, K. (1992). The current state of psychiatry in the treatment of violent patients. *Archives of General Psychiatry, 49,* 493–499.

Tuinier, S., Verhoeven, W. M. A., & van Praag, H. M. (1995). Cerebrospinal fluid 5-hydroxyindolacetic acid and aggression: A critical reappraisal of the clinical data. *International Clinical Psychopharmacology, 10*(3), 147–156.

van den Bree, M. B., Svikis, D. S., & Pickens, R. W. (1998). Genetic influences in antisocial personality and drug use disorders. *Drug and Alcohol Dependence, 49*(3), 177–187.

van Praag, H. M. (1992). About the centrality of mood lowering in mood disorders. *European Neuropsychopharmacology, 2*(4), 393–404.

Verkes, R. J., Fekkes, D., Zwinderman, A. H., Hengeveld, M. W., Van der Mast, R. C., Tuyl, J. P., Kerkhof, A. J. F. M., & Van Kempen, G. M. J. (1997). Platelet serotonin and [–3H] paroxetine binding correlate with recurrence of suicidal behavior. *Psychopharmacology, 132*(1), 89–94.

Virkkunen, M., Goldman, D., Nielsen, D. A., & Linnoila, M. (1995). Low brain serotonin turnover rate (low CSF 5-HIAA) and impulsive violence. *Journal of Psychiatry and Neurosciences, 20*(4), 271–275.

Wessely, S. C., Castle, D., & Douglas, A. J. (1994). The criminal careers of incident cases of schizophrenia. *Psychological Medicine, 24*, 483–502.

Wetzler, S., & Sanderson, W. C. (1997). *Treatment strategies for patients with psychiatric comorbidity.* New York: Wiley.

Widom, C. S. (1989). The cycle of violence. *Science, 244*(4901), 160–166.

Wong, S. (1995). Recidivism and criminal career profiles of psychopaths: A longitudinal study. *Issues in Criminological and Legal Psychology, 24*, 147–152.

Zamble, E., & Palmer, W. (1995). Prediction of recidivism using psychopathy and other psychologically meaningful variables. *Issues in Criminological and Legal Psychology, 24*, 153–156.

Zuckerman, M. (1986). Serotonin, impulsivity, and emotionality. *Behavioural and Brain Sciences, 9*(2), 348–349.

Index

adolescence
  aggression development, 47–8, 74,
    79
  cortisol effects, 34
  homicide, *see* filicide
  hormonal effects, 29–32
  parricide risk, *see* parricide
adrenal androgens, antisocial
    behavior relationship, 32–3
adult violence, prediction, 66–85
  behavioral predictors, 74–6, 90
  Cambridge Study in Delinquent
    Development, 68–70
  conviction records, 70–2, 74, 95,
    263
  explanatory predictors, 76–8
  multivariate analysis, 78–80
  overview, 66, 83–5
  previous analysis, 72–4
  research, 67–8
  risk scores, 81–3
age (*See also* adolescence; middle
    childhood years; preschool
    years)
  age–crime curve, 47–50
  alcoholism, 201
  filicide victims, 159–60
  risk assessment relationship, 7
aggression (*See also* intimate partner
    homicide)

prediction, 47–61
  adolescent years, 47–8, 74, 79
  correlations, 48–50, 55–9
  middle childhood years, 48–51
  overview, 59–61
  preschool years, 51–5
alcohol use
  alcohol-related crimes, 202–5,
    264–6
  antisocial behavior relationship,
    205–8
  conceptual issues, 208–10
  criminal behavior link, 196–202
  historical perspectives, 197–9
  overview, 195
  recidivistic violent behavior, 121,
    123, 131
  short-term dangerousness
    prediction, 115–16
antisocial behavior (*See also* violent
    behavior)
  alcohol use relationship, 205–8
  antisocial parricide perpetrator,
    190–1
  antisocial personality disorder,
    104–5
  biological systems effects, 28–38
  adrenal androgens, 32–3
  cortisol, 33–4
  endocrine system, 29

antisocial behavior *(continued)*
  estrogen, 31–2
  neurotransmitters, 34–7
  psychophysiology, 37–8, 115
  serotonin, 34–7, 104, 106, 272
  testosterone, 29–31
  clinical implications, 38–40
  developmental models, 25–6
  examples, 26–7
  overview, 23–4
  personality scales, 83
assessment, *see* risk assessment
axis II disorders, 103–18
  antisocial personality disorder,
    104–5
  borderline personality disorder,
    105–7
  histrionic personality disorder,
    107–8
  narcissistic personality disorder,
    108–10
  overview, 103–4, 118
  paranoid personality disorder,
    110–11
  short-term dangerousness
    prediction factors, 111–17
    alcohol use, 115–16
    background, 116–17
    degree of formulation, 113
    history, 114–15
    information sources, 113
    intent, 113
    organicity, 116
    psychosis, 115
    substance abuse, 115–16
    treatment compliance, 117
    victim availability, 114
    weapons, 114
  threats toward clinicians, 117–18

battering, *see* intimate partner
  homicide

behavioral predictors, *see* prediction;
  risk assessment
behaviors, *see* antisocial behavior;
  specific behaviors
biological processes
  antisocial behavior
    biological systems, 28–38
    adrenal androgens, 32–3
    cortisol, 33–4
    endocrine system, 29
    estrogen, 31–2
    neurotransmitters, 34–7
    psychophysiology, 37–8, 115
    serotonin, 34–7, 104, 106, 272
    testosterone, 29–31
    clinical implications, 38–40
    developmental models, 25–6
    examples, 26–7
    behavioral domains, 23–4
    overview, 23
  borderline personality disorder,
    description, 105–7

Cambridge Study in Delinquent
  Development, adult violence
  prediction, 68–70
child abuse
  filicide risk, 158–78
    neonaticide, 162–5
    overview, 158–9, 176–8
    perpetrators
      characteristics, 170–2
      fathers, 165
      gender, 165–76
      mental illness role, 174–6
      mothers, 165
      Munchausen syndrome by
        proxy, 172–3
      predictors, 173–4
      stepfathers, 165–6
      typologies, 166–70
    victim characteristics, 159–62

age, 159–60
gender, 160–1
obstetric risk factors, 161–2
parricide response, 184–5
childhood, *see* adolescence; middle
childhood years; preschool
years
clinical assessment, *see* risk
assessment
conviction records, adult violence
prediction, 70–2, 74, 95, 263
cortisol, antisocial behavior
relationship, 33–4
criminal harassment, *see* stalking
criminal records, adult violence
prediction, 70–2, 74, 95, 263

dangerousness (*See also* specific
aspects)
definition, 2–7
domestic violence, *see* intimate
partner homicide; stalking
driving fatalities, alcohol use link,
204
drugs, *see* alcohol use; pharmacology; substance abuse

economic crime
parricide motivation, 191–2
socioeconomic status role, 7, 76,
79, 266
substance abuse association, 220,
228–30
education, risk assessment
relationship, 76, 266
endocrine system, antisocial
behavior relationship, 29–32
epidemiology, mental illness
future research directions, 97–9
overview, 89, 99–100
violence, 89–94

estrogen, antisocial behavior
relationship, 31–2
explanatory predictors, *see*
prediction; risk assessment

femicide (*See also* intimate partner
homicide)
risk assessment, 141–6
filicide, parental risk, 158–78
neonaticide, 162–5
overview, 158–9, 176–8
perpetrators
characteristics, 170–2
fathers, 165
gender, 165–76
mental illness role, 174–6
mothers, 165
Munchausen syndrome by
proxy, 172–3
predictors, 173–4
stepfathers, 165–6
typologies, 166–70
victim characteristics, 159–62
age, 159–60
gender, 160–1
obstetric risk factors, 161–2

gender
childhood aggression
development, 48–51
estrogen effects, 31–2
filicide risk
perpetrators, 165–76
victims, 160–1
mental illness relationship, 94
overkill, 140–1
partner homicide, *see* intimate
partner homicide
restraining order effectiveness, 252
risk assessment relationship, 7, 68,
94

gender *(continued)*
  stalking
    typologies, 243–4
    victims, 245–6
  substance abuse association, 232–3
  testosterone effects, 29–31

harassment, *see* stalking
historical factors
  criminal history, 70–2, 74, 95, 263
  medical history, 8, 258–61
  personal history, 266
  professional history, 266
  psychiatric history, 8, 244–5, 261–3
  psychosexual history, 267
  relational history, 266–7
  risk assessment relationship, 8,
    114–15, 263
  short-term prediction, 114–15
  social history, 266–7
histrionic personality disorder,
  description, 107–8
homicide, *see* filicide; intimate
  partner homicide; parricide;
  suicide
hormones, 29–32
hospitalization, risk management,
  269–70

infants, *see* filicide; preschool years
intimate partner homicide
  restraining orders, 251–3
  risk assessment, 136–53
    danger assessment, 146–52
    domestic femicide, 141–6
    homicide-suicide, 141–6
    K-SID, 146–52
    lethality risk domestic violence
      instruments, 145–6
    mental disorders, 142
    overview, 136–7, 152–3

perpetrators, 139–40
  recidivism, 145–6
  risk factors, 142–4
  SARA, 146–52
  substance abuse, 142
  victim–perpetrator relationship,
    138–9, 141–6
  weapons, 140–1
stalking, 248, 251

K-SID, intimate partner homicide
  risk assessment, 146–52

legal considerations, risk
  management, 270–1

medical history, risk assessment, 8,
  258–61
mental illness
  axis II disorders, 103–18
    antisocial personality disorder,
      104–5
    borderline personality disorder,
      105–7
    histrionic personality disorder,
      107–8
    narcissistic personality disorder,
      108–10
    overview, 103–4, 118
    paranoid personality disorder,
      110–11
    short-term dangerousness
      prediction factors, 111–17
        alcohol use, 115–16
        background, 116–17
        degree of formulation, 113
        history, 114–15
        information sources, 113
        intent, 113
        organicity, 116

psychosis, 115
substance abuse, 99, 115–16
treatment compliance, 117
victim availability, 114
weapons, 114
threats toward clinicians,
117–18
epidemiology
future research directions, 97–9
overview, 89, 99–100
violence, 89–94
recidivistic violent behavior,
121–32
association, 122–5
overview, 121–2, 131–2
predictors, 126–31
prevention, 126–31
risk assessment
filicide risk, 174–6
future research directions, 18,
97–9
intimate partner homicide, 142
overview, 3–5, 9, 89, 99–100
parricide, 188–90
psychiatric history, 8, 261–3
violence, 94–7
middle childhood years
aggression development, 48–51
homicide risk, *see* filicide
multivariate analysis, adult violence
prediction, 78–80
Munchausen syndrome by proxy,
filicide risk, 172–3

narcissistic personality disorder,
description, 108–10
neonaticide (*See also* filicide)
parental risk, 162–5
neurological pathways, substance
abuse effects, 12–13
neurotransmitters, antisocial
behavior relationship, 34–7

outpatient follow-up, risk
management, 270–1

paranoid personality disorder,
description, 110–11
parricide, 181–93
antisocial parricide perpetrator,
190–1
child abuse response, 184–5
economical motivation, 191–2
family conspiracy, 186–8
incidence, 183–4
mental illness association, 188–90
overview, 181–3
perpetrator–victim relationship,
184
risk assessment, 192–3
risk factors, 185–6
personality disorders
antisocial, 104–5
borderline, 105–7
histrionic, 107–8
narcissistic, 108–10
paranoid, 110–11
pharmacology
psychopharmacological violence,
220, 224–8
risk management, 272
treatment compliance, 117
physical aggression, *see* aggression;
intimate partner homicide
prediction (*See also* risk assessment)
adult violence, 66–85
behavioral predictors, 74–6, 90
Cambridge Study in Delinquent
Development, 68–70
conviction records, 70–2, 74, 95,
263
explanatory predictors, 76–8
multivariate analysis, 78–80
overview, 66, 83–5
previous analysis, 72–4

prediction *(continued)*
  previous relevant research, 67–8
  risk scores, 81–3
aggression development, 47–61
  adolescent years, 47–8, 74, 79
  correlations, 48–50, 55–9
  middle childhood years, 48–51
  overview, 59–61
  preschool years, 51–5
clinical issues
  alcohol use, 264–6
  criminal history, 263
  education, 76, 266
  future violent behavior
    diagnoses association, 267
  medical history, 8, 258–61
  personal history, 266
  professional history, 266
  psychiatric history, 261–3
  psychosexual history, 267
  relational history, 266–7
  social history, 266–7
  sociodemographic data, 7,
    116–17, 258
  substance abuse, 264–6
  violence characteristics, 268–73
filicide risk, 173–4
overview, 5–7
short-term dangerousness
  prediction, axis II disorders,
    111–17
  alcohol use, 115–16
  background, 116–17
  degree of formulation, 113
  history, 114–15
  information sources, 113
  intent, 113
  organicity, 116
  psychosis, 115
  substance abuse, 115–16
  treatment compliance, 117
  victim availability, 114
  weapons, 114

stalking behavior, 253–4
preschool years
  aggression development, 51–5
  homicide risk, *see* filicide
psychiatric history
  clinical issues, 8, 261–3
  stalking behavior, 244–5
psychophysiology, antisocial
  behavior relationship, 37–8,
  115
psychosexual history, risk
  assessment relationship, 267

race
  alcoholism, 201
  intimate partner homicide, 150
  parricide risk, 184, 193
  risk assessment relationship, 7, 68,
    116
recidivistic violent behavior, 121–32
  intimate partner homicide risk
    assessment, 145–6
  mental disorder association, 122–5
  overview, 121–2, 131–2
  persons without major mental
    disorders association, 125–6,
    130–1
  predictors, 126–31
  prevention, 126–31
risk assessment *(See also* prediction)
  clinical issues
    alcohol use, 264–6
    criminal history, 263
    education, 76, 266
    future violent behavior
      diagnoses association, 267
    management strategies, 269–73
      administrative considerations,
      271
      collaboration, 271
      counseling considerations, 272
      hospitalization, 269–70

institutional considerations, 271

legal considerations, 270–1

outpatient follow-up, 270–1

pharmacological considerations, 272

reevaluation, 270

medical history, 8, 258–61

overview, 14–17, 258

personal history, 266

professional history, 266

psychiatric history, 261–3

psychosexual history, 267

relational history, 266–7

social history, 266–7

sociodemographic data, 7, 116–17, 258

substance abuse, 264–6

violence characteristics, 268–73

dangerousness definition, 2–7

equation components, 7

future research directions, 18, 97–9

intimate partner homicide, *see* intimate partner homicide

mental illness relationship, *see* mental illness

methods, 13–14

overview, 1–2, 17–18

parricide, 185–6, 192–3

risk scores, 81–3

situational factors, 8–9

substance abuse, *see* substance abuse

SARA, intimate partner homicide risk assessment, 146–52

serotonin, antisocial behavior relationship, 34–7, 104, 106, 272

sex, *see* gender; psychosexual history

social history, risk assessment relationship, 266–7

sociodemographics, risk assessment relationship, 7, 116–17, 258

socioeconomic status, risk assessment relationship, 7, 76, 79, 266

spousal abuse, *see* intimate partner homicide

stalking

demographics, 242–3

dramatic moments, 250–1

escalation, 251

motivations, 246–7

overview, 238–9, 254

predictive factors, 253–4

property damage, 251

protection, 251–3

psychiatric diagnosis, 244–5

pursuit characteristics, 246

threats, 239–42

typologies, 243–4

victims, 245–6

violence, 247–51

stepfathers

filicide risk, 165–6

parricide risk, 184

substance abuse

abuser profile, 221–2

economic crime, 220, 228–30

gender association, 232–3

genetics, 11–12

intimate partner homicide risk assessment, 142

mental illness relationship, 99, 115–16

neurological pathways, 12–13

organic factors, 11

overview, 216–18, 233–5

psychopharmacological violence, 220, 224–8

short-term dangerousness prediction, 115–16

systemic violence, 230–2

theoretical assumptions, 218–24

substance abuse *(continued)*
   violence conditions, 222–4, 264–6
suicide
   borderline personality disorder,
      105–7
   histrionic personality disorder,
      107–8
   homicide-suicide risk, 141–6
   short-term prediction, 114–15

testosterone, antisocial behavior
   relationship, 29–31
third-party violence, 249–50
threatening communication
   clinician threats, 117–18
   evaluation, 241–2
   research limitations, 241
   stalking relationship, 239–42

violent behavior (*See also* antisocial
   behavior)

alcohol use link, *see* alcohol use
   characteristics, 268–73
   mental disorder link, *see* mental
      illness
   prediction, *see* prediction; risk
      assessment
   recidivism, 121–32
      mental disorder association,
         122–6
      overview, 121–2, 131–2
      prevention, 126–31
   stalking-related violence, 247–51
   substance abuse link, *see*
      substance abuse

weapons
   intimate partner homicide risk
      assessment, 140–1
   short-term dangerousness
      prediction, 114
wife battering, *see* intimate partner
   homicide